Have Dog Will Travel

Oregon & Washington, Second Edition

Comprehensive Guide to 2,000 Dog-Friendly Lodgings in the Pacific Northwest

PLUS
First Aid Guide, Packing & Traveling Tips

Barbara Whitaker

Ginger & Spike Publications

Printed in the United States of America.
First printing

Publisher's Cataloging-In-Publication Data
   (Prepared by The Donohue Group, Inc.)

Whitaker, Barbara.
 Have dog will travel : Oregon & Washington : comprehensive guide to 2,000 dog-friendly lodgings in the Pacific Northwest plus first aid guide, packing & travelling tips / Barbara Whitaker ; cover and interior illustrations by Kristin Johnson and Bob Sleeper. – 2nd ed.

 p. : ill., maps ; cm.

Includes index.
ISBN: 978-0-9660544-4-6

1. Hotels–Pet accommodations–Northwest, Pacific–Directories. 2. Dogs–Housing–Northwest, Pacific–Directories. 3. Pets and travel–Northwest, Pacific. I. Summers, Kristin. II. Sleeper, Bob. III. Title.

TX907.3.N96 W45 2009
917.95

Cover and interior illustrations by Kristin (Johnson) Summers and Bob Sleeper

Ginger & Spike Publications
PO Box 937, Wilsonville OR 97070-0937
Phone 503-625-3001, Fax 503-625-3076
Email barbw@havedogwilltravel.com
Web www.havedogwilltravel.com

This book is dedicated to my "forever pets" Ginger and Spike, for giving me the initial nudge to create the *Have Dog Will Travel* guidebook series.

Their loving presence has been evident each and every day during the preparation of this latest book, in their new roles as Dog and Cat Angels.

Acknowledgments

I want to express my appreciation to all the wonderful people who helped me to complete this book, the fifth volume in the *Have Dog Will Travel* series.

Heartfelt thanks to dear friends Susan Foster, Randi Goodrich and Bonnie Vorenberg for your never-flagging encouragement and support, and for keeping me focused (and sane!) throughout the long process.

Kudos also to Carol Beck, Cassie Freitas, Linda Beattie Inlow, Tracie Ploeger, Shanon Tilyer Schlegel and Liz Smith for your invaluable help during the research and editing stages.

As always, special thanks to my husband Linn for your ongoing encouragement and support. And of course, I need to acknowledge my four-footed buddies Rocky and Mooshka, whose companionable presence, as I sat at the computer day after day, kept me motivated to finish this book.

Many thanks, one and all—I couldn't have done it without you!

Table of Contents

1: Touring With Your Well-behaved Traveler

So you plan to travel in Oregon or Washington by car, and you want to take your dog along? Well, you're in good company—lots of dogs travel with their owners. Rocky, our 90-lb Hound/German Shepherd mix, sure does. After all, he's part of our family, and a vacation just wouldn't be the same without him.

Traveling with a well-behaved dog can be great fun and a minimum of fuss. But it does involve some advance planning and effort on your part. It also requires extra consideration for your fellow travelers and for the friendly people who provide your accommodations.

Chapters 1–6 in this book are packed with common-sense information you can use to make sure your dog is a well-behaved traveler—making your trips more fun for both of you. There's even a common-sense first aid guide, for your pet's safety and your own peace of mind.

Chapter 7 contains maps of each state, showing the location of every town that has at least one dog-friendly hotel, motel, B-&-B, cabin or vacation home.

In Chapter 8 you'll find detailed listings for more than 2,200 hotels, motels, and bed & breakfast inns throughout California where you and your well-behaved dog are welcome guests.

At the back of the book you'll find two separate indexes:

- A: Business Name Index—an alphabetical list of all the business names, cross-referenced to their detailed listings in Chapter 8

- B: Topics Index—an alphabetical list of the pet travel topics discussed in Chapters 1 through 6

How to have fun and get invited back

Sad to say, it appears that the numbers of hotels, motels, cabins and B-&-Bs that allow dogs have dwindled in recent years. This unfortunate trend is due largely to a few irresponsible dog owners who permit their dogs to damage furnishings and landscaping, or to behave aggressively toward other guests and their pets. Or, they fail to make sure their pet, his travel bed, and his cleanup towels are freshly washed in preparation for their trip.

As responsible dog owners, we can all help to reverse this trend. Preparing in advance and taking appropriate equipment along with us not only ensures more enjoyable trips for ourselves and our dogs; it also provides positive examples of well-behaved traveling dogs. Good examples help to encourage more establishments to accept pets.

This book will help you prepare for a great trip with your dog, by following these easy but important steps:

- Attend obedience training classes with your dog *before* you travel. When you are both familiar with the basic commands for good behavior, you'll be ready when the unexpected happens. (And believe me, it *does* eventually happen!)

- Prepare a canine first aid kit and read the first aid guide in Chapter 5 to learn (in advance) how to handle a medical emergency

- Pack the appropriate pet travel supplies

- Call ahead to reserve a dog-friendly room—be aware that most of the hotels, motels and bed-and-breakfast inns included in this book allow dogs in some, but not all, of their rooms

- Always pay attention to your dog's impact on other guests and on the facilities (both indoors and outside) where you're staying—in short, be well-behaved travelers!

When to bring your dog—and when NOT to

Obviously you want your dog to travel with you, or you wouldn't be reading this book. But also ask yourself whether or not he *wants* to come along.

Your dog will probably enjoy the trip if:

🐾 You're traveling by car.

🐾 Driving time will be fairly short, so he won't be in the car for hours.

🐾 You've planned lots of activities that your dog can share, like hiking or walking on the beach.

But consider traveling *without* your dog when:

🐾 Adverse weather conditions could make him miserably hot or cold.

🐾 You'd be traveling by plane or train—these are more of an ordeal for your pet than a vacation.

🐾 Most of your time would be spent in activities that your dog could not share—after all, would you want to spend your entire vacation locked in an empty car or motel room while your companion attended meetings all day long?

And now, a word from Mooshka

The feline member of our family ("She Who Must Be Obeyed") wants to point out that she prefers to stay home while Rocky goes traveling. Call her a homebody if you like, but Mooshka insists that most cats would much rather stay behind in their own familiar surroundings.

On Mooshka's advice, then, this book focuses on traveling with dogs only. Obviously you'll be making arrangements for your cats to be properly cared for in your absence. So, you can rest assured that they will be just fine while you're gone. Though it may hurt to admit it, they probably won't even miss you.

As Mooshka puts it, "I'm staying here. And as long as I'm properly fed and admired, my servants *[that's us mere humans]* can go wherever they like!"

2: Puppy, Pack Your Bags

It has been said that every successful vacation begins with careful packing. This is just as true for your dog as for yourself—you need to bring along the proper pet supplies. Use the handy checklist on page 21 to be sure nothing important gets left behind.

Many of these supplies are as close as your local pet store. You can also check dog magazines at your library or newsstand for the names of mail order pet supply houses and then go online, telephone or write to request their catalogs. You'll be amazed at the variety of new gadgets available to make traveling with your pet easy and fun.

Collar and leash

Every dog should wear a sturdy leather or woven collar at all times, with your pet's license, identification and rabies tags attached.

Don't use a choke collar as a permanent collar! Properly used, it can be helpful during training sessions, but if left on your dog all the time, the choke collar could snag on a low branch or other obstruction. Don't let your beloved pet become one of the sad stories of dogs who choked to death when their owners were not there to rescue them.

If your dog is really hard to control, check with a reputable trainer about using a *prong collar* during your training sessions. This type of collar has blunt metal prongs that momentarily pinch the dog's neck when he pulls against the leash or when you administer a correction. Again, this is for use during training sessions only; don't leave it on your dog all the time!

You'll need a 1-ft to 6-ft long leash for walking with your dog close to your side. Woven nylon or leather works better than metal chain, which is noisy and hard to hold onto. Also check out the retractable leashes that extend to 16 feet or more so your pet can investigate his surroundings without dragging you every which way, then they retract fully for walking close to your side.

🐾 Attending a basic obedience class with your dog is one of the very best ways to help him master the fine art of walking on leash.

All the proper ID tags

As important as your dog's license and ID tags are at home, they're even more vital when you travel. If you and your pet lose track of each other, those ID tags will enable his finders to contact you.

Any number of companies can create ID tags for you. Veterinary offices often have brochures from several of them. Dog magazines are full of ads for this service—check your library or newsstand. Some mail order catalogs also offer custom tags. Do-it-yourself tag-making machines are available in many pet stores. Dog shows and pet fairs and even holiday bazaars often include a booth where they'll make your tags "while you wait."

Dog license tag—Among the many good reasons for licensing your dog, one of the best is that the license number and phone number of your county dog control department appears on the tag. Those numbers offer yet another way to trace your dog back to you if he becomes lost.

Permanent identification tag—This should include your name, address, phone number, and perhaps your dog's name. (Rocky's tag even lists his veterinarian's phone number.) If you don't care to reveal your full street address, just list the city and state. Ideally, this information should be permanently engraved or stamped onto a metal tag. The rectangular-style tag that fastens at both ends of the tag lays flat to the collar and doesn't add to the jingling of the other tags.

Rabies tag—Provided by your veterinarian. This tag displays a serial number that can be traced back to the veterinarian and then to the dog's owner. There could be dire consequences if your dog were to get picked up as a stray and not have proof of current rabies vaccination.

Travel tag—Very important! This tag shows where you can be reached during your vacation. Several styles are available; one is a two-part set consisting of a round cardboard tag that you write on, which then fits inside a clear plastic snap-together case. Another type consists of a tiny metal "barrel" that unscrews to hold a rolled-up slip of paper—just be sure to tighten the two halves together very securely to keep them from jiggling loose.

Whichever type you choose, write or type in your name and cell phone number, plus the name, street address, city and phone number where you'll be staying. As an alternative, list the name and phone number of someone who can receive messages for you.

Microchip ID system

Microchipping is one of the newest and most promising ways to identify a lost pet. While tags or collars can fall off or be removed, a microchip stays with your pet forever. Each chip is programmed with a unique ID code that can be detected by a hand-held scanning device, similar to the UPC scanners used in retail stores to read product barcodes.

Your veterinarian can implant the microchip, no bigger than a grain of rice, beneath your pet's skin in a safe, quick office procedure. Then all you have to do is register your pet's unique code and your contact information with the national database agency to receive coverage anywhere you travel in the USA.

Microchip scanners are now used at thousands of animal control agencies, shelters and veterinary clinics across the country. Once the chip's code has been retrieved, the staff simply calls it in to the national database agency, which is accessible 24 hours a day, 365 days a year via a toll-free number. The database agency then notifies you that your dog has been found.

The cost of implanting the microchip and the onetime database registration fee add up to about $50—pretty inexpensive insurance for your dog's safe return if he should ever get lost. Pet fairs or veterinary associations sometimes sponsor lower-cost microchip clinics.

Health certificate and vaccinations

Get this certificate from your veterinarian no sooner than 10 days before your trip. Effective for 30 days, it states that your pet is in good health and includes a list of his current vaccinations. While not strictly required when traveling by car, you'll definitely need this if you plan to travel by air (even just within your state) or to cross an international border. Before traveling to any other countries, check with their embassies for specific vaccinations and other requirements.

If your pet takes medication or has other health problems, get a copy of his medical records along with the certificate. Make sure the paperwork includes your veterinarian's name, address and phone number, in case follow-up information is needed.

The most well-known canine vaccination is for rabies. In fact, you can't get a dog license without proof of a current rabies vaccination. And as a caring, responsible pet owner, *of course* you license your dog, right?

In addition, your pet should be immunized against distemper, hepatitis, parainfluenza, leptospirosis and possibly parvovirus. Depending on where you'll be traveling, your veterinarian may also recommend a preventive for heartworm or Lyme disease.

Also ask about periodic booster shots for corona and bordetella. These vaccines safeguard your pet against kennel cough and other infectious diseases that he might be exposed to from contact with other dogs. They are often required before your dog can attend obedience classes or stay in a boarding kennel.

Bottom line on vaccinations: Your traveling dog is exposed to many new health hazards at rest stops, parks and other public areas. Along with the stresses of drinking unfamiliar water and meeting new dogs, these factors add up to very real dangers for the non-vaccinated dog. So be safe—vaccinate!

🐾 Some vaccines can take up to 30 days to develop full protective strength, so check with your veterinarian and *plan ahead!*

First aid kit

A basic first aid kit is easy to put together and enables you to deal with emergencies until you can get to a local veterinarian. You'll find a list of the items that belong in your first aid kit on pages 38–39.

Of course you'll also bring along any special medication your veterinarian may have prescribed. If fleas are a problem in the area you're visiting, you may want to include flea-and-tick spray or powder—just be sure to apply it to your dog only when outdoors, never in your motel room. Or ask your veterinarian about the monthly flea and tick treatments that protect your pet "from the inside out."

Travel crate

Many trainers, breeders and veterinarians recommend using a portable kennel, or *crate,* when your dog travels in the car. Obviously, this is more practical with small dogs than with larger ones—it is much easier to fit a Beagle-sized crate into the back seat than one for a Rottweiler.

Several types of crate are available, from collapsible wire mesh panels, to soft-sided carriers, to rigid molded plastic. A wire crate works well in the flat back of a van or station wagon, while the plastic carriers often fit better into the back seat of a sedan. Of course, when traveling by plane, your dog *must* be in an airline-approved travel crate.

The crate should be large enough for your dog to turn around, lie down, and stand or sit up without hitting his head. If he's still a puppy, get a crate that will be large enough for his full adult stature. Think of this as his den—*cozy* and *secure*—so don't get anything larger than your adult pet will need. To cushion and provide traction underfoot, place a folded blanket on the bottom of the crate. Or better yet, cut a thick piece of carpet to fit snugly without slipping—ask a local carpet dealer for a remnant or sample square.

Restraints and safety barriers

If a travel crate isn't the answer for your situation, not to worry—there are a number of other safety options you can use instead.

Seat belts—Available for dogs of all sizes, these consist of a chest harness and a strap that fastens to the car seat or to the regular seat belt. These allow your dog to sit up or lie down as he chooses, yet prevent him from being thrown forward in the event of a sudden stop. Various sizes and types are available. And it keeps him from jumping around in the car while you're trying to concentrate on safe driving.

Metal barriers—These allow you to close off the back seat or the back of a station wagon, and can be ordered for specific makes of cars, other models are adjustable to fit a variety of vehicles. Your dog can see and hear you through the barrier, but is securely restrained from jumping or being thrown into the front seat. Metal barriers may be either temporarily or permanently installed.

Mesh barriers—These stretchy nets create a temporary barrier between the front and back seats. Mesh nets are available in generic sizes and shapes to fit most car models.

Food

First and foremost, you'll need to bring along dog food and a bowl to serve it in. Unless you're absolutely certain that your dog's preferred brand of food is available wherever you plan to travel, you should pack enough dog food for the entire trip.

If your dog typically nibbles at his food without finishing it all right away, bring a bowl with a snap-on lid that can go back into your dog's tote bag without spilling kibble everywhere. The shallow containers used for whipped toppings or margarine work very well.

You may also want to bring along a vinyl placemat for catching spills under the food and water bowls. This is an item you can pick up for pennies at garage sales. Or, you can buy fancy mats and bowls decorated with pet pictures or paw prints in pet stores or mail order catalogs.

Remember to pack a can opener for canned food, along with a serving spoon and a snap-on lid for covering any portion to be saved for the next meal. If your dog is accustomed to frequent dog treats or snacks, pack those too. A small cooler is helpful in hot weather for keeping drinking water and leftover canned food cool.

Water

Pack a plastic gallon jug of water and an unbreakable bowl where they'll be accessible during your travels, since your dog will need a drink of water every few hours. Don't let him drink from streams or puddles, because drinking unfamiliar or polluted water can lead to stomach upsets or diarrhea.

Many veterinarians recommend bringing enough water from home to last at least halfway through your trip. By gradually mixing local tap water in with your own water, you can prevent an unpleasant digestive reaction for your dog. You can also buy distilled water for about a dollar a gallon at most grocery stores.

Never allow your dog to drink from the toilet in your motel room—some establishments put slow-release cleaning chemicals into the toilet tank, which could make him very sick.

Bedding & towels

You should always travel with your dog's own bedding and cleanup towels. Your dog will thank you—and so will the hotel and motel managers, for sparing their furnishings. If your dog is accustomed to sleeping on the bed with you, or on other furniture, bring a clean sheet from home to protect bedspreads and upholstery. And do consider training your dog to stay off the furniture, at home *and* when traveling.

A travel crate, so useful in the car, also makes the perfect bed. It is reassuringly cozy and safe. If you're not using a crate, then bring along a *familiar* washable blanket or other bedding. Rocky travels with the same trusty sleeping bag that he sleeps on at home. Zipped up and folded in half, it makes a thick, soft bed. Opened out full-length, it protects his favorite spot in the back seat of the car from dirt, mud and beach sand.

An absolute must is a pair of cleanup towels especially for your dog. Use these to rub down a wet coat or wipe muddy or sandy paws. If your dog is a messy drinker, use one under his water bowl.

You can spend a lot of money on "designer" travel supplies if you choose to, but the sheet, dog towels, and bedding can also be found very inexpensively at garage sales or secondhand stores. Rocky's sleeping bag cost us a couple of dollars, and his towels were a quarter each. The tote bag which holds his travel supplies was another garage sale find—making the cost of his entire travel set less than four dollars.

Grooming aids

Pack your dog's brush or comb, since you'll probably be going to fun places that will result in a happy but dirty or sandy pet! A quick brushing *before* going indoors will keep your motel room clean, and will endear you to the housekeeping staff—not to mention how much your pet probably enjoys being groomed. Rocky relaxes so completely while his coat is being brushed that he practically falls asleep.

Take care of your pet's major grooming chores *before* your trip—trim those too-long toenails and brush the loose hair out of his coat. Also pack a bottle of pet shampoo if he has any tendency to roll in smelly things. I'll never forget the day Jeremiah, my husband's 100-pound Great Pyrenees, found a dead seal on the beach—enough said!

Cleaning up

Even seasoned canine travelers occasionally have car sickness accidents, so it's a good idea to pack supplies in the car for quick cleanups. Paper towels, pre-moistened towelettes, or just a wet washcloth in a plastic bag are all good options. Stash them in an easy-to-reach spot in the car, such as under the front seat.

Many hotels and motels now offer pet amenities such as pooper scoopers or disposable cleanup bags, as well as pet towels and even sheets to cover the furnishings in case your pet has a tendency to jump up. However, it is up to us as dog owners to take full responsibility for cleaning up after our dogs, so always pack your own cleanup bags.

Please, please be considerate of others by cleaning up after your dog's rest stops—whether in a park, on the motel grounds, or at a roadside rest area. You can use either disposable pooper scoopers, or a reusable scooper with disposable bags—plus another bag for storing the scooper between uses.

For a low cost, low tech method, use a plastic produce bag saved from a trip to the grocery store. Place your hand inside the bag and use this "glove" to pick up the doggie doo. With your other hand, turn the bag inside out, then twist the top shut and secure it with a knot. Properly dispose of the bag in a trash can.

Keep several clean, folded bags in your car, ready for the next rest stop. And *always* tuck one in your pocket when taking your dog out for a walk. Zip-top plastic bags also work well.

Last but not least, a flashlight

You probably already have a flashlight stashed in your vehicle for emergencies. Keep another one in your dog's tote bag for those just-before-bedtime walks.

Tote bag checklist

🐾 First aid kit, health certificate/medical records

🐾 Dog bed (sleeping bag or blanket) and towels

🐾 Dog food, bowl, serving spoon, can opener
    and snap-on lid, vinyl placemat

🐾 Jug of water, drinking bowl

🐾 Dog brush or comb, shampoo

🐾 Pooper scoopers (reusable or disposable)
    or a supply of plastic bags

🐾 Paper towels, pre-moistened towelettes,
    or wet washcloth in a plastic bag

🐾 Flashlight

🐾 A favorite chew toy!

3: Good Behavior is a TEAM Effort

Which sort of pet would you rather vacation with: a barky, uncontrollable bundle of energy, or a well-behaved traveler? The answer is obvious, and basic obedience training is the key.

"Obedience" simply means that your dog is reliably under your control, both on and off the leash. Mastering just a few useful commands and reviewing them often with your pet can make all the difference in his behavior. The practice sessions can be a lot of fun, and they help to strengthen the bond between you and your dog.

What commands are necessary?

According to noted dog trainer Bruce Sessions, only two commands are truly required for the traveling dog: *come* and *no*. Rocky and I have also learned in obedience class that a few more commands come in handy: *sit, down, stay* and *heel*. Does your dog absolutely have to know all these commands before he can travel with you? No, but they will definitely make your trips more relaxed. Compare the following two scenarios...

Before obedience training...

It's early morning at the motel, and you've just let your dog off his leash in the designated corner of the motel grounds for a rest stop. Another guest and her pet suddenly appear and your dog runs to investigate the newcomer, ignoring your call to *"Come back here right now!"* You have to chase after him and grab his collar. The other guest glares as your two dogs bristle and circle around each other in the traditional "I'm a tougher dog than you are" dance. Back on the leash again, your dog lunges along the path at full speed, dragging you behind him.

In the motel room, he runs back and forth between the window and the closed door, barking at the sounds of people and cars outside in spite of your repeated scolding to *"Stop that barking and lie down."* Loaded down with luggage, you open the door and he runs out ahead of you, nearly tripping another guest in his excitement.

...and after

Let's try this again after you and your dog have completed a course of obedience classes. You take him outside *on the leash* for his morning rest stop. If he moves toward an approaching dog, you tell him *"Heel"* and you walk together in the opposite direction. If he makes any aggressive move or sound, you say *"No!"* sharply and he continues walking with you—without any pulling on the leash.

Back in the motel room, if your dog barks at a sound outside, you say *"No!"* followed by *"Down."* He lies down—and stays down—quietly. When checking out of the room, you put him on the leash *before* opening the door, tell him *"Heel"* and he walks politely beside you to the car. Once he's safely inside, you can finish loading the luggage.

What a difference!

Feel the change in stress levels between these two scenarios? And that's just the beginning of the day—imagine spending your whole vacation with an uncontrollable dog versus a well-behaved traveler.

Obedience 101

You *can* learn about obedience training from books, and there are some excellent ones available. However, I definitely recommend that you and your dog attend at least a beginners' obedience class. A trained instructor can get you off to a great start, avoiding behavior problems before they begin.

Professional dog trainers usually offer both group and one-on-one sessions—check the Yellow Pages under "Dog Training" or ask for referrals at your veterinary clinic. Beginning, intermediate and advanced levels of obedience classes may also be available through your local school district or community college. Call the school office and ask about their Continuing Education or Community Education programs. Class schedules may also be available at your local bank, library or post office.

Train BEFORE you travel

The time to begin obedience training is before your trip—so that your dog can learn the basic commands in a controlled area without distractions. Once he understands the commands, start practicing with him in a public area like a park, surrounded by people and other dogs. He'll soon learn that you expect the same good behavior wherever he goes, regardless of distractions in the background.

Relax and have fun with this training time. Your dog will love the extra attention and he'll try to please you. Be patient and upbeat even if he gets confused at first. If you reach a stumbling block, go back to an earlier command that he knows well, to get his confidence level back up before you try the more difficult command again.

Keep your training sessions short so that they don't turn into torture for either one of you. And always end with a few minutes of plain old playing—toss a ball for your dog to fetch, or lead him on a run around the yard to release any leftover tension. After all, good behavior is supposed to make your time together more fun, right?

Basic commands

The following discussion is based on the collective expertise of a number of well-known trainers and authors. For more detailed training information, check your local library or bookstore.

Come—This is an easy command that most dogs pick up very quickly. You want to get your dog's attention in such an inviting way that there's nothing else he'd rather do than come running to you. While he's on a leash or long cord, call his name followed by the command *"Come."* As soon as he starts toward you, praise him lavishly. Giving a small food treat at first for every positive response helps to reinforce the idea that coming when called is a wonderful idea.

No—There is no specific routine for teaching this command. Just belt it out in a very firm tone of voice, whenever your dog is doing something you *really* don't want him to do. Don't overuse it though—save it for when he does something you absolutely will not tolerate; otherwise you risk losing its impact. The sudden loud command should startle him out of whatever he's doing. Then as soon as he begins to pay attention to you, praise him. You may even want to call him over to you for a pat on the head or a good ear-scratching.

Sit—With your dog on the leash, say his name and then *"Sit."* At the same time, pull up gently on the leash and push down on his hindquarters to guide him into the sit position. Praise him *("Good sit")* and then release him from this position with *"Okay"* or *"Release."* (Use the same word consistently.) Only after you give the release command is he allowed to stand up again. Then give lots of praise, both verbal and hands-on. Most dogs will be so delighted with themselves by this time that they'll happily repeat the exercise over and over as long as you keep telling them how wonderful they are.

Down—With your dog on the leash, say his name and the command *"Down"* while you pull downward on his leash. At first, you may also need to push down on his hindquarters or shoulders until he is lying down. Again, give lots of praise to reassure him that he's doing well. Use patience and lots of repetition here.

Stay—With your dog in the Sit or Down position, hold your hand in front of his face, palm toward him, while saying *"Stay."* Praise lavishly for even the shortest compliance, then release. Gradually increase the time your dog is expected to hold this position, then practice keeping him in the Stay position as you step further and further away. Always remember to release him from this position before going on to another command or ending the practice session, so he doesn't get the idea that *he* can decide when this command is over.

Heel (walking on leash)—Start with your dog sitting at your left side, leash in your left hand. Say his name and the command *"Heel"* just before you step out with your left foot. Take just a few steps the first time, then say *"Sit"* as you stop walking. You want him to learn to stay right at your side rather than rushing ahead of you, and to immediately sit down when you stop.

Say *"Heel"* and start walking again, and so on. He'll soon learn to follow your steps. In fact, he'll probably anticipate your takeoff and start too soon at first, so be patient. Once he catches on to the routine, stop giving the Sit command every time, so that he learns to do it automatically.

Try carrying a small food treat right in front of his nose to keep him at your side. Give him the treat after he has successfully walked a few steps and then stopped with you. And of course, give lots of praise. (If you think it's starting to sound like practice and praise are the secrets to successful obedience training, you're absolutely right!)

Controlling aggression

If you intend to take your well-behaved traveler out in public, he must be reliably *not* aggressive toward people or dogs. Some dogs don't start out being comfortable with other dogs. Their reactions range from defensive postures such as raised fur along the back of the neck and fierce stares, to outright barking or growling.

The best way to overcome aggressive tendencies is to socialize your dog at an early age, that is, to get him accustomed to being in the presence of other dogs. Simply attending obedience classes will go a long way toward helping him relax around dogs and people. Your instructor can also offer specialized help for problem dogs.

Dog behaviorists say that once you establish yourself as the "pack leader," your dog will follow your lead on whether to charge ahead or hold back. The most important step in preventing aggression is to *always* have your dog under your control—this means on the leash—whenever you venture outside your car or motel room.

If your dog is a barker

Simply put, barking is *not* to be tolerated. A barking dog makes everyone around you miserable. You should train your dog to stop barking as soon as you give the all-purpose command *"No!"*

A really insistent barker may at first need more than a spoken command to break through his mental barriers. I've had good luck with plain water in a plastic squirt bottle. One good squirt in the face (aim for the forehead) doesn't hurt your dog, but it certainly interrupts his train of thought, especially when accompanied by a loud *"No!"* and followed with praise the minute he stops barking.

Of course, a dog left behind in a motel room, barking incessantly, is unacceptable. That kind of barking is a sign of stress, as in "They left me here all alone and I'm scared/bored/frustrated." It isn't fair to your dog or to the unfortunate neighbors who have to endure the noise.

Never leave your dog alone in the motel room. He should be going with you—isn't that why you brought him on the trip in the first place? If he can't be with you for a short time, such as while you're in a restaurant, then let him wait in your car, not in the room. (See page 32 for safety tips when *briefly* leaving your pet in a parked car.)

If you already use a travel crate, your dog should be accustomed to sitting or lying down quietly when he's inside it. Put him in the crate for a few minutes to calm down when he becomes upset and barky. Be sure to practice this "time-out in the crate" exercise at home before you travel, so that your dog knows exactly what is expected of him when he is put into his little den.

Learning to love car rides

Many dogs just naturally love going anywhere in the car with you, but others have difficulty getting used to the sound and motion. Pacing back and forth, drooling, panting excessively or throwing up are all signs that your dog is anxious about being in the car. Some advance preparations will help to ensure a comfortable trip for all concerned.

Getting used to the car—Practice rides can help to reassure him that riding in the car can be fun rather than intimidating. In extreme cases, you may need to start by sitting quietly with him in the car, not even starting the engine. Ignore him for a few minutes—perhaps read a magazine article—then let him out of the car with a simple word of praise and a pat on the head.

Repeat this exercise until he can enter the car, sit quietly, and exit without any problems. Then try starting the car but not going anywhere. Next, try driving just around the block, and so on. By the time you've progressed to taking him with you on short errands, such as to the grocery store and back, he'll probably just take a nap while you drive.

Arrange some of your practice trips to include a fun destination or activity, like a brisk walk in the park. Rocky loves riding to the drive-up window at our bank, because the teller keeps a bowl of treats handy for canine customers.

Avoiding a "nervous stomach"—Stress can trigger car sickness, so don't give food or water for at least an hour before a practice ride. Allow time for a few minutes of exercise and a chance to relieve himself just before you leave. If he still gets carsick, see page 50 for some simple remedies.

Riding politely—Train your dog to sit or lie down quietly—no jumping around, and no barking in your ear or out the window. Consider using one of the safety restraints described on pages 17–18. Reassure him by remaining calm yourself. Don't keep asking anxiously if he's all right—he'll pick up on your tension and get even more nervous. Praise him for sitting politely, then ignore him as long as he behaves himself.

Loading and unloading—For his own safety, your dog *must* learn to wait for your command before getting into or out of the car. Never open the door without checking that the leash is attached to his collar, and that you have a firm grasp on the other end of the leash. Losing control of an excited dog in unfamiliar territory can be disastrous—so use the Stay command to keep him safely in the car until you are ready for him to get out.

Reviewing what your dog already knows

A brief practice session makes a great exercise break during your trip. It also helps to reinforce the idea that obedience is expected even when surrounded by unfamiliar distractions. Start by walking your dog on the leash. Pause periodically to practice the Sit or Down command, then release him and continue your walk. Or tell him to Sit and Stay while you walk ahead a few steps—still holding the leash, of course. Then call him to you once more with lots of praise.

A few minutes of this activity at each rest stop will leave you with a happy dog who settles down comfortably as soon as you resume driving.

4: The Well-Behaved Traveler on the Road

Okay, you've faithfully completed your dog's obedience training, assembled his first aid kit (see page 38) and packed his food, water, and other traveling supplies. You've made your advance room reservations, you're ready to go, and your ecstatic pet is running in circles around the car. This is the payoff for all your preparations—it's time to hit the road!

Tips for traveling in the car

The safest way for a smaller dog to ride in the car is in a travel crate. This protects him in case of a sudden stop and keeps him from jumping around in the car or getting underfoot while you're trying to drive. If your pet is too large for a travel crate, consider using a doggie seat belt that offers similar protection but still allows him to sit or stand up, as he chooses.

Don't leave your dog's leash attached to his collar while the car is in motion. Take the leash off once he's safely inside the car, and remember to put it on again *before* you open the door to let him out.

If you feel you must open a car window, roll it down just enough for your dog to put his nose into the fresh air, not his whole face. *Never* let him hang his head out the window of a moving car—not only could he squeeze his whole body out if he decided to chase something, but airborne objects such as insects or flying gravel could injure his ears and eyes. The force of the wind could actually give him an earache.

It goes without saying that your pet belongs *inside* the vehicle. A dog riding in the open bed of a pickup truck is an accident just waiting to happen. He's exposed to wind-borne hazards and harsh weather, and could even be thrown out of the vehicle if you swerve or brake suddenly.

If you need to briefly leave your dog in the parked car—while you stop for lunch, for example—be sure he won't suffer from heat buildup in the car, which can lead to heatstroke or even death. Park in a covered lot, or at least in the shade, and check frequently to be sure the temperature in the car is still comfortable. Or better yet, have an outdoor picnic lunch and let him lounge in the shade with you. See tips for dealing with heat problems on page 51.

Rest stop pointers

When traveling a long distance, stop every few hours to give both you and your pet a chance to stretch and relax. Keep him on the leash while you're at the rest stop, and stay in the designated pet areas.

He'll probably be ready for a drink of water. Give him a few minutes to relieve himself and walk around a bit. Be considerate of others by *always* cleaning up after your dog—use plastic bags or pooper scoopers and dispose of the waste in a garbage can.

This is a great time for a short exercise break, especially if you combine it with a brief review of obedience commands. Try walking a few steps and then tell him to sit or lie down, walk for another minute and practice a different command, and so on. A few minutes of activity will have you both feeling refreshed and ready to continue your trip.

Checking into your room

When you check in at your overnight destination, remind the staff that your dog is with you. Of course, you should already have stated this when making your advance reservation, but tell them again now that you have arrived. That way, they can be sure not to put you in a "no-pets, ever" room by mistake. Many establishments reserve certain rooms for guests who suffer from allergies. Sneaking a dog into a no-pets room hurts all dog owners by jeopardizing the management's willingness to accept dogs in the future.

Ask where on their grounds you can exercise your dog, whether or not they provide cleanup bags or pooper scoopers, and which trash cans you should use for disposal. A growing number of public parks and beaches either do not allow dogs, or only allow them at certain times. So, when you check in, also ask for directions to the dog-friendly parks or beaches in the area.

Room etiquette

Place your pet's bed on the floor in a corner of the room and show him where it is. Make sure that he uses his own bed and not the furniture. If your pet sleeps on your bed or other furniture at home, bring along a sheet to cover the motel furnishings—and resolve to begin breaking that habit as soon as your trip is over.

If your dog gets bored or rambunctious while in the room, offer a favorite chew toy to play with. Watch that he doesn't damage the furnishings—remember, you are legally and financially responsible for any damage he does to motel property, both indoors and out.

While it's natural for dogs to bark at unfamiliar sounds, don't tolerate any barking in the room, no matter what's going on outside. Barking is the single most common reason managers give for not allowing dogs to stay.

Never leave your pet alone in the room when you go out, for example, to dinner. Take him along and let him wait for you in the car rather than in the room. He'll feel safer in the familiar vehicle and will probably settle right down for a nap. More and more establishments are offering onsite dogsitting services (for a fee), or can recommend local dog sitters or even "doggie day care" facilities.

Before you and your dog leave the room, make him sit down by the door while you put his leash on. He should remain sitting while you open the door and step outside, then he can follow you out. Don't let him charge through the door ahead of you.

When you and your pet return to the room, check him over before stepping inside. Use the dog towel you brought from home to wipe any mud or sand off his feet. This small courtesy only takes a second, helps to keep the room clean, and has a very positive effect on the manager's willingness to continue accepting pets as guests.

Mealtime arrangements

Put the food and water bowls on your dog towel or vinyl placemat in the bathroom. If your pet is a messy eater, the placemat is easy to rinse off and drip-dry in the bathtub, and the smooth bathroom floor is much easier to clean than the bedroom carpet. Don't let him drink out of the toilet—cleaning chemicals that may have been added to the toilet tank could make him sick.

On checkout day, it's a good idea to withhold food and water for at least an hour before starting a long drive. If your pet tends to suffer car sickness, you may need to do this up to six hours beforehand, meaning the night before an early morning departure.

Walking on the grounds

Shortly after eating or drinking, your dog will need a walk outside in the designated pet relief area. This is also true after he has been waiting in the car while you were out having your dinner. Just before bedtime is another important walking time.

Always keep your dog leashed while on the premises. And be courteous when taking him for a "relief walk." Use the designated pet area or at least go to the far end of the grounds away from buildings, major footpaths and children's play areas. Remember to always take along the pooper scooper or plastic bag for cleaning up after him. Don't let him romp in landscaped flower beds, decorative ponds or streams. Be aware of your pet's energy level and potential for destruction, and seek out areas where he can play harmlessly.

On the trail

When you go out for the day's activities, be sure to bring along your dog's water jug and bowl, just as you would pack your own water bottle for a hike. And of course, the first aid kit should be in your car, not left behind in the room.

Pay attention to your pet's effect on other people and animals when you're out in public. You are responsible for making sure that he doesn't cause anyone else discomfort. If you're walking along a trail, for example, rein him in to walk closely beside you when you encounter other hikers. Don't let him monopolize the whole walkway or run up to greet them—or worse yet, to challenge their pet.

Remember that although your dog is the apple of your eye, not everyone shares your enchantment. In fact, some people are uncomfortable around even the smallest, meekest dog. So keep your pet on the leash unless you're in a clearly marked "off-leash" area.

Watch out for potential hazards underfoot: broken glass, nails or other sharp objects, burning hot pavement, melted road tar, chemical sprays or wet paint could all injure his feet or poison him if he licks his paws later. Also, remember to clean his feet after walking on snow or ice that may have been treated with salt or other de-icing chemicals.

At the beach

Many dogs love playing in the ocean, and few scenes are more enjoyable to watch than a happy dog chasing waves up and down the beach. However, don't allow your pet to chase the shore birds, as that can cause them severe or even fatal stress. You could also be cited and fined for endangering the wildlife.

Keep a close eye on your pet while he's in the water—don't let him wade or swim out too far, as dangerous currents can arise unexpectedly that could carry him away from the shore.

Also watch that he doesn't drink a lot of salt water, or else he may be throwing up later in the car. A little bit won't hurt him, and he'll soon learn that he doesn't like the taste after all. Offer him a drink of fresh water when he gets back to your parked car, and then wait a few minutes before bundling him inside—he may still need to throw up any salt water already in his stomach.

After walking your dog on the beach, brush off any sand clinging to his feet or coat. Salt water that dries on his skin can cause lasting irritation, so if he's been in the surf, rinse the salt away as soon as possible—definitely *before* returning to your room. This is where those dog towels you packed in his tote bag come in handy. And of course, the motel's bath towels should *never* be used on your dog!

5: First Aid for Your Traveling Dog

Whether your pet sustains a minor scratch or a life-threatening injury, you need to know what first aid measures to take. Then, for all but the most minor problems, your immediate next step is to get him to the nearest veterinary clinic. If you're not sure just how serious the problem is, call them. Most clinics are happy to answer questions over the phone, and they can give you exact directions for getting there if it becomes necessary.

Before first aid is needed

Put together your dog's first aid kit in advance (see page 38) and *always* bring it (and this book) along when he travels with you. Keep it in your car when you're out and about, not back in the motel room.

Read through this chapter *now* to get a basic idea of what to do in an emergency, and how to use the supplies in the first aid kit.

Knowing your dog's healthy state will help you to recognize when something is wrong. Sit down on the floor with your dog—he'll love the attention—and listen to his breathing. Place your palm on his chest just behind his "elbow" and feel his heartbeat. Check the size and color of his pupils, the color of his gums and tongue, and how warm his body feels normally.

In an emergency, refer to specific sections in this chapter for the proper first aid steps to take. Or better yet, have another person read the steps aloud to you while you perform them on your pet. As soon as you complete the emergency procedures, take him to a veterinary clinic, or at least call the clinic for further instructions.

➤ As a precaution, it's a good idea to identify nearby veterinary clinics at your vacation destination *before* the need arises. Check in the local Yellow Pages, which are usually available in your room.

Your dog's first aid kit

This list includes the emergency supplies you'll need until you can get to the clinic. All items are available from your veterinarian or local pharmacy. The dosage of some medicines varies according to body weight, so write your pet's correct dose on a piece of masking tape attached to each medicine container. Pack everything into a sturdy carrier, such as a fishing tackle box or cosmetics travel case.

Travel papers—copies of your dog's license, health certificate, veterinary records if he has special medical problems, and a master Lost-and-Found poster with extra photos of your dog as described on page 55; store all this paperwork in a zip-top plastic bag

Any medication your dog takes—and the written prescription

Honey packets (available in restaurants) or **small hard candies** such as butterscotch or fruit flavors (no chocolate)—for treating carsickness or upset stomach (page 50)

Antibacterial ointment—such as *Panalog* from your veterinarian, or *Neosporin* from any pharmacy, for treating wounds (page 48)

Tranquilizers—but *only* if prescribed by your veterinarian *and* you've tested the dosage on your pet before the trip. Please note that the ASPCA discourages tranquilizer use because the effects can be unpredictable.

Plastic dosage spoon—for measuring liquid medicines (available at any pharmacy, often for free)

Paper or **flexible plastic cup**—for administering liquid medicines; can be squeezed into the shape of a pouring spout

Slip-on muzzle—for restraining an injured dog (page 43)—the kind that fastens with hook-and-loop tape is especially easy to use

Emergency stretcher—flat piece of wood or cardboard stored in your car's trunk— for moving an injured dog (page 47)

Kaopectate—for treating diarrhea

Hydrogen peroxide, 3% solution—for treating poison (page 46) and cleaning wounds (page 48)

Activated charcoal—for treating poison (page 46)

Olive oil—for treating poison (page 46)

Petroleum jelly—for taking rectal temperature (see below)

Sterile saline solution—for rinsing eyes (page 49)

Zip-top plastic bags—for collecting a sample of poison (page 45)

Sterile gauze pads—for bandaging wounds and burns (page 44, 48)

Adhesive tape and **elastic bandages**—for wounds (page 44, 48)

Cotton-tipped swabs—for cleaning wounds (page 48)

Rectal thermometer—for taking dog's temperature (see below)

Ice pack—for treating heatstroke (page 52)

Tweezers—for removing foreign objects (page 49, 50)

Pliers—for removing foreign objects (page 49)

Blunt-tipped scissors—for bandaging wounds (page 44, 48)

Taking your dog's temperature

Have another person restrain your dog while you take his temperature, if at all possible. Coat the rectal thermometer with a bit of petroleum jelly or hand lotion to make insertion easier.

Firmly grasp your dog's tail and very gently insert the thermometer about one inch while rotating it back and forth slightly. After one minute, remove it to read the temperature. Wash the thermometer with soap and *cool* water before returning it to its protective case. Normal canine body temperature is 100° to 101°—anything over 102.5° deserves a phone call to the veterinary clinic for further advice.

What to do in a life-threatening emergency

Your pet is depending on you for the first aid that he needs to survive until you reach a veterinarian. Remain calm and focused on what you need to do. Speak to him reassuringly as you work.

Each step listed here is described in greater detail in the sections that follow—exact page numbers are indicated for each step.

1. *Do not move your dog* until you have checked his injuries. The only exception is when it's unsafe to leave him where he is, such as in the middle of a busy street.

2. Check for a heartbeat—if there is none, start cardiac massage *immediately* (page 42).

3. Check whether he is breathing—if not, begin artificial respiration *immediately* (page 42).

4. Muzzle and restrain him if he's in obvious pain, seems dazed or starts to struggle (page 43).

5. Check for obvious injuries; control severe bleeding (page 44).

6. Check for symptoms of internal bleeding (page 44).

7. Check for signs of poisoning—depending on the type of poison, induce vomiting or make him swallow an antidote (page 45–46).

8. Move him to your vehicle using a board, stiff cardboard or a blanket as a stretcher (page 47).

9. Treat for shock by keeping him warm (page 47).

10. Rush him to the nearest veterinary clinic. If possible, have another person call ahead so they can prepare for your pet's arrival.

If your dog is choking

The traveling dog may encounter chicken bones at picnic areas, fishing line at the river's edge—even more dangerous if a fishhook is still attached—or any number of other choking hazards that can be potentially fatal unless you act quickly.

Signs of choking include violent pawing at his mouth or throat and loud gasping or gagging sounds. In his panic, he may even snap at your hand when you try to help.

If possible, have another person hold your pet while you open his mouth wide and pull his tongue out straight with your fingers or a cloth. If you can see the entire object, pull it out. But *never* pull on a fishline that extends out of sight down his throat—there could be a hook at the other end. Instead, take him immediately to a veterinary clinic for an x-ray.

If you can't see what he's choking on, place your hands on each side of his chest and squeeze in a sudden, forceful movement. The air expelled from his lungs may dislodge the object in his throat.

If he is still choking, head straight for the emergency clinic. Keep him as immobile as possible during the trip, and speak reassuringly to calm him.

If your dog is drowning

If your pet is in the water and can't make it back to shore, *do not* swim out to him. Try to help him from shore by extending out a board, rope or any floating thing that he can hold or climb onto. If you still can't reach him, wade part of the way out and try again. If you absolutely must swim all the way out to him, bring something he can cling to other than your own body—otherwise you could be seriously clawed or even pulled under in his panic to get out of the water.

After you get him onto the shore, lift his back legs as high above his head as possible for fifteen seconds and give three or four downward shakes to drain his airway. Gently pull his tongue out straight, and clear any debris from his mouth with your hand or a cloth.

If his heart has stopped, start cardiac massage *immediately* (page 42). If he has a heartbeat but is not breathing, give artificial respiration *immediately* (page 42).

Once he begins breathing on his own, dry him off and keep him warm. If he's willing to drink, give him warm liquids. If his body temperature doesn't quickly return to normal, check with a veterinarian for follow-up treatment.

Cardiac massage

Place your palm on your dog's chest just behind the elbow. (Practice this at home until you can easily detect his normal heartbeat.) If his heart has stopped beating, you must restart it *immediately.* Gently lay your dog on his side with head extended—don't move him suddenly, as that can further deepen his shock. Pull his tongue out straight to clear the airway.

Place your hands on each side of his chest just behind the elbow. In a sudden forceful movement, squeeze your hands together to compress the chest, then release. Repeat once every second for one minute, then check for heartbeat again. If there still is none, repeat the steps above. As soon as his heart starts beating, give artificial respiration to restore his breathing.

Artificial respiration

Check your pet's heartbeat before beginning this procedure. If his heart has stopped, you must perform cardiac massage (see above) before giving artificial respiration.

If your dog has swallowed water while drowning, or choked on vomit or other liquids, lift his back legs as high above his head as possible for fifteen seconds and give three or four downward shakes to drain his airway. Gently pull his tongue out straight and clear any debris from his mouth with your hand or a cloth.

Place your hands on both sides of his chest just behind the elbow. Squeeze hard, then release. Repeat once every five seconds for one minute. If the movement of air in and out of the lungs seems blocked, open his mouth wide to see if an object is lodged in his throat, and remove it.

If he doesn't start breathing within one minute, grasp his muzzle firmly to hold his mouth shut. Take a deep breath, place your mouth over his nose, forming a tight seal, and blow gently. You should see his chest rise as air enters his lungs.

Listen for air leaving the lungs, then repeat every five seconds for one minute (ten to fifteen breaths). Check to see if he's breathing on his own, then repeat for another ten to fifteen breaths, and so on.

Have someone drive you and your dog to the veterinary clinic while you continue helping him to breathe. Don't give up even if there is no immediate response—dogs have been successfully revived after extended periods of artificial resuscitation, as long as the heart continues beating.

Restraining an injured dog

An injured dog is also frightened, disoriented and in pain. He may not recognize you and could even snap at your hand when you try to help him. Unless he's unconscious, you'll need to muzzle him before you can safely check his injuries.

Use the slip-on muzzle in your first aid kit or improvise one from a handkerchief, scarf, or his own leash—whatever is handy. Since a muzzle doesn't work well on a short-nosed dog, loosely place a coat or blanket over his head instead. Whatever you use, be sure not to restrict his breathing. And be ready to remove the muzzle *immediately* if your dog starts to vomit or has obvious difficulty in breathing.

Broken bones

If your dog is unable to move his leg (or tail) or holds it at an odd angle, the bone may be fractured. Muzzle and restrain him before checking for broken bones, and handle the injured leg as little as possible.

If the bone is protruding from an open wound, cover with a clean cloth and control the bleeding with direct pressure.

If you can find a rigid stretcher (page 47) for moving your dog, don't waste time applying a splint. But if you have to jostle him in a blanket stretcher or carry him in your arms, you should immobilize the broken ends of the bone before moving him.

To apply a temporary splint, wrap a clean cloth around the leg for padding. Fold a newspaper, magazine or piece of cardboard in a U-shape around the leg or lay a strip of wood alongside it. Hold it all in place with adhesive tape or strips of cloth. The splint should extend beyond the joints above and below the fracture in order to hold the broken bones still.

External bleeding

Your first concern is to stop any major bleeding. Minor wounds that are oozing only a small amount of blood can wait for the veterinarian. But if blood is spurting out or flowing steadily, you must act *now.* Cover the wound with a sterile gauze pad or a clean cloth, or just place your hand directly over it and apply firm, steady pressure until the bleeding stops. Secure with adhesive tape or an elastic bandage.

If the wound is on the leg (or tail) and you cannot slow down the blood loss after a few minutes of direct pressure, you must apply a tourniquet. This may result in having to amputate the limb, so use this method only as a last resort—always try direct pressure first. And *never* place the tourniquet over a joint or a fractured bone.

Wrap a handkerchief or other strip of cloth in a loose loop around the leg about one inch above the wound. Tie it with a double knot, then place a strong, short stick in the loop. Twist the stick to tighten the loop until the blood flow stops.

Now take him to the emergency clinic *fast.* On the way there, you *must* loosen the tourniquet every ten minutes to allow some blood to flow through the limb. Apply direct pressure to the wound to prevent further bleeding, and tighten the tourniquet again only if absolutely necessary.

If you suspect internal bleeding

Hidden bleeding inside your dog's body can result from a fall or other traumatic blow or from certain kinds of poison. Even if he has no visible wounds, his internal organs may be seriously damaged. He may go into fatal shock without immediate veterinary care.

Signs of internal bleeding include: pale skin, gums and tongue; bleeding from ears, mouth or anus; bloody vomit or stool; difficulty breathing; or extreme sleepiness from which you cannot rouse him. Symptoms may appear immediately after the accident or hours later, even if he seemed fine initially.

Use a rigid stretcher (page 47) if at all possible to move your dog to and from your car on the way to the emergency clinic. Keep him warm and try not to jostle him any more than you absolutely have to.

Poisoning

Your dog can be poisoned by eating or drinking a toxic substance, inhaling it, licking it off his coat or paws or absorbing it through his skin. Poisons that your pet might encounter when traveling include spilled antifreeze, toxic bait intended for insects or rodents (or their dead bodies), garbage that contains poisonous substances, or chemical sprays that have been applied to plants that your dog chews or rolls in. Even your own prescription medicine can poison your pet if he discovers it in your luggage and accidentally swallows some while playing with this new "rattle toy."

Signs of poisoning include: drooling or difficulty swallowing; trembling; vomiting; shallow rapid breathing; twitching; seizure or coma.

Contact poisoning

Rinse his coat immediately with lots of water—fresh water, sea water, a mud puddle by the side of the road, whatever it takes to dilute the chemical and wash it away. Wear rubber gloves, if available, to avoid getting the toxic chemicals on your own skin. Then wash him with mild hand soap or shampoo and rinse thoroughly with clean water. Repeat until all traces of the chemicals are removed.

See or call a veterinarian for further instructions.

Swallowed poisons

Depending on the type of poison, you must choose between two very different first aid treatments—for **corrosive chemicals (Method A on the next page)** or **noncorrosive substances (Method B)**.

Your first step is to determine what kind of poison your pet has swallowed. If the product container is available, it may identify the ingredients, the antidote and whether or not to induce vomiting.

If you can't identify the type of poison, check inside your dog's mouth and throat. If the tissues look burned or raw as if from a corrosive substance, use Method A. Otherwise use Method B.

Bring the poison container itself if at all possible, or else try to collect a sample of the poison in a zip-top plastic bag from your first aid kit. Also, collect any material your dog vomits up. These samples can help the veterinarian identify the exact antidote that your dog will need.

Method A. When the poison is CORROSIVE, such as an acid, alkali, or petroleum product: NEUTRALIZE THE POISON BUT DO NOT INDUCE VOMITING!

These poisons will injure your dog's mouth and throat even further if he throws up. Instead, rinse his mouth thoroughly with water to wash away any remaining chemicals. Then make him swallow two to three tablespoons of olive oil or up to one cup of milk.

Keep him warm with a blanket or coat while you rush him to the nearest veterinary clinic.

Method B. When the poison is NOT corrosive: INDUCE VOMITING IMMEDIATELY!

Mix equal parts of hydrogen peroxide and water. Make him swallow 1½ tablespoonfuls of this mixture for each ten pounds of body weight.

Example: the dose for a 60-lb dog would be 6 x 1½ = 9 tablespoons

If he doesn't vomit within ten minutes, repeat this dosage, but not more than three doses altogether.

After he vomits, make him swallow a mixture of three to four tablespoonfuls of activated charcoal in a cup of warm water. Wrap him in a blanket or coat while you rush him to the nearest veterinary clinic.

A special warning about antifreeze

Every year, dogs die from ingesting antifreeze that has dripped from leaking car radiators. This coolant has a sweet smell and taste that attracts many pets to drink it—but even a tiny spoonful can be deadly.

If your dog has swallowed even the tiniest amount of antifreeze, induce vomiting *immediately* and then rush him to a veterinarian for an antidote injection—but you must work *fast*. Minutes can make the difference between losing him or saving his life.

🐾 Pet-safe antifreeze is now available at auto supply stores and service centers—ask for it the next time your car's radiator fluid is changed.

Moving an injured dog

The safest way to move your pet is on a *stretcher,* a flat rigid surface that won't flex under his weight. A piece of wood or heavy cardboard will do, or even an air mattress blown up as firm as you can make it. If that's unavailable, use a blanket, tarp or piece of clothing that you can carry by its corners to make as flat a surface as possible.

Slide your dog onto the stretcher without twisting or shaking him. If possible, have a helper lift his hindquarters and abdomen at exactly the same moment that you lift his head and shoulders.

If you are alone and can't find a rigid stretcher, you'll have to carry him in your arms. Place one arm around his hindquarters and the other around his front legs at the shoulder, supporting his head on your arm. Keep his spine as straight as possible.

Treating for shock

"Shock" refers to a sudden collapse of your dog's circulatory system, which can be brought on by serious injury or other trauma. All his bodily functions are shutting down. You must be very careful not to jostle or quickly move him, because any rapid movement can bring on the *fatal* stages of shock.

Symptoms of shock include: extreme muscle weakness; loss of bladder and bowel control; shallow, rapid breathing and pulse; pale or whitish gums and mouth; he feels cold to the touch; he appears asleep or semiconscious.

Pull his tongue out straight to clear the airway—but be very cautious, as even the most gentle dog may bite when dazed from great pain or fear. Try to get his head lower than his body to encourage circulation, unless he has a head injury, in which case you should keep his head level with his body.

Cover him with a blanket or coat to stabilize his body temperature; the only exception would be if his temperature is already too high (as in heatstroke). Now take him to a veterinary clinic for follow-up care. If possible, call ahead so the staff can prepare for the emergency procedures that your pet will need as soon as he gets there.

Treating burns

Watch for hazards that can lead to your dog being accidentally burned—sparks from a beach bonfire, hot liquids spilled from a tiny kitchen unit, licking meat juices from a hot barbecue grill or brushing against a space heater.

Chewing on an electrical cord can lead to burns in the mouth as well as unconsciousness, shock, and even death. Be sure to *unplug the cord* before touching your dog.

If the burned skin is red but not broken, gently run cold water over the affected area or cover it with an ice pack or a cold wet towel.

If the burned area is heavily blistered, raw, weeping or bleeding, blackened or whitish, *do not apply ice or water*—just cover with a sterile gauze pad or clean cloth. Treat for shock (page 47) and take your dog to the nearest veterinarian *immediately.*

Minor cuts and scrapes

Rinse away any dirt in your pet's wound with sterile saline solution or clean water, then swab with hydrogen peroxide. If the wound is still bleeding, cover with a gauze pad and apply pressure until the bleeding stops. Then lightly apply an antibiotic ointment such as *Panalog* or *Neosporin.*

If the wound is more than just a scratch, or your dog just won't leave it alone, cover the area with a gauze pad held in place with adhesive tape or an elastic wrap bandage. Elastic bandages are much easier to work with than sticky tape, especially after your dog starts fiddling with it and you have to readjust things.

And of course, for anything more than a minor scratch or scrape, you should have a veterinarian take a look at it.

Removing foreign objects

Use common sense on whether or not to try removing an embedded object such as a burr or porcupine quill. Sometimes, incorrect removal can do more harm than waiting to let the veterinarian do the job right. In that case, just keep your dog as motionless as possible during the trip to the nearest clinic.

From the ears

Use tweezers to gently remove seeds or burrs from the *outer* ear canal. If your dog still shakes his head or scratches repeatedly at his ear, seeds or other tiny intruders may also be deeper inside the ear canal and must be removed by a veterinarian.

From the eyes

If your pet paws at his eye or rubs his face along the ground, gently hold the eyelid open and check for seeds or debris. Use sterile saline solution to wash away a loose object. Don't try to remove any object that is embedded into the surface of the eye. Instead, take him to the nearest veterinary clinic *immediately.*

From everywhere else

You're already familiar with this routine if your dog loves to crash through the underbrush. Run your hands gently over his face, body and feet to check for thorns. If he's limping or holding up his paw, he has already zeroed in on the problem for you.

Use tweezers to pull out embedded thorns or splinters. When a foreign object is buried too deeply to find, either soak the affected body part in salt water (one teaspoon salt per cup of lukewarm water) several times a day until the object works its way up to the surface where you can remove it, or else have a veterinarian remove it.

Sharp objects such as porcupine quills or a fishhook can be removed with pliers. First use the wire cutter notches at the center of the pliers to clip off the tip of each porcupine quill or the barbed point of the fishhook *if it is exposed.* But if the fishhook point is hidden below the skin surface, or if your dog won't submit to having the objects pulled out, take him straight to a veterinarian.

When finished, rinse any open wounds with hydrogen peroxide.

Watch out for ticks

If you're traveling in tick country, examine your dog closely after any outdoor activity, especially around his head, shoulders and feet. If found early (before the ticks have had a chance to bite deeply into the skin), they can be picked off with tweezers without causing the dog any discomfort.

Forget the old wives' tales about using a match to burn the tick off, applying gasoline or petroleum jelly to loosen its grip, and so on. Dousing the tick with rubbing alcohol or nail polish remover just *might* make it easier to remove. A new method I've seen recommended but haven't tried yet is to cover the tick with liquid hand or dishwashing soap, which is supposed to make the tick release its hold within a few minutes.

If the tick is already deeply attached below the skin surface, use tweezers to grab the tick *by its head* and firmly pull it away from the bite wound. Above all, don't squeeze the fat abdomen—doing so might force disease-carrying blood back into the bite wound. *And don't use your fingers!* Ticks can carry Lyme disease or Rocky Mountain spotted fever, both of which are dangerous to humans.

Swab the bite area with hydrogen peroxide. If the skin becomes red or irritated, see a veterinarian for follow-up treatment.

Treating an upset stomach

Car sickness is one of the most common complaints for the traveling dog—whether it's because he's fearful of the car, or just overly excited about coming along. Try reducing his stress level with practice rides as described on page 28. Don't give him food or water for at least an hour before traveling. And always allow him a few minutes of exercise and a last-minute chance to relieve himself before loading him back into the car.

If your dog still gets carsick, try giving him a small spoonful of honey, a piece of hard candy or a spoonful of plain vanilla ice cream to calm his stomach.

🐾 Warning—never give your dog any food containing chocolate, as it can be toxic!

If these simple remedies don't help, ask your veterinarian about stronger medicines for motion sickness.

An upset stomach can also be caused by eating unfamiliar or spoiled food, or drinking unfamiliar water—contaminants in the water or a different mineral content can throw your pet's system for a loop.

Give two teaspoons of Kaopectate for each ten pounds of body weight, once every four hours.

If the problem doesn't clear up within 24 hours, this may be a symptom of a more serious illness—see a veterinarian.

Treating diarrhea

This may be a temporary upset caused by the stress of unfamiliar surroundings, food or water, or a symptom of a more serious illness. Give two teaspoons of Kaopectate for each ten pounds of body weight, once every four hours.

If the diarrhea doesn't clear up within 24 hours or if other symptoms appear, such as labored breathing, bloody stool, either a rise or a drop in body temperature, listlessness or loss of appetite, consult a veterinarian for follow-up care.

Dealing with heat problems

Summer can mean added hazards for your pet. Shorthaired dogs can become sunburned just as easily as people can. Older or overweight pets are more prone to heat problems, as are short-nosed breeds and dogs who are taking certain medications. Heat problems are even more likely if the humidity is also high.

When walking your dog, pay special attention to the surface underfoot—if it's too hot for your bare feet, then it's too hot for your dog's paws as well.

Heatstroke can be caused by too much exercise in the hot sun, not drinking enough water, or simply from sitting in a hot car. On a sunny 80° day, the temperature inside your parked car (even with the windows partly rolled down) will climb well above 100° in just minutes. Your pet is in danger of permanent damage to the brain and internal organs, and even death.

Recognizing the danger signs

Symptoms of heatstroke may include some or all of the following: frenzied barking; a vacant expression or wild-eyed stare; rapid or heavy panting; rapid pulse; dizziness or weakness; vomiting or diarrhea; deep red or purple tongue and gums (the normal color is light pink, except in breeds where the gums and tongue are naturally black); twitching, convulsions or coma.

Use a rectal thermometer to check your dog's body temperature. Normal body temperature is 100° to 101°—but it can rise to 106° or more with heatstroke.

Treating for heatstroke

First, get your dog out of the sun. Then cover him with towels soaked in cool water, or pour cool water over him every few minutes. *Do not* immerse him in ice water or apply ice directly to his skin, but an ice pack is okay if wrapped in a towel.

Give him a small amount of cool water to drink, or let him lick ice cubes or a bit of plain vanilla ice cream. (Remember—no chocolate!) As soon as his body temperature begins to come down, take him to the nearest veterinarian for follow-up care.

Keeping your pet safe in cold weather

Many dogs, Rocky included, love outdoor activities in the snow. But don't assume that your dog is as safe and comfortable as you are in your insulated boots and down-filled clothing. Wintertime hazards include hypothermia, frostbite, and irritation from road salt and other de-icing chemicals.

After playing outside, wash off any remaining ice or road salt and towel him dry. Then give him a well-deserved rest in a warm place— but not too close to a fireplace or space heater. If he's really chilled, he could burn himself without even feeling the heat.

Treating for hypothermia

Smaller or older dogs are most likely to suffer from hypothermia. However, exposure to the cold *when he's wet* can be extremely hazardous for any dog, especially if immersed in icy water for even a few minutes. When your pet starts lagging behind you instead of bounding ahead, that's the signal to take him indoors and let him rest.

If he becomes listless, ignores your calls or just wants to lie down in the snow, you need to warm him up right away.

Dry him off and boost his circulation by rubbing vigorously with a towel. Wrap him in a warm blanket and offer warm (not hot) water if he's willing to drink it. If his body temperature has dropped below 98.5° take him to a veterinarian *immediately.*

Treating for frostbite

When the weather turns windy, check frequently to see if your dog's feet, ears, and tail are getting pale or numb. If so, bring him indoors right away.

Massage the affected areas *very gently* to encourage circulation—rough handling can bruise damaged tissues. Soak frostbitten paws or tail in barely lukewarm (90°) water to gradually restore circulation. Dry him off and keep him warm; then check with a veterinarian for follow-up care.

6: If Your Dog Gets Lost

You've heard the saying "carry an umbrella and you'll never get rained on." Hopefully, being prepared in case your dog gets lost will work the same way for you. And it will remind you of how important—and easy—it is to *prevent* losing him.

The basic prevention measures (you've seen all these before) include:

- Make sure your dog is *always* wearing his collar with ID tags attached. (See page 14-15 for information on proper travel tags.)

- Attach the leash to his collar *before* letting him out of your car or motel room—and hold onto the other end!

- *Never* leave him alone and unrestrained—he should be in his travel crate or at least inside your car, with adequate ventilation and shade.

That said, if by some chance you and your dog do get separated, don't panic. Your cool-headed actions now, plus a few advance preparations that you wisely made before leaving home, will maximize your chances of finding him as quickly as possible.

Preparing a Lost Dog poster

Your first advance effort should be in creating a master lost-and-found poster, complete with your dog's photo and detailed description. Feel free to copy the fill-in-the-blanks poster on the following page and use it to create your own poster. (Enlarge it to 8.5" x 11" or even bigger for better visibility.)

First, write a brief description of your pet. Include his name, age,

LOST DOG

Name:

Breed:

Age:

Sex:

Ht: Wt:

Eye color:

Coat color & length:

Collar & ID tags:

Distinctive markings or behaviors:

Last seen at:

Owners:

Home address:

Home Phone (call COLLECT!):

Staying locally at:

Dates at this location:

Local phone:

(Call collect or leave message and we will reimburse you.)

REWARD!

Attach photo here

breed, sex (and if neutered or spayed), coat and eye color, height (at top of head or ears when standing), weight, and any special characteristics, such as a crooked ear or a limp.

Second, find a recent close-up photo of your pet, or take a new one right now. It should clearly show his color, any distinctive markings and his relative size. For example, photograph your dog standing beside a person or a car—if you personally appear in the photo alongside your dog, that also provides visual proof of ownership.

List your cell phone as well as a home phone number or another person's phone number who can receive and relay messages for you. Leave blank spaces for the name, address and phone number of your motel. You'll add that information if and when you actually use the poster.

Store the poster and photo with your dog's other travel papers, which I recommend keeping in a plastic bag inside his first aid kit. Also tuck in a broad tipped marking pen.

Searching for your lost dog

As soon as you realize your pet is missing, begin searching the immediate area in an ever-widening spiral pattern. Keep calling your dog's name—if he's within the sound of your voice, *he'll* most likely find *you*. Try to enlist the aid of other people in your search.

It's important to search *on foot,* not in your car, for several reasons. First, if you're walking, your dog is more likely to catch your scent and come back to you. Second, if you're cruising along in the car, your pet may hear you call him, but by the time he runs to that location, you could be a block—or a mile—away, missing him altogether.

When to call for reinforcements

If you've already searched for an hour or two without finding your dog, it's time to move on to public announcements. Phone the police or county sheriff's office, the animal control department (dog pound) or humane society, and the local veterinary clinics to see if anyone has already found your pet.

Tell them whether or not your dog has been implanted with an identification microchip (see page 15 for more information).

Leave your phone numbers with everyone you speak to, and check back with them periodically. Also ask if any local radio or TV station makes on-the-air "lost pet" announcements as a public service. (Then after you find your dog, be sure to let everyone know, so they don't continue to broadcast the alert.)

Putting up Lost Dog posters

If you have already checked with the local authorities and still haven't found your dog, you'll need to start posting "Lost Dog" notices around the area. That way, when someone does find him, they'll know how to contact you.

Get out your master poster. Attach your pet's photo and fill in the name, address, and phone number of the place where you're staying. Then take it to the local quick print shop and run off *color copies* for posting around town. If you can't find a print shop, pharmacies and "one-stop shopping" stores are also likely to have copy machines these days, though you may have to settle for black-and-white rather than color copies.

Beginning at the location where your dog was last seen and spiraling outward again, start putting up your posters wherever people congregate (ask for permission before posting on privately owned bulletin boards):

🐾 On bulletin boards in parks, shopping malls, or in front of convenience stores

🐾 In store windows—be sure to ask for permission first!

🐾 At bus stops or parking lot entrances

🐾 On street signs or light posts, especially where cars are likely to be stopping or moving slowly

🐾 Near schools or churches

Since your motel's phone number appears alongside your own phone numbers on each poster, notify them of your situation right away. If you can, have a family member stay by the phone in your room in case that all-important "Found Dog" call comes in while you're out searching. If not, ask if the front desk can take messages for you.

Continue to check back periodically at the place where your dog disappeared, in case he returns there. By the end of the day, he'll be hungry, thirsty, and anxious about being separated from you. Leave a handful of his food there, along with something that has your scent on it, such as an already-worn sock. Finding this sign of you during the night may encourage him to stay there until you come back in the morning.

Stay in the local area as long as possible. Even if you don't find your pet right away, he may well turn up after a day or two. A local citizen may take him in overnight, then deliver him to the local animal shelter the next day.

If you do have to leave town without finding your dog, be sure to leave your phone numbers with everyone—motel management, police, dog pound, local veterinarians—along with instructions to call you "COLLECT" if necessary.

And of course, check your phone often for messages. If your dog is picked up and traced by his license number, rabies tag number or microchip ID, you'll probably be contacted at your home phone number, so keep that line of communication open as well.

May your dog never be lost

Your pet is a treasured member of your family, and I sincerely hope you never lose him. Please, spend just a minute or two reviewing the simple steps at the beginning of this chapter to prevent losing him in the first place.

Happy travels to you and your dog!

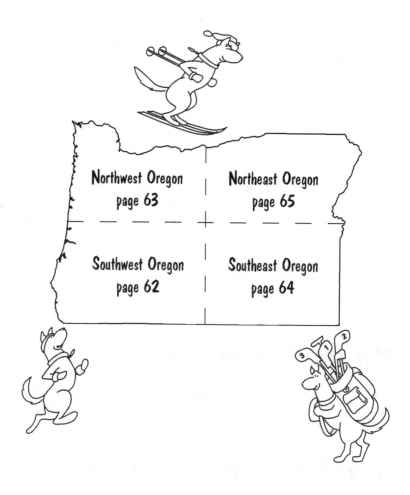

Northwest Oregon
page 63

Northeast Oregon
page 65

Southwest Oregon
page 62

Southeast Oregon
page 64

7: Maps of Oregon & Washington

Each map on the following pages represents one quarter of the state (with a small band of overlap from one map to the next). The maps show all the cities and towns in which one or more dog-friendly lodgings are located.

To make the names as easy as possible to read, roads and other landmarks have been eliminated. (I'm assuming that all of you seasoned travelers bring your own road maps along for planning your route.)

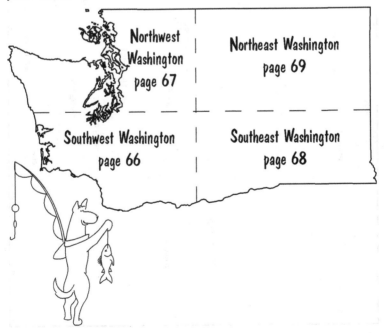

Northwest Washington
page 67

Northeast Washington
page 69

Southwest Washington
page 66

Southeast Washington
page 68

Southwest Oregon

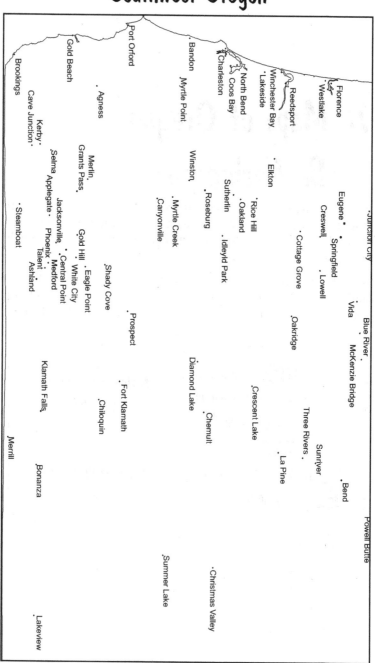

Florence
Westlake
Reedsport
Winchester Bay
Lakeside
North Bend
Coos Bay
Charleston

Port Orford

Gold Beach

Brookings

Bandon

Myrtle Point

Agness

Cave Junction
Kerby

Steamboat

Selma
Applegate
Grants Pass
Merlin

Winston

Elkton

Rice Hill
Oakland

Sutherlin
Roseburg

Myrtle Creek
Canyonville

Jacksonville
Phoenix
Talent
Ashland

Gold Hill
Medford
Central Point
White City
Eagle Point

Shady Cove

Prospect

Junction City

Eugene
Creswell
Springfield
Lowell

Cottage Grove

Idleyld Park

Oakridge

Klamath Falls

Fort Klamath

Chiloquin

Blue River
Vida
McKenzie Bridge

Diamond Lake

Crescent Lake

Chemult

Three Rivers
Sunriver

La Pine

Bend

Powell Butte

Merrill

Bonanza

Summer Lake

Christmas Valley

Lakeview

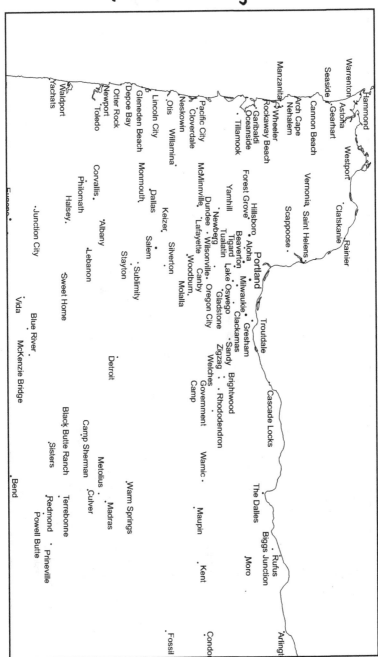

Hammond
Warrenton
Astoria
Seaside
Gearhart
Westport
Clatskanie
Rainier

Manzanita
Arch Cape
Nehalem
Wheeler
Rockaway Beach
Cannon Beach
Vernonia, Saint Helens
Scappoose

Garibaldi
Oceanside
Tillamook
Pacific City
Cloverdale
Neskowin

Otis
Willamina
Lincoln City
Glenedon Beach
Depoe Bay
Otter Rock
Newport
Toledo
Yachats
Waldport

Corvallis
Philomath
Monmouth
Dallas
Keizer
Silverton
Salem
Stayton
Sublimity
Molalla

Hillsboro
Forest Grove
Aloha
Beaverton
Yamhill
Tigard
Newberg
Tualatin
McMinnville
Dundee
Wilsonville
Oregon City
Lafayette
Woodburn
Lake Oswego
Gladstone
Canby
Portland
Milwaukie
Gresham
Clackamas
Troutdale

Halsey
Sweet Home
Lebanon
Albany
Junction City

Detroit
Vida
McKenzie Bridge
Blue River

Sandy
Brightwood
Zigzag
Welches
Rhododendron
Government
Camp

Cascade Locks

Wamic
Warm Springs

Camp Sherman
Black Butte Ranch
Sisters
Metolius
Culver
Madras
Terrebonne
Redmond
Powell Butte
Prineville

Maupin

The Dalles
Moro

Biggs Junction
Rufus

Kent

Bend

Fossil

Condo

Arling

Eugene

Southeast Oregon

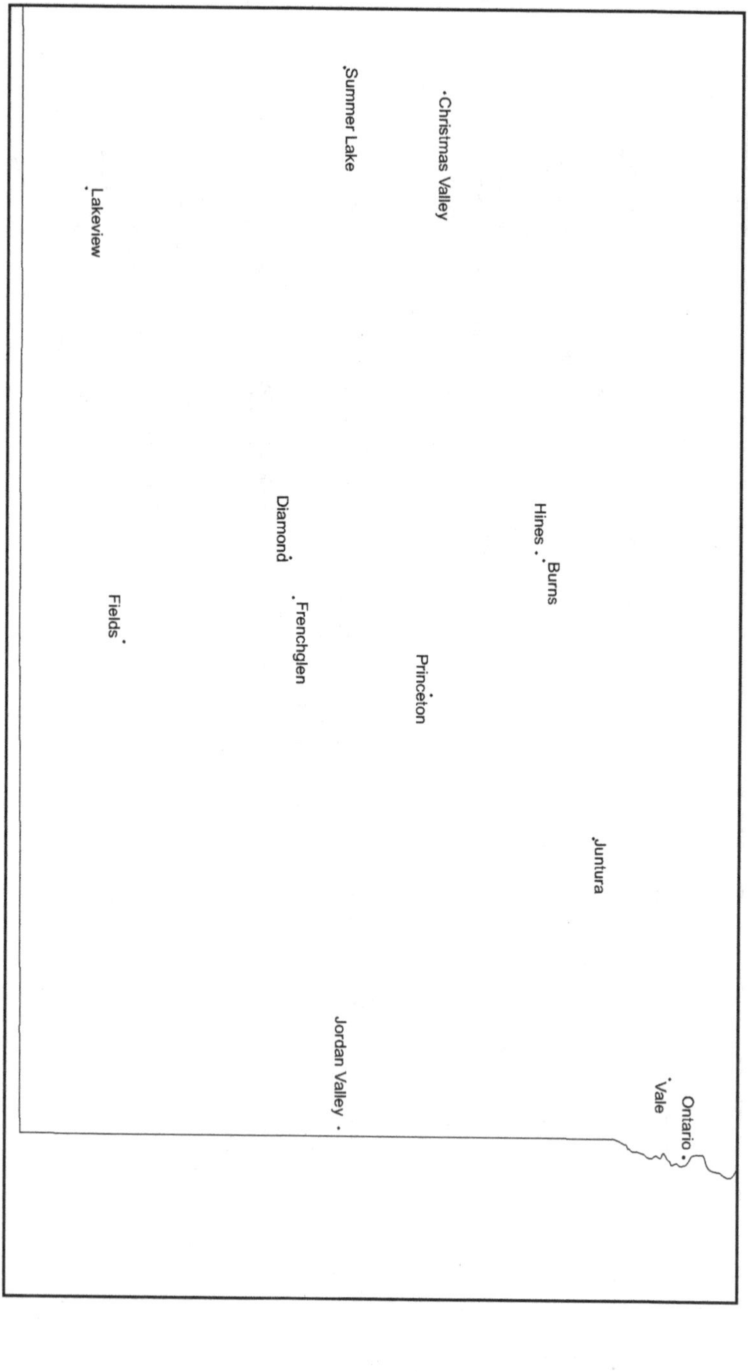

Summer Lake

·Christmas Valley

Lakeview

Diamond

Hines · .Burns

Fields ·

· Frenchglen

Princeton

·Juntura

Jordan Valley ·

Ontario ·
·Vale

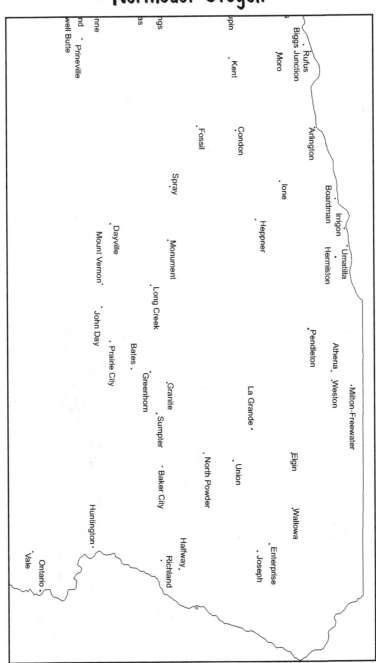

Biggs Junction
Rufus
Moro
Kent
Arlington
Condon
Fossil
Spray
Ione
Boardman
Irrigon
Umatilla
Hermiston
Heppner
Dayville
Mount Vernon
Monument
Long Creek
John Day
Prairie City
Bates
Greenhorn
Granite
Sumpter
Pendleton
Athena
Weston
Milton-Freewater
La Grande
North Powder
Union
Elgin
Wallowa
Enterprise
Joseph
Baker City
Huntington
Halfway
Richland
Ontario
Vale
Prineville
well Butte

Southwest Washington

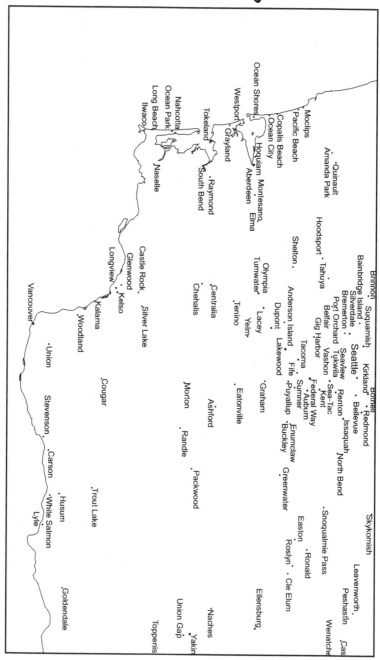

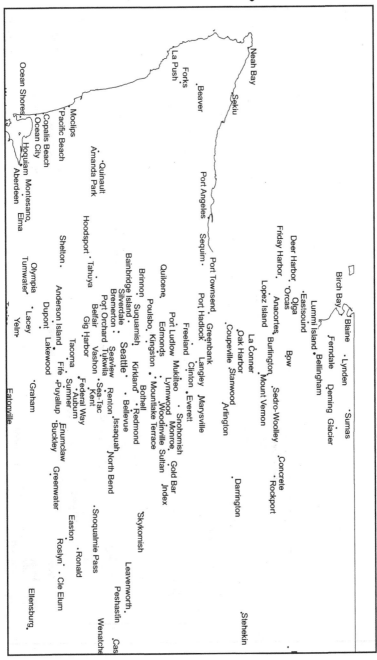

Neah Bay

La Push
Forks
·Beaver
Sekiu

Ocean Shores
·Copalis Beach
·Ocean City
Pacific Beach
Moclips
Hoquiam
Aberdeen
Montesano·
Elma
·Quinault
Amanda Park
Port Angeles

Birch Bay
·Blaine
·Lynden
·Sumas
·Ferndale
Deming
Glacier
Lummi Island
·Bellingham

Deer Harbor
Friday Harbor·
Olga
·Orcas
·Eastsound
Anacortes·
Lopez Island
·Bow
Burlington·
·Sedro-Woolley
·Concrete
·Rockport
Oak Harbor
·La Conner
Coupeville
·Stanwood
Mount Vernon
·Arlington
·Darrington
·Stehekin

Port Townsend
Sequim·
Shelton·
Hoodsport·
·Tahuya
Quilcene·
Olympia
Tumwater·
·Lacey
Yelm·
Anderson Island
Dupont
Lakewood
Brinnon·
Poulsbo·
Kingston·
Bainbridge Island·
Silverdale·
Bremerton·
Port Orchard·
Belfair
Gig Harbor
Vashon
Tacoma
Fife
·Puyallup
·Graham
Eatonville

Greenbank
Port Hadlock
Freeland
Langley
Clinton
Mukilteo
Port Ludlow
Suquamish
Seaview
Tukwila
Edmonds
Lynnwood
Kirkland·
Bothell
·Redmond
·Marysville
·Snohomish
Monroe,
Gold Bar
·Everett
·Woodinville
Sultan
·Mountlake Terrace
Index
Seattle·
Sea-Tac
Kent
·Federal Way
·Auburn
Sumner
·Buckley
·Enumclaw
Greenwater
Renton
·Bellevue
·Issaquah
North Bend
·Skykomish
·Snoqualmie Pass
Easton
Roslyn
·Ronald
·Cle Elum
Leavenworth
·Cas
Peshastin·
Wenatche
Stehekin.
Ellensburg.

Southeast Washington

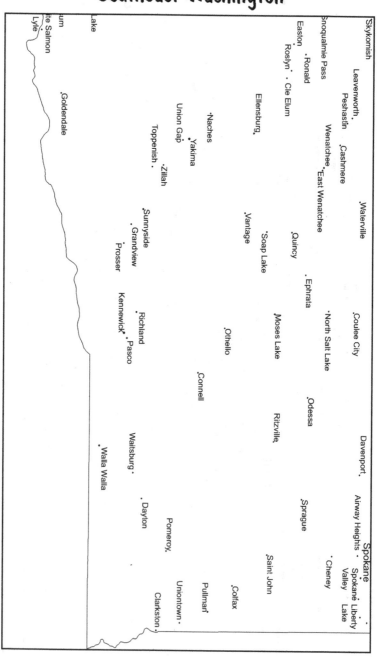

Skykomish

Snoqualmie Pass

Easton
  Roslyn   · Cle Elum
      · Ronald

Leavenworth·
      Peshastin·

      Wenatchee·
          ·East Wenatchee

          ·Cashmere

Lake

ium
te Salmon ·
Lyle·

·Goldendale

          Ellensburg·

          ·Naches
            ·Yakima
    Union Gap·
      Toppenish·
          ·Zillah

·Waterville

          ·Vantage

      Sunnyside·
      · Grandview
        Prosser

·Quincy

·Soap Lake

          · Ephrata

          ·Coulee City

          · North Salt Lake

    Richland
  Kennewick·
      · Pasco

      ·Moses Lake

          ·Othello

          ·Connell

·Odessa

      Davenport·

          Ritzville·

  Walla Walla·

      Waitsburg ·

          · Dayton

·Sprague

            Spokane ·
  Airway Heights ·   Spokane· Liberty
                          Valley Lake

                      · Cheney

      Pomeroy·

              ·Saint John

          Pullman·

          ·Colfax

      Uniontown ·
          Clarkston·

Skykomish

Snoqualmie Pass

Easton
Roslyn · · Cle Elum
· Ronald

Leavenworth ·

Peshastin ·

Ellensburg,

Stehekin

Mazama

· Winthrop
· Twisp
· Carlton

Wenatchee · · East Wenatchee
· Cashmere

· Quincy

Vantage

· Soap Lake

Manson
· Chelan
· Waterville

· Pateros

Brewster

· Mansfield

· Ephrata

Moses Lake

Oroville

· Conconully

· Tonasket

· Omak
· Okanogan

· North Salt Lake

· Coulee City

Coulee Dam
Grand Coulee

· Nespelem

· Wilbur

· Odessa

Ritzville,

Sprague

Saint John

Curlew

Republic

Inchelium
·

Davenport,

· Fruitland

Airway Heights ·

· Cheney

Ione

Kettle Falls
· Colville

Cusick
·

· Chewelah
· Valley

Newport

Loon Lake
·

Deer Park
·

Newman Lake

Spokane
Spokane Liberty
Valley Lake
Otis Orchards
·

Colfax

8: Dog-Friendly Lodgings

This directory chapter is organized by state, then city, then business name. If you know the business name but not the city, see the cross-referenced list in Appendix A: Business Name Index, beginning on page 349. All the lodgings listed here have reported that they allow dogs in some, but not necessarily all, of their rooms or cabins, etc.

🐾 Always call ahead to specifically request a dog-friendly room (or cabin or vacation home, etc.).

Please be aware that the stated policy of some of these lodgings is that they accept dogs "with manager's approval only," meaning they reserve the right to refuse pets that they deem to be overly large, dirty or otherwise disruptive. Another reason might be if they feel that they already have a full quota of pets staying that night.

The daily rates shown here represent a range from off-season low rate to peak-season high rate for 2 people. In most cases, these are the "before tax" prices. These rates are accurate as of the time each business was contacted during the preparation of this book. However, as in most other industries, **all rates and fees shown are "subject to change without notice."** So be sure to verify the current prices when you call to reserve your pet-friendly room.

If you don't see one of your favorite dog-friendly establishments listed in the directory, don't despair. Some managers said that although they do accept dogs, they didn't wish to "go public" with that information in this book. However, most of them also said they will continue to accept customers who have stayed there in the past with their well-behaved dogs. Again, the key is to call ahead.

Lastly, a note about several terms you'll see in this directory: "kitchenette" means a coffeemaker, microwave, refrigerator and stovetop burners (but no oven); "kitchen" means all of those AND a conventional oven.

Oregon's Dog-Friendly Lodgings

Agness, OR

Cougar Lane Lodge   541-247-7233
4219 Agness Rd   6 units, $50–$70
each pet $8/day, full kitchen or microwave, restaurant, lounge,
service station, convenience store, waterfront walking area, open
May thru October

Singing Springs Ranch   541-247-6162, 877-330-3777
34501 Agness Illahe Rd   33 units, $75–$110
pet fee $15/stay, riverside cabins & cottages, continental breakfast,
restaurant, walking trail, 1 block to river, open May thru October,
www.singingspringsresort.com

Albany, OR

Budget Inn   541-926-4246
2727 Pacific Blvd SE   50 units, $55–$66
each pet $20/day, microwave, refrigerator, continental breakfast,
large open walking area, short walk to lakefront hiking trail

Comfort Suites   541-928-2053, 866-625-4884
100 Opal Ct NE   86 units, $89–$104
$15/day 1st pet, $10/day 2nd pet, coffeemaker, microwave,
refrigerator, full breakfast, indoor pool, sauna, hot tub, fitness
room, RV sites, grassy walking area, 1/2 mile to public park,
www.comfortsuites.com/hotel/or100

Econo Lodge   541-926-0170, 888-321-3352
1212 Price Rd SE   78 units, $60–$86
1 to 2 dogs allowed, $10/day, microwave, refrigerator, coffee in
lobby, continental breakfast, grassy walking area, close to public
park, www.econolodge.com/hotel/or158

Holiday Inn Express   541-928-8820, 800-465-4329
105 Opal Ct NE   71 units, $89–$169
pet fee $15/day ($30 maximum), coffeemaker, microwave,
refrigerator, full breakfast, indoor pool, sauna, hot tub, fitness
room, designated pet walking area, 1/4 mile to public park,
www.hiexpress.com/albanyor

KOA Albany/Corvallis   541-967-8521, 800-562-8526
33775 Oakville Road S   6 units, $25–$49
rustic kamping kabins with refrigerator, RV & tent sites, small pet
walking area, nature trail, www.koa.com/where/or/37176/

La Quinta Inn & Suites   541-928-0921, 800-531-5900
251 Airport Rd SE   62 units, $82–$125
1 to 2 dogs, coffeemaker, microwave, refrigerator, full breakfast,
indoor pool, sauna, hot tub, pet walking area, park, www.lq.com

Motel 6   541-926-4233, 800-466-8356
2735 Pacific Blvd SE   42 units, $44–$65
dogs under 50 lbs only, microwave, refrigerator, coffee in lobby,
next to 14-acre park with paved walking path, www.motel6.com

Phoenix Inn Suites   541-926-5696, 888-889-0208
3410 Spicer Dr SE   93 units, $99–$129
pet fee $15/day, coffeemaker, microwave, refrigerator, freshly
baked cookies, full breakfast, indoor pool, hot tub, fitness room,
grassy walking area, short drive to riverfront park,
www.phoenixinn.com/albany

Quality Inn   541-928-5050
1100 Price Rd SE   74 units, $70–$110
pet fee $10/day, extended continental breakfast, indoor pool,
hot tub, next to public park, www.qualityinn.com/hotel/or165

Super 8 Motel   541-928-6322, 866-890-0519
315 Airport Rd SE   71 units, $59–$149
1 to 2 dogs allowed, $10/day, coffeemaker, microwave,
refrigerator, full breakfast, seasonal pool, hot tub, fitness room,
½-acre fenced walking area, short walk to public park, close
to fairgrounds & lakeside walking trail, www.super8.com

Valu Inn   541-926-1538, 800-547-0106
3125 Santiam Hwy SE   78 units, $44
pet fee $10-$20/day, microwave, refrigerator, coffee in lobby,
restaurant, small pet walking area, close to public park

Aloha, OR

America's Best Inns & Suites 503-642-4531, 800-237-8466
3333 SW 198th Ave   52 units, $53–$104
dogs under 30 lbs only, $20/stay, microwave, refrigerator,
extended continental breakfast, grassy walking area, close to
off-leash dog park, www.americasbestinn.com

Applegate, OR

Applegate River Lodge   541-846-6690
15100 Hwy 238   7 units, $145–$165
1 to 2 dogs, $15/day each pet, each room has private spa tub &
deck overlooking river, continental breakfast, lawn for walking
dogs, close to riverside walkway, www.applegateriverlodge.com

Arch Cape, OR

Arch Cape House B & B   503-436-2800, 800-436-2848
31970 E Ocean Lane   9 units, $129–$299
pet fee $35/day, dog-friendly room with private entrance to patio,
full breakfast, wine & appetizers in evening, "welcome bag" of pet
supplies, lawn, 1 block to beach, www.archcapehouse.com

Arch Cape Property Service   503-436-1607, 866-436-1607
32009 E Shingle Mill Lane   30 units, $125–$675
1 to 2 dogs, $30-$60/stay each pet, fully equipped vacation homes,
close to beach, www.archcaperentals.com

Inn at Arch Cape   503-436-0429, 800-352-8034
79340 Hwy 101   6 units, $105–$205
1 to 2 dogs, $15/day each pet, studios & 1-bdrm suites, kitchen,
courtyard & gardens, 1 block to beach, www.innatarchcape.com

Shaw's Oceanfront B & B   503-436-1422
79924 Cannon Rd   1 unit, $175–$195
pet fee $35/stay, beachfront guest suite with kitchen sleeps 5, full
breakfast, deck, close to park, www.shawsoceanfrontbb.com

Arlington, OR

Village Inn   541-454-2646
410 Beech St   34 units, $52
each pet $10/day, microwave, refrigerator, restaurant, lounge,
across street to public park

Ashland, OR

Albion Inn   541-488-3905, 866-933-5688
34 Union St   5 units, $124–$154
each pet, $20/stay, private suite with courtyard entry, full breakfast,
landscaped gardens, large courtyard, sidewalks & alley for
walking dogs, 1¾ miles to off-leash dog park, www.albion-inn.com

Anne Hathaway's Cottage   541-488-1050, 800-643-4434
586 E Main St   14 units, $125–$180
1 to 2 dogs, $10/day each pet, resident labrador greets all visiting
dogs, B & B rooms include full gourmet breakfast, garden suites
with kitchenette include continental breakfast (full breakfast
available for nominal fee), grassy walking area, ½ mile to public
park & off-leash dog park, www.ashlandbandb.com

Ashland Creek Inn   541-482-3315
70 Water St   10 units, $120–$450
pet fee $10/day, rooms & suites, private decks overlooking creek,
full kitchen or coffeemaker-microwave-refrigerator, full breakfast,
next to river & vacant lot for walking dogs, 1 mile to off-leash dog
park, pet sitting service available, www.ashlandcreekinn.com

Ashland Lodges   541-488-2826
170 Emigrant Lake Rd   3 units, $175–$450
2-bdrm cabins sleep 6 to 8, 3-bdrm lodge sleeps 12, sauna, hot tub,
exercise room, lakefront walking area, www.ashlandlodges.com

Ashland Motel   541-482-2561, 800-460-8858
1145 Siskiyou Blvd   27 units, $45–$68
pet fee $10/day, microwave, refrigerator, kitchen, outdoor pool,
garden area for walking dogs, 5 blocks to public park,
www.ashlandmotel.com

Ashland Springs Hotel   541-488-1700, 888-795-4545
212 E Main St   70 units, $89–$259
1 to 2 dogs, $30/stay each pet, refrigerator, continental breakfast,
restaurant, lounge, grassy walking area, ¾ mile to off-leash dog
park, www.ashlandspringshotel.com

Best Western Bard's Inn   541-482-0049, 800-533-9627
132 N Main St   91 units, $81–$226
each pet $15/day, coffeemaker, microwave, refrigerator,
continental breakfast, lounge, outdoor pool, hot tub, next to
off-leash dog park, www.bardsinn.com

Best Western Windsor Inn   541-488-2330, 800-334-2330
2520 Ashland St   92 units, $99–$170
1 to 2 dogs, $15/day, continental breakfast, outdoor pool, hot tub,
fitness room, grassy walking area, 1 mile to walking trail,
www.bestwesternwindsor.com

Ashland, OR (continued)

Blue Moon Bed & Breakfast　　541-482-9228, 800-460-5453
312 Helman St　　　　　　　　　　6 units, $100–$225
dogs allowed in one cottage by advance arrangement only,
$10/day each pet, kitchen, full breakfast & afternoon tea, 5-minute
walk to off-leash dog park, www.bluemoonbandb.com

Callahan's Siskiyou Lodge　　　　　　　　541-482-1299
7100 Old Hwy 99 S　　　　　　　　　19 units, $160–$270
dogs allowed by advance arrangement only, $25/day each pet,
coffeemaker, microwave, refrigerator, restaurant, whirlpool tub in
every room, grassy walking area, next to open field & trail,
www.callahanslodge.com

Cedarwood Inn　　　　　　　541-488-9429, 800-547-4141
1801 Siskiyou Blvd　　　　　　　　58 units, $59–$148
1 to 2 dogs, $10/day each pet, full kitchen or coffeemaker,
continental breakfast, sidewalks for walking dogs, 2½ blocks to
off-leash dog park, www.ashlandcedarwoodinn.com

Chanticleer Inn　　　　　　　541-482-1919, 800-898-1950
120 Gresham St　　　　　　　　　　6 units, $145–$199
1 to 2 small to medium dogs allowed, $15/day each pet, full
breakfast, landscaped yard & butterfly garden, 15-minute walk to
off-leash dog park, www.ashland-bed-breakfast.com

Econo Lodge　　　　　　　　541-482-4700, 800-424-6423
50 Lowe Rd　　　　　　　　　　　　43 units, $55–$90
each pet $10/day, continental breakfast, restaurant, seasonal pool,
grassy walking area, close to trail,
www.econolodge.com/hotel/or137

Flagship Inn of Ashland　　　　541-488-8428, 800-547-6414
1193 Siskiyou Blvd　　　　　　　　64 units, $59–$128
1 to 2 dogs under 80 lbs only, $10/day each pet, coffeemaker,
microwave, refrigerator, continental breakfast, outdoor pool, BBQ,
grassy walking area, short drive to off-leash dog park,
www.ashlandflagshipinn.com

Green Springs Inn　　　　　　　　　　　541-482-0614
11470 Hwy 66　　　　　　　　　　　8 units, $79–$109
some rooms have spa tub & private deck or veranda, restaurant,
grassy walking area, next to trail, www.greenspringsinn.net

Green Springs Box R Ranch   541-482-1873
16799 Hwy 66   4 units, $95–$175
1 to 2 dogs allowed with advance approval only, $25/stay, 2-bdrm
log houses sleep 10, tipis & tent sites, pond, on 1600-acre livestock
ranch, open May thru mid-October, www.boxrranch.com

Hersey House Bed & Breakfast   541-482-4563, 888-343-7739
451 N Main St   4 units, $95–$225
pets allowed in separate 2-bdrm cottage only, kitchen, continental
breakfast delivered to your door, pet treats provided, lawn,
2 blocks to off-leash dog park, www.herseyhouse.com

Historic Pinehurst Inn   541-488-1002
17250 Hwy 66   6 units, $85–$100
1 to 2 dogs, $25/stay each pet, evening reception with beverages &
snacks, on 20 wooded acres with creek for walking dogs,
www.thepinehurstinn.com

Holiday Inn Express   541-201-0202, 800-465-4329
565 Clover Lane   65 units, $99–$119
1 to 2 dogs, $15/day each pet, coffeemaker, microwave,
refrigerator, full breakfast, indoor pool, hot tub, fitness room, lawn,
3 miles to off-leash dog park, www.hiexpress.com/ashlandor

Hyatt Lake Resort   541-482-3331
7979 Hyatt Prairie Rd   54 units, $129–$169
1 large or 2 small dogs only, $10/day each pet, wooded & open
grassy areas for walking dogs, close to lake & trails

Knights Inn   541-482-5111, 800-547-4566
2359 Ashland St   40 units, $52
1 to 2 dogs, $10/day each pet, coffeemaker, microwave,
refrigerator, restaurant, lounge, outdoor pool, hot tub, lawn,
1½ miles to off-leash dog park, www.ashlandknightsinn.com

La Quinta Inn & Suites   541-482-6932, 800-527-5331
434 E Valley View Rd   71 units, $69–$169
coffeemaker, microwave, refrigerator, continental breakfast,
freshly baked cookies, indoor pool, fitness room, open field for
walking dogs, 4-minute walk to public park, www.lq.com

Manor Motel   541-482-2246, 866-261-9733
476 N Main St   12 units, $45–$125
1-bdrm to 2-bdrm suites, kitchen, shaded picnic area, pet walking
area, 15-minute walk to off-leash dog park, www.manormotel.net

Ashland, OR (continued)

Palm Motel   541-482-2636, 800-691-2360
1065 Siskiyou Blvd   13 units, $69–$95
dogs under 45 lbs allowed with advance approval from November
thru February only, $18/day, rooms, suites, kitchen, seasonal pool,
landscaped gardens & large yard for walking dogs,
www.palmcottages.com

Plaza Inn & Suites at Ashland Creek   541-488-8900
98 Central Ave   888-488-0358
1 to 2 dogs allowed, $25/day   91 units, $130–$289
coffeemaker, microwave, refrigerator, coffee in lobby, continental
breakfast, hot tub, fitness room, afternoon snacks & cookies, wine
reception in summer on Thursday thru Saturday evenings,
massage therapy available, grassy walking area, 1 block to public
park, www.plazainnashland.com

Relax Inn   541-482-4423
535 Clover Lane   18 units, $45–$70
pet fee $10/day, microwave, refrigerator, seasonal pool, small pet
walking area, 3 miles to off-leash dog park

Timbers Motel   541-482-4242, 866-550-4400
1450 Ashland St   29 units, $46–$115
kitchen, outdoor pool, across street to public park,
www.ashlandtimberslodging.com

Astoria, OR

Best Western Lincoln Inn   503-325-2205, 800-621-0641
555 Hamburg Ave   75 units, $79–$169
each pet $15/day, kitchenette, full breakfast, indoor pool, sauna,
steam room, hot tub, fitness room, 6 blocks to riverside walking
trail, www.bestwesternastoria.com

Cannery Pier Hotel   503-325-4996, 888-325-4996
10 Basin St   46 units, $179–$375
1 to 2 dogs, $25/stay each pet, coffeemaker, microwave,
refrigerator, continental breakfast, sauna, hot tub, fitness room,
complimentary wine & lox nightly, private decks overlooking river,
bicycles for guest use, pet bed-treats-leash available at front desk,
grassy walking area, 1/4 block to river, www.cannerypierhotel.com

Clementine's B & B   503-325-2005, 800-521-6801
847 Exchange St   8 units, $85–$160
pet fee $15/stay, 3 dog-friendly suites next door to the B & B, full
kitchen or kitchenette, full breakfast, evening wine & light
appetizers, pet treats & bowls, small pet walking area, 1 block to
park, 3 blocks to river walk, www.clementines-bb.com

Crest Motel   503-325-3141, 800-421-3141
5366 Leif Erickson Dr   40 units, $53–$100
on 2½ acres overlooking Columbia River, coffeemaker,
microwave, refrigerator, continental breakfast, hot tub, lawn,
½ mile to riverside walkway, www.astoriacrestmotel.com

Holiday Inn Express   503-325-6222, 888-898-6222
204 W Marine Dr   78 units, $149–$229
each pet $15/day, coffeemaker, microwave, continental breakfast,
restaurant, indoor pool, hot tub, fitness room, lawn for walking
dogs, www.astoriahie.com

Hotel Elliott   503-325-2222, 877-378-1924
357 12th St   32 units, $109–$279
each pet $25/stay, hotel rooms & 4-bdrm 2-bath waterfront suite
that sleeps up to 14, continental breakfast, 2 blocks to riverside
walkway, www.hotelelliott.com

Lamplighter Motel   503-325-4051, 800-845-8847
131 W Marine Dr   29 units, $42–$102
each pet $10/day, continental breakfast, microwave, refrigerator,
complimentary soup & stews on Monday thru Thursday evenings,
area for walking dogs, close to waterfront,
www.astoria-usa.com/lamplighter

Red Lion Inn   503-325-7373, 800-733-5466
400 Industry St   150 units, $99–$150
each pet $20/stay, coffeemaker, microwave, refrigerator,
restaurant, lounge, fitness room, grassy walking area, close to
public park & riverfront walkway, www.redlion.com/astoria

Rosebriar Inn B & B   503-325-7427, 800-487-0224
636 14th St   12 units, $160–$205
dogs under 70 lbs allowed with advance reservation only, $25/stay,
full breakfast, grassy walking area, 3 blocks to riverfront,
www.rosebriar.net

Baker City, OR

Baker City Motel & RV Park   541-523-6381, 800-931-9229
880 Elm St   17 units, call for current rates
1 to 2 small dogs only, $10/stay each pet, designated pet walking
area, 10-minute walk to public park

Best Western Sunridge Inn   541-523-6444, 800-233-2368
1 Sunridge Lane   154 units, $65–$95
each pet $15/day, coffeemaker, microwave, refrigerator,
restaurant, lounge, seasonal pool, hot tub, designated pet walking
area, 1 mile to public park, www.bestwestern.com/sunridgeinn

Bridge Street Inn   541-523-6571
134 Bridge St   41 units, $37–$47
1 to 2 dogs, $5/day each pet, hot breakfast served 3 times/week,
microwave, refrigerator, large open area for walking dogs, across
street to paved walking trail, www.bridgestreetinn.net

Budget Inn   541-523-6324
2205 Broadway St   36 units, $38–$45
pet fee $10/stay, microwave, refrigerator, coffee in lobby, extended
continental breakfast, seasonal pool, grassy walking area, ½ mile
to public park, www.bakercitybudgetinn.com

Eldorado Inn   541-523-6494, 800-537-5756
695 Campbell St   54 units, $52–$81
coffeemaker, refrigerator, continental breakfast, indoor pool,
grassy walking area, ¾ mile to public park, www.eldoradoinn.net

Geiser Grand Hotel   541-523-1889, 888-434-7374
1996 Main St   30 units, $79–$249
each pet $15/day, coffee in lobby, restaurant, lounge, gift shop,
guest pass to gym & pool across street, small pet walking area,
3 blocks to public park & walkway, www.geisergrand.com

Oregon Trail Motel & Restaurant   541-523-5844, 800-523-5882
211 Bridge St   54 units, $42–$81
pet fee $10/day, extended continental breakfast, seasonal pool,
restaurant, sauna, fenced yard, next to trail, 6 blocks to public park

Rodeway Inn   541-523-2242
810 Campbell St   53 units, $66–$80
each pet $10/stay, coffeemaker, refrigerator, small pet walking
area, ½ mile to public park, www.rodewayinn.com/hotel/or047

Super 8 Motel   541-523-8282
250 Campbell St   72 units, $60–$85
each pet $10/day, kitchenette or coffeemaker-microwave-
refrigerator, continental breakfast, indoor pool, hot tub, open field
for walking dogs, 1 mile to public park, www.bakercitysuper8.com

Trail Motel   541-523-4646
2815 10th St   4 units, $35–$50
pet fee $5/day, kitchen in some units

Western Motel   541-523-3700, 800-481-3701
3055 10th St   14 units, $30–$80
1 to 3 dogs, $5/day each pet, coffeemaker, refrigerator, grassy
walking area, next to open field

Bandon, OR

Bandon Beach Motel   541-347-9451, 866-945-0133
1090 SW Portland Ave   23 units, $75–$135
pet fee $10-$15/day, full kitchen or coffeemaker-microwave-
refrigerator, continental breakfast, indoor pool, hot tub, on bluff
overlooking sea, stairway to beach, www.bandonbeachmotel.com

Bandon Inn   541-347-4417, 800-526-0209
355 Hwy 101   57 units, $139–$150
1 to 2 dogs under 50 lbs only, $15/day each pet, coffeemaker,
microwave, refrigerator, continental breakfast, lawn for walking
dogs, ⅓ mile to beach & boardwalk, www.bandoninn.com

Bandon Wayside Motel & RV Park 541-347-3421, 866-670-7199
1175 2nd St SE   10 units, $50–$70
dogs allowed with advance approval only, $5/day each pet,
coffeemaker, microwave, refrigerator, BBQ, picnic area, RV sites,
pet walking area, short drive to beach & off-leash dog park,
www.myspace.com/bandonwaysidemotel

Best Western Inn at Face Rock   541-347-9441, 800-638-3092
3225 Beach Loop Rd   74 units, $136–$261
each pet $25-$40/day, coffeemaker, microwave, refrigerator, full
breakfast, restaurant, indoor pool, sauna, hot tub, fitness room,
lawn for walking dogs, beach access, www.innatfacerock.com

La Kris Inn   541-347-3610, 888-496-3610
940 Oregon Ave SW   12 units, $55–$95
pet fee $10/day, coffeemaker, microwave, refrigerator, ¼ mile to
ocean & park, short drive to off-leash dog park, www.lakrisinn.com

Bandon, OR (continued)

Lamplighter Motel   541-347-4477, 800-650-8817
40 North Ave NE   16 units, $42–$90
kitchenette or microwave, grassy pet walking area, 3 miles to
beach, www.lamplighterbandon.com

Sea Star Guest House   541-347-9632, 888-732-7871
370 1st St SE   5 units, $65–$150
dogs allowed with advance approval only, $10/stay, studios to
2-bdrm suites sleep up to 6, full kitchen or coffeemaker-
microwave-refrigerator, BBQ, deck, grassy walking area,
5-minute drive to beach, www.seastarbandon.com

Shooting Star Motel   541-347-9192
1640 Oregon Ave SW   15 units, $50–$100
each pet $5/day, coffeemaker, microwave, refrigerator, large open
area for walking dogs, www.shootingstarmotel.com

Sunset Oceanfront Lodging   541-347-2453, 800-842-2407
1865 Beach Loop Dr SW   70 units, $65–$150
each pet $10/day, 18 pet-friendly motel units, kitchen, private deck
or patio, continental breakfast, indoor pool, hot tub, beach access,
also cabins & beach houses, www.sunsetmotel.com

Table Rock Motel & Coquille Point Vacation Rentals
840 Beach Loop Rd   541-347-2700, 800-457-9141
1 to 2 dogs, $10/day each pet   26 units, $40–$139
kitchenette or coffeemaker-microwave-refrigerator, grassy walking
area, beach access, www.tablerockmotel.com

Bates, OR

Boulder Creek Ranch   541-421-3031
72585 Middle Fork Lane   1 unit, $53–$70
fully equipped 1-bdrm cabin with kitchen sleeps 4, on 160 acres
surrounded by national forest & hiking trails, horses welcome too,
www.bouldercreekranch.net

Beaverton, OR

Budget Inn   503-646-2155
13295 SW Canyon Rd   32 units, $72–$88
1 to 2 dogs under 35 lbs only, $8/day each pet, microwave,
refrigerator, coffee in lobby, lawn, 3 blocks to public park

Comfort Inn & Suites   503-643-9100, 866-572-6232
13455 SW Tualatin Valley Hwy   105 units, $95
1 to 2 dogs under 35 lbs only, $15/day each pet, coffeemaker,
microwave, refrigerator, extended continental breakfast,
restaurant, seasonal pool, fitness room, grassy walking area,
www.portlandcomfortinn.com

Extended StayAmerica   503-439-1515, 800-398-7829
18665 NW Eider Ct   122 units, $85–$96
pet fee $25/day ($150 maximum), studios with kitchenette,
www.extendedstayamerica.com/795

Homestead Studio Suites   503-690-3600, 800-804-3724
875 SW 158th Ave   142 units, $70–$113
1 to 2 dogs, $25/day ($75 maximum), kitchenette, pet walking
area, ¼ mile to walking trail, www.homesteadhotels.com/105

Homewood Suites   503-614-0900
15525 NW Gateway Ct   123 units, $99–$189
1 to 2 dogs under 50 lbs only, $15/day each pet ($75 maximum),
suites with kitchenette, full breakfast, Monday thru Thursday
evenings complimentary beer-wine-salad-hot entree, fitness room,
small grassy area for walking dogs, 1 block to public park,
www.homewoodsuites.com

Peppertree Inn   503-641-7477
10720 SW Allen Blvd   73 units, $79–$84
1 to 2 dogs, $15/day each pet, coffeemaker, microwave,
refrigerator, full breakfast, outdoor pool, hot tub, walking path to
pond, 3 miles to off-leash dog park, www.peppertreeinn.com

Phoenix Inn Suites   503-614-8100, 888-944-8100
15402 NW Cornell Rd   98 units, $99–$129
1 to 2 dogs under 50 lbs only, $15/stay, coffeemaker, microwave,
refrigerator, continental breakfast, indoor pool, hot tub, fitness
room, freshly baked cookies, lawn for walking dogs, short walk to
public park, www.phoenixinn.com/beaverton

Bend, OR

A Bend Cottage Experience   541-317-8595
22122 Neff Rd   3 units, $99–$255
pet fee $7.50/day, 2-bdrm to 3-bdrm cottages with full kitchen
sleep up to 10, some with hot tub-BBQ-picnic area-fenced yard,
close to public park, www.bendcottages.com

Bend, OR (continued)

A Stone's Throw Bungalow   206-339-6422
NW Elgin Ave   1 unit, $93–$99
pet fee $10/day, fully equipped 2-bdrm bungalow sleeps 6, deck,
BBQ, fenced backyard, 5 blocks to public park & river, short drive
to off-leash dog park, www.astonesthrowbungalow.com

Absolutely Bend Vacation Homes   541-280-1813
61185 Larsen Rd   6 units, $150–$195
1 to 2 dogs, fully furnished 3-bdrm to 5-bdrm vacation homes,
some with hot tub or fenced yard, close to riverside walking trail,
www.absolutelybend.com

Alpenglow Vacation Rentals   541-385-7100
1 to 2 dogs, $100-$150/stay   5 units, $150–$275
1-bdrm to 4-bdrm vacation homes sleep up to 9, BBQ, patio, deck,
close to off-leash dog park, www.alpenglowvacationrentals.com

Bend Dutch Vacation Rentals   541-322-0218, 866-322-0218
61198 Tall Timber Ct   20 units, $125–$300
each pet $10/day, condos-cottages-vacation homes, some with pool
or hot tub, close to public parks, www.benddutchrentals.com

Bend Inn & Suites   541-388-4114, 888-678-2363
15 NE Butler Market Rd   99 units, $69–$139
each pet $15/stay, coffeemaker, microwave, refrigerator, extended
continental breakfast, seasonal pool, hot tub, freshly baked
cookies, small pet walking area, www.bendinnsuites.com

Bend Riverside Motel & Suites   541-389-2363, 800-284-2363
1565 NW Hill St   80 units, $72–$169
pet fee $25/day, kitchenette or coffeemaker, indoor pool, sauna,
hot tub, lawn, 5 blocks to park, www.bendriversidemotel.com

Bend Vacation Rentals   541-385-9492, 877-385-9492
377 SW Century Dr # D2   40 units, $105–$425
pet fee $25-$50/day, townhouses, vacation homes, close to parks-
trails-open areas for walking dogs, www.bendvacationrentals.com

Best Western Inn & Suites   541-382-1515, 800-937-8376
721 NE 3rd St   100 units, $69–$159
pets allowed with manager's approval only, each pet $10/day,
coffeemaker, microwave, refrigerator, continental breakfast,
seasonal pool, hot tub, fitness room, small pet walking area, 1 mile
to off-leash dog park, www.bestwestern.com/prop_38096

Budget Inn   541-389-1448
1300 SE 3rd St   24 units, $28–$68
full kitchen or microwave & refrigerator, next to river

Cascade Lodge   541-382-2612
420 SE 3rd St   33 units, $39–$99
each pet $10/day, kitchenette or microwave & refrigerator,
continental breakfast, seasonal pool, small pet walking area,
5-minute walk to public park, www.cascadelodgemotel.com

Central Oregon Accommodations   541-617-0179, 866-617-0179
dogs allowed with advance approval only   30 units, $110–$320
each pet $10/day, condos-townhouses-vacation homes, outdoor
pool, hot tub, www.centraloregonaccomm.com

Chalet Motel   541-382-6124
510 SE 3rd St   22 units, $28–$40
each pet $10/day, kitchenette, continental breakfast, 10-minute
walk to public park, www.cascadelodgemotel.com

Country Inn the City   541-385-7639
1776 NE 8th St   2 units, $89
1 to 2 dogs, $20/stay, full breakfast, on 1 acre, close to off-leash
dog park, http://home.bendbroadband.com/thecountryinnthecity

Crane Prairie Resort & RV Park   541-383-3939
                                                     3 units, $45–$60
rustic cabins sleep 4 to 8, RV sites, small pet walking area, next to
reservoir, www.crane-prairie-resort-guides.com

Cricketwood Country B & B's Champagne Chalet
63520 Cricketwood Rd   541-330-0747, 877-330-0747
pet fee $10/day   1 unit, $140
kitchen, private hydrotherapy spa, on 5 acres, next door to their
B & B (no dogs allowed in that facility), www.cricketwood.com

Cultus Lake Resort   541-389-3230, 800-616-3230
Hwy 46 Century Dr   23 units, $80–$145
each pet $10/day, studios to 1-bdrm cabins, kitchen, lakefront &
forest land for walking dogs, www.cultuslakeresort.com

Days Inn   541-383-3776, 866-388-7972
849 NE 3rd St   75 units, $64–$169
each pet $6/day, coffeemaker, microwave, refrigerator, continental
breakfast, seasonal pool, hot tub, fitness room, grassy walking
area, ½ mile to public park, www.daysinn.com/hotel/15567

Bend, OR (continued)

Dunes Motel   541-382-6811, 800-681-9336
1515 NE 3rd St   30 units, $40–$125
2 small dogs or 1 larger dog per room, $7/day each pet,
coffeemaker, microwave, refrigerator, continental breakfast,
lawn for walking dogs, 5-minute walk to public park

Econo Lodge   541-382-7711, 800-304-4050
437 NE 3rd St   58 units, $59–$99
1 to 2 dogs under 25 lbs only, $10/stay, kitchen or coffeemaker-
microwave-refrigerator, continental breakfast, restaurant, seasonal
pool, 3 blocks to park, www.econolodge.com/hotel/or173

Elk Lake Resort   541-480-7378 or 541-480-7228
Cascade Lakes Hwy   10 units, $150–$325
1 to 2 dogs, rustic camping cabins (no water or electricity) to
modern cabins with full kitchen & bathroom that sleep up to 6,
tent sites, restaurant, www.elklakeresort.net

Entrada Lodge   541-382-4080, 888-505-6343
19221 SW Century Dr   79 units, $79–$129
each pet $10/day, coffeemaker, continental breakfast, seasonal
pool, hot tub, walking trail, www.entradalodge.com

Fairfield Inn & Suites   541-318-1747, 800-228-2800
1626 NW Wall St   80 units, $89–$219
pet fee $75/stay, coffeemaker, extended continental breakfast,
light dinner, freshly baked cookies, indoor pool, hot tub, fitness
room, across street to public park, www.marriott.com/rdmfi

Hillside Inn Bed & Breakfast   541-389-9660, 800-550-1821
1744 NW 12th St   2 units, $168
pet fee $20/day, private entrance to pet-friendly studio suite, full
breakfast, BBQ, patio, hot tub, landscaped garden, open area for
walking dogs, 2 blocks to public park, www.bendhillsideinn.com

Holiday Inn Express   541-317-8500, 800-261-9168
20615 Grandview Dr   99 units, $99–$139
each pet $10/day, kitchenette or coffeemaker-microwave-
refrigerator, extended continental breakfast, indoor pool, hot tub,
fitness room, small pet walking area, 2 miles to public park,
www.hiexpress.com/bendor

Holiday Motel 541-382-4620, 800-252-0121
880 SE 3rd St 25 units, $35–$59
each pet $10/day, kitchen, continental breakfast, hot tub,
10-minute walk to public park, www.cascadelodgemotel.com

Home Spun Vacation Rentals 541-389-2278
1630 SE Tempest Dr Ste 6 3 units, $99–$255
each pet $25/day, 2-bdrm to 3-bdrm vacation homes sleep up to 10,
BBQ, deck, picnic area, hot tub, www.homespunvacations.com

KOA Sisters/Bend 541-549-3021, 800-562-0363
67667 Hwy 20 3 units, $60–$99
1 to 2 dogs, $10/stay, 1-room to 2-room kamping kabins, seasonal
pool, mini-golf, park & trails, www.koa.com/where/or/37151/

La Quinta Inn & Suites 541-388-2227
61200 S Hwy 97 65 units, $79–$209
coffeemaker, continental breakfast, indoor pool, small pet walking
area, ½ mile to public park, www.lq.com

Lavabelles Downtown Vacation Rentals 541-497-3242
888-820-5084
each pet $20/stay 11 units, $125–$400
1-bdrm to 4-bdrm bungalows & vacation homes sleep 2 to 10, hot
tub, fenced yard, 2 blocks to riverfront park, www.lavabelles.com

Motel 6 541-382-5961, 800-466-8356
201 NE 3rd St 60 units, $45–$80
1 to 2 dogs, no fee for 1st dog, $5/day for 2nd dog, microwave,
refrigerator, seasonal pool, ½ mile to park, www.motel6-bend.com

Motel West 541-389-5577, 800-282-5577
228 NE Irving Ave 39 units, $36–$49
each pet $10/day, microwave, refrigerator, coffee in lobby,
10-minute walk to public park, www.cascadelodgemotel.com

Mount Bachelor Motel 541-382-6365
2359 NE Division St 19 units, $35–$40
1 to 2 dogs, $5/day each pet, microwave, refrigerator, across street
to riverside public park

Quality Inn 541-318-0848, 800-831-3537
20600 Grandview Dr 58 units, $79–$119
each pet $10/day, microwave, refrigerator, coffee in lobby,
continental breakfast, indoor pool, hot tub, small pet walking area,
next to open field, www.qualityinn.com/hotel/or079

Bend, OR (continued)

Red Lion Hotel Bend   541-382-7011, 800-733-5466
1415 NE 3rd St   75 units, $81–$166
pet fee $10/day, coffeemaker, microwave, refrigerator, full
breakfast, restaurant, seasonal pool, hot tub, fitness room, pet
walking area, 2-minute walk to park, www.redlion.com/bendnorth

RentConnect.com Central Oregon Rentals
60970 Alpine Lane   541-383-1780, 888-702-0761
1 to 3 dogs, $50/stay   200+ units, $85–$450
fully equipped vacation homes in Bend & surrounding areas, close
to national park land & trails, www.rentconnect.com

Riverhouse Resort   541-389-3111, 800-547-3928
3075 N Hwy 97   220 units, $89–$285
coffeemaker, microwave, refrigerator, continental breakfast,
restaurant, lounge, indoor & outdoor pools, sauna, hot tub, fitness
room, nature trails, 1/2 block to park, www.riverhouse.com

Royal Gateway Motel   541-382-5631
475 SE 3rd St   21 units, $45–$100
each pet $10/stay, microwave, refrigerator, coffee in lobby,
continental breakfast, lawn, 1 mile to off-leash dog park

Shilo Inn   541-389-9600, 800-222-2244
3105 NE O B Riley Rd   151 units, $109–$249
pet fee $25/stay, kitchen or coffeemaker-microwave-refrigerator,
continental breakfast, restaurant, indoor pool, seasonal pool,
sauna, hot tub, fitness room, 4 blocks to park, www.shiloinns.com

Sleep Inn   541-330-0050
600 NE Bellevue Dr   59 units, $69–$139
pet fee $10/stay, microwave, refrigerator, continental breakfast,
seasonal pool, hot tub, open field for walking dogs, 4 miles to
off-leash dog park, www.sleepinn.com/hotel/or420

Sonoma Lodge   541-382-4891
450 SE 3rd St   17 units, $39–$79
each pet $6/day, kitchenette, continental breakfast, pet walking
area, short drive to public park, www.sonomalodge.com

Sugarloaf Mountain Motel   541-330-5998, 866-499-3971
62980 N Hwy 97   146 units, $49–$110
small petsonly, $15/day, coffeemaker, microwave, refrigerator,
coffee in lobby, seasonal pool, www.sugarloafmtmotel.com

Suite Escapes   541-389-0222
61 SW Taft Ave   4 units, $170–$265
1 to 2 dogs, kitchen, hot tub, patio & grassy walking area,
1 block to public park, www.suiteescapes.net

Sunriver Retreats   541-593-3162
55755 Cone Place   4 units, call for current rates
dogs allowed with manager's advance approval only, smallest of
their vacation homes is 5-bdrm, most sleep 14 to 30, large open
areas for walking dogs, www.sunriverretreats.com

Super 8 Motel   541-388-6888, 800-800-8000
1275 S Hwy 97   79 units, $74–$95
1 to 2 dogs, $10/stay each pet, coffeemaker, continental breakfast,
indoor pool, hot tub, 2 miles to off-leash dog park,
www.super8.com

Tom Tom Motel   541-382-4734
3600 N Hwy 97   10 units, $49–$79
1 to 2 dogs allowed with manager's approval only, $6-$10/stay,
coffeemaker, refrigerator, continental breakfast, pet walking area,
across street to open field, www.jbmailroom.com/tomtom

Towneplace Suites   541-382-5006, 800-257-3000
755 SW 13th Place   71 units, $89–$229
1 to 3 dogs, $75/stay, kitchen, extended continental breakfast, pet
walking area, close to public park, www.marriott.com/rdmts

Westward Ho Motel   541-382-2111, 800-999-8143
904 SE 3rd St   65 units, $32–$99
each pet $5/stay, microwave, refrigerator, indoor pool, hot tub,
small walking area, 1/4 mile to park, www.westwardhomotel.com

Biggs Junction, OR

Dinty's Motor Inn at Biggs Junction   541-739-2596
91581 Biggs-Rufus Hwy   800-218-5913
call ahead to reserve a pet-friendly room   26 units, $45–$75
seasonal pool, gravel & grassy pet walking areas, 3 miles to public
park

Nu Vu Motel   541-739-2525
91495 Biggs-Rufus Hwy   16 units, $46–$56
each pet $10/day, coffeemaker, microwave, refrigerator, small pet
walking area, short drive to public park

Biggs Junction, OR (continued)

Three Rivers Inn   541-739-2501
91484 Biggs-Rufus Hwy   40 units, $59–$89
1 to 2 small dogs only, $15/day, coffeemaker, microwave, refrigerator, continental breakfast, grassy walking area, next to river & walking trails, www.biggsthreeriversinn.com

Black Butte Ranch, OR

Black Butte Ranch   541-595-6211, 866-901-2961
8 miles west of Sisters, OR on Hwy 20   120+ units, $340–$385
6 vacation homes are dog-friendly, full kitchen, grassy areas & paved trails for walking dogs, www.blackbutteranch.com

Blue River, OR

Belknap Hot Springs Lodge & Gardens   541-822-3512
59296 N Belknap Springs Rd   19 units, $60–$100
pet fee $10/day, dogs allowed in rustic cabins with kitchen, large open area for walking dogs, 2 manmade soaking pools filled from the hot springs, www.belknaphotsprings.com

McKenzie River Mountain Resort   541-822-6272
51664 Blue River Dr   6 units, $80–$160
dogs under 40 lbs only, $15/day each pet, 2-bdrm to 3-bdrm cottages & bunkhouse, on 8 wooded acres, close to riverfront park, www.rivermountainresort.com

Boardman, OR

Dodge City Inn   541-481-2441
100 1st St NW   39 units, $48
continental breakfast, outdoor pool, lounge, near off-leash dog park

Rodeway Inn   541-481-2375, 800-336-4485
105 Front St   51 units, $69
coffeemaker, microwave, refrigerator, continental breakfast, seasonal pool, riverside trail, www.rodewayinn.com/hotel/or097

Brightwood, OR

Mountain Retreats Vacation Homes 503-622-3212, 800-622-4080
63045 E Brightwood Bridge Rd   20 units, $135–$450
each pet $25/stay, cabins-condos-vacation homes, some with hot tub, surrounded by national forest, www.mtnretreats.com

Rainbow Bungalow 503-789-7206
64125 E Relton Lane 1 unit, $219–$399
each pet $25/stay, 2-bdrm plus loft cabin sleeps 8, kitchen, hot tub,
short walk to riverfront meadow for walking dogs, 4 miles to
public park & walking trail, www.mthoodlifestyle.com

Brookings, OR

Best Western Beachfront Inn 541-469-7779, 800-468-4081
16008 Boat Basin Rd 102 units, $129–$230
each pet $10/day, coffeemaker, microwave, refrigerator, outdoor
pool, hot tub, grassy walking area, pet cleanup stations, beach
access, www.bestwestern.com/beachfrontinnbrookings

Blue Coast Inn 541-469-2161
1216 Chetco Ave 36 units, $55–$80
each pet $5-$15/day, coffeemaker, microwave, refrigerator,
continental breakfast, seasonal pool, small walking area, close to
hiking trail, 1/4 mile to beach access, www.brookingsmotel.com

Harbor Inn Motel 541-469-3194, 800-469-8444
15991 Hwy 101 S 30 units, $69–$94
each pet $12/day, coffeemaker, microwave, refrigerator, fish
freezers for guest use, across street to open field for walking dogs,
1/4 mile to beach, www.harborinnmotel.com

Pacific Sunset Inn 541-469-2141, 800-469-2141
1144 Chetco Ave 38 units, $49–$59
dogs under 20 lbs only, $10/day each pet, full kitchen, short drive
to ocean & state park, www.pacificsunsetinn.com

Westward Inn 541-469-7471, 888-521-6020
1026 Chetco Ave 30 units, $75–$100
pet fee $12/day, coffeemaker, microwave, refrigerator, continental
breakfast, sidewalks for walking dogs, 2 blocks to beach,
www.westwardinn.com

Whaleshead Beach Resort 541-469-7446, 800-943-4325
19921 Whaleshead Rd 142 units, $95–$195
each pet $10/day, cottages sleep 2 to 8, full kitchen, restaurant,
lounge, hot tub, grassy walking area, convenience store, RV sites,
700-ft-long tunnel under road for access to beach, short drive to
park, www.whalesheadresort.com

Brookings, OR (continued)

Wild Rivers Motor Lodge   541-469-5361
437 Chetco Ave   30 units, $59–$99
each pet $10-$20/stay, coffeemaker, microwave, refrigerator, pet
towels & bedding, pet walking area, 4 blocks to public park, 1 mile
to beach, www.wildriversmotorlodge.com

Burns, OR

Burns America's Best Inn   541-573-1700, 800-237-8466
999 Oregon Ave   38 units, $38–$70
each pet $5/day, coffeemaker, microwave, refrigerator, continental
breakfast, indoor pool, hot tub, open field for walking dogs, ½ mile
to public park, www.bestinnoregon.com

City Center Motel   541-573-5100
73 W Monroe St   20 units, $37–$64
full kitchen or coffeemaker, open field, 5 blocks to public park

Crystal Crane Hot Springs   541-493-2312
59315 Hwy 78   5 units, $45
pet fee $7/day, rustic cabins, camp kitchen, shared bathhouse with
showers & private hot tubs fed by natural hot springs, RV & tent
sites, small pet walking area, www.cranehotsprings.com

Horseshoe Inn   541-573-2034, 866-834-2034
30868 Hwy 20 E   32 units, $45–$69
pet fee $5-$10/day, coffeemaker-microwave-refrigerator, open field

Lone Pine Guest Ranch   541-573-2103
72172 Long Pine Rd   2 units, $95–$135
1 pet-friendly room with kitchenette, full breakfast, large open area
for walking dogs, bike riding area

Silver Spur Motel   541-573-2077, 800-400-2077
789 N Broadway Ave   26 units, $47–$66
each pet $5/day, coffeemaker, microwave, refrigerator, continental
breakfast, grassy walking area, near park, www.silverspurmotel.net

Camp Sherman, OR

Black Butte Resort   541-595-6514
25635 SW Forest Svc Rd 1419   6 units, $65–$85
each pet $10/day, motel rooms, kitchenette, BBQ, picnic tables,
RV & tent sites, riverfront park, www.blackbutterv.com

Cold Springs Resort   541-595-6271
25615 Cold Springs Resort Lane   7 units, $120–$162
each pet $8/day, cabins with full kitchen, covered porch
overlooking river, BBQ, fire pit, RV sites, 1-acre lawn & trails for
walking dogs, www.coldsprings-resort.com

Lake Creek Lodge   541-595-6331, 800-797-6331
13375 SW Fourth Service Rd 1419   18 units, $99–$400
1 to 2 dogs, $10/day each pet, cabins with full kitchen sleep 2 to 7,
seasonal restaurant & pool open in summer only,
www.lakecreeklodge.com

Canby, OR

Canby Country Inn   503-266-5400, 888-825-6343
463 SW 1st Ave   35 units, $69–$84
1 to 2 dogs, coffeemaker, microwave, refrigerator, continental
breakfast, small pet walking area, 1 mile to public park,
www.canbycountryinn.com

Cannon Beach, OR

Cannon Beach Ecola Creek Lodge   503-436-2776, 800-873-2749
208 5th St   22 units, $55–$230
1 to 2 dogs, $20/day each pet, full kitchen or coffeemaker-
microwave-refrigerator, across street to public park, 1/4 block to
beach, www.cannonbeachlodge.com

Cannon Beach Property Management   503-436-2021
3188 S Hemlock   877-386-3402
each pet $40/stay   41 units, $110–$390
ocean-view & oceanfront condos-cottages-vacation homes, indoor
pool, lawn for walking dogs, close to ocean, www.cbpm.com

Cannon Beach Vacation Rentals   503-436-0940, 866-436-0940
1 to 2 dogs, $50/stay each pet   60 units, $150–$550
fully equipped condos (located at Sandcastle Condominiums) &
vacation homes, close to ocean, www.visitcb.com

Ecola Inn   503-436-2457
1164 Ecola Ct   13 units, $101
1 small dog only, full kitchen in all units, 7-night minimum stay,
next to beach, www.ecolainn.com

Cannon Beach, OR (continued)

Hallmark Resort   503-436-1566, 888-448-4449
1400 S Hemlock   142 units, $104–$369
1 to 2 dogs, $20/day each pet, full kitchen or coffeemaker-
microwave-refrigerator, indoor pool, sauna, hot tub, fitness room,
pet basket with frisbee-bowl-bones, dog washing station, pooper
scooper stations, beachfront walking area, www.hallmarkinns.com

Haystack Lodgings   503-436-2714, 800-507-2714
487 S Hemlock St   50 units, $59–$375
each pet $15/day, rooms-suites-vacation homes, grassy walking
area, close to beach, www.haystacklodgings.com

Haystack Resort   503-436-1577, 800-499-2220
3339 S Hemlock St   23 units, $60–$260
1 to 2 dogs under 50 lbs only, $15/day, studios, 1-bdrm to 2-bdrm
suites, full kitchen or coffeemaker-microwave-refrigerator, indoor
pool, grassy walking area, across street to public park, short walk
to beach, www.haystackresort.com

Hearthstone Inn   503-436-1392, 800-438-4107
107 E Jackson St   4 units, $115–$185
each pet $15/day, kitchenette, 1 block to beach,
www.hearthstoneinncannonbeach.com/index.asp

Hidden Villa Cottages   503-436-2237
188 E Van Buren St   6 units, $85–$165
pet fee $10/stay, 1-bdrm cottages with full kitchen, pet bowls-
treats-towels-waste bags provided, designated pet walking area,
2 blocks to beach, www.hiddenvillacottages.com

Inn at Cannon Beach   503-436-9085, 800-321-6304
3215 S Hemlock St   40 units, $139–$259
1 to 2 dogs, $10/day each pet, coffeemaker, microwave,
refrigerator, extended continental breakfast, guest pass to local
fitness center, gravel walking area, 1 block to public park & beach,
www.atcannonbeach.com

Land's End Beachfront Motel   503-436-2264, 800-793-1477
263 2nd St   15 units, $130–$295
1 to 2 dogs under 50 lbs only, $15/day, full kitchen or coffeemaker-
microwave-refrigerator, hot tub, large open area for walking dogs,
www.landsendmotel.com

McBee Motel Cottages   503-436-2569, 800-238-4107
888 S Hemlock St   10 units, $85–$185
each pet $15/day, 1940s shingled cottages with kitchenette,
picnic area, BBQ, fire pit, flower gardens, 1 block to beach,
www.cannonbeachhotellodgings.com

Ocean Lodge   503-436-2241, 888-777-4047
2864 Pacific St   45 units, $179–$369
1 to 2 dogs, $15/day each pet, coffeemaker, microwave,
refrigerator, continental breakfast, guest pass to fitness center,
dog washing station, beachfront, www.theoceanlodge.com

Surfsand Resort   503-436-2274, 800-547-6100
148 W Gower St   83 units, $159–$379
1 to 2 dogs, $15/day each pet, coffeemaker, microwave,
refrigerator, apples & freshly baked cookies, restaurant, lounge,
indoor pool, sauna, hot tub, fitness room, pet blanket-towel-bowls-
treats, www.surfsand.com

Tolovana Inn   503-436-2211, 800-333-8890
3400 S Hemlock St, Tolovana Park   175 units, $69–$419
1 to 3 dogs under 80 lbs only, $15/day each pet, beachfront
studios, 1-bdrm to 2-bdrm suites, full kitchen or coffeemaker,
beach fire pit, indoor pool, sauna, hot tub, fitness room,
www.tolovanainn.com

Van Buren Lighthouse Inn   503-436-2929, 866-265-1686
963 S Hemlock   8 units, $109–$219
pet fee $10/day, pets allowed in 4 rooms, coffeemaker, microwave,
refrigerator, continental breakfast, small pet walking area, 1 block
to beach, www.vblinn.com

Canyonville, OR

Best Western Canyonville Inn & Suites   541-839-4200
200 Creekside Dr   73 units, $79–$120
pet fee $15/day, coffeemaker, microwave, refrigerator, extended
continental breakfast, indoor pool, hot tub, fitness room, walking
area, close to park, www.bestwestern.com/canyonvilleinnandsuites

Leisure Inn   541-839-4278
554 SW Pine St   36 units, $50–$55
pet fee $10/stay, full kitchen or coffeemaker, continental breakfast,
outdoor pool, small pet walking area, 1 block to public park,
www.canyonvilleleisureinn.net

Canyonville, OR (continued)

Riverside Lodge   541-839-4557
1786 Stanton Park Rd   12 units, $55–$80
each pet $10/stay, coffeemaker, microwave, refrigerator, BBQ,
riverside picnic area, close to park, www.riverside-lodgemotel.com

Valley View Motel   541-839-4550
1926 Stanton Park Rd   11 units, $59–$65
pet fee $10/stay, coffeemaker, microwave, refrigerator, BBQ,
picnic tables, open field for walking dogs, next to riverside
walkway, www.valleyview-motel.com

Cascade Locks, OR

Best Western Columbia River Inn   541-374-8777, 800-595-7108
735 NW WaNaPa St   62 units, $79–$169
small pets only, $10/day each pet, coffeemaker, microwave,
refrigerator, continental breakfast, indoor pool, fitness room,
grassy walking area, www.bwcolumbiariverinn.com

Bridge of the Gods Motel & RV Park   541-374-8628
630 SW WaNaPa St   15 units, $69–$99
each pet $10/day, motel rooms & cabins, kitchenette, jacuzzi tubs,
www.bridgeofgodsmotel.com

Columbia Gorge Inn   541-374-0015, 866-497-6474
404 SW WaNaPa St   30 units, $59–$99
pet fee $10/day, coffeemaker, microwave, refrigerator, lawn,
5-minute walk to river, www.columbiagorgemotelor.com

KOA Cascade Locks/Portland East   541-374-8668,
841 NW Forest Lane   800-562-8698
                                              11 units, $43–$129
kamping kabins range from rustic sleeping rooms with shared
bathhouse to larger units with full kitchen & bathroom, BBQ,
seasonal pool, hot tub, RV sites, on 10 acres for walking dogs,
1/4 mile to river, www.koa.com/where/or/37105/

Cave Junction, OR

Country Hills Resort   541-592-3406, 888-592-3406
7901 Caves Hwy   11 units, $59–$90
pet fee $5/day, motel rooms, cabins with full kitchen sleep 2 to 6,
continental breakfast, RV & tent sites, on 22 acres next to creek &
trails, www.countryhillsresort.com

Junction Inn   541-592-3106
406 Redwood Hwy   60 units, $60–$85
pet fee $5/day, microwave, refrigerator, restaurant, outdoor pool,
pet walking area, 1 mile to public park

Central Point, OR

Holiday Inn Express Medford/Central Point
285 Penninger St   541-423-1010, 888 465 4329
1 to 2 dogs, $25/day ($75 maximum)   84 units, $85–$104
coffeemaker, microwave, refrigerator, full breakfast, indoor pool,
hot tub, fitness room, grassy walking area, 30-minute drive to lake,
www.hiexpress.com

KOA Medford/Gold Hill   541-855-7710, 800-562-7608
12297 Blackwell Rd   4 units, $50–$60
kamping kabins, 1/2 mile to river, www.koa.com/where/or/37109/

Charleston, OR

Captain John's Motel   541-888-4041
63360 Kingfisher Rd   44 units, $59–$72
each pet $10/day, rooms & 1-bdrm to 2-bdrm apartments with
kitchenette, complimentary coffee & donuts, crab-cooking & fish
cleaning facility, 2 miles to beach, www.captainjohnsmotel.com

Chemult, OR

Budget Inn   541-365-2266
109482 Hwy 97 N   25 units, $58
1 to 2 dogs, $5/stay each pet, microwave, refrigerator, on 2 acres
with paved walking area, 1/2 mile to off-leash dog park

Chemult Motel   541-365-2228
109256 Hwy 97 S   16 units, $30–$44
pet fee $5/day, coffeemaker, microwave, refrigerator, on 3 acres
for walking dogs, next to snowmobile & hiking trail

Dawson House Lodge   541-365-2246
109455 Hwy 97 N   9 units, $45–$110
lodge rooms, 2-bdrm suite with full kitchen sleeps 8, continental
breakfast, small pet walking area, 1/4 mile to public park, 1/2 mile to
walking trails, www.dawsonhouse.net

Chemult, OR (continued)

Featherbed Inn   541-365-2235
108915 Hwy 97 N   14 units, $45–$120
rooms with coffeemaker-microwave-refrigerator, 2-bdrm house
with full kitchen, on 5 acres next to national forest & trails, 4-stall
stable & corral for guests' horses, www.thefeatherbedinn.com

Holiday Village Motel & RV Park   541-365-2394
100220 Hwy 97 N   8 units, $35–$80
A-frame cabins with kitchen, RV sites, large open area for walking
dogs, next to national forest & walking trails

Whispering Pines Motel   541-365-2259
94400 Hwy 97   11 units, $35–$55
each pet $10/day, kitchenette, large open area for walking dogs,
close to national forest, grocery store next door

Chiloquin, OR

Melita's Motel & Cafe   541-783-2401
39500 Hwy 97 N   14 units, $45–$95
each pet $5/day, restaurant, lounge, RV sites, large open area for
walking dogs, 2 miles to river

RaGin Ranch B & B   541-783-3815, 877-783-3815
24305 Hwy 97 N   2 units, $90
1 to 2 dogs, 1925 home on 37 acres, full breakfast, guest use of
kitchen, close to lakefront walking trail, www.raginranch.com

Winema Rapids Motel   541-783-2271
33551 Hwy 97 N   10 units, $55
1 to 2 dogs per room, on 80 acres of open land for walking dogs,
close to hiking trails, open April thru mid-November

Christmas Valley, OR

Christmas Valley Desert Inn   541-576-2262
87217 Christmas Valley Hwy   16 units, $35–$53
pets allowed if kept in kennels while in room, kitchenette, large
open area for walking dogs, 1 mile to public park

Lakeside Terrace Motel   541-576-2309
89275 Spruce Lane   10 units, $40–$60
pet fee $5/day, private patios, restaurant, RV sites, small pet
walking area next to lake, golf course nearby

Clackamas, OR

Best Western Sunnyside Inn   503-652-1500, 800-547-8400
12855 SE 97th Ave   139 units, $85
1 to 2 dogs under 100 lbs only, $25/stay, coffeemaker, continental
breakfast, seasonal pool, fenced off-leash walking area, next to
paved jogging path, 10-minute drive to off-leash dog park,
www.bestwestern.com/sunnysideinn

Clackamas Inn   503-650-5340, 800-874-6560
16010 SE 82nd Dr   45 units, $64–$104
1 to 2 dogs, $10/day, coffeemaker, microwave, refrigerator,
extended continental breakfast, outdoor pool, grassy walking area,
across highway to walking trail, www.clackamasinn.com

Comfort Suites   503-723-3450, 800-424-6423
15929 SE McKinley Ave   50 units, $70–$113
1 to 2 dogs under 50 lbs only, $30/stay, coffeemaker, microwave,
refrigerator, full breakfast, freshly baked cookies, indoor pool,
sauna, hot tub, fitness room, grassy pet walking area, across street
to walking trail, www.comfortsuites.com/hotel/or006

Clatskanie, OR

Clatskanie River Inn   503-728-9000
600 E Columbia River Hwy   40 units, $89–$129
1 to 2 dogs, $20/stay, coffeemaker, microwave, refrigerator,
continental breakfast, indoor pool, hot tub, close to public park,
www.clatskanie.com

Cloverdale, OR

Raines Resort   503-965-6371
33555 Ferry St   7 units, $55–$85
pet fee $5/stay, fully equipped cabins with kitchen, picnic tables,
RV sites, convenience store, close to river, 1 mile to beach

Condon, OR

Condon Motel   541-384-2181
216 N Washington St   18 units, $48–$71
pet fee $10/day, coffeemaker, microwave, refrigerator, large open
area for walking dogs, short walk to public park

Coos Bay, OR

Annie's Cottage   541-269-2473
489 Nichols Ave   1 unit, $110–$150
1 to 2 dogs, 1-bdrm 1½ bath 1908 house sleeps 4, jacuzzi tub, lawn
for walking dogs, 1 block to bayfront, www.anniescottage.org

Bayshore Motel   541-267-4138, 800-621-0641
1685 N Bayshore Dr   44 units, $45
1 to 2 dogs, $5/day each pet, microwave, refrigerator, coffee in
lobby

Best Western Holiday Motel   541-269-5111, 800-228-8655
411 N Bayshore Dr   83 units, $99–$169
dogs under 35 lbs only, $15/day each pet, kitchenette or coffeemaker-
microwave-refrigerator, continental breakfast, indoor pool, hot tub,
fitness room, www.bestwestern.com/holidaymotelcoosbay

Coos Bay Manor B & B   541-269-1224, 800-269-1224
955 S 5th St   5 units, $135
dogs up to 30 lbs $10/stay (dogs over 30 lbs may also be allowed
but must be preapproved by innkeepers), full breakfast, short walk
to public park, www.coosbaymanor.com

Edgewater Inn   541-267-0423, 800-233-0423
275 E Johnson Ave   82 units, $90–$149
each pet $10/day, kitchenette or coffeemaker-microwave-
refrigerator, picnic area, waterfront deck, continental breakfast,
indoor pool, tanning bed, hot tub, fitness room, grassy walking
area, close to walking trail, www.theedgewaterinn.com

Motel 6   541-267-7171, 800-466-8356
1445 N Bayshore Dr   94 units, $49–$79
kitchenette, coffee in lobby, sauna, hot tub, small pet walking area,
1 mile to public park, 2 miles to beach, www.motel6.com

Pacific Empire Motel   541-888-3281
155 S Empire Blvd   40 units, $50–$60
pet fee $5/day, microwave & refrigerator available on request,
grassy walking area, 2 blocks to beach

Plainview Motel & RV Park   541-888-5166, 800-962-2815
91904 Cape Arago Hwy   9 units, $74–$179
1 to 2 dogs under 30 lbs only, $10/day each pet, 1-bdrm bayfront
vacation cottage, kitchenette, RV sites, across street to beach,
www.plainviewmotel.com

Red Lion Hotel 541-267-4141, 800-733-5466
1313 N Bayshore Dr 145 units, $89–$136
pet fee $10/day, restaurant, lounge, seasonal pool, hot tub, fitness
room, grassy walking area, across street to bay,
www.redlion.com/coosbay

This Olde House B & B 541-267-5224
202 Alder Ave 5 units, $105–$185
small to medium dogs only $15/stay, coffeemaker, microwave,
refrigerator, full breakfast, complimentary wine & appetizers, hot
tub, 2 blocks to bayfront & boardwalk, www.thisoldehousebb.com

Corvallis, OR

Best Western Grand Manor Inn 541-758-8571, 800-626-1900
925 NW Garfield Ave 55 units, $95–$170
1 to 2 dogs, $10/day each pet, coffeemaker, microwave,
refrigerator, continental breakfast, seasonal pool, fitness room,
lawn, 4 blocks to public park, www.bestwestern.com/prop_38111

Days Inn 541-754-7474, 800-432-1233
1113 NW 9th St 76 units, $54–$65
pet fee $10/day, microwave & refrigerator available upon request,
coffeemaker, continental breakfast, seasonal pool, next to walking
& biking path, www.daysinn.com/hotel/14682

Donovan Guest Houses 541-758-6237
5720 SW Donovan Place 2 units, $150
dogs allowed with advance approval only, $5/day each pet,
2-bdrm & 4-bdrm farmhouses on 13-acre Christmas tree farm,
kitchen, hot tub, fenced dog run, large doghouse,
www.donovanplace.com/guesthouses.htm

Hanson Country Inn 541-752-2919
795 SW Hanson St 4 units, $125
each pet $10/day, suites with private decks, full breakfast, on 6
acres for walking dogs, also 2-bdrm cottage, 1 mile to riverfront
park, www.hcinn.com

Holiday Inn Express 541-752-0800, 800-465-4329
781 NE 2nd St 93 units, $99–$209
1 to 2 dogs, $25/day, coffeemaker, microwave, refrigerator,
continental breakfast, riverside picnic area, indoor pool, hot tub,
fitness room, small barkdust area for walking dogs, next to
riverside walkway, www.hiexpress.com/corvallisor

Corvallis, OR (continued)

Motel 6   541-758-9125, 800-626-1900
935 NW Garfield Ave   61 units, $58–$70
1 to 2 dogs, coffeemaker, microwave, refrigerator, hot tub, 2 blocks
to public park, www.motel6-corvallis.com

Super 8 Motel   541-758-8088, 800-800-8000
407 NW 2nd St   101 units, $70–$80
1 to 2 dogs, $10/day each pet, coffeemaker, microwave &
refrigerator on request, continental breakfast, indoor pool, hot tub,
grassy walking area, next to riverside walkway, www.super8.com

Towne House Motor Inn   541-753-4496, 800-898-4496
350 SW 4th St   65 units, $55–$60
1 to 2 dogs, $5-$7/day, microwave, refrigerator, restaurant, lounge,
2 blocks to public park, www.townehousemotorinn.8k.com

Cottage Grove, OR

City Center Motel   541-942-8322
737 Hwy 99 S   15 units, $45
pet fee $5/day, coffeemaker, kitchen in some units, next to park

Comfort Inn   541-942-9747, 800-944-0287
845 Gateway Blvd   64 units, $80–$140
1 to 2 dogs, $10/day each pet, coffeemaker, microwave,
refrigerator, continental breakfast, seasonal pool, hot tub, open
field across street, www.comfortinn.com/hotel/or038

Gray Cat Inn   541-942-1900, 866-696-2814
337 N 9th St   2 units, $75–$95
1 to 2 dogs under 20 lbs allowed with advance approval only,
full breakfast, hot tub, large yard & garden for walking dogs,
5-minute drive to paved trail, www.graycatinn.com

Holiday Inn Express   541-942-1000, 800-465-4329
1601 Gateway Blvd   41 units, $79–$150
each pet $15/day, coffeemaker, microwave, refrigerator,
continental breakfast, indoor pool, hot tub, fitness room, lawn for
walking dogs, 1/4 mile to public park, www.hiexpress.com

Relax Inn   541-942-5132
1030 N Pacific Hwy   24 units, $45–$65
each pet $5/day, coffeemaker, microwave, refrigerator, small pet
walking area, 1 mile to public park

Stardust Motel   541-942-5706
455 Bear Creek Rd   18 units, $49
each pet $5/day, small pet walking area, 5-minute walk to park

Village Green Resort   541-942-2491, 800-343-7666
725 Row River Rd   96 units, $49–$119
1 to 3 dogs, coffeemaker, extended continental breakfast,
restaurant, lounge, outdoor pool, hot tub, chew toys & cleanup
bags provided, on 14 acres for walking dogs, 1 block to lakeside
trail, www.villagegreenresortandgardens.com

Crescent Lake, OR

Crescent Creek Cottages & RV Park   541-433-2324
19100 Hwy 58   5 units, $70–$90
each pet $5/stay, creekside cabins sleep 2 to 6, kitchen, picnic
table, campfire ring, RV sites, on 4 acres with trails for walking
dogs, www.crescentcreekcottages.com

Crescent Lake Lodge & Resort   541-433-2505
Crescent Lake Hwy   18 units, $75–$225
studios to 3-bdrm cabins sleep up to 11, most cabins have full
kitchen, all linens provided, restaurant, lounge, grocery store, boat
rentals, surrounded by national forest, trails for walking dogs,
www.crescentlakeresort.com

Odell Lake Lodge   541-433-2540, 800-434-2540
21501 E Odell Rd   19 units, $95–$265
each pet $10/day, cabins sleep 4 to 16, fully equipped kitchen,
linens provided, woodstove, BBQ, RV & tent sites, restaurant,
surrounded by national forest, www.odelllakeresort.com

Shelter Cove Resort & Marina   541-433-2548, 800-647-2729
West Odell Lake Rd, Hwy 58   13 units, $80–$250
cabins sleep 2 to 8, kitchen, RV & tent sites,
www.sheltercoveresort.com

Creswell, OR

Super 8 Creswell Inn   541-895-3341, 877-895-3341
345 E Oregon Ave   69 units, $64–$138
1 to 2 dogs, $15/stay each pet, coffeemaker, microwave,
refrigerator, continental breakfast, outdoor pool, large courtyard
for walking dogs, 2 blocks to public park, www.creswellinn.com

Culver, OR

KOA Central Oregon   541-546-3046, 800-562-1992
2435 SW Jericho Lane   5 units, $44–$67
1 to 2 dogs, no fee for 1st dog, $2/day for 2nd dog, rustic kamping
kabins, seasonal pool, convenience store, pet walking area,
www.koa.com/where/or/37149/

Dallas, OR

Best Western Dallas Inn & Suites   503-623-6000
250 Orchard Dr   42 units, $100–$160
1 to 2 dogs, $10/day each pet, coffeemaker, continental breakfast,
hot tub, fitness room, open field for walking dogs, 3 miles to public
park, www.bestwestern.com/dallasinnandsuites

Riverside Inn & Suites   503-623-8163
517 Main St   22 units, $55–$60
each pet $10/day, full kitchen or coffeemaker-microwave-
refrigerator, grassy walking area, ½ mile to public park

Dayville, OR

Country Inn Last Resort   541-987-2128
150 Schoolhouse St   6 units, $55
1 to 2 dogs, cabins, decks, coffeemaker, microwave available on
request, RV & tent sites, grassy area, trail, across street to river

Fish House Inn   541-987-2124, 888-286-3474
110 E Franklin Ave   6 units, $70
1 to 2 dogs allowed in 1 cottage only, coffeemaker, microwave,
refrigerator, BBQ, outside seating areas, lawn for walking dogs,
close to national park, www.fishhouseinn.com

Depoe Bay, OR

Crown Pacific Inn   541-765-7773, 877-765-7773
Hwy 101 & Bechill St   32 units, $65–$115
pet fee $10/stay, coffeemaker, microwave, refrigerator, continental
breakfast, hot tub, grassy walking area, across street to beach,
www.crownpacificinn.com

Four Winds Motel   541-765-2793, 888-875-2936
356 NE Hwy 101   22 units, $39–$69
microwave, refrigerator, continental breakfast, open field for
walking dogs, 1 block to beach access, www.the4windsmotel.com

Harbor Lights Inn B & B   541-765-2322, 800-228-0448
235 SE Bay View Ave   13 units, $89–$109
1 to 2 small dogs, $10/day each pet, full breakfast, food served in
lounge Thursday thru Saturday evenings, please bring your pet's
bedding, extra dog towels provided, grassy walking area, next to
harbor, www.theharborlightsinn.com

Inn at Arch Rock   541-765-2560, 800-767-1835
70 Sunset St   14 units, $69–$299
dogs under 20 lbs only, $10/day each pet, full kitchen or
coffeemaker-microwave-refrigerator, continental breakfast,
grassy walking area, private beach, www.innatarchrock.com

Oregon Shores Vacation Rentals   541-764-3300, 800-800-7108
3885 N Hwy 101   100 units, $79–$695
fully equipped vacation homes in multiple locations along the
central Oregon coast, www.orshores.com

Pana-Sea-Ah Bed & Breakfast   541-764-3368, 866-829-3368
4028 Lincoln Ave   4 units, $119–$149
1 to 2 dogs allowed in 1 suite only, $25/stay, full breakfast, hot tub,
beach towels, lounge, next to beach, www.panaseah.com

Surfrider Oceanfront Resort   541-764-2311, 800-662-2378
3115 N Hwy 101   50 units, $69–$199
1 to 2 dogs under 25 lbs only, $20/stay, deck overlooking cove,
full kitchen or microwave & refrigerator, restaurant, lounge,
indoor pool, hot tub, www.surfriderresort.com

Trollers Lodge   541-765-2287, 800-472-9335
355 SW Hwy 101   16 units, $84–$210
each pet $10-$15/day, lodge rooms, 1-bdrm to 2-bdrm suites,
vacation house, kitchen, BBQ, picnic tables, lawn for walking dogs,
1/2 mile to beach, www.trollerslodge.com

Vacation Rentals Bella Beach   541-764-5700, 866-994-7026
24 Bella Beach Dr   47 units, $119–$495
1 to 2 dogs, $50/stay each pet, fully equipped vacation homes, hot
tubs, 1/4 mile to beach & walking trail, www.bellabeach.com

Whale Inn at Depoe Bay   541-765-2789, 866-569-4253
416 N Hwy 101   10 units, $62–$129
1 to 2 dogs under 25 lbs only, $20/stay each pet, coffeemaker,
microwave, refrigerator, extended continental breakfast, pet basket
with dog biscuits-towels-cleanup bags, across street to cove beach,
close to off-leash dog park

Detroit, OR

All Seasons Motel   503-854-3421, 877-505-8779
130 Breitenbush Rd   15 units, $56–$150
each pet $10/day, kitchen, across street to lakefront walking trail,
www.allseasonsmotel.net

Detroit Lake Motel   503-854-3344
175 Detroit Ave   11 units, $45–$60
each pet $17/stay, full kitchen or coffeemaker-microwave-
refrigerator, restaurant, grassy walking area, ½ block to lake,
www.detroitlakemotel.com

Diamond, OR

Hotel Diamond   541-493-1898
49130 Happy Valley Rd   8 units, $75–$97
dogs allowed with manager's approval only, $15/day each pet,
continental breakfast, restaurant, lounge, convenience store, also
3-bdrm house, surrounded by open area for walking dogs, open
March thru October, www.central-oregon.com/hoteldiamond

Diamond Lake, OR

Diamond Lake Resort   541-793-3317, 800-733-7293
350 Resort Dr   92 units, $79–$99
each pet $10/day, motel rooms & cabins with full kitchen,
restaurant, lounge, large open area for walking dogs, surrounded
by national forest beside 3,000-acre lake, www.diamondlake.net

Dundee, OR

Inn at Red Hills   503-495-5825
1410 N Hwy 99W   20 units, $150–$300
1 to 2 dogs, restaurant, lounge, across street to public park,
www.innatredhills.com

Eagle Point, OR

Fish Lake Resort   541-949-8500
Hwy 140 Mile Marker 30   11 units, $75–$225
1 to 2 dogs, $15/day, rustic cottages with hot plate & refrigerator,
larger cabins with full kitchen, RV & tent sites, restaurant,
convenience store, game room, boat rentals, moorage on quiet
lake, waterfront walking area, hiking trails, www.fishlakeresort.net

Elgin, OR

Stampede Inn   541-437-2441, 877-769-7600
51 S 7th St   11 units, $40–$75
pet fee $5-$10/day, microwave, refrigerator, restaurant, 3 blocks to
public park & swimming pool, www.stampedeinn.com

Elkton, OR

Big K Guest Ranch   541-584-2295, 800-390-2445
20029 Hwy 138 W   20 units, $369–$399
1 to 3 dogs, $15/day each pet, lodge rooms & private cabins,
coffeemaker, microwave, refrigerator, on 2,500-acre guest ranch,
per-person nightly rate includes breakfast-lunch-dinner, hot tub,
river float trips & trail rides available, www.big-k.com

Enterprise, OR

Barking Mad Farm B & B   541-215-2758 or 541-426-0360
65156 Powers Rd   3 units, $120–$175
full breakfast, on 8 acres with resident pets & livestock, fenced off-
leash dog park, horses welcome, www.barkingmadfarm.com

North End Crossing   541-828-7010, 888-897-8020
80903 College Lane   3 units, $85
each pet $15/day, located in the old ghost town of Flora, full
breakfast, accommodations based on authentic pioneer lifestyle,
guests are invited to participate in daily activities such as soap-
making, large open walking area, www.northendcrossing.com

Ponderosa Motel   541-426-3186
102 E Greenwood St   33 units, $69–$154
coffeemaker, microwave, refrigerator, small pet walking area,
2 blocks to park, www.ponderosamotel.hotels.officelive.com

Wallowa Lake Vacation Rentals   541-426-2039, 800-709-2039
82240 Fish Hatchery Lane   17 units, $95–$430
dogs allowed with advance approval only, $10/day each pet, fully
equipped cabins & vacation homes, most are within 5 blocks of
walking trails or parks, www.wallowalakevacationrentals.com

Wilderness Inn   541-426-4535, 800-965-1205
301 W North St   29 units, $71–$92
each pet $10/day, kitchenette, 2 blocks to public park & open field
at fairgrounds

Eugene, OR

America's Best Value Inn   541-343-0730, 877-646-2466
1140 W 6th Ave   40 units, $50–$75
1 to 2 dogs, $8-$14/day each pet depending on its size, microwave,
refrigerator, coffee in lobby, continental breakfast, fitness room,
1 block to public park, www.bestvalueinneugene.com

Augusta House Bed & Breakfast   541-342-8615
2585 Bowmont Dr   2 units, $239–$300
each pet $25/stay, pet-friendly suites with outdoor entrances,
coffeemaker, microwave, refrigerator, full breakfast, guest use of
kitchen, hot tub, fenced backyard, close to off-leash dog park,
1 mile to wetlands, www.augustahouse.net

Best Western Greentree Inn   541-485-2727, 800-937-8376
1759 Franklin Blvd   65 units, $84–$110
dogs under 20 lbs only, coffeemaker, microwave, refrigerator,
continental breakfast, restaurant, lounge, outdoor pool, hot tub,
fitness room, next to walking trail that leads to public park,
www.bestwestern.com/greentreeinneugene

Best Western New Oregon Motel   541-683-3669, 800-780-7234
1655 Franklin Blvd   129 units, $95–$170
coffeemaker, refrigerator, continental breakfast, restaurant, indoor
pool, sauna, hot tub, fitness room, next to walking & biking path,
short walk to park, www.bestwestern.com/neworegonmotel

Boon's Red Carpet Motel   541-345-0579
1055 W 6th Ave   24 units, $50–$66
1 to 2 dogs, microwave, refrigerator, continental breakfast,
2 blocks to public park

Broadway Inn   541-344-5233
476 E Broadway   47 units, $60–$80
pet fee $15 for 1st day, $5 each additional day, coffeemaker,
microwave, refrigerator, continental breakfast, seasonal pool,
grassy walking area, across street to riverfront park, 3 blocks to
riverside walkway, www.eugenebroadwayinn.com

C'est la Vie Inn   541-302-3014, 866-302-3014
1006 Taylor St   5 units, $120–$250
dogs allowed with advance approval only, $25/stay, full breakfast,
2 blocks to public park, www.cestlavieinn.com

Campbell House Inn   541-343-1119, 800-264-2519
252 Pearl St   20 units, $143–$386
small pets only, $50/day, microwave, refrigerator, coffee in lobby,
full breakfast, complimentary wine in evening, guest pass to local
fitness center, lawn for walking dogs, next to natural park area,
2 blocks to riverside walkway, www.campbellhouse.com

Days Inn Eugene/Springfield   541-342-6383, 800-444-6383
1859 Franklin Blvd   60 units, $83–$110
each pet $10/day, coffeemaker, microwave, refrigerator,
continental breakfast, sauna, hot tub, grassy walking area, 2 blocks
to public park, www.daysinn.com/hotel/prop_06248

Express Inn & Suites   541-868-1520
990 W 6th Ave   24 units, $60–$80
each pet $10/day, microwave, refrigerator, coffee in lobby,
continental breakfast, 1 mile to public park, www.expressinn.net

Hilton Eugene & Conference Ctr   541-342-2000, 800-937-6660
66 E 6th Ave   269 units, $119–$234
1 to 2 dogs under 100 lbs only, $35/stay, coffeemaker, microwave,
refrigerator, restaurant, lounge, indoor pool, hot tub, fitness room,
small walking area, close to riverfront park, www.hilton.com

La Quinta Inn & Suites   541-344-8335, 800-531-5900
155 Day Island Rd   73 units, $119–$139
coffeemaker, microwave, refrigerator, extended continental
breakfast, indoor pool, hot tub, off-leash dog park, www.lq.com

Motel 6 Eugene South   541-687-2395, 800-466-8356
3690 Glenwood Dr   59 units, $43–$55
coffee in lobby, outdoor pool, lawn, 1½ miles to walking trail,
www.motel6.com

Red Lion Hotel   541-342-5201, 800-733-5466
205 Coburg Rd   137 units, $129–$180
pet fee $20/day, coffeemaker, microwave, refrigerator, restaurant,
lounge, outdoor pool, hot tub, fitness room, small pet walking area,
short walk to park & walking path, www.redlion.com/eugene

Residence Inn Eugene/Springfield   541-342-7171
25 Club Rd   108 units, $159–$179
1 to 2 dogs, $75/stay, coffeemaker, microwave, refrigerator, full
breakfast, Monday thru Thursday evenings complimentary
beverages & dinner, outdoor pool, hot tub, fitness room, lawn,
riverfront park & walkway, www.marriott.com/eugri

Eugene, OR (continued)

Sixty-Six Motel   541-342-5041
755 E Broadway   66 units, $48–$61
1 to 2 dogs, refrigerator available upon request, designated pet walking area, 300 ft to walking trail

University Inn & Suites   541-342-4804, 800-424-5213
1857 Franklin Blvd   45 units, $64–$89
dogs under 20 lbs only, $10/day each pet, coffeemaker, microwave, refrigerator, continental breakfast, seasonal pool, freshly baked cookies, grassy walking area, close to walking & biking path, www.eugeneuniversityinn.com

Valley River Inn   541-743-1000, 800-543-8266
1000 Valley River Way   257 units, $149–$169
coffeemaker, microwave, refrigerator, restaurant, lounge, seasonal pool, sauna, hot tub, fitness room, pet welcome basket provided with a map of local dog parks, pet stores & veterinary clinics; restaurant features a doggie appetizer menu, grassy walking area, next to riverside walkway, www.valleyriverinn.com

Value Inn Motel   541-688-2733
595 Hwy 99 N   25 units, $60–$300
pet fee $10/stay, kitchenette, www.eugenevalueinn.com

Fields, OR

Fields Motel & General Store   541-495-2275
22276 Fields Dr   4 units, $45–$85
each pet $10/day, restaurant, large open area for walking dogs

Florence, OR

Action Realty   541-997-8277
1720 Hwy 101   5 units, $105–$175
fully equipped vacation homes, close to ocean

Best Western Pier Point Inn   541-997-7191, 800-435-6736
85625 Hwy 101   57 units, $107–$200
1 to 2 dogs, $10/day each pet, coffeemaker, microwave, refrigerator, full breakfast, indoor pool, sauna, hot tub, large riverside walking area, www.bestwestern.com/pierpointinn

Coastal Property Management 541-997-1351, 866-997-1351
Hwy 101 & 20th S 35 units, $95–$425
1 to 2 dogs allowed with advance approval only, $15/day, fully
equipped vacation homes & condos, hot tub, short drive to beach
& public parks, www.florence4rent.com

Economy Inn 541-997-7115, 800-630-2689
3829 Hwy 101 29 units, $80–$120
each pet $10/day, coffeemaker, microwave, refrigerator, indoor
pool, hot tub, small pet walking area, 2 miles to beach,
www.economyinnflorence.com

Le Chateau Motel 541-997-3481, 800-451-1688
1084 Hwy 101 49 units, $60–$104
pet fee $16/stay, microwave, refrigerator, continental breakfast,
seasonal pool, sauna, hot tub, fitness room, lawn for walking dogs,
short drive to beach, www.lechateaumotel.com

Lighthouse Inn 541-997-3221, 866-997-3221
155 Hwy 101 26 units, $59–$149
dogs under 35 lbs only, $5-10/day, microwave, refrigerator,
restaurant, pet packet provided that includes the official pet policy
plus dog biscuits-dog towel-cleanup bag, grassy walking area,
1 block to riverside walkway, www.lighthouseinn-florence.com

Mercer Lake Resort 541-997-3633, -800-355-3633
88875 Bayberry Lane 10 units, call for current rates
dogs allowed with manager's approval only, $5/day each pet,
cabins with kitchenette, RV sites, boat ramp & moorage, fishing
boats for rent, covered fish-cleaning area & freezer, lakefront
walking area, www.mlroregon.com

Ocean Breeze Motel 541-997-2642, 800-753-2642
85165 Hwy 101 13 units, $50–$120
each pet $10/day, coffeemaker, microwave, refrigerator, across
street to target golf range, small pet walking area, ½ mile to
beach, close to dunes & state park, www.oceanbreezemotel.com

Old Town Inn 541-997-7131, 800-570-8738
170 Hwy 101 40 units, $65–$99
each pet $7/stay, coffeemaker, microwave, refrigerator, designated
pet walking area, 3 blocks to public park, www.old-town-inn.com

Florence, OR (continued)

Park Motel   541-997-2634, 800-392-0441
85034 Hwy 101   21 units, $45–$135
each pet $10/day, rooms & suites with kitchenette, 2-bdrm cabins
with full kitchen & private decks, one RV site, on 5 wooded acres,
grassy walking area, 1/2 mile to beach, www.parkmotelflorence.com

Silver Sands Motel   541-997-3459
1449 Hwy 101   50 units, $40–$88
pet fee $7/day, microwave, refrigerator, grassy walking area,
5 miles to beach, www.silver-sandsmotel.com

Villa West Motel   541-997-3457
901 Hwy 101   22 units, $68–$92
1 to 2 dogs, $10/day, coffeemaker, microwave, refrigerator, grassy
walking area, 2 miles to beach, www.villawestmotelflorence.com

Whales Watch Vacation Rentals   541-999-1493, 800-760-1866
88572 2nd Ave   13 units, $150–$350
each pet $10/day, fully equipped 1-bdrm to 4-bdrm vacation
homes, hot tub, fenced dog run, most are beachfront or only a
short walk to beach, www.whaleswatch.com

Woahink Lake Suites   541-997-6516, 800-962-4465
83693 Hwy 101   6 units, $60–$99
pet fee $15/stay, kitchenette, BBQ, private frontage on Woahink
Lake, across street to the dunes, 2 miles to beach access,
www.woahinklakesuites.com

Forest Grove, OR

America's Best Value Inn & Suites   503-357-9000, 888-670-2960
3306 Pacific Ave   40 units, $59–$89
1 to 2 dogs under 50 lbs only, $10/day each pet, coffeemaker,
microwave, refrigerator, continental breakfast, indoor pool, hot
tub, fitness room, small lawn for walking dogs, 2 miles to park,
www.bestvalueinn.com

Best Western University Inn & Suites   503-992-8888
3933 Pacific Ave   800-937-8376
dogs under 50 lbs only, $15/day each pet   54 units, $105–$150
coffeemaker, microwave, refrigerator, continental breakfast,
indoor pool, sauna, hot tub, 2 miles to public park,
www.bestwestern.com/prop_38137

Forest Grove Inn   503-357-9700, 800-240-6504
4433 Pacific Ave   20 units, $60–$80
dogs under 20 lbs only, $10/day each pet, coffeemaker,
microwave, refrigerator, ½ mile to park, www.forestgroveinn.com

Holiday Motel   503-357-7411
3224 Pacific Ave   14 units, $50–$75
dogs under 20 lbs only, $7/day each pet, microwave, refrigerator,
grassy walking area, 2-minute walk to public park

Fort Klamath, OR

Aspen Inn Motel   541-381-2321
52250 Hwy 62   12 units, $59–$95
each pet $10/day, microwave, refrigerator, coffee in lobby,
large open area for walking dogs, short walk to river,
www.theaspeninn.com

Crater Lake Bed & Breakfast   541-381-9711, 866-517-9560
52395 Weed Rd   3 units, $110–$140
full breakfast, kitchen available for guest use, garden, pond, close
to hiking trails & fishing, 15-minute drive to south entrance of
Crater Lake National Park, www.craterlakebandb.com

Crater Lake Resort   541-381-2349
50711 Hwy 62   9 units, $60–$100
each pet $5/day, cabins sleep 2 to 4, kitchen, deck, BBQ, RV sites,
open woods for walking dogs, www.craterlakeresort.com

Jo's Motel & Campground   541-381-2234
52851 Hwy 62   7 units, $110
1 to 3 dogs, $5/day each pet, suites & cabins sleep up to 6, kitchen,
BBQ, RV & tent sites, organic grocery & deli, large yard for
walking dogs, 5-minute drive to walking trail, www.josmotel.com

Wilson's Cottages   541-381-2209
57997 Hwy 62   10 units, $75–$110
fully equipped 2-bdrm to 3-bdrm cottages sleep up to 7, on 130
wooded acres with large open area for walking dogs, lots of
walking trails, 1 mile to Crater Lake National Park,
www.wilsonscottages.com

Fossil, OR

Bridge Creek Flora Inn & Fossil Lodge   541-763-2355
828 Main   12 units, $75–$95
pet fee $10/stay, full breakfast, large yard for walking dogs,
2 blocks to public park, www.fossilinn.com

Fossil Motel & Trailer Park   541-763-4075
105 1st St   10 units, $45–$60
full kitchen or microwave & refrigerator, continental breakfast,
BBQ, patio, picnic tables, large open area for walking dogs, next to
public park, www.fossilmotelandrvpark.com

Frenchglen, OR

Frenchglen Hotel   541-493-2825
39184 Hwy 205   8 units, $65–$90
pet fee $10/stay, resident dog, historic hotel, full breakfast, family-
style dinners also available, screened porch, large yard for walking
dogs, 2 miles to river, open mid-March thru October

Steens Mountain Resort   541-493-2415, 800-542-3765
35678 Resort Lane   6 units, $75
each pet $10/day, 1-bdrm air-conditioned cabins with kitchenette,
bring your own bedding & towels, RV & tent sites, large riverside
area for walking dogs, www.steensmountainresort.com

Garibaldi, OR

Bayshore Inn   503-322-2552, 877-537-2121
227 Garibaldi Ave   22 units, $64–$110
each pet $10/day, kitchen or kitchenette, coffee in lobby, large
open area for walking dogs, close to walking trail & Tillamook Bay

Comfort Inn   503-322-3338, 877-322-6489
502 E Garibaldi Ave   50 units, $79–$179
1 to 2 dogs under 50 lbs only, $20/day each pet, coffeemaker,
microwave, refrigerator, extended continental breakfast, indoor
pool, sauna, hot tub, fitness room, grassy walking area,
www.comfortinn.com/hotel/or145

Edgewater Vacation Rentals   503-842-1300, 888-425-1050
1110 Bay Lane   2 units, $109–$267
each pet $10/day, duplex overlooking ocean, 3-bdrms on each side
sleep 6, fully equipped kitchen, large open area for walking dogs,
close to ocean, www.oregoncoastvacrentals.com

Harbor View Inn & RV Park   503-322-3251
302 S 7th St   20 units, $49–$75
microwave, refrigerator, RV sites, bayfront access & walking trails,
grassy walking area, next to harbor

Gearhart, OR

Gearhart by the Sea Resort   503-738-8331, 800-547-0115
1157 N Marion Ave   85 units, $93–$185
each pet $10/day, fully equipped condos, indoor pool, hot tub,
close to public golf course, next to beach, www.gearhartresort.com

Gearhart Ocean Inn   503-738-7373, 800-352-8034
67 N Cottage Ave   13 units, $100–$240
1 to 2 dogs, $15/day each pet, full kitchen or microwave &
refrigerator, coffee in lobby, backyard with BBQ, croquet, 1 block
to historic ridge path & tennis court, 3 blocks to beach,
www.gearhartoceaninn.com

Lodge at Gearhart's Little Beach   503-288-7318, 888-502-5588
715 H St   1 unit, $850–$875
8-bdrm 4-bath lodge sleeps up to 26 people, on 2 acres for walking
dogs, 4 blocks to beach, www.lodgeatgearhart.com

Pat Ordway Vacation Rentals   503-738-0837
810 Avenue G   30 units, $185–$300
pet fee $50/stay, fully equipped vacation homes, close to beach,
www.patordwayvacationrentals.com

Surfside Condo Rental   503-738-6384
PO Box 2591   1 unit, $100–$125
small dogs allowed with advance approval only, $9/stay,
fully equipped condo, 2-minute walk to beach

Gladstone, OR

Oxford Suites   503-722-7777, 877-558-7710
75 82nd Dr   98 units, $99–$140
pet fee $15/stay, coffeemaker, microwave, refrigerator, full
breakfast, indoor pool, steam room, hot tub, fitness room,
1/2 mile to public park, www.oxfordsuitesportlandsoutheast.com

Gleneden Beach, OR

Beachcombers Haven   541-764-2252, 800-428-5533
7045 NW Glen Ave   15 units, $135–$235
dogs allowed with advance approval only, $25/stay, 1-bdrm to
3-bdrm units, kitchen, lawn for walking dogs, close to beach,
www.beachcombershaven.com

Salishan Lodge   541-764-3605, 800-452-2300
7760 N Hwy 101   205 units, $199–$309
pet fee $35/day, coffeemaker, restaurant, lounge, hot tub, fitness
room, lap pool, hydrotherapy pool, 3 miles of private beach for
walking dogs, www.salishan.com salishan.com

Glide, OR

Illahee Inn   541-496-4870
170 Wild Thyme Lane (formerly Bar L Ranch Rd)   6 units, $75
each pet $10/day, coffeemaker, microwave, refrigerator,
restaurant, lawn, close to riverside walkway, www.illaheeinn.net

Steelhead Run Bed & Breakfast   541-496-0563, 800-348-0563
23049 N Umpqua Hwy   6 units, $65–$125
pet fee $5-$10/day, kitchen, extended continental breakfast, BBQ,
picnic area, on 4 acres overlooking river, www.steelheadrun.com

Gold Beach, OR

Chart House   541-247-0909, 800-290-6208
94169 Wedderburn Loop   2 units, $95–$150
vacation apartments in 2-story riverfront house, RV sites, 4-minute
walk to beach, www.lexslanding.com/vacation.html

Gold Beach Inn   541-247-7091, 888-663-0608
29346 Ellensburg Ave   82 units, $48–$149
each pet $5-$10/day, kitchenette or coffeemaker, continental
breakfast, 2 large enclosed spas, grassy walking area, private
beach paths, also see sister facility Ireland's Rustic Lodges for
additional pet-friendly lodgings, www.goldbeachinn.com

Inn of the Beachcomber   541-247-6691, 888-690-2378
29266 Ellensburg Ave   48 units, $64–$154
pet fee $15/day, microwave, refrigerator, extended continental
breakfast, indoor pool, hot tub, grassy beachfront walking area,
www.innofthebeachcomber.com

Ireland's Rustic Lodges   541-247-7718, 877-447-3526
29346 Ellensburg Ave   42 units, $70–$169
pet fee $5-$10/day, cabins & vacation homes, full kitchen or
coffeemaker-microwave-refrigerator, private beach paths,
www.irelandsrusticlodges.com

Jot's Resort   541-247-6676, 800-367-5687
94360 Wedderburn Loop   140 units, $50–$315
each pet $15/day, kitchen, restaurant, indoor pool, outdoor pool,
hot tub, grassy walking area next to river, www.jotsresort.com

Motel 6   541-247-4533, 800-759-4533
94433 Jerrys Flat Rd   50 units, $49–$80
1 to 2 dogs, microwave, refrigerator, coffee in lobby, hot tub,
grassy walking area, across street to trail, www.motel6.com

Oregon Trail Lodge   541-247-6030
29855 Ellensburg Ave   18 units, $45–$65
pet fee $5/day, 1-bdrm to 3-bdrm units, microwave, refrigerator,
2 blocks to beach, www.u-s-history.com/or/o/ortrlodg.htm

Pacific Reef Resort   541-247-6658, 800-808-7263
29362 Ellensburg Ave   41 units, $59–$219
pet fee $10/day, coffeemaker, microwave, refrigerator, continental
breakfast, small lawn, close to beach, www.pacificreefresort.com

Rogue Landing Resort   541-247-7183
94764 Jerrys Flat Rd   13 units, $85–$165
cabins & vacation homes, hot tub, on 15 riverfront acres, RV sites,
restaurant, lounge, fish cleaning station, boat ramp, lawn for
walking dogs, 1 mile to ocean, www.roguelandingresort.com

Rogue Pacific Motel   541-247-7444
29450 Ellensburg Ave   15 units, $35–$95
motels rooms, cottages with kitchen, close to high school field for
walking dogs, 1 block to beach

Rogue Reef Vacation Rentals   541-247-6700, 888-807-6483
29851 Colvin St   25 units, $165–$450
1-bdrm to 7-bdrm fully equipped vacation homes sleep up to 28,
hot tub, close to beach, www.roguereefvacationrentals.com

Sand Dollar Inn   541-247-6611, 866-726-3657
29399 Ellensburg Ave   26 units, $39–$125
each pet $10/stay, microwave, refrigerator, continental breakfast,
across street to beach, www.sanddollar-inn.com

Gold Beach, OR (continued)

Turtle Rock Resort   541-247-9203, 800-353-9754
28788 Hunter Creek Loop   15 units, $129–$179
1 to 2 dogs allowed by advance reservation only, $15/day each pet,
cottages sleep up to 6, private hot tubs, BBQ, lawn, 5-minute walk
to beach, www.turtlerockresorts.com

Wild Coast Vacation Rentals   541-247-0898
                                          52 units, $78–$475
condos-cabins-beach homes in Gold Beach & Port Orford, some
with hot tub or fenced yard, www.wildcoastvacations.com

Gold Hill, OR

Lazy Acres Motel & RV Park   541-855-7000
1550 2nd Ave   4 units, $75
1 to 2 dogs allowed, coffeemaker, microwave, refrigerator,
riverfront walking area, dock

Rogue River Guest House   541-855-4485, 877-764-8322
41 Rogue River Hwy   3 units, $160
full breakfast, dinner available on request, fenced yard, 100 yards
to river & walking trails, www.rogueriverguesthouse.com

Government Camp, OR

Mount Hood Inn   503-272-3205, 800-443-7777
87450 E Government Camp Loop   57 units, $89–$169
each pet $10/day, coffeemaker, microwave, refrigerator, continental
breakfast, hot tub, walking area, close to trail, www.mthoodinn.com

Summit Meadow Cabins   503-272-3494
Summit Meadow   5 units, $165–$275
1-bdrm to 3-bdrm cabins, kitchen, BBQ, grassy walking area,
surrounded by national forest & trails, www.summitmeadow.com

View House LLC   503-272-3295
1 to 2 dogs allowed   1 unit, $225
2-bdrm cabin with full kitchen sleeps 8, linens provided, next to
national forest, www.mthoodviewhouse.com

Granite, OR

Granite Lodge   541-755-5200
1525 McCann St   9 units, $65–$132
continental breakfast, large open area for walking dogs

Grants Pass, OR

Angels Rest Vacation Rentals   541-476-7400
305 NE 6th St   10 units, $80–$110
kitchen, seasonal pool, hot tub, open field for walking dogs, 2 miles
to public park, www.rogueweb.com/angelsrest

Best Western Grants Pass Inn   541-476-1117, 800-553-7666
111 NE Agness Ave   84 units, $70–$140
pet fee $10/day, coffeemaker, continental breakfast, lounge,
outdoor pool, hot tub, www.bestwestern.com/grantspassinn

Best Western Inn at the Rogue   541-582-2200, 800-238-0700
8959 Rogue River Hwy   53 units, $79–$130
dogs up to 20 lbs $10/day, dogs over 20 lbs $20/day, coffeemaker,
microwave, refrigerator, continental breakfast, restaurant, outdoor
pool, steam room, hot tub, fitness room, large yard, across street
to riverfront park, www.bestwestern.com/innattherogue

Comfort Inn   541-479-8301, 800-626-1900
1889 NE 6th St   59 units, $65–$125
each pet $10/stay, coffemaker-microwave-refrigerator, continental
breakfast, seasonal pool, designated pet walking area, 1/2 mile to
public park, www.comfortinn.com/hotel/or004

Holiday Inn Express   541-471-6144, 800-838-7666
105 NE Agness Ave   80 units, $101–$109
each pet $10/day, coffeemaker, microwave, refrigerator, full
breakfast, outdoor pool, hot tub, large yard for walking dogs,
www.hiexpress.com/grantspassor

Knights Inn   541-479-5595
104 SE 7th St   32 units, $45–$60
pet fee $5/day, coffeemaker, microwave, refrigerator, continental
breakfast, open walking area, 3 blocks to public park

La Quinta Inn & Suites   541-472-1808
243 NE Morgan Lane   59 units, $69–$150
coffeemaker, microwave, refrigerator, continental breakfast, indoor
pool, hot tub, fitness room, small pet walking area, www.lq.com

Motel 6   541-474-1331, 800-466-8356
1800 NE 7th St   122 units, $35–$65
microwave, refrigerator, coffee in lobby, outdoor pool, small pet
walking area, close to riverside dock, 3 miles to public park,
www.motel6.com

Grants Pass, OR (continued)

Motel Del Rogue   541-479-2111, 866-479-2111
2600 Rogue River Hwy   15 units, $90–$145
each pet $10/day, kitchen or kitchenette, BBQ, picnic area on
several acres, riverside walking trails, www.moteldelrogue.com

Redwood Motel   541-476-0878, 888-535-8824
815 NE 6th St   28 units, $50–$180
each pet $10/day, coffeemaker-microwave-refrigerator, extended
continental breakfast, seasonal pool, hot tub, pet walking area,
10 blocks to public park, www.redwoodmotel.com

Restful Nest on the Rogue B & B   541-582-8259
6015 Rogue River Hwy   2 units, $75–$105
dogs under 50 lbs allowed by advance arrangement only, $10/day,
full breakfast, evening snacks provided, close to riverfront walking
area, www.restfulnestbandb.com

Riverside Inn   541-476-6873, 800-334-4567
986 SE 6th St   63 units, $80–$149
each pet $10/day, continental breakfast, outdoor pool, hot tub,
private balconies overlooking river, short walk to riverfront park
& walkway, www.riverside-inn.com

Rod & Reel Motel   541-582-1516
7875 Rogue River Hwy   10 units, $40–$50
cabins, coffeemaker, microwave, refrigerator, river frontage &
woods for walking dogs, trails to river & up the mountain

Rogue River Inn   541-582-1120
6285 Rogue River Hwy   21 units, $45–$85
full kitchen or coffeemaker, outdoor pool, open field for walking
dogs, across street to riverside walkway

Shilo Inn   541-479-8391, 800-222-2244
1880 NW 6th St   70 units, $60–$95
pet fee $25/stay, coffeemaker, microwave, refrigerator, continental
breakfast, seasonal pool, sauna, pet beds & dog treats available at
front desk, small pet walking area, 2 blocks to public park,
www.shiloinns.com

Sunset Inn   541-479-3305
1400 NW 6th St   30 units, $55–$95
pet fee $7/day, continental breakfast, seasonal pool, grassy
walking area next to river, www.sunset-inn.net

Super 8 Motel   541-474-0888, 800-800-8000
1949 NE 7th St   79 units, $54–$103
1 to 2 dogs, coffeemaker, microwave, refrigerator, continental
breakfast, indoor pool, hot tub, open area for walking dogs,
www.super8.com

Sweet Breeze Inn   541-471-4434, 800-349-4434
1627 NE 6th St   21 units, $45–$60
dogs under 20 lbs only, $5/day, microwave, refrigerator,
continental breakfast, open field for walking dogs,
www.sweetbreezeinn.com

Travelodge   541-479-6611, 800-578-7878
1950 NW Vine St   61 units, $59–$79
dogs under 35 lbs only, $10/day each pet, coffeemaker,
microwave, refrigerator, extended continental breakfast,
seasonal pool, large open area for walking dogs, 5 blocks to park,
www.travelodge.com

Wild River Inn   541-479-5381, 888-337-6925
110 NE Morgan Lane   60 units, $35–$65
1 to 2 dogs under 20 lbs only, $10/day each pet, restaurant, lounge,
outdoor pool, sauna, hot tub, small pet walking area,
www.wildriverinn.com

Gresham, OR

Best Western Pony Soldier Inn   503-665-1591, 888-766-9476
1060 NE Cleveland Ave   74 units, $90–$125
each pet $10/day, coffeemaker, microwave, refrigerator,
continental breakfast, seasonal pool, steam room, hot tub, fitness
room, lawn, 1 mile to park, www.bestwestern.com/prop_38112

Days Inn   503-465-1515
24124 SE Stark St   53 units, $59–$72
1 to 2 dogs, $10/day each pet, coffeemaker, microwave,
refrigerator, continental breakfast, indoor pool, hot tub, fitness
room, lawn, 1 block to park, www.daysinn.com/hotel/14358

Extended StayAmerica Portland/Gresham   503-661-0226
17777 NE Sacramento St   800-326-5651
pet fee $25/day ($75 maximum)   104 units, $70–$90
suites with kitchen, grassy walking area, close to walking trail,
www.extendedstayamerica.com/794

Gresham, OR (continued)

Holiday Inn Portland/Gresham   503-907-1777, 800-465-4329
2752 NE Hogan Dr   168 units, $107–$170
small dogs only, $30/day each pet, coffeemaker, restaurant,
lounge, indoor pool, hot tub, fitness room, small pet walking area,
1 block to public park, www.portlandhi.com

Howard Johnson Inn   503-666-9545, 888-422-9545
1572 NE Burnside Rd   73 units, $59–$179
pet fee $20/day, coffeemaker, continental breakfast, outdoor pool,
fitness room, 1 mile to park, www.greshamhowardjohnson.com

Super 8 Motel   503-661-5100
121 NE 181st Ave   44 units, $60–$63
1 to 2 dogs, $10/day each pet, coffeemaker, microwave, refrigerator,
continental breakfast, hot tub, short walk to park, www.super8.com

Halfway, OR

Birch Leaf Guest House   541-742-2990, 800-727-9977
47830 Steele Hill Rd   1 unit, $195
pet fee $50/stay, 6-bdrm farmhouse, on 40 acres with swimming
pond, 3 miles to wilderness trailhead, www.thebirchleaf.com

Cornucopia Lodge   541-742-4500
1 to 2 dogs, $15-$30/stay   1 unit, $140–$195
lodge rooms & 1-bdrm to 2-bdrm cabins, kitchenette, restaurant,
trails, surrounded by national forest, www.cornucopialodge.com

Halfway Motel & RV Park   541-742-5722
170 S Main St   31 units, $45–$65
coffeemaker, microwave, refrigerator, large yard, 4 blocks to park,
www.hellscanyonchamber.com/halfway_motel_rv_park.htm

Pine Valley Lodge   541-742-2027
163 N Main St   8 units, $75–$150
pet fee $10/stay, kitchen or coffeemaker-microwave-refrigerator,
continental breakfast, walking area, national forest, www.pvlodge.com

Halsey, OR

Travelodge Pioneer Villa   541-369-2804
33180 Hwy 228   57 units, $65–$72
1 to 2 dogs, $5/day each pet, coffeemaker, microwave, refrigerator,
full breakfast, restaurant, lounge, seasonal pool, hot tub, open
field, www.travelodge.com/hotel/18208

Hammond, OR

KOA Astoria/Seaside   503-861-2606, 800-562-8506
1100 NW Ridge Road   55 units, $72–$186
1 to 2 dogs, $2/day, 1-room to 1-bdrm kamping kabins sleep up to
6, some with full kitchen & private bath, restaurant, indoor pool,
hot tub, mini-golf, bike rentals, www.astoriakoa.com

Officer's Inn Bed & Breakfast   503-861-2524, 888-861-2524
540 Russell Place   8 units, $125–$150
pet fee $25/stay, 1 pet-friendly suite, full breakfast, ½-acre yard,
across street to playground & park, 5-minute drive to off-leash
dog park, www.officersinn.com

Heppner, OR

Northwestern Motel & RV Park   541-676-9167
389 N Main St   15 units, $50
each pet $5/day, coffeemaker, microwave, refrigerator, large open
walking area, across street to park, www.heppnerlodging.com

Hermiston, OR

Comfort Inn & Suites   541-564-5911
77514 Hwy 207   65 units, $90–$100
1 to 2 dogs, $20/day, coffeemaker, microwave, refrigerator,
extended continental breakfast, indoor pool, hot tub, fitness room,
grassy area for walking dogs, www.comfortinn.com/hotel/or167

Economy Inn   541-567-5516, 888-567-9521
835 N 1st St   39 units, $59
each pet $5/day, coffeemaker, microwave, refrigerator, continental
breakfast, seasonal pool, grassy walking area, next to public park

Motel 6   541-567-7777, 800-466-8356
655 N 1st St   90 units, $46–$59
microwave, refrigerator, coffee in lobby, grassy walking area,
¼ mile to public park, www.motel6.com

Oxford Suites   541-564-8000, 888-545-7848
1050 N 1st St   126 units, $89–$109
1 to 2 dogs under 30 lbs only, $25/stay each pet, coffeemaker,
microwave, refrigerator, full breakfast, complimentary evening
reception, indoor pool, hot tub, fitness room, BBQ, lawn, 3-minute
walk to park, www.oxfordsuiteshermiston.com

Hermiston, OR (continued)

Way Inn   541-567-5561, 888-564-8767
635 S Hwy 395   30 units, $50–$55
dogs under 80 lbs only, $5/day each pet, coffeemaker, microwave,
refrigerator, continental breakfast, seasonal pool

Hillsboro, OR

Dunes Motel   503-648-8991
452 SE 10th Ave   39 units, $55–$66
1 to 2 dogs under 50 lbs only, $15/day each pet, microwave,
refrigerator, coffee in lobby, 1 block to public park

Econo Lodge   503-640-4791
622 SE 10th Ave   60 units, $60–$73
dogs under 15 lbs only, $10-$15/day each pet, microwave,
refrigerator, continental breakfast, close to public park,
www.econolodge.com/hotel/or183

Extended Stay Deluxe Portland/Hillsboro   503-439-0706
19311 NW Cornell Rd   800-398-7829
    136 units, $105–$140
dogs under 25 lbs only, $25/day ($75 maximum), kitchenette,
fitness room, outdoor pool, large open area for walking dogs,
1 block to park & walking path, www.extendedstaydeluxe.com/916

Hotel B   503-648-3500, 800-325-4000
3500 NE Cornell Rd   123 units, $79–$156
each pet $20/day, coffeemaker, microwave, refrigerator,
restaurant, lounge, seasonal pool, hot tub, fitness room, large
open area for walking dogs, next to county fairgrounds, 1 mile to
park & walking path, www.hotelb-hillsboro.com

Larkspur Landing Hillsboro Hotel   503-681-2121
3133 NE Shute Rd   124 units, $119–$169
pet fee $10/day plus $75 cleaning fee, kitchen, extended
continental breakfast, hot tub, fitness room, freshly baked cookies,
across street to public park, www.larkspurlanding.com/hillsboro

Orenco Station Manor Suites   503-358-5683
1459 NE Orenco Station Parkway   10 units, $110–$165
1 to 2 small dogs with advance approval only, $10/day each pet,
coffeemaker, refrigerator, continental breakfast, guest pass to local
fitness center, across street to public park, www.orencomanor.com

Residence Inn Portland West/Hillsboro   503-531-3200
18855 NW Tanasbourne Dr   122 units, $109–$219
1 to 2 dogs, $10/day each pet, kitchen, full breakfast, seasonal
pool, hot tub, fitness room, designated pet walking area, ½ mile to
public park, www.marriott.com/pdxhb

Towneplace Suites Portland/Hillsboro   503-268-6000
6550 NE Brighton St   800-257-3000
1 to 2 dogs, $10/day each pet   136 units, $89–$179
kitchen, extended continental breakfast, outdoor pool, hot tub,
fitness room, BBQ, lawn, 2 blocks to park, www.marriott.com/pdxts

Hines, OR

Best Western Rory & Ryan Inns   541-573-5050
534 N Hwy 20   63 units, $89–$99
dogs under 25 lbs only, $15/stay, coffeemaker, microwave,
refrigerator, continental breakfast indoor pool, small walking area,
½ mile to park, www.bestwestern.com/prop_38144

Comfort Inn   541-573-3370, 800-228-5150
504 N Hwy 20   51 units, $89–$98
1 to 3 dogs, $10/day each pet, coffeemaker, microwave,
refrigerator, full breakfast, indoor pool, hot tub, large walking area,
¼ mile to public park, www.comfortinn.com/hotel/or072

Knotty Pine Motel   541-573-7440, 866-689-9695
104 S Hwy 395 & 20   8 units, $50–$55
1 to 2 dogs, $5/day, coffeemaker, microwave, refrigerator, grassy
walking area, next to public park, www.knottypinemotel-or.com

Hood River, OR

Best Western Hood River Inn   541-386-2200, 800-828-7873
1108 E Marina Way   149 units, $80–$269
each pet $12/day, coffeemaker, microwave, refrigerator,
restaurant, lounge, outdoor pool, hot tub, fitness room, lawn,
short walk to river, private beach, bicycles for guest use,
www.hoodriverinn.com

Columbia Gorge Vacation Rentals   541-490-8198
4205 Summitview Dr   8 units, $150–$900
1 to 2 dogs, $25/stay each pet, 2-bdrm to 4-bdrm condos &
vacation homes sleep up to 8, hot tub, lawn, close to trails &
doggie day care center, www.columbiagorgevacationrentals.com

Hood River, OR (continued)

Gorge Rentals   541-387-4080, 800-387-4787
610 Oak St   29 units, $95–$690
fully equipped studios-condos-vacation homes sleep 2 to 12, close
to trails, community swimming pool, www.gorgerentals.com

Hood River B & B   541-387-2997
918 Oak St   4 units, $85–$135
dogs allowed with advance approval only, full breakfast, backyard
for walking dogs, 1 mile to river, www.hoodriverbnb.com

Hood River Hotel   541-386-1900, 800-386-1859
102 Oak Ave   41 units, $139–$169
1 to 2 dogs, $25/stay, kitchenette, restaurant, sauna, hot tub,
fitness room, pet bowls-treats-bones, lawn for walking dogs,
2 blocks to riverfront park, www.hoodriverhotel.com

Lincoln Street Guest House   541-387-2687, 888-403-2687
1322 Lincoln St   2 units, $98–$210
well-behaved dogs allowed with advance approval only, 3-bdrm
2½-bath house can be rented as separate 1-bdrm & 2-bdrm suites
or as complete home, www.hoodriverretreat.com

Lost Lake Resort & Campground   541-386-6366
9000 Lost Lake Rd   13 units, $60–$125
pet fee $10/stay, lodge rooms or rustic lakeside cabins with
electricity & shared restrooms (no indoor plumbing), RV & tent
sites, national forest & trails, www.lostlakeresort.org

Panorama Lodge B & B   541-387-2687, 888-403-2687
dogs allowed with advance approval only   5 units, $80–$520
7-bdrm rustic log home sleeps 23 or can be rented as 5 separate
1-bdrm to 3-bdrm suites, full breakfast, close to walking trail,
www.panoramalodge.com

Prater's Motel   541-386-3566
1306 Oak St   7 units, $59–$75
pet fee $10/day, full kitchen or microwave & refrigerator, across
street to public park

Sunset Motel   541-386-6322, 800-705-0597
2300 W Cascade Ave   14 units, $80
each pet $15/day, coffeemaker, microwave, refrigerator, grassy
walking area, 1 mile to riverfront park

Vagabond Lodge   541-386-2992, 877-386-2992
4070 Westcliff Dr   42 units, $55–$102
1 to 3 dogs, $5/day each pet, full kitchen or microwave & refrigerator,
coffee in lobby, on 5 acres overlooking Columbia river, picnic area
& playground, www.vagabondlodge.com

Huntington, OR

Joy Motor Inn   541-869-2211
5945 Hwy 30   42 units, $39–$81
pet fee $10/day, continental breakfast, restaurant, lounge, open
area for walking dogs, ½ mile to public park

Idleyld Park, OR

Dogwood Motel   541-496-3403
28866 N Umpqua Hwy   6 units, $65–$70
1 to 2 dogs, $10/day each pet, each log cabin duplex unit sleeps 4,
full kitchen or coffeemaker, microwave, refrigerator, on 3 acres
with picnic area & large meadow, trails, www.dogwoodmotel.com

Idleyld Lodge   541-496-0088
23834 N Umpqua Hwy   4 units, $67–$77
pet fee $10/stay, 2-bdrm theme-decorated suites in 120-year-old
lodge, small dog allowed in separate cabin, continental breakfast
(full country breakfast $6), riverside trail, www.idleyldlodge.com

Lemola Lake Resort   541-643-0750
2610 Birds Point Rd   11 units, $80–$250
pet fee $10/day, hotel rooms, 2-bdrm cabins, kitchenette or
coffeemaker-microwave-refrigerator, restaurant, convenience
store, gas station, boat & snowmobile rentals, large open area &
lakefront trails for walking dogs, www.lemololakeresort.com

River Vista Vacation Homes   541-496-0506
138 River Vista Ct   3 units, $125
each pet $15/day, 1-bdrm vacation homes sleep up to 6, fully
equipped kitchen, deck overlooking river, BBQ, riverfront walking
area, www.rivervista-vacationhomes.com

Swiftwater Park Guest House   541-496-3333, 888-454-9696
121 Tioga Lane   3 units, $105–$195
each pet $10/day, 3-bdrm vacation home & 2 fully furnished
studios, kitchen, hot tub, open field for walking dogs, short walk to
riverfront park, www.northumpquariverguesthouse.com

Ione, OR

Woolery House B & B   541-422-7218
170 E 2nd   5 units, $65–$105
full breakfast, 2 blocks to public park, www.wooleryhouse.com

Irrigon, OR

Bake's Motel   541-922-2681
W Hwy 730   9 units, $50
microwave, refrigerator, 4 blocks to riverfront park

Jacksonville, OR

Jacksonville Inn   541-899-1900, 800-321-9344
175 E California St   12 units, $159–$270
rooms & cottages, coffeemaker, microwave, refrigerator, full
breakfast, restaurant, small pet walking area, 2-minute walk to
public park, www.jacksonvilleinn.com

Jacksonville's Magnolia Inn   541-899-0255
245 N 5th St   9 units, $95–$160
pet fee $25/stay, extended continental breakfast, guest use of
kitchen, veranda, landscaped yard, close to public park & walking
path, www.magnolia-inn.com

Stage Lodge   541-899-3953, 800-253-8254
830 N 5th St   27 units, $88–$175
1 to 2 dogs, $12/day each pet, continental breakfast, small pet
walking area, 2 blocks to public park, www.stagelodge.com

John Day, OR

America's Best Value Inn   541-575-1462, 888-315-2378
390 W Main St   44 units, $60–$80
each pet $5/day, coffeemaker, microwave, refrigerator, restaurant,
lounge, outdoor pool, hot tub, 1 block to public park,
www.bestvalueinn.com

Best Western John Day Inn   541-575-1700, 800-243-2628
315 W Main St   39 units, $53–$100
each pet $5/day, coffeemaker, microwave, refrigerator, continental
breakfast, indoor pool, fitness room, small pet walking area,
2 blocks to public park, www.bestwestern.com/johndayinn

Budget 8 Motel   541-575-2155
711 W Main St   14 units, $39–$59
each pet $10/day, coffeemaker, microwave, refrigerator, small pet
walking area, 1 mile to public park

Dreamers Lodge   541-575-0526, 800-654-2849
144 N Canyon Blvd   25 units, $45–$99
1 to 2 dogs, $5/day each pet, full kitchen or coffeemaker-
microwave-refrigerator, coffee in lobby, grassy walking area, close
to public park, www.dreamerslodge.com

Little Pine Inn   541-575-2100
250 E Main St   13 units, $45–$60
fenced yard, 4 blocks to public park

Sonshine Bed & Breakfast   541-575-1827
210 NW Canton St   2 units, $75–$85
full breakfast, next to park, www.sonshinebedandbreakfast.com

Jordan Valley, OR

Basque Station Motel   541-586-2244
801 Main St   16 units, $54–$64
small pet walking area, 4 blocks to public park

Joseph, OR

Chandler's Inn B & B   541-432-9765
700 S Main St   3 units, $80–$100
full breakfast, guest use of kitchen, grassy area, close to walking
trail, 5-minute drive to lakefront, www.josephbedandbreakfast.com

Eagle Cap Chalets   541-432-4704
59879 Wallowa Lake Hwy   35 units, $65–$180
pet fee $20-$30/day, condos-cabins-chalets, full kitchen or
microwave & refrigerator, indoor pool, hot tub, riverfront walking
area, ¼ mile to national forest & trails, www.eaglecapchalets.com

Little Ranch Bed & Breakfast   541-432-3706
62483 Little Ranch Rd   1 unit, $60–$80
1 to 2 dogs, $10/day each pet, private bungalow with kitchenette,
continental breakfast, on 10 acres, www.littleranchbb.com

Mountain View Motel & RV Park   541-432-2982, 866-262-9891
83450 Joseph Hwy   9 units, $63–$89
coffeemaker, microwave, refrigerator, BBQ, grassy walking area,
1 mile to lake & national forest, www.rvmotel.com

Joseph, OR (continued)

Ninebark Outfitters & Lodge   541-426-4855, 877-646-3275
65881 Dobbin Rd   2 units, $250–$400
2-bdrm ranch house & bunkhouse sleep up to 9, full kitchen or
microwave & refrigerator, will host only one group at a time in
private wilderness setting, www.ninebarkoutfitters.com

Strawberry Wilderness B & B   541-432-3125
406 W Wallowa   3 units, $75–$95
outside entrances, full breakfast, lawn, 1 mile to Wallowa Lake

Wallowa Lake Resort   541-432-2391
84681 Ponderosa Lane   25 units, $65–$160
1 to 2 dogs, $8/day each pet, cabins & vacation homes, kitchen or
kitchenette, hot tub, trails, close to lake, www.wallowalakeresort.com

Junction City, OR

Guest House Inn   541-998-6524
1335 Ivy St   22 units, $70–$85
each pet $10/day, coffeemaker, microwave, refrigerator, grassy
walking area, 2 blocks to public park

Regency Inn   541-998-6551
1575 Ivy St   17 units, $58–$65
microwave, refrigerator, 1 block to public park

Western Motel & RV Park   541-952-0161, 866-952-0161
1714 Ivy St   10 units, $45–$80
small pets only, coffeemaker, microwave, refrigerator,
www.junctioncity.com/western

Juntura, OR

Oasis Motel   541-277-3605
5838 Hwy 20   8 units, $34–$75
each pet $5/day, coffeemaker, microwave, refrigerator, restaurant,
gravel walking area, 1 mile to 1,000 acres BLM land to walk dogs

Keizer, OR

Keizer Renaissance Inn   503-390-4733, 800-299-7221
5188 Wittenberg Lane   86 units, $84–$94
1 to 2 dogs, $10/day each pet, coffeemaker, microwave, refrigerator,
continental breakfast, restaurant, lounge, indoor pool, hot tub, fitness
room, lawn, 1 mile to park, www.keizerrenaissanceinn.com

Kerby, OR

Holiday Motel   541-592-3003
24810 Redwood Hwy   11 units, $49–$90
each pet $6/day, kitchenette or microwave & refrigerator, large
open area for walking dogs, next to walking trail

Kerbyville Inn Bed & Breakfast   541-592-4689
24304 Redwood Hwy   5 units, $59–$105
suites with private entrance, coffeemaker, microwave, refrigerator,
continental breakfast, grassy walking area, 2 miles to public park,
www.bridgeviewwine.com

Klamath Falls, OR

America's Best Value Inn & Suites   541-882-8844, 888-315-2378
3939 Hwy 97 N   24 units, $48–$69
1 to 2 dogs, $10–$15/day, microwave, refrigerator, coffee in lobby,
continental breakfast, outdoor pool, BBQ, picnic area, large area
for walking dogs, 2 miles to lakefront park, www.bestvalueinn.com

Best Western Klamath Inn   541-882-1200, 877-882-1200
4061 S 6th St   52 units, $107–$118
each pet $10/day, coffeemaker, microwave, refrigerator,
continental breakfast, indoor pool, lawn for walking dogs, next to
walking & biking path, www.bestwestern.com/klamathinn

Cimarron Motor Inn   541-882-4601, 800-742-2648
3060 S 6th St   163 units, $69–$85
small dogs preferred, $10/day, coffeemaker, microwave,
refrigerator, outdoor pool, next to walking trail, 7-minute drive to
public park, www.cimarroninnklamathfalls.com

Crystalwood Lodge   541-381-2322, 866-381-2322
38625 Westside Rd   7 units, $85–$182
historic lodge, full breakfast, restaurant, lounge, guest use of
kitchen, dog crate provided in every room, on 133 acres with pond,
near wildlife refuge & national forest, www.crystalwoodlodge.com

Days Inn   541-882-8864
3612 S 6th St   108 units, $89–$120
coffeemaker, microwave, refrigerator, extended continental
breakfast, seasonal pool, hot tub, next to walking trail,
www.daysinn.com/hotel/31672

Klamath Falls, OR (continued)

Econo Lodge   541-884-7735, 800-553-2666
75 Main St   49 units, $40–$100
each pet $10/day, coffeemaker, microwave, refrigerator, continental
breakfast, waterfront park, www.econolodge.com/hotel/or051

Golden West Motel   541-882-1758
6402 S 6th St   14 units, $38–$54
microwave, refrigerator, BBQ, on ½ acre for walking dogs,
2 blocks to walking trail, www.goldenwestmotel.us

Klamath Travel Inn   541-882-4675
5440 N Hwy 97   33 units, $42–$60
coffeemaker, microwave, refrigerator, grassy area, close to trail

Lake of the Woods Resort   541-949-8300, 866-201-4194
950 Harriman Rt   26 units, $139–$259
pet fee $5/stay, cabins, full kitchen or kitchenette, hot tub, RV & tent
sites, restaurant, lounge, general store, marina, beach, lakefront trail,
open May thru September, www.lakeofthewoodsresort.com

Majestic Inn & Suites   541-883-7771, 866-488-0088
5543 S 6th St   16 units, $34–$85
1 to 2 dogs under 30 lbs only, $5/day each pet, microwave,
refrigerator, continental breakfast, large yard for walking dogs,
¾ mile to public park, www.majesticinn.info

Maverick Motel   541-882-6688, 800-404-6690
1220 Main St   49 units, $39–$99
pet fee $10/stay, microwave, refrigerator, continental breakfast,
small pet walking area, close to trail, www.maverickmotel.com

Microtel Inn & Suites   541-273-0206
2716 Dakota Ct   57 units, $79–$125
pet fee $35/stay, coffeemaker, microwave, refrigerator, continental
breakfast, indoor pool, hot tub, www.microtelinn.com

Motel 6   541-884-2110, 800-466-8356
5136 S 6th St   62 units, $45–$70
coffee in lobby, outdoor pool, lawn for walking dogs, 6 blocks to
park & walking path, www.motel6.com

Olympic Lodge   541-883-8800
3006 Green Springs Dr   32 units, $50
full kitchen or coffeemaker-microwave-refrigerator, lawn, next to
walking trail, 1 mile to public park

Oregon 8 Motel & RV Park   541-883-3431
5225 N Hwy 97   28 units, $35–$87
each pet $10/day, coffeemaker, microwave, refrigerator,
continental breakfast, seasonal pool, on 6 acres, 2 miles to park

Quality Inn & Suites   541-882-4666
100 Main St   80 units, $59–$149
pet fee $10/day, coffeemaker, continental breakfast, outdoor pool,
hot tub, lawn, 1 block to park, www.klamathfallsqualityinn.com

Rivers Inn Motel   541-273-8668
11 Main St   47 units, $35–$50
pet fee $5/day, coffeemaker, microwave, refrigerator, continental
breakfast, across street to public park

Rocky Point Resort   541-356-2242
128121 Rocky Point Rd   4 units, $120–$160
each pet $5/day, 1-bdrm to 2-bdrm cabins, kitchen, restaurant,
BBQ, lakefront walking area, www.rockypointoregon.com

Running Y Ranch Resort   541-850-5500, 888-850-0275
5500 Running Y Rd   82 units, $139–$249
pet fee $25/stay, lodge rooms & vacation homes, full kitchen or
coffeemaker-microwave-refrigerator, restaurant, lounge, indoor
pool, sauna, fitness room, 8 miles of paved trails,
www.runningy.com

Shilo Inn   541-885-7980, 800-222-2244
2500 Almond St   143 units, $99–$135
1 to 2 dogs, $25/stay, coffeemaker, microwave, refrigerator,
restaurant, fitness room, pet beds & treats, designated pet walking
area, next to walking & biking path, www.shiloinns.com

Super 8 Motel   541-884-8880, 800-800-8000
3805 Hwy 97 N   61 units, $60–$88
microwave, refrigerator, continental breakfast, hot tub, lawn,
2 blocks to public park & walking path, www.super8.com

La Grande, OR

All American Inn   541-962-7143, 877-962-7143
402 Adams Ave   32 units, $48–$71
pet fee $10/stay, microwave, refrigerator, coffee in lobby,
continental breakfast, seasonal pool, small pet walking area in
alley, 3 blocks to public park, www.allamericaninnoregon.com

La Grande, OR (continued)

America's Best Value Sandman Inn 541-963-3707, 888-315-2378
2410 East R Ave   63 units, $80–$109
pet fee $25/stay, coffeemaker, microwave, refrigerator, continental breakfast, indoor pool, hot tub, pet treats & cleanup bags provided, lawn, 3 miles to public park, www.bestvalueinn.com

Grande Ronde Cow Camp B & B   541-428-2199
58303 Grande Ronde River Rd   4 units, $60–$135
dogs allowed by advance arrangement only, bunkhouse, cabin with microwave & refrigerator, 1-bdrm plus loft in main house, country-style full breakfast, horses also welcome, close to forest land & trails, www.granderondecowcamp.com

Greenwell Motel   541-963-4134, 888-963-9889
305 Adams Ave   33 units, $35–$46
microwave, refrigerator, open field, 2 blocks to public park

La Grande Inn   541-963-7195
2612 Island Ave   146 units, $59–$69
1 to 2 dogs $15/stay, 3 or more dogs $20/stay, coffeemaker, refrigerator, continental breakfast, seasonal pool, sauna, hot tub, fitness room, BBQ, picnic area, lawn & courtyard for walking dogs, ½ mile to public park, www.lagrandeinn.com

Moon Motel   541-963-2724
2116 Adams Ave   9 units, $40–$45
pet fee $5/day, coffeemaker, across street to public park

Orchard Motel   541-963-6160
2206 E Adams Ave   10 units, $39–$49
pet fee $10/stay, coffeemaker, microwave, refrigerator, very small pet walking area, 2 blocks to public park

Quail Run Motor Inn   541-963-3400, 877-782-4576
2400 Adams Ave   17 units, $35–$39
1 to 2 dogs, $5-$10/day each pet, kitchenette or microwave & refrigerator, BBQ, picnic area, trails, www.quailruninn.net

Travelodge   541-963-7116
2215 Adams Ave   35 units, $45–$60
pet fee $10/stay, coffeemaker, microwave, refrigerator, continental breakfast, freshly baked cookies, guest pass to local fitness center, small sandy pet walking area, 5-minute drive to public park, www.travelodge.com/hotel/12290

La Pine, OR

Best Western Newberry Station   541-536-5130, 800-210-8616
16515 Reed Rd   40 units, $80
1 to 2 dogs under 25 lbs only, $10/stay, coffeemaker, refrigerator,
continental breakfast, indoor pool, hot tub, lawn for walking dogs,
4 blocks to park & walking path,
www.bestwestern.com/newberrystation

DiamondStone Guest Lodge   541-536-6263, 866-626-9887
16693 Sprague Loop   8 units, $90–$165
dogs allowed by advance arrangement only, $10/day each pet,
coffeemaker, microwave, refrigerator, full breakfast, hot tub, on
5 acres for walking dogs, 5-minute walk to river, vacation homes
also available, www.diamondstone.com

Highlander Motel & RV Park   541-536-2131
51511 Hwy 97   9 units, $42–$65
coffeemaker, microwave, refrigerator, large open area for walking
dogs, 3 blocks to public park

Paulina Lake Lodge   541-536-2240
each pet $10/day   13 units, $90–$250
rustic cabins with kitchen sleep up to 8, all linens provided,
restaurant, lounge, general store, boat rentals, moorage, open area
& woods for walking dogs, www.paulinalakelodge.com

Timbercrest Inn   541-536-1737
52560 Hwy 97   22 units, $50–$90
each pet $10/day, microwave, refrigerator, continental breakfast,
small pet walking area, close to lakes & walking trails

West View Motel   541-536-2115
51371 Hwy 97   9 units, $53
full kitchen or coffeemaker-microwave-refrigerator, large open
area for walking dogs, close to riverfront park

Lafayette, OR

Kelty Estate Bed & Breakfast   503-864-3740, 800-867-3740
675 E 3rd St   5 units, $99–$179
full breakfast, complimentary wine & cheese in evening, on 1 acre
with lawn-gardens-pond, close to public park, www.keltyestate.com

Lake Oswego, OR

Crowne Plaza Hotel   503-624-8400, 866-565-4062
14811 Kruse Oaks Dr   161 units, $149–$259
pet fee $25/day, coffeemaker, restaurant, lounge, indoor & outdoor
pools, sauna, hot tub, fitness room, pet treats-beds-toys, paved
walking path, www.crowneplaza.com/lakeoswegoor

Residence Inn Portland South/Lake Oswego   503-684-2603
15200 SW Bangy Rd   112 units, $109–$209
pet fee $10/day, kitchen, extended continental breakfast, Monday
thru Wednesday complimentary beverages & appetizers, outdoor
pool, hot tub, lawn, 1/4 mile to park, www.marriott.com/pdxlo

Lakeside, OR

Lakeshore Lodge   541-759-3161, 800-759-3951
290 S 8th St   20 units, $75–$95
1 to 2 small dogs or 1 large dog, coffeemaker, microwave, refrigerator,
restaurant, lawn, 1 mile to beach, www.lakeshorelodgeor.com

Lakeview, OR

Best Western Skyline Motor Lodge   541-947-2194, 800-780-7234
414 North G St   38 units, $85
small pets only, $10/stay each pet, coffeemaker, microwave,
refrigerator, continental breakfast, indoor pool, hot tub, 4 blocks to
public park, www.bestwestern.com/skylinemotorlodge

Budget Inn   541-947-2201
411 North F St   15 units, $49–$59
pet fee $10/stay, open field, www.budgetinnlakeview.com

Interstate 8 Motel   541-947-3341
354 North K St   32 units, $50–$59
refrigerator, continental breakfast, small barkdust walking area,
1/4 mile to open field for walking dogs, www.interstate8motel.com

Lakeview Lodge Motel   541-947-2181
301 North G St   39 units, $60–$100
coffeemaker, microwave, refrigerator, hot tub, grassy walking
area, 4 blocks to public park, www.lakeviewlodgemotel.com

Rim Rock Motel   541-947-2185
727 South F St   28 units, $40–$100
each pet $5/day, coffeemaker, microwave, refrigerator, continental
breakfast, large yard for walking dogs, 1 block to public park

Lebanon, OR

Cascades City Center Motel   541-258-8154
1296 S Main St   16 units, $45–$52
pet fee $7/day, full kitchen or microwave & refrigerator,
small pet walking area, 1 mile to public park

Shanico Inn   541-259-2601, 888-815-4408
1840 S Main St   40 units, $66–$72
1 to 3 dogs, $10/day each pet, coffeemaker, microwave,
refrigerator, large walking area, www.shanicoinnlebanon.com

Valley Inn   541-258-8184
2885 S Santiam Hwy   18 units, $59–$89
1 to 3 dogs, $10/day each pet, coffeemaker, microwave,
refrigerator, lawn, short drive to public park, www.valleyinn.us

Lincoln City, OR

Ashley Inn   541-996-7500, 888-427-4539
3430 NE Hwy 101   75 units, $99–$189
each pet $20/stay, coffeemaker, microwave, refrigerator, full
breakfast, freshly baked cookies, salt water whirlpool tub &
swimming pool, fitness room, open area for walking dogs, 2 blocks
to beach, www.ashley-inn.com

Beachfront Vacation Rentals   541-996-2955, 800-224-7660
2110 NE 36th St Suite 1300   9 units, $150–$450
dogs allowed with advance approval, $35/stay each pet, 2-bdrm to
5-bdrm fully equipped oceanfront vacation homes sleep 4 to 20,
some with hot tub or large yard, www.beachfrontrentals.net

Bella Beach Vacation Rentals   503-292-2599, 800-667-7607
1 to 2 dogs, $25/day ($100 maximum)   18 units, $99–$670
beach cottages & vacation homes sleep 2 to 14, fully equipped
kitchen, hot tub, next to beach, www.bellabeachrentals.com

Captain Cook Inn   541-994-2522, 800-809-4275
2626 NE Hwy 101   17 units, $49–$169
1 to 2 dogs allowed with advance approval only, rooms & suites
with full kitchen or coffeemaker-microwave-refrigerator, 3-bdrm
fully equipped oceanfront home sleeps 6, dog treats provided,
picnic area, lawn for walking dogs, short walk to beach,
www.captaincookinn.com

Lincoln City, OR (continued)

Chinook Winds Casino Resort Hotel   541-994-3655
1501 NW 40th Place   888-244-6665
each pet $20/day   247 units, $80–$174
coffeemaker, microwave, refrigerator, restaurant, lounge, indoor
pool, sauna, hot tub, fitness room, pet walking area, beachfront,
www.chinookwindscasino.com/stay_home_hotel_casino_resort

Coast Inn Bed & Breakfast   541-994-7932, 888-994-7932
4507 SW Coast Ave   4 units, $99–$135
full breakfast, evening reception with wine-cheese-smoked salmon,
pet walking area, 2 blocks to beach, www.oregoncoastinn.com

Coastal Hideaways Vacation Rentals   541-994-6468
3691 NW Highway 101   1 unit, $290
pet fee $80/stay, fully equipped 3-bdrm vacation home, small yard,
beach for walking dogs, www.coastproperty.com/vacationrentals

Coho Inn   541-994-3684, 800-848-7006
1635 NW Harbor Ave   51 units, $61–$250
dogs under 25 lbs only, $10/day each pet, kitchenette, continental
breakfast, indoor pool, sauna, hot tub, fitness room, grassy walking
area, 1/2 block to beach, www.thecohoinn.com

Comfort Inn   541-994-8155, 800-423-6240
136 NE Hwy 101   62 units, $69–$249
dogs under 25 lbs only, $20/day each pet, kitchenette or coffeemaker-
microwave-refrigerator, continental breakfast, indoor pool, hot tub,
small park, 2 blocks to beach, www.comfortinn.com/hotel/or105

Crown Pacific Inn Express   541-994-7559, 800-359-7559
1070 SE 1st St   41 units, $40–$89
1 to 2 dogs, $10/day each pet, kitchenette or coffeemaker-
microwave-refrigerator, continental breakfast, hot tub, across
street to beach & park, www.crownpacificinn.com

Dolphin Motel   541-994-2124
1018 SE Hwy101   10 units, $185–$200
weekly rentals only, microwave, refrigerator, 3/4 mile to beach

Econo Lodge   541-994-5281
1713 NW 21st St   50 units, $80–$232
1 to 2 dogs under 30 lbs only, $10/day each pet, coffeemaker,
microwave, refrigerator, continental breakfast, restaurant, 3-minute
walk to beach, www.econolodge.com/hotel/or143

Edgecliff Motel   541-996-2055, 888-750-3636
3733 SW Hwy 101   56 units, $50–$110
1 to 2 dogs, $5/day each pet, studios-suites-condos, kitchen,
continental breakfast, ½ block to beach, www.edgecliffmotel.com

Ester Lee Motel   541-996-3606, 888-996-3606
3803 SW Hwy 101   53 units, $61–$159
1 to 2 dogs, $9/day each pet, 1-bdrm to 2-bdrm cottages sleep 2 to
7, full kitchen or coffeemaker-microwave-refrigerator, dog blankets
provided to protect furniture, small pet walking area on bluff
overlooking ocean, paved path to beach, www.esterleemotel.com

Hideaway Motel   541-994-8874
810 SW 10th St   6 units, $80–$150
pet fee $10/day, full kitchen or coffeemaker, microwave, grassy
walking area overlooking ocean, 1 block to beach access,
http://oregon-coastdirectory.com/lodging/oregoncoast/central/
lincolnc/hideaway/hideaway.htm

Horizon Rentals Vacation Homes 541-994-2226, 800-995-2411
1225 SE 1st St   85 units, $110–$525
pet fee $35/stay, fully equipped condos & vacation homes sleep 2
to 25, kitchen, seasonal pool, hot tub, www.horizonrentals.com

Lincoln City Inn   541-996-4400, 800-870-7067
1091 SE 1st St   59 units, $79–$119
pet fee $11/stay, coffeemaker, microwave, refrigerator, continental
breakfast, hot tub, small pet walking area, across street to beach,
www.lincolncityinn.com

Lincoln City Vacation Homes   541-994-8778, 866-396-0404
3303 SW Anchor Ave Ste 4   18 units, $110–$215
small dogs only, fully equipped condos & vacation homes are
beachfront or across the street to beach, picnic tables,
www.getaway2thecoast.com

Looking Glass Inn   541-996-3996, 800-843-4940
861 SW 51st St   36 units, $69–$249
1 to 2 dogs, $10/day each pet, kitchen, continental breakfast,
pet sheets-towels-bowls-treats, small pet walking area, easy beach
access, www.lookingglass-inn.com

Motel 6   541-996-9900, 800-466-8356
3517 NW Hwy 101   72 units, $52–$91
microwave, refrigerator, coffee in lobby, 6 blocks to beach,
www.motel6.com

Lincoln City, OR (continued)

O'dysius Hotel 541-994-4121, 800-869-8069
120 NW Inlet Ave 30 units, $159–$365
1 to 3 dogs under 20 lbs only, $25/day each pet, kitchen, complimentary wine tasting nightly, grassy walking area, close to beach, www.odysius.com

Oregon Beach House Rentals 541-921-3101, 888-755-7783
4741 SW Hwy 101 22 units, $99–$499
1 to 2 dogs allowed with advance approval only, $50-$100/stay, fully equipped cottages & vacation homes in Depoe Bay-Lincoln City-Newport, www.cottagesbythebeach.com

Oregon Beach Vacations 503-528-7480, 800-723-2383
690 SE 39th St 230 units, $69–$795
pet fee $50/stay, studios, condos, up to 8+ bdrm homes, some with hot tub, located in Depoe Bay-Gearhart-Gleneden Beach-Lincoln City-Neskowin-Newport-Seaside-Waldport, www.oregonbeachvacations.com

Overlook Motel 541-996-3300
3521 SW Anchor Dr 8 units, $80–$232
1 to 2 dogs, $10/day each pet, kitchen, pet cleanup towels-disposal bags-sheet for covering pet's sleeping area, 3-minute walk to beach, www.overlookmotel.net

Pacific Retreats Vacation Homes 541-994-4833, 800-473-4833
3126 NE Hwy 101 # A 4 units, $85–$160
pet fee $50/stay, fully equipped vacation homes in Lincoln City-Pacific City-Gleneden Beach sleep up to 8, some with hot tub or fenced yard, all within easy walking or driving distance to public parks & beach, www.pacificretreats.com

Palace Inn & Suites 541-996-9466, 866-996-9466
550 SE Hwy 101 51 units, $49–$229
1 to 2 dogs, $25/stay, coffeemaker, microwave, refrigerator, continental breakfast, sauna, hot tub, fitness room, grassy walking area, 2 blocks to beach, www.thepalaceinn.com

Sailor Jack Oceanfront Motel 541-994-3696, 888-432-8346
1035 NW Harbor Ave 40 units, $50–$150
coffeemaker, microwave, refrigerator, sauna, small pet walking area, beach access, www.sailorjack.com

Sea Echo Motel   541-994-2575
3510 NE Hwy 101   18 units, $55–$70
1 to 3 dogs, $5/day for each pet under 30 lbs or $10/day for each pet over 30 lbs, microwave, refrigerator, coffee in lobby, grassy walking area, 1/4 mile to beach

Sea Horse Oceanfront Lodging   541-994-2101, 800-662-2101
1301 NW 21st St   60 units, $76–$269
1 to 2 dogs, rooms-cabins-vacation homes, full kitchen or coffeemaker, microwave, refrigerator, continental breakfast, indoor pool, hot tub, stairway to beach, miles of open sandy beach for walking dogs, www.seahorsemotel.com

Seagull Beach Front Motel   541-994-2948, 800-422-0219
1511 NW Harbor Ave   25 units, $55–$225
1 to 2 dogs, $15-$20/stay, rooms-suites-cottage, full kitchen or microwave & refrigerator, www.seagullmoteloregon.com

Seahaven Vacation Rentals   541-996-8800
2110 NE 36th Dr Suite 1000   17 units, $125–$350
dogs allowed with advance approval only, $35/stay, fully equipped vacation homes sleep up to 16, some with hot tub, close to beach for walking dogs, www.seahavenrentals.com

Surftides Inn on the Beach   541-994-2191, 800-452-2159
2945 NW Jetty Ave   141 units, $79–$209
dogs under 30 lbs only, $25/stay, coffeemaker, microwave, refrigerator, restaurant, lounge, indoor pool, sauna, hot tub, fitness room, parking lot for walking dogs, close to beach, www.surftidesinn.com

Westshore Oceanfront Motel   541-996-2001, 800-621-3187
3127 SW Anchor Ave   20 units, $59–$179
1 to 2 dogs, $10/day each pet, kitchen, beach access for walking dogs, www.westshoremotel.com

Long Creek, OR

Ritter Hot Springs   541-421-3846
40035 Ritter Rd   8 units, $34
historic stage stop hotel, private rooms with shared bath, veranda, BBQ, picnic tables, hot tub & soaking tubs, swimming pool, shower with water piped in from the hot springs, surrounded by wilderness area & trails, open Memorial Day thru Labor Day

Madras, OR

Best Western Madras Inn   541-475-6141, 888-726-2466
12 SW 4th St   47 units, $99–$109
small pets only, $20/day each pet, microwave, refrigerator,
continental breakfast, seasonal pool, hot tub, 2 blocks to public
park, www.bestwestern.com/madrasinn

Budget Inn   541-475-3831
133 NE 5th St   30 units, $45–$85
each pet $10/day, full kitchen or microwave & refrigerator, grassy
walking area, 1 block to public park

Madras Chateau Inn   541-475-4633, 800-227-6865
600 N Hwy 26   99 units, $49–$69
pet fee $12/stay, continental breakfast, indoor pool, large open
area for walking dogs

Sonny's Motel   541-475-7217, 800-624-6137
1539 SW Hwy 97   43 units, $80–$135
pet fee $10/stay, coffeemaker, microwave, refrigerator, continental
breakfast, restaurant, lounge, outdoor pool, hot tub, small pet
walking area, 1 mile to public park, www.sonnysmotel.net

Manzanita, OR

Coast Cabins   503-368-7113, 800-435-1269
635 Laneda Ave   5 units, $125–$375
each pet $25/day, cabins & luxury condos, full kitchen or
kitchenette, 6 blocks to beach, www.coastcabins.com

Manzanita Rental Company   503-368-6797, 800-579-9801
686 Manzanita Ave   75 units, $90–$370
each pet $15/day, fully equipped vacation homes, some with yard
or fenced dog run, close to beach, www.manzanitarentals.com

Ocean Edge Vacation Rentals   503-368-3343, 866-368-3343
330 Laneda Ave   25 units, $100–$300
1 to 2 dogs, $30/stay, fully equipped vacation homes sleep 2 to 12,
hot tub, close to beach, www.oceanedge-vacation-rentals.com

Ocean Inn   503-368-7701, 866-368-7701
32 Laneda Ave   10 units, $145–$165
1 to 2 dogs, $15/day each pet, oceanfront 1-bdrm apartments,
pet cleanup bags provided, outside hose for washing dogs, beach
access, www.oceaninnatmanzanita.com

Ribbon Vacation Rentals   503-368-6009, 888-503-6009
423 Dorcas Lane   2357 units, $95–$225
1 to 2 dogs, $10/day each pet, fully equipped vacation homes in
Manzanita & Nehalem, www.ribbonvacationrentals.com

San Dune Motel   503-368-5163, 888-368-5163
428 Dorcas Lane   14 units, $65–$105
each pet $10/stay, full kitchen or coffeemaker-microwave-
refrigerator, BBQ, dog treats & cleanup bags, small pet walking
area, 4 blocks to beach access, www.sandune-inn-manzanita.com

Spindrift Inn   503-368-1001, 877-368-1001
114 Laneda Ave   14 units, $60–$120
each pet $10/day, kitchenette or coffeemaker-microwave-
refrigerator, 1 block to beach, close to several public parks,
www.spindrift-inn.com

Sunset Surf Oceanfront Motel   503-368-5224, 800-243-8035
248 Ocean Rd   40 units, $39–$169
1 to 2 dogs, $10/day each pet, full kitchen or coffeemaker-
microwave-refrigerator, outdoor pool, across street to beach,
www.sunsetsurfocean.com

Sunset Vacation Rentals   503-368-7969, 800-883-7784
186 Laneda Ave   92 units, $99–$600
1 to 4 dogs, $10/day each pet, fully equipped vacation homes in
Manzanita-Neahkanie-Rockaway Beach-Twin Rocks, www.ssvr.com

Maupin, OR

Deschutes Motel   541-395-2626, 877-899-6608
616 Mill St   8 units, $61–$96
1 to 3 dogs, $10/stay, refrigerator or kitchenette, coffee in lobby,
1 block to public park, www.deschutesmotel.com

Imperial River Company   541-395-2404, 800-395-3903
304 Bakeoven County Rd   25 units, $69–$279
each pet $15/day, coffeemaker, refrigerator, continental breakfast,
restaurant, lounge, riverside walking area, fishing from the river
bank, www.deschutesriver.com

Oasis Resort   541-395-2611
609 Hwy 197 S   11 units, $40–$80
each pet $5/day, private cottages, coffeemaker, microwave,
refrigerator, restaurant, lawn for walking dogs, riverside walkway,
guided fishing packages, tent sites, www.deschutesriveroasis.com

Maupin, OR (continued)

River Run Lodge   541-395-2747, 877-335-8867
210 Hartman Ave   6 units, $50–$105
1 to 2 dogs, $10/day each pet, rustic lodge sleeps 16, kitchen,
BBQ, riverview courtyard, lawn for walking dogs, next to riverside
walkway, www.riverrunlodge.net

McKenzie Bridge, OR

Caddisfly Resort   541-822-3556
56404 McKenzie Hwy   3 units, $95
dogs allowed with manager's approval, each pet $10/stay, cabins
with kitchen sleep 2 to 7, riverfront lawn, www.caddisflyresort.com

McMinnville, OR

Baker Street B & B   503-472-5575, 800-870-5575
129 SE Baker St   4 units, $159–$179
dogs allowed in separate cottage with advance approval, $20/stay,
coffeemaker, microwave, refrigerator, full breakfast, dog run
available, 1/2 block to public park, www.bakerstreetinn.com

Best Western Vineyard Inn Motel 503-472-4900, 800-285-6242
2035 SW Hwy 99W   65 units, $100–$115
each pet $10/day, coffeemaker, microwave, refrigerator,
continental breakfast, indoor pool, hot tub, fitness room, lawn,
1/2 mile to public park, www.bestwestern.com/prop_38128

Comfort Inn   503-472-1700
2520 SE Stratus Ave   66 units, $98–$179
1 to 2 dogs under 50 lbs only, $10/day each pet, coffeemaker,
microwave, refrigerator, extended continental breakfast, indoor
pool, hot tub, fitness room, lawn for walking dogs, short drive to
public park, www.comfortinn.com/hotel/or177

Paragon Motel   503-472-9493, 800-525-5469
2065 S Hwy 99W   55 units, $54–$75
1 to 2 dogs, $9/day each pet, microwave, refrigerator, continental
breakfast, seasonal pool, 1/2 mile to park, www.paragonmotel.com

Red Lion Inn & Suites   503-472-1500, 888-489-1600
2535 NE Cumulus Ave   67 units, $108–$114
each pet $10/day, coffeemaker, microwave, refrigerator,
continental breakfast, indoor pool, hot tub, open field for walking
dogs, 1/2 mile to walking trail, www.redlion.com/mcminnville

Safari Motor Inn   503-472-5187, 800-321-5543
345 NE Hwy 99W   59 units, $62–$77
dogs under 35 lbs only, $10/day each pet, coffeemaker,
microwave, refrigerator, extended continental breakfast, grassy
walking area, 1 mile to park & walking path

Twisted Willow Inn   503-472-5787
509 NE 9th St   2 units, $85–$95
full breakfast, lawn & sidewalks for walking dogs, 1 mile to public
park, www.twistedwillowinn.com

Medford, OR

Best Western Horizon Inn   541-779-5085, 800-452-2255
1154 E Barnett Rd   122 units, $74–$119
each pet $20/day, coffeemaker, microwave, refrigerator, extended
continental breakfast, seasonal pool, steam room, hot tub, fitness
room, across street to off-leash dog park,
www.bestwestern.com/horizoninn

Budget Inn   541-494-8088
345 S Central Ave   36 units, $36–$50
pet fee $5/day, coffeemaker, microwave, refrigerator, continental
breakfast, paved walking area

Candlewood Suites Airport   541-772-2800, 888-226-3539
3548 Heathrow Way   72 units, $99–$119
dogs under 80 lbs only, $10/day each pet ($75 maximum),
kitchenette, fitness room, 10-minute walk to public park,
www.candlewoodsuites.com

Capri Motel   541-773-7796
250 E Barnett Rd   36 units, $44
dogs under 20 lbs only, $20/stay, coffeemaker, microwave,
refrigerator, outdoor pool, 3 blocks to public park

Cedar Lodge Motor Inn   541-773-7361, 800-282-3419
518 N Riverside Ave   80 units, $45–$65
each pet $5/day, microwave, refrigerator, continental breakfast,
outdoor pool, picnic tables, small pet walking area, 1½ blocks to
public park, close to walking & biking paths

Cobblestone Cottages B & B   541-772-0898
2281 Ross Lane   2 units, $94–$129
dogs allowed by advance arrangement only, full breakfast, private
entrance, fenced 1-acre yard, www.cobblestonecottagesbnb.com

Medford, OR (continued)

Homewood Suites   541-779-9800
2010 Hospitality Way   109 units, $149–$229
pet fee $75/stay, studios to 2-bdrm suites, kitchen, full breakfast,
complimentary light dinner & beverages on weeknights, indoor
pool, hot tub, fitness room, pet walking area, 2 blocks to off-leash
dog park, close to trail, www.medford.homewoodsuites.com

Knights Inn   541-773-3676, 800-531-2655
500 N Riverside Ave   84 units, $50–$65
pet fee $15/day, microwave, refrigerator, seasonal pool, lawn,
1 mile to off-leash dog park, www.knightsinn-medford.com

Medford Inn   541-773-8266, 877-473-7444
1015 S Riverside Ave   105 units, $40–$85
each pet $15/stay, coffeemaker, microwave, refrigerator,
continental breakfast, outdoor pool, fitness room, large yard,
6 blocks to park, www.medfordinn.com

Mill Wood Inn   541-773-1152
1030 N Riverside Ave   34 units, $40
pet fee $10/stay, microwave, refrigerator, large yard, 5-minute walk
to public park

Motel 6 North   541-779-0550, 800-466-8356
2400 Biddle Rd   116 units, $56–$66
microwave, refrigerator, coffee in lobby, seasonal pool, small pet
walking area, 1 mile to walking & biking path, www.motel6.com

Motel 6 South   541-773-4290, 800-466-8356
950 Alba Dr   101 units, $46–$66
microwave, refrigerator, coffee in lobby, seasonal pool, next to
off-leash dog park

Paradise Lodge   541-842-2822, 888-667-6483
3140 Juanipero Way Suite 201   20 units, $145–$155
lodge is at Mile 58 on the Rogue River, 76 miles downriver from
Grants Pass, access by boat or on foot only, lodge rooms & cabins,
nightly rate includes breakfast-lunch-dinner, restaurant, sauna,
open May thru November, www.paradise-lodge.com

Plaza Motel   541-772-5404
1102 N Riverside Ave   19 units, $45
pet fee $10/day, full kitchen or microwave & refrigerator,
1 block to off-leash dog park

Quality Inn & Suites   541-779-0050, 877-779-0050
1950 Biddle Rd   123 units, $90–$104
coffeemaker, microwave, refrigerator, extended continental
breakfast, seasonal pool, sauna, hot tub, fitness room, dog biscuits
available in lobby, grassy walking area, close to walking & biking
path, www.qualityinnmedford.com

Ramada Inn & Convention Center   541-779-3141, 800-779-7829
2250 Biddle Rd   164 units, $69–$82
pet fee $20/stay, coffeemaker, microwave, refrigerator, full
breakfast, indoor pool, grassy walking area, 6-minute drive to
off-leash dog park, www.ramada.com/hotel/16509

Red Lion Hotel   541-779-5811, 800-733-5466
200 N Riverside Ave   185 units, $70–$260
pet fee $10/day, coffeemaker, microwave, refrigerator, restaurant,
lounge, seasonal pool, fitness room, grassy walking area, next to
park & walking path, www.redlion.com/medford

Rogue Regency Inn   541-770-1234, 800-535-5805
2345 Crater Lake Hwy   203 units, $81–$111
dogs allowed by advance reservation only, coffeemaker,
microwave, refrigerator, continental breakfast, restaurant, lounge,
indoor pool, hot tub, fitness room, lawn for walking dogs, close to
creekside walking & biking trail, www.rogueregency.com

Shilo Inn   541-770-5151, 800-222-2244
2111 Biddle Rd   48 units, $79–$114
pet fee $25/stay, coffeemaker, microwave, refrigerator, continental
breakfast, sauna, paved walking area, pet beds & treats available,
next to walking paths, 3/4 mile to public park, www.shiloinns.com

Super 8 Central Point/Medford   541-664-5888, 800-800-8000
4999 Biddle Rd   75 units, $80–$115
each pet $25/day, coffeemaker, microwave, refrigerator,
continental breakfast, hot tub, indoor heated pool with 80-ft
waterslide, lawn, 3 blocks to public park, www.super8.com

TownePlace Suites   541-842-5757, 800-257-3000
1395 Center Dr   76 units, $99–$189
pet fee $25/day ($75 maximum), full kitchen or coffeemaker,
continental breakfast, seasonal pool, lawn for walking dogs,
1 mile to off-leash dog park, www.marriott.com/mfrts

Medford, OR (continued)

Travelodge   541-773-1579, 800-578-7878
954 Alba Dr   60 units, $45–$75
pet fee $5/day, coffeemaker, microwave, refrigerator, continental
breakfast, seasonal pool, small pet walking area, close to public
park & walking trail, www.travelodge.com/hotel/13396

Under the Greenwood Tree B & B   541-776-0000
3045 Bellinger Lane   4 units, $120–$140
1 to 2 dogs allowed, full breakfast, afternoon tea & treats, bicycles
for guest use, on 10 acres with gardens & lawn for walking dogs,
10-minute drive to off-leash dog park, www.greenwoodtree.com

Valli Hai Motel   541-772-6183
1034 Court St   20 units, $55–$65
kitchenette or microwave & refrigerator, grassy walking area,
across street to public park

Merlin, OR

Doubletree Ranch   541-476-0120
6000 Abegg Rd   4 units, $95–$165
dogs allowed with advance approval only, $25/stay, 1-bdrm to
5-bdrm cabins & vacation homes, kitchen, riverside walkway,
www.doubletree-ranch.com

Galice Resort   541-476-3818
11744 Galice Rd   4 units, $109–$609
cabins & lodges sleep 2 to 16, kitchen or kitchenette, restaurant,
lounge, riverside trails for walking dogs, riverside walkway, 4 miles
to public park, open May thru September, www.galice.com

Rogue Forest B & B   541-472-1052
12035 Galice Rd   2 units, $225–$245
full breakfast, riverfront park & walkway, www.rogueforest.com

Merrill, OR

Wild Goose Motel   541-798-5826
105 E Court Dr   13 units, $53–$90
each pet $5/day, coffeemaker, microwave, refrigerator,
1 block to public park

Metolius, OR

Sweet Virginia's B & B   541-546-3031, 800-546-3031
407 6th St   3 units, $75–$115
full breakfast, large yard for walking dogs, across street to park,
1 block to walking path, www.sweetvirginiasbedandbreakfast.com

Milton-Freewater, OR

Morgan Inn   541-938-5547, 866-938-6369
104 N Columbia St   37 units, $64–$125
1 to 4 dogs, $20/stay each pet, kitchen or coffeemaker, microwave,
refrigerator, continental breakfast, lawn, 5 blocks to public park

Out West Motel   541-938-6647, 800-881-6647
84040 Hwy 11   12 units, $45–$75
each pet $10/stay, coffeemaker, microwave, refrigerator, small pet
walking area, across street to open field, www.outwestmotel.net

Milwaukie, OR

Budget Lodge Milwaukie Inn   503-659-2125, 800-255-1553
14015 SE McLoughlin Blvd   39 units, $45–$103
1 to 2 dogs under 30 lbs only, $10/day each pet, microwave,
refrigerator, 1/2 mile to public park, www.milwaukieinn.com

Molalla, OR

Stage Coach Inn Motel   503-829-4382
415 Grange Ave   32 units, $50–$60
each pet $10/day, kitchenette or coffeemaker-microwave-
refrigerator, open field for walking dogs, 2 blocks to public park,
www.stagecoachinnmolalla.com

Monmouth, OR

Courtesy Inn   503-838-4438
270 N Pacific Ave   35 units, $70
1 to 2 dogs, $10/day each pet, coffeemaker, microwave,
refrigerator, grassy walking area, 1/2 mile to public park

Monument, OR

Monument Motel & RV Park   541-934-2242
780 Hwy 402   10 units, $58–$68
pet fee $10/day, kitchenette, BBQ, 1/3 mile to public park,
www.monumentmotel.com

Moro, OR

Tall Winds Motel   541-565-3519
301 Main St (Hwy 97)   12 units, $44–$59
each pet $15/stay for up to 3 days, kitchenette or coffeemaker-
microwave,-refrigerator, continental breakfast, next to city park,
www.shermcty.biz/tallwinds/tallwinds.htm

Mount Hood/Parkdale, OR

Cooper Spur Mountain Resort   541-352-6692
10755 Cooper Spur Rd   16 units, $99–$440
pet fee $25/day, rooms-condos-cabins sleep up to 8, kitchen or
kitchenette, hot tub, BBQ, picnic area, dog run available, on 750
acres next to national forest & hiking trails, www.cooperspur.com

Mount Hood Hamlet B & B   541-352-3574, 800-407-0570
6741 Hwy 35   4 units, $140–$160
pets allowed by advance arrangement only, full breakfast, hot tub,
lawn & open field, close to walking trail, www.mthoodhamlet.com

Mount Vernon, OR

Blue Mountain Lodge   541-932-4451
150 W Main St   14 units, $46
each pet $5/day, microwave, refrigerator, coffee in lobby,
dog run available, 1 block to public park

Inn at Juniper Ridge   503-537-7570
23121 Hwy 395 N   2 units, $125
1 to 2 dogs allowed with advance approval only, $10/day,
kitchenette, full breakfast, BBQ, hot tub, private deck,
on 1,000 acres for hiking & fishing, www.innatjuniperridge.com

Mount Vernon Motel & Trailer Park   541-932-4712
195 N Mountain Blvd   5 units, $37–$49
each pet $5/day, 1-bdrm cabins & mobile homes, full kitchen or
microwave & refrigerator, fitness room, shaded yard for walking
dogs, 2 blocks to public park

Myrtle Creek, OR

Quick Stop Motel & Market   541-863-4689
6453 Dole Rd   12 units, $42–$48
pet fee $5/day, microwave, refrigerator, large open area for
walking dogs, convenience store

Rose Motel	541-863-3581
316 N Main St	4 units, $42

small dogs only, microwave, refrigerator, coffee in lobby, fenced yard, next to city park

Myrtle Point, OR

Myrtle Trees Motel	541-572-5811
1010 8th St	28 units, $60–$66

dogs under 20 lbs only, $15/day each pet, kitchenette or microwave & refrigerator, coffee in lobby, BBQ, picnic tables, 2½ acres overlooking wetlands area, www.myrtletreesmotel.com

Nehalem, OR

Beach Break Vacation Rentals	503-368-3865, 877-655-0623
35690 Hwy 101 N	60 units, $75–$750

each pet $5/day, vacation homes in Cape Meares-Fallon Cove-Manzanita-Pacific City-Rockaway, www.beach-break.com

North Coast Beach Rentals	503-368-4867, 866-355-0733
pet fee varies	12 units, $69–$359

1-bdrm to 7-bdrm suites-cottages-vacation homes on the north Oregon coast sleep up to 20, www.northcoastbeachrentals.com

Ripple Run Resort & Marina	503-368-3865, 877-655-0623
35345 Riverside Dr	7 units, $75–$550

each pet $5/day, fully equipped cottages & houseboats sleep up to 11, BBQ, fire pit, short drive to beach, www.ripplerunresort.com

Neskowin, OR

Breakers Condominiums	503-392-3417
48060 Breakers Blvd	10 units, $130–$245

each pet $20/day, 3-bdrm 2-bath fully equipped condos sleep 6+, beachfront location for walking dogs, www.breakersoregon.com

Grey Fox Vacation Rentals	503-392-4355, 888-720-2154
48880 Hwy 101 S	88 units, $75–$700

each pet $40/stay, fully equipped condos & vacation homes in Neskowin & Pacific City, www.oregoncoast.com/greyfox

Neskowin Resort Condominiums	503-392-4850
48990 Hwy 101 S	9 units, $72–$209

pet fee $20/stay, studios to 3-bdrm suites & townhouses, waterfront walking area, www.neskowinvacationrentals.com

Neskowin, OR (continued)

Proposal Rock Inn   503-392-3115, 866-404-4974
48988 Hwy 101 S   32 units, $59–$190
1 to 2 dogs, $15/stay, rooms-suites-condos, easy beach access,
www.proposalrockneskowin.com

Netarts, OR

Edgewater Vacation Rentals   503-842-1300, 888-425-1050
1020 1st St W   8 units, $109–$279
1 to 2 dogs, $10/day each pet, bayview suites & cabins sleep 4 to
10, kitchen, dog blankets & towels provided, large open area for
walking dogs, beach access, www.oregoncoastvacrentals.com

Sea Lion Inn   503-842-5477, 800-689-8923
4951 Netarts Hwy W   7 units, $60
each pet $5/day, rooms & 1-bdrm to 2-bdrm suites with full
kitchen or kitchenette, 1 block to beach, www.sealioninn.com

Terimore Lodging by the Sea   503-842-4623
5105 Crab Ave   26 units, $56–$125
$7/day for 1 pet, $10/day for 2 pets, rooms-cabins-cottages, full
kitchen or coffeemaker-microwave-refrigerator, across street to
beach, www.oregoncoast.com/terimore

Newberg, OR

Avellan Inn Bed & Breakfast   503-537-9161
16900 NE Hwy 240   2 units, $125–$155
pet-friendly "bed & biscuit" program: 5-course full breakfast,
refrigerator in each room, fenced yard on 12 acres with
landscaped gardens-woods-pond, www.avellaninn.com

Shilo Inn   503-537-0303, 800-222-2244
501 Sitka Ave   61 units, $60–$100
pet fee $25/stay, full kitchen or coffeemaker-microwave-
refrigerator, continental breakfast, seasonal pool, sauna, hot tub,
fitness room, pet beds & treats available, grassy walking area,
1½ blocks to public park, www.shiloinns.com

Towne & Country Motel   503-538-2800
1864 Portland Rd (99W)   22 units, $65
pet fee $7/day, large open walking area, 3 blocks to public park

Travelodge   503-537-5000, 800-578-7878
2816 Portland Rd   41 units, $75–$95
1 to 2 dogs under 50 lbs only, $7/day each pet, coffeemaker,
microwave, refrigerator, continental breakfast, restaurant, lounge,
indoor pool, hot tub, fitness room, paved walking area, short drive
to public park, www.travelodge.com/hotel/09113

VineRoost at McKinlay Vineyards   503-625-2534
                                          1 unit, $125–$200
dogs allowed with advance approval, 3-bdrm cottage sleeps 8, full
kitchen, covered patio with BBQ, outdoor fireplace, large yard for
walking dogs, surrounded by vineyards, www.vineroost.com

Newport, OR

America Inn & Suites   541-265-6631
710 N Coast Hwy   49 units, $50–$150
pet fee $10/day, theme-decorated rooms, kitchen, continental
breakfast, grassy walking area, 7 blocks to beach,
www.americainnandsuites.com

Beach Cottage at Nye   541-265-3537, 800-895-7170
115 SW Coast St   1 unit, $90
1-bdrm cottage, kitchenette, 2-person whirlpool tub in bathroom,
deck with ocean view, small fenced yard, short walk to beach,
www.beachcottageatnye.com

Beach Retreat   541-487-4966, 877-820-6132
423 SW Elizabeth St   2 units, $110–$125
dogs allowed with advance approval only, 2-bdrm upstairs/
downstairs duplex units sleep 15, deck & patio, kitchen, BBQ,
lawn, across street to beach, www.beachretreatoregon.com

Best Western Agate Beach Inn   541-265-9411, 800-547-3310
3019 N Coast Hwy   148 units, $99–$275
1 to 3 dogs by advance arrangement only, $20/stay each pet,
coffeemaker, microwave, refrigerator, restaurant, lounge, indoor
pool, hot tub, fitness room, small pet walking area, 1/4 mile to
beach, www.agatebeachinn.com

Driftwood Village Motel   541-265-5738
7947 N Coast Hwy   9 units, $85–$170
dogs allowed with manager's approval only, $10/day each pet,
studios with kitchenette, 1-bdrm suites with kitchen sleep up to 6,
pet walking area, trail to beach, www.driftwoodvillagemotel.com

Newport, OR (continued)

Econo Lodge   541-265-7723, 866-211-5107
606 SW Coast Hwy 101   43 units, $45–$99
dogs under 25 lbs only, $5/day each pet, microwave, refrigerator,
continental breakfast, lawn for walking dogs, 2 blocks to beach,
www.econolodge.com/hotel/or106

Embarcadero Resort Hotel   541-265-8521, 800-547-4779
1000 SE Bay Blvd   80 units, $89–$189
hotel rooms to townhouses with full kitchen, restaurant, lounge,
indoor pool, hot tub, on 13 acres for walking dogs, private crabbing
& fishing dock, 1½ miles to beach, www.embarcadero-resort.com

Fairhaven Vacation Rentals   541-574-0951, 888-523-4179
1109 SW Fall St   4 units, $145–$295
pet fee $10/day, 2-bdrm to 4-bdrm vacation homes in Nye Beach
neighborhood, some with hot tub or yard, 1 block to public park,
www.fairhavenvacationrentals.com

Hallmark Resort   541-265-2600, 888-448-4449
744 SW Elizabeth St   158 units, $99–$234
each pet $15/day, full kitchen or coffeemaker-microwave-
refrigerator, restaurant, lounge, indoor pool, sauna, hot tub, fitness
room, children's play area, complimentary basket of pet supplies,
dog washing & pooper scooper stations, pet walking areas, trails to
beach, www.hallmarkinns.com

House of Rogue Bed & Beer   (541) 961-0142
748 SW Bay Blvd   3 units, $90–$130
1-bdrm to 2-bdrm fully furnished apartments above Rogue Ales
Public House, paved walking area, ¼ block to waterfront,
www.rogue.com/locations/bb.php

La Quinta Inn & Suites Newport   541-867-7727
45 SE 32nd St   71 units, $69–$150
coffeemaker, microwave, refrigerator, extended continental
breakfast, indoor pool, sauna, hot tub, fitness room, small pet
walking area, 1 mile to beach, www.lq.com

Landing at Newport Condominium Hotel & Resort
890 SE Bay Blvd   541-574-6777, 800-749-4993
1 to 2 dogs allowed   57 units, $218–$418
$25 each pet for 1st day, $10 each pet each additional day, bayfront
condos, full kitchen, fitness room, www.thelandingatnewport.com

Money Saver Motel   541-265-2277, 888-461-4031
861 SW Coast Hwy   42 units, $45–$55
dogs allowed with advance reservation only, $10/day each pet,
microwave, refrigerator, coffee in lobby, grassy walking area,
20-minute walk to beach, www.newportoregonmotel.com

Newport Bay Motel   541-265-4533
1823 N Coast Hwy   49 units, $49–$129
1 to 2 dogs, $10/day each pet, coffeemaker, microwave,
refrigerator, 4 blocks to public park, www.newportbaymotel.com

Newport City Center Motel   541-265-7381, 800-687-9099
538 SW Coast Hwy   30 units, $25–$140
each pet $10/stay, kitchen or microwave & refrigerator,
continental breakfast, lawn, 3-minute walk to beach,
www.newportcitycentermotel.com

Newport Motor Inn   541-265-6363 or 541-265-8516
1311 N Coast Hwy   39 units, $28–$68
pet fee $5/stay, microwave, refrigerator, coffee in lobby, gravel
walking area, 6 blocks to beach, www.newportmotorinn.net

Park Motel   541-265-2234
1106 SW 9th St   13 units, $45–$78
each pet $7/day, full kitchen or coffeemaker-microwave-refrigerator,
lawn, 5-minute walk to beach, www.newportparkmotel.com

Shilo Inn   541-265-7701, 800-222-2244
536 SW Elizabeth   179 units, $105–$230
pet fee $25/stay, coffeemaker, microwave, refrigerator, grassy
walking area, stairway to beach, www.shiloinns.com

Starfish Point   541-265-3751, 800-870-7795
140 NW 48th St   6 units, $190–$215
1 to 2 dogs, $17/day each pet, 2-bdrm condos with jacuzzi tubs,
decks, dog treats & towels, beach access, www.starfishpoint.com

Summer Wind Budget Motel   541-265-8076
728 N Coast Hwy   33 units, $39–$45
1 to 2 dogs, $10/stay, microwave, refrigerator, coffee in lobby,
parking lot for walking dogs, 3 blocks to public park

Vikings Cottages & Condos   541-265-2477, 800-480-2477
729 NW Coast St   18 units, $135
pets allowed in one 2-bdrm cottage with kitchen, large open area
for walking dogs, stairway to beach, www.vikingsoregoncoast.com

Newport, OR (continued)

Waves of Newport Motel   541-265-4661, 800-282-6993
820 NW Coast St   64 units, $99–$114
small pets only, $10/day, rooms with microwave & refrigerator,
2-bdrm to 3-bdrm cottages with full kitchen, continental breakfast,
grassy walking area, 4 blocks to beach, www.wavesofnewport.com

Whaler Motel   541-265-9261, 800-433-9444
155 SW Elizabeth St   73 units, $99–$169
each pet $10/day, motel rooms with coffeemaker-microwave-
refrigerator, continental breakfast, indoor pool, hot tub, fitness
room, pet sheet & cleanup bags, across street to beach, beach
house rentals also available, www.whalernewport.com

Yaquina Bay Property Management   541-265-3537
146 SE 1st St   800-895-7170
     24 units, $90–$285
fully equipped oceanfront & oceanview vacation homes, beachfront
or short walk to beach, www.yaquinabayproperties.com

North Bend, OR

Bay Bridge Motel   541-756-3151, 800-557-3156
66304 Hwy 101   16 units, $60–$90
dogs under 25 lbs only, $5/day, kitchenette, continental breakfast,
grassy walking area

City Center Motel   541-756-5118
750 Connecticut St   18 units, $40–$55
pet fee $10/stay, microwave, refrigerator, continental breakfast,
next to public park

Comfort Inn   541-756-3191, 877-424-6423
1503 Virginia Ave   96 units, $105–$149
1 to 2 dogs, $15/day, coffeemaker, microwave, refrigerator,
extended continental breakfast, hot tub, fitness room, picnic area,
courtyard & grassy walking area, 4 miles to public park, 5 miles to
beach, www.coosbayinn.com

Itty Bitty Inn B & B Motel   541-756-6398
1504 Sherman Ave   5 units, $35–$45
pets allowed with manager's approval only, microwave,
refrigerator, grassy walking area, ½ block to public park

Mill Casino Hotel 541-756-8800, 800-953-4800
3201 Tremont St   202 units, $120–$140
dogs under 50 lbs only, $25/day, coffeemaker, refrigerator,
restaurant, lounge, indoor pool, hot tub, small pet walking area,
2 miles to public park, www.themillcasino.com

Parkside Motel 541-756-4124
1480 Sherman Ave   16 units, $39–$80
pet fee $5/day, microwave, refrigerator, coffee in lobby, grassy
walking area, 2 blocks to public park, www.parkside-motel.com

North Powder, OR

North Powder Motel 541-898-2829
850 2nd St   12 units, $40–$50
each pet $8/day, coffeemaker, microwave, refrigerator, large open
walking area, 1 block to off-leash dog park, 2 blocks to river

Oakland, OR

Ranch Motel Inn 541-849-2126
581 John Long Rd   25 units, $45–$75
coffeemaker, microwave, refrigerator, seasonal pool, small pet
walking area, www.ranchmotelinn.com

Oakridge, OR

Arbor Inn Motel 541-782-2611
48229 Hwy 58   14 units, $45–$65
1 to 2 dogs, $10/day each pet, kitchenette or coffeemaker-
microwave-refrigerator, next to walking & biking path, RV park
next door, arborinnmotel.net

Best Western Oakridge Inn 541-782-2212, 800-780-7234
47433 Hwy 58   40 units, $99
1 to 2 small pets only, $10/day each pet, coffeemaker, microwave,
refrigerator, continental breakfast, seasonal pool, hot tub, gravel
walking area, 1/4 mile to river, www.bestwestern.com/oakridgeinn

Bluewolf Motel 541-782-5884
47465 Hwy 58   12 units, $40–$49
each pet $10/stay, coffeemaker, microwave, refrigerator, lawn for
walking dogs, 1/4 mile to river & walking trail, 9 lakes within
a 30-minute drive, www.bluewolfmotel.com

Oakridge, OR (continued)

Cascade Motel   541-782-2489
47487 Hwy 58   10 units, $51–$70
1 to 2 dogs under 35 lbs only, $10/day, continental breakfast,
designated pet walking area, 6 blocks to riverfront park & walkway

Oakridge Motel   541-782-2432
48197 Hwy 58 East   12 units, $45–$200
rooms & suites with coffeemaker-microwave-refrigerator, also
vacation homes with full kitchen, bring your dog's own bedding, large
open walking area, 1/2 mile to park, www.theoakridgemotel.com

Oceanside, OR

Clifftop Inn   503-842-6030, 866-254-3386
1816 Maxwell Mountain Rd   14 units, $45–$159
pet fee $20/day, kitchen or kitchenette, sauna, massage therapist,
paved walking area, 2 blocks to beach, www.clifftopinn.com

Oceanfront Cabins   503-842-6081, 888-845-8470
1610 Pacific NW   7 units, $55–$110
pet fee $10/day, cabins with kitchen or kitchenette, small pet
walking area, 200 feet to beach, www.oceanfrontcabins.com

Ontario, OR

Budget Inn   541-889-3101
1737 N Oregon St   26 units, $55
each pet $5/day, coffeemaker, microwave, refrigerator, outdoor
pool, small pet walking area, 3 blocks to public park

Colonial Inn   541-889-9615, 800-727-5014
1395 Tapadera Ave   89 units, $42–$72
pet fee $5/stay, continental breakfast, indoor pool, hot tub, small
pet walking area, 2 miles to riverfront park

Creek House B & B   541-823-0717
717 SW 2nd St   4 units, $89–$129
dogs allowed with advance approval, $25/stay, full breakfast,
outside kennel available, www.creekshouse.com

Economy Inn   541-889-6449
88 N Oregon St   32 units, $36–$39
pet fee $6/day, microwave, refrigerator, continental breakfast,
seasonal pool, large open walking area, 1 block to public park

Holiday Inn   541-889-8621, 800-525-5333
1249 Tapadera Ave   96 units, $89–$129
pet fee $10/stay, coffeemaker, restaurant, lounge, seasonal pool,
hot tub, large open area for walking dogs, 1 mile to riverside
walkway, www.holidayinn.com/ontarioor

Motel 6   541-889-6617, 800-466-8356
275 NE 12th St   104 units, $36–$52
microwave, refrigerator, coffee in lobby, seasonal pool, open field
for walking dogs, 3 miles to riverfront park, www.motel6.com

Ontario Inn   541-823-2556
1144 SW 4th Ave   22 units, $39–$45
each pet $5/day, microwave, refrigerator, continental breakfast,
large open area for walking dogs, 1 block to public park,
www.ontarioinnmotel.com

Oregon Trail Motel   541-889-8633
92 E Idaho Ave   30 units, $35–$38
pet fee $5/stay, full kitchen or coffeemaker, lawn for walking dogs,
3 blocks to public park

Rodeway Inn   541-889-9188
615 E Idaho Ave   71 units, $60–$80
1 to 3 dogs, $5/day each pet, coffeemaker, refrigerator,
full breakfast, restaurant, outdoor pool, hot tub, picnic area,
small pet walking area, 1 mile to riverside walkway,
www.rodeway.com/hotel/or178

Sleep Inn   541-881-8771 or 541-881-0007, 800-424-6423
1221 SE 1st Ave   65 units, $59–$109
dogs under 35 lbs only, $10/day each pet, microwave, refrigerator,
continental breakfast, indoor pool, hot tub, gravel pet walking area,
5 miles to public park, www.sleepinn.com/hotel/or060

Oregon City, OR

Best Western Rivershore Hotel   503-655-7141, 800-443-7777
1900 Clackamette Dr   114 units, $85–$115
1 to 3 dogs, $5/day each pet, coffeemaker, microwave, refrigerator,
restaurant, lounge, seasonal pool, hot tub, fitness room, small
walking area, across street to park, www.rivershorehotel.com

Otis, OR

Anna's Falls B & B   541-994-8785
7212 Hwy 18   3 units, $89
cabins, full breakfast, special dinners available by advance
arrangement, RV & tent sites, on 6½ acres overlooking Salmon
River & 20-ft wide waterfall, 10-minute walk to beach,
www.annasfalls.com

Otter Rock, OR

Alpine Chalets   541-765-2572, 800-825-5768
7045 Otter Crest Loop   11 units, $135–$150
each pet $10/day, chalets with full kitchen sleep 5 to 8, studio
apartment with kitchenette sleeps 6, BBQ, fire pit, private park &
picnic area, private beach access, www.oregonalpinechalets.com

Pacific City, OR

Anchorage Motel & Vacation Rentals   503-965-6773
6585 Pacific Ave   800-941-6250
pet fee $10 for 1st day, $5 each additional day   12 units, $49–$195
rooms with coffeemaker, 1-bdrm to 2-bdrm apartments & vacation
home with full kitchen, BBQ, picnic area, pet towels provided,
fenced yard, 4 blocks to beach, www.oregoncoast.com/anchorage

Inn at Cape Kiwanda   503-965-7001, 888-965-7001
33105 Cape Kiwanda Dr   35 units, $129–$329
1 to 3 dogs, $20/day each pet, rooms with coffeemaker-microwave-
refrigerator, 2-bdrm to 3-bdrm beachfront cottages with kitchen,
private decks & balconies, complimentary wine & appetizers every
Friday evening, fitness room, across street to beach,
www.innatcapekiwanda.com

Inn at Pacific City   503-965-6366, 888-722-2489
35215 Brooten Rd   15 units, $60–$110
1 to 2 dogs, $15/day each pet, kitchenette or coffeemaker-
microwave-refrigerator, grassy walking area, 5 blocks to beach,
www.innatpacificcity.com

Pacific City Inn   503-965-6464, 866-567-3466
35280 Brooten Rd   17 units, $70–$180
1 to 3 dogs, $15/day each pet, kitchenette or coffeemaker-
microwave-refrigerator, restaurant, lounge, www.pacificcityinn.com

Riverview Lodge & RV Park   503-965-6000
36220 Resort Dr   5 units, $55–$95
each pet $15/day, 1-bdrm to 2-bdrm units with kitchen, deck
overlooking river, on 5 acres with open field for walking dogs,
RV & tent sites, moorage facility, 2 miles to beach,
www.ifish.net/riverview.html

Sea View Vacation Rentals   503-965-7888, 888-701-1023
6340 Pacific Ave   71 units, $75–$360
1 to 2 dogs, $25/stay each pet, fully equipped vacation homes in
Neskowin-Pacific City-Tierra Del Mar, some with hot tub,
beachfront or close to beach, www.seaview4u.com

Shorepine Village Vacation Rentals 503-965-5776, 877-549-2632
5975 Shorepine Dr   38 units, $129–$269
1 to 2 dogs, $20/day each pet, beach homes sleep 4 to 10, BBQ,
bicycles for guest use, close to beach, www.shorepinerentals.com

Pendleton, OR

America's Best Value Inn   541-276-1400, 888-315-2378
201 SW Court Ave   53 units, $50–$89
pet fee $10/day, coffeemaker, refrigerator, continental breakfast,
outdoor pool, riverfront area for walking dogs, close to paved
walking trail, www.bestvalueinn.com

Best Western Pendleton Inn   541-276-2135, 800-528-1234
400 SE Nye Ave   71 units, $70–$90
dogs under 20 lbs only, $10/stay each pet, coffeemaker,
microwave, refrigerator, continental breakfast, seasonal pool, hot
tub, fitness room, open field for walking dogs, 1 mile to riverside
walkway, www.bestwestern.com/pendletoninn

Econo Lodge   541-276-8654
620 SW Tutuilla Rd   51 units, $47–$110
each pet $10/day, coffeemaker, microwave, refrigerator,
continental breakfast, creekside area for walking dogs, close to
walking path, www.econolodge.com/hotel/or109

Holiday Inn Express   541-966-6520, 800-465-4329
600 SE Nye Ave   62 units, $129–$139
pet fee $10/day, extended continental breakfast, restaurant,
indoor pool, hot tub, large open area for walking dogs,
www.hiexpress.com/pendletonor

Pendleton, OR (continued)

Knights Inn	541-276-3231
105 SE Court Ave	46 units, $45–$65

dogs under 30 lbs only, $10/day each pet, microwave, refrigerator, continental breakfast, restaurant, lounge, ½ block to public park, www.knightsinn.com/hotel/15531

Motel 6	541-276-3160, 800-466-8356
325 SE Nye Ave	92 units, $39–$55

microwave, refrigerator, coffee in lobby, seasonal pool, large open area for walking dogs, www.motel6.com

Neigh-bors Horse Motel, Bed & Barn	541-276-6737
543 NW 21st St	1 unit, $75

fully equipped apartment sleeps 5, breakfast supplies provided, 4-stall horse barn, large open area & trails for off-leash walking, guests' horses welcome too, www.neigh-bors.com

Oxford Suites	541-276-6000, 877-545-7848
2400 SW Court Place	87 units, $109–$149

pet fee $20/stay, coffeemaker, microwave, refrigerator, full breakfast, indoor pool, hot tub, fitness room, evening reception with beverages & appetizers, lawn & open field for walking dogs, 1 mile to public park, www.oxfordsuitespendleton.com

Pendleton House	541-276-8581, 800-700-8581
311 N Main St	6 units, $100–$140

small dogs allowed with advance approval, $25/stay, full gourmet breakfast, please bring your pet's bedding, large backyard, ½ block to riverside walkway, www.pendletonhousebnb.com

Pillars Motel	541-276-6241
1816 SE Court Ave	14 units, $34–$37

dogs allowed by advance reservation only, $2/day each pet, microwave, refrigerator, open area for walking dogs, 3 blocks to riverfront park & walkway

Red Lion Hotel	541-276-6111, 800-733-5466
304 SE Nye Ave	170 units, $102

dogs allowed by advance arrangement only, $20/stay, coffeemaker, microwave, refrigerator, restaurant, lounge, seasonal pool, hot tub, fitness room, lawn for walking dogs, www.redlion.com/pendleton

Relax Inn   541-276-3293
205 SE Dorion Ave   36 units, $45–$50
each pet $7/day, coffeemaker, microwave, refrigerator, 4 blocks to
public park

Rodeo City Inn   541-276-4711, 800-734-7466
74149 Barnhart Rd   50 units, $40–$44
pet fee $10/stay, full kitchen or coffeemaker-microwave-
refrigerator, continental breakfast, on 2 acres in quiet country
setting, close to walking trail, www.rodeocityinn.com

Rugged Country Lodge   541-966-6800, 877-778-4433
1807 SE Court Ave   28 units, $62–$72
pet fee $10/stay, extended continental breakfast, freshly baked
cookies, coffee & tea always available, small pet walking area,
4-minute walk to riverfront park, www.ruggedcountrylodge.com

Super 8 Motel   541-276-8881, 800-800-8000
601 SE Nye Ave   50 units, $65–$120
pet fee $10/stay, coffeemaker, microwave, refrigerator, continental
breakfast, indoor pool, hot tub, lawn, www.super8.com

Travelers Inn   541-276-6231, 866-349-8232
310 SE Dorion Ave   40 units, $39–$79
coffeemaker, microwave, refrigerator, continental breakfast,
seasonal pool, hot tub, grassy walking area, 2 blocks to public
park, www.pendletontravelersinn.com

Travelodge   541-276-7531, 800-578-7878
411 SW Dorion Ave   36 units, $56–$89
pet fee $10/stay, microwave, refrigerator, continental breakfast, lawn,
1 block to riverside walkway, www.travelodge.com/hotel/11283

Philomath, OR

Galaxie Motel   541-929-4334
104 S 20th St   15 units, $45–$60
pet fee $7/day, microwave, refrigerator, small pet walking area,
1 block to public park

Phoenix, OR

Bavarian Motel   541-535-1678
636 N Main St   22 units, $40–$52
1 to 2 dogs allowed with manager's approval only, $100/stay,
coffeemaker, microwave, refrigerator, 1 block to riverfront park

Port Orford, OR

Arizona Beach Lodge   541-332-1001
37015 Arizona Ranch Rd   11 units, $40–$120
coffeemaker, microwave, refrigerator, across street to public park,
www.arizonabeachlodge.com

Castaway-by-the-Sea Motel   541-332-4502
545 W 5th St   13 units, $85–$185
1 to 2 dogs, $10/day, rooms & suites with kitchen, small pet
walking area, 1 block to beach, also 2-bdrm+loft vacation lodge
sleeps 10, on 7½ oceanview acres next to the motel,
www.castawaybythesea.com

Sea Crest Motel   541-332-3040, 888-332-3040
44 Hwy 101 S   18 units, $69–$82
each pet $7/day, coffeemaker, refrigerator, located on clifftop
overlooking ocean, small pet walking area, ¼ mile to beach &
harbor, www.seacrestoregon.com

Shoreline Motel   541-332-2903
206 6th St   10 units, $55–$85
coffeemaker, microwave & refrigerator also available for small
additional fee, short walk to beach

Portland, OR

Ace Hotel   503-228-2277
1022 SW Stark St   32 units, $75–$250
continental breakfast, 2 blocks to public park, www.acehotel.com

Aloft Portland Airport at Cascade Station   503-200-5678
9920 NE Cascade Parkway   800-325-3535
    136 units, $89–$144
coffeemaker, refrigerator, restaurant, lounge, indoor pool, fitness
room, barkdust walking area, close to park & walking path,
www.alofthotels.com/portland

Banfield Motel   503-280-1400
1525 NE 37th Ave   53 units, $65–$85
1 to 2 well-behaved dogs allowed with manager's approval only,
$5/day, coffeemaker, microwave, refrigerator, outdoor pool, gravel
walking area, 4 blocks to public park, www.banfieldvalueinn.com

Benson Hotel   503-228-2000, 888-523-6766
309 SW Broadway   287 units, $129–$309
pet fee $75/stay, coffeemaker, complimentary wine tasting,
restaurant, lounge, fitness room, dog beds-bowls-treats provided,
dog walking service also available, list of local dog parks-walking
routes-day care providers available at front desk, 3 blocks to city
park, www.bensonhotel.com

Best Western Inn at the Meadows   503-286-9600
1215 N Hayden Meadows   146 units, $85–$110
1 to 2 dogs under 25 lbs only, $20/day, coffeemaker, microwave,
refrigerator, extended continental breakfast, hot tub, lawn,
2 blocks to park, www.bestwestern.com/innatthemeadows

Best Western Pony Soldier Inn Airport   503-256-1504
9901 NE Sandy Blvd   800-634-7669
                                    103 units, $99–$159
coffeemaker, microwave, refrigerator, extended continental
breakfast, seasonal pool, steam room, fitness room, pet treats
available, lawn, close to walking trail, www.ponysoldierinns.com

Briarwood Suites   503-788-9394, 800-578-7878
7740 SE Powell Blvd   40 units, $84–$101
each pet $10/day, coffeemaker, microwave, refrigerator,
continental breakfast, 2 blocks to park, www.briarwoodsuites.com

Budget Value Viking Motel   503-285-6687, 800 308-5097
6701 N Interstate Ave   25 units, $50–$65
dogs under 50 lbs only, $10/day each pet, coffeemaker,
microwave, refrigerator, lawn for walking dogs, 5-minute walk to
public park, www.vikingmotelportland.com

Days Inn East Portland/Gresham   503-618-8400, 866-753-3796
2261 NE 181st Ave   75 units, $63–$75
1 to 2 dogs under 50 lbs only, $15/day each pet, coffeemaker,
microwave, refrigerator, continental breakfast, indoor pool, fitness
room, freshly baked cookies, 2 miles to public park,
www.sleepgresham.com

Days Inn   503-289-1800, 800-833-1800
9930 N Whitaker Rd   208 units, $74–$95
1 to 3 dogs, $15/stay, kitchenette or coffeemaker, extended
continental breakfast, fitness room, open field for walking dogs,
next to public park, www.daysinn.com/hotel/11544

Portland, OR (continued)

Heathman Hotel   503-241-4100, 800-551-0011
1001 SW Broadway   150 units, $159–$319
1 to 2 dogs, $35/day each pet, coffeemaker, restaurant, lounge,
fitness room, 1 block to park, http://portland.heathmanhotel.com

Hilton Portland & Executive Tower 503-226-1611, 800-445-8667
921 SW 6th Ave   782 units, $139–$259
1 to 2 dogs under 50 lbs only, $25/stay, coffeemaker, restaurant,
lounge, indoor pool, sauna, hot tub, fitness room, ½ mile to
riverfront park, www.portland.hilton.com

Holiday Inn Express East   503-252-7400
9707 SE Stark St   84 units, $90–$109
dogs under 30 lbs only, $20/stay, coffeemaker, refrigerator,
extended continental breakfast, hot tub, fitness room, 1 block to
walking path, www.hiexpress.com/portland-stark

Holiday Inn Portland Airport   503-256-5000
8439 NE Columbia Blvd   284 units, $79–$179
pet fee $25/stay, coffeemaker, restaurant, lounge, indoor pool, hot
tub, fitness room, 7-minute walk to open area for walking dogs,
www.portlandairporthi.com

Holiday Motel   503-285-3661
8050 NE MLK Jr Blvd   22 units, $65–$90
1 to 2 dogs, $10/day each pet, microwave, refrigerator, grassy
walking area, 1 mile to public park

Hospitality Inn   503-244-6684, 800-929-4442
10155 SW Capitol Hwy   53 units, $72–$90
dogs under 30 lbs only, $10/day each pet, coffeemaker,
microwave, refrigerator, extended continental breakfast, fitness
room, ½ mile to public park, www.hospitalityinnportland.com

Hotel deLuxe   503-219-2094, 866-895-2094
729 SW 15th Ave   130 units, $160–$350
each pet $65/stay, coffeemaker, refrigerator, restaurant, lounge,
fitness room, pet bowls & toys provided, pet room service menu-
day care-grooming available, sidewalks for walking dogs,
10-minute drive to public park, www.hoteldeluxeportland.com

Hotel Fifty   503-221-0711, 877-505-7220
50 SW Morrison St   140 units, $149–$399
1 to 2 dogs under 40 lbs only, $50/stay each pet, coffeemaker,
restaurant, lounge, guest pass to local fitness center, across street
to waterfront park, www.hotelfifty.com

Hotel Lucia   503-225-1717, 877-225-1717
400 SW Broadway   127 units, $149–$369
1 to 2 dogs, $45/stay each pet, coffeemaker & refrigerator,
restaurant, lounge, fitness room, pet beds-toys-bowls-cleanup bags
provided, 2 blocks to public park, www.hotellucia.com

Hotel Monaco   503-222-0001, 800-207-2201
506 SW Washington St   221 units, $159–$399
hosted evening wine hour, coffeemaker, refrigerator, restaurant,
lounge, fitness room, pet bowl-bed-treats-bottled water-cleanup
bags, 2 blocks to public park, pet walking service-massage-even a
pet psychic available, www.monaco-portland.com

Hotel Vintage Plaza   503-228-1212, 800-243-0555
422 SW Broadway   117 units, $159–$300
hosted evening wine hour, refrigerator, restaurant, lounge, fitness
room, pet treats-bowls-bed-cleanup bags, designated pet walking
area, 8 blocks to riverfront park, pet walking service-massage-
daycare-grooming service available, www.vintageplaza.com

Howard Johnson Inn Portland Airport   503-256-4111
8247 NE Sandy Blvd   866-440-7700
each pet $15/day   120 units, $70–$80
coffeemaker, microwave, refrigerator, continental breakfast,
restaurant, lounge, outdoor pool, guest pass to local fitness center,
grassy walking area, across street to park & walking path,
www.hotelpdxairport.com

Inn at the Convention Center   503-233-6331
420 NE Holladay St   97 units, $79–$105
1 to 3 dogs under 25 lbs only, $10/day, coffeemaker, 4 blocks to
public park, www.innatcc.com

Jupiter Hotel   503-230-9200, 877-800-0004
800 E Burnside St   80 units, $109–$144
1 to 3 dogs, $35/stay, restaurant, lounge, paved walking area,
5-minute drive to public park, www.jupiterhotel.com

Portland, OR (continued)

La Quinta Inn & Suites Portland Airport   503-382-3820
11207 NE Holman St   98 units, $94–$134
coffeemaker, microwave, refrigerator, extended continental
breakfast, indoor pool, hot tub, fitness room, lawn for walking
dogs, next to walking & biking path, www.lq.com

La Quinta Inn Portland Convention Center   503-233-7933
431 NE Multnomah St   79 units, $85–$130
coffeemaker-microwave-refrigerator, extended continental
breakfast, indoor pool, hot tub, fitness room, pet treats available,
4 blocks to public park, www.lq.com

La Quinta Inn Portland NW   503-497-9044
4319 NW Yeon Ave   84 units, $150–$189
coffeemaker, microwave, refrigerator, continental breakfast, indoor
pool, hot tub, fitness room, 3 miles to riverfront park & walkway,
www.lq.com

Mark Spencer Hotel   503-224-3293, 800-548-3934
409 SW 11th Ave   102 units, $99–$209
pet fee $10/day, kitchen, continental breakfast, freshly baked
cookies, guest pass to local fitness center, pet bowls-furniture
covers-cleanup bags, 4 blocks to park, www.markspencer.com

Motel 6   503-491-4444
18323 SE Stark St   40 units, $44–$62
1 to 2 dogs, 1st pet free, 2nd pet $10/stay, microwave, refrigerator,
coffee in lobby, near public park, www.motel6.com

Motel 6 Portland Downtown   503-234-4391
518 NE Holladay St   36 units, $66–$76
microwave, refrigerator, coffee in lobby, barkdust walking area,
10-minute walk to public park, www.motel6.com

Motel 6 Mall 205/Airport   503-255-0808
9225 SE Stark St   63 units, $49–$69
1 to 2 dogs, 1st pet free, 2nd pet $10/day, microwave, refrigerator,
coffee in lobby, 2 blocks to park, www.motel6-portland-mall.com

Motel 6 Portland Central   503-238-0600, 800-466-8356
3104 SE Powell Blvd   68 units, $45–$69
coffee in lobby, outdoor pool, grassy walking area, across street to
school field for walking dogs, 5 blocks to public park,
www.motel6.com

Motel 6 Portland North   503-247-3700, 800-466-8356
1125 N Schmeer Rd   65 units, $69–$75
dogs up to 30 lbs free, dogs over 30 lbs $10/day, refrigerator,
coffee in lobby, hot tub, lawn, www.motel6-portland-north.com

Oxford Suites Jantzen Beach   503-283-3030, 800-548-7848
12226 N Jantzen Dr   200 units, $139–$199
1 to 3 dogs, $10-$25/day, coffeemaker, microwave, refrigerator, full
breakfast, indoor pool, sauna, hot tub, fitness room, convenience
store, small pet walking area, short drive to public park,
www.oxfordsuitesportland.com

Paramount Hotel   503-223-9900, 800-663-1144
808 SW Taylor St   154 units, $115–$185
dogs under 50 lbs only, $50/stay each pet, refrigerator, continental
breakfast, restaurant, barkdust walking area, close to public park,
www.portlandparamount.com

Park Lane Suites   503-226-6288, 800-532-9543
809 SW King Ave   44 units, $119–$189
1 to 2 dogs under 50 lbs only, $15/day each pet ($45 maximum),
kitchenette, continental breakfast, guest pass to local fitness
center, sidewalks for walking dogs, 3 blocks to public park,
www.parklanesuites.com

Portland Value Inn & Suites   503-244-0151
10450 SW Barbur Blvd   43 units, $55–$70
1 to 2 dogs, $10/day, suites with kitchenette, standard rooms with
coffeemakers on request, outdoor pool, small pet walking area,
next door to school field, 1½ miles to public park,
www.portlandvalueinn.com

Portlander Inn & Marketplace   503-345-0300, 800-523-1193
10350 N Vancouver Way   100 units, $75–$120
pet fee $10/day, coffeemaker, microwave, refrigerator, restaurant,
fitness room, full service market, 1 block to walking trail &
off-leash dog park, www.portlanderinn.com

Quality Inn & Suites   503-492-4000
2323 NE 181st Ave   70 units, $55–$93
1 to 2 dogs under 40 lbs only, $15/day each pet, microwave,
refrigerator, continental breakfast, indoor pool, hot tub, fitness
room, lawn for walking dogs, www.qualityinn.com/hotel/or160

Portland, OR (continued)

Ramada Inn Portland Airport   503-255-6511, 877-726-2326
6221 NE 82nd Ave   202 units, $59–$191
1 to 2 dogs under 20 lbs only, $20/day each pet, coffeemaker,
microwave, refrigerator, restaurant, lounge, outdoor pool, sauna,
hot tub, small grassy areas, www.ramada.com/hotel/01642

Red Lion Hotel Convention Center 503-235-2100, 800-323-1877
1021 NE Grand Ave   174 units, $110–$120
1 to 2 dogs under 50 lbs only, $20/day, coffeemaker, refrigerator,
restaurant, lounge, fitness room, sidewalks for walking dogs,
5 blocks to public park, www.redlion.com/conventioncenter

Red Lion Hotel Jantzen Beach   503-283-4466, 800-733-5466
909 N Hayden Island Dr   320 units, $118–$149
pet fee $20/stay, full kitchen or coffeemaker-microwave-
refrigerator, restaurant, lounge, seasonal pool, hot tub, fitness
room, tennis courts, next to paved riverside walking trail,
www.redlion.com/jantzenbeach

Red Lion Hotel Portland Airport   503-255-6722, 800-345-3896
7101 NE 82nd Ave   136 units, $89–$139
1 to 2 dogs, $20/stay, coffeemaker, microwave, refrigerator,
restaurant, lounge, seasonal pool, hot tub, fitness room, courtyard
& lawn for walking dogs, close to open field, www.redlion.com

Residence Inn Downtown/Riverplace   503-552-9500
2115 SW River Parkway   258 units, $209–$309
each pet $10/day, kitchenette, full breakfast, Monday thru
Wednesday evenings complimentary beverages & appetizers,
indoor pool, hot tub, fitness room, 24-hr convenience store, across
street to public park, www.marriott.com/pdxri

Residence Inn Lloyd Center   503-288-1400, 800-331-3131
1710 NE Multnomah St   168 units, $169–$234
pet fee $75/stay, kitchen, full breakfast, Monday thru Thursday
evenings complimentary beverages & light meal, BBQ, picnic
area, outdoor pool, hot tub, fitness room, small pet walking area,
4 blocks to public park, www.marriott.com/pdxlc

Residence Inn North Harbour   503-285-9888
1250 N Anchor Way   102 units, $119–$269
pet fee $75/stay, kitchen, full breakfast, restaurant, lounge, outdoor
pool, hot tub, fitness room, public park, www.marriott.com/pdxph

Riverplace Hotel   503-228-3233, 800-227-1333
1510 SW Harbor Way   84 units, $259–$550
1 to 2 dogs under 50 lbs only, $50/stay, coffeemaker, refrigerator, apples & freshly baked cookies in lobby, restaurant, lounge, guest pass to local fitness center, convenience store, next to waterfront park, www.riverplacehotel.com

Rose Cottage B & B   503-292-5475, 877-292-5475
3392 SW Delaney Place   2 units, $130–$155
1 well-behaved dog under 30 lbs allowed by advance arrangement only, $25/stay, coffeemaker, microwave, refrigerator, full breakfast, hot tub, private covered patio, www.rosecottagebb.com

Sheraton Airport Hotel   503-281-2500, 800-325-3535
8235 NE Airport Way   213 units, $129–$450
1 to 2 dogs under 50 lbs only, $25/stay, coffeemaker, evening beverages & appetizers, restaurant, lounge, indoor pool, sauna, hot tub, fitness room, gift shop, small pet walking area, 1/2 mile to open field for walking dogs, www.sheratonportland.com

Shilo Inn Portland/Beaverton   503-297-2551, 800-222-2244
9900 SW Canyon Rd   142 units, $95–$200
1 to 2 dogs under 50 lbs only, $25/stay, coffeemaker, microwave, refrigerator, full breakfast, fruit-popcorn-coffee in lobby, restaurant, lounge, seasonal pool, hot tub, fitness room, lawn for walking dogs, 2 1/2 miles to public park, www.shiloinns.com

Shilo Inn Rose Garden   503-736-6300
1506 NE 2nd Ave   44 units, $99–$160
1 to 2 dogs, $25/stay, coffeemaker, microwave, refrigerator, continental breakfast, sauna, parking lot for walking dogs, 5-minute walk to waterfront park, www.shiloinns.com

Shilo Inn Portland Airport   503-252-7500, 800-222-2244
11707 NE Airport Way   200 units, $109–$209
1 to 2 dogs, $25/stay, coffeemaker, microwave, refrigerator, continental breakfast, restaurant, indoor pool, hot tub, fitness room, parking lot for walking dogs, www.shiloinns.com

Staybridge Suites Portland Airport   503-262-8888, 877-238-8889
11936 NE Glenn Widing Dr   106 units, $140–$230
each pet $75/stay, kitchen, full breakfast, Tuesday thru Thursday evenings complimentary beverages-salad bar-hot entree, indoor pool, sauna, hot tub, fitness room, convenience store, open field for walking dogs, 5 blocks to walking trail, www.staybridge.com

Portland, OR (continued)

Super 8 Portland Airport   503-257-8988, 800-800-8000
11011 NE Holman St   78 units, $72–$100
1 to 2 dogs under 50 lbs only, $10/day, continental breakfast,
grassy walking area, 3 blocks to bike path, www.super8.com

The Nines Hotel   503-222-9996, 877-229-9995
525 SW Morrison   331 units, $129–$385
1 to 2 dogs under 80 lbs only, refrigerator, restaurant, lounge, pet
bed-bowls-treats, 5 blocks to riverfront park, www.thenines.com

Travelodge Airport   503-256-2550
3828 NE 82nd Ave   52 units, $75–$85
1 to 3 dogs, $10/day each pet, coffeemaker, continental breakfast,
outdoor pool, fitness room, grassy area, 11 blocks to off-leash dog
park, www.travelodge.com/hotel/15493

Union Ave Motel   503-285-3909
59 NE Gertz Rd   18 units, $45–$80
hot tub, paved walking area

University Place Hotel & Conference Center   503-221-0140
310 SW Lincoln St   235 units, $119–$149
dogs under 40 lbs only, $75/stay, coffeemaker, restaurant, lounge,
seasonal pool, fitness room, gift shop, large courtyard for walking
dogs, park & walking path, www.cegs.pdx.edu/stay/upl/

Washington Park Inn   503-226-2722, 800-532-9543
840 SW King Ave   39 units, $59–$69
1 to 2 dogs under 30 lbs only, $10/day, refrigerator, continental
breakfast, 4 blocks to public park

Westin Portland Hotel   503-294-9000, 800-937-8461
750 SW Alder St   205 units, $159–$349
1 to 2 dogs under 40 lbs only, coffeemaker, refrigerator, fitness room,
small lawn, 7 blocks to riverfront park, www.westin.com/portland

Powell Butte, OR

Brasada Ranch & Canyons Golf Course   541-526-6865
16986 SW Brasada Ranch Rd   888-701-2987
each pet $25/day   80 units, $195–$495
studios to 3-bdrm 3-bath suites, restaurant, lounge, indoor &
outdoor pools, sauna, hot tub, fitness room, lawn for walking dogs,
private golf course, www.brasada.com

Prairie City, OR

Historic Hotel Prairie   541-820-4800
112 W Front St   9 units, $75–$135
rooms & suites with private or shared bath, garden sitting area,
2 public parks within 3 blocks,
www.prairiecityoregon.com/prairie-city-oregon-hotel-prairie.html

Riverside School House B & B   541-820-4731
28076 N River Rd   2 units, $125
dogs allowed by advance arrangement only, $20/stay, full
breakfast, large yard & riverfront walking area on working cattle
ranch, www.riversideschoolhouse.com

Princeton, OR

Malheur Field Station (Hostel)   541-493-2629
34848 Sodhouse Lane   10 units, $40–$110
each pet $5/day, education & research center with mobile homes
& dormitory units, shared kitchen, cafeteria-style meals available,
bring your own bedding & towels, fenced yard, RV sites,
www.malheurfieldstation.org

Steens Country Cabin   541-495-2344
30192 Penland Rd   1 unit, $95
dogs allowed with advance approval only, 2-bdrm air-conditioned
cabin with full kitchen, continental breakfast, large open area for
walking dogs, www.steenscountrycabin.com

Prineville, OR

Best Western Prineville Inn   541-447-8080, 800-937-8376
1475 NE 3rd St   67 units, $80–$95
pet fee $15/day, coffeemaker, microwave, refrigerator, indoor pool,
hot tub, lawn, 2 blocks to park, www.bestwestern.com/prinevilleinn

City Center Motel   541-447-5522
509 NE 3rd St   20 units, $45–$57
1 to 2 dogs, $5/day, coffeemaker, microwave, refrigerator,
continental breakfast, large yard for walking dogs, next to park

Econo Lodge   541-447-6231
123 NE 3rd St   34 units, $60–$70
1 to 2 dogs, $10/stay each pet, coffeemaker, microwave,
refrigerator, continental breakfast, across street to grassy walking
area, 1 block to public park, www.econolodge.com/hotel/or140

Prineville, OR (continued)

Inn at Ochoco Creek (formerly Executive Inn)   541-447-4152
1050 NE 3rd St   26 units, $70–$85
1 to 2 dogs, $10/stay each pet, full kitchen or coffeemaker-microwave-refrigerator, continental breakfast, creekside walking area, close to public park & waterfall

Rustler's Inn   541-447-4185
960 NW 3rd St   20 units, $55
1 to 2 dogs, $10/day each pet, coffeemaker, microwave, refrigerator, continental breakfast provided or discount vouchers for full breakfast at restaurant next door, across street to grassy walking area, 2 blocks to riverfront park & walkway, www.rustlersinn.com

Stafford Inn   541-447-7100
1773 NE 3rd St   63 units, $75–$117
coffeemaker, microwave, refrigerator, extended continental breakfast, indoor pool, hot tub, fitness room, dog treats available at front desk, grassy walking area, 5 blocks to public park, www.staffordinn.com

Prospect, OR

Prospect Historic Hotel & Motel   541-560-3664, 800-944-6490
391 Mill Creek Dr   14 units, $80–$110
dogs allowed in motel rooms only, $10/day each pet, coffeemaker, microwave, refrigerator, restaurant, on 5 acres with field & walking paths, several waterfalls within walking distance, www.prospecthotel.com

Union Creek Resort   541-560-3565, 866-560-3565
56484 Hwy 62   23 units, $48–$225
pet fee $10/day, cabins with full kitchen or coffeemaker-microwave-refrigerator, restaurant, on 12 acres surrounded by national forest & walking trails, www.unioncreekoregon.com

Rainier, OR

Budget Inn   503-556-4231
120 West A St   26 units, $55
pet fee $5/day, full kitchen or microwave & refrigerator, across street to riverfront park & walkway

Redmond, OR

Comfort Suites Airport   541-504-8900, 877-424-6423
2243 SW Yew Ave   92 units, $89–$149
pets under 25 lbs only, $25/stay, coffeemaker, microwave,
refrigerator, extended continental breakfast, indoor pool, hot tub,
grassy area, walking trail, www.comfortsuites.com/hotel/or113

Eagle Crest Resort   541-923-2453, 800-682-4786
1522 Cline Falls Rd   100+ units, $125–$145
1 to 2 dogs, $75/stay in hotel rooms, $250/stay in condos,
coffeemaker, microwave, refrigerator, restaurant, hot tub, fitness
center, grassy area & walking trail, www.eagle-crest.com

Hub Motel & Restaurant   541-548-2101, 800-784-3482
1128 NW 6th St   30 units, $42–$52
pet fee $5/day, full kitchen or coffeemaker-microwave-refrigerator,
restaurant, grassy walking area, close to walking trail & county
fairgrounds, www.thehubmotel.com

Marr Management Vacation Rentals   541-923-8222
515 SW Cascade Ave # 4   70 units, $100–$400
fully equipped condos & vacation homes at multiple locations in
central Oregon, some with hot tub, most have yard for walking
dogs, close to local parks, www.marrmanagement.com

Motel 6   541-923-2100, 800-466-8356
2247 S Hwy 97   83 units, $59–$81
1 small pet per room, microwave, refrigerator, coffee in lobby, hot
tub, open field for walking dogs, close to walking trail,
www.motel6-redmond.com

Redmond Inn   541-548-1091, 800-833-3259
1545 Hwy 97 S   46 units, $45–$210
pet fee $5/day, microwave, refrigerator, continental breakfast,
seasonal pool, large open area for walking dogs, 1 block to public
park, www.redmondinn.net

Sleep Inn & Suites   541-504-1500, 800-424-6423
1847 N Hwy 97   72 units, $95–$110
1 to 3 dogs, $10/day each pet, coffeemaker, microwave,
refrigerator, extended continental breakfast, indoor pool, hot tub,
fitness room, large open area for walking dogs, 3/4 mile to park &
walking path, www.sleepinn.com/hotel/or188

Redmond, OR (continued)

Super 8 Motel   541-548-8881, 800-800-8000
3629 SW 21st Place   85 units, $80–$90
each pet $10/stay, continental breakfast, indoor pool, hot tub,
grassy walking area, 1 mile to public park, www.super8.com

Village Squire Motel   541-548-2105, 800-548-2102
629 SW 5th St   24 units, $36–$60
small pets only, microwave, refrigerator, coffee in lobby, small pet
walking area, 1 block to park, www.villagesquiremotel.com

Reedsport, OR

Anchor Bay Inn   541-271-2149, 800-767-1821
1821 Winchester Ave   21 units, $50–$90
pet fee $7/day, kitchenette or microwave & refrigerator,
continental breakfast, seasonal pool, garden area for walking dogs,
3-minute walk to river levee, www.ohwy.com/or/a/anchobin.htm

Best Western Salbasgeon Inn & Suites   541-271-4831
1400 Hwy 101 S   57 units, $90–$136
dogs allowed with advance approval, $10/day each pet, full kitchen
or coffeemaker, continental breakfast, indoor pool, fitness room,
small pet walking area, 5-minute drive to beach,
www.bestwestern.com/prop_38115

Economy Inn   541-271-3671, 800-799-9970
1593 Hwy 101   39 units, $75–$85
1 to 3 dogs, $10/stay each pet, microwave, refrigerator, continental
breakfast, seasonal pool, lawn for walking dogs, 5 miles to beach,
www.economyinnreedsport.com

Fir Grove Motel   541-271-4848
2178 Winchester Ave (Hwy 101 at 2nd St)   19 units, $40–$95
1 to 2 dogs, $10/day each pet, kitchenette or microwave &
refrigerator, continental breakfast, alley for walking dogs, 1 block
to public park

Loon Lake Lodge   541-599-2244, 866-360-3116
9011 Loon Lake Rd   15 units, $50–$260
1 to 2 dogs, $25/stay, lakefront motel rooms, 1-bdrm to 2-bdrm
cabins, kitchen or coffeemaker-microwave-refrigerator, restaurant,
RV & tent sites, yurts, boat launch & boat rentals, wooded area for
walking dogs, www.loonlakerv.com

Salbasgeon Inn of the Umpqua   541-271-2025
45209 State Hwy 38   14 units, $85–$98
1 to 2 dogs, $10/stay, full kitchen or coffeemaker, riverside
outdoor seating area, fire pit, open field for walking dogs

Rhododendron, OR

Snowline Motel   503-622-3188
73270 E Hwy 26   12 units, $65–$180
each pet $5-$10/day, rooms & log cabins sleep up to 11, full
kitchen or coffeemaker-microwave-refrigerator, BBQ, next to
riverfront park, www.snowlinemotel.com

Rice Hill, OR

Best Western Rice Hill Inn   541-849-3335
621 John Long Rd   48 units, $85
1 to 2 dogs, $10/day, microwave, refrigerator, continental
breakfast, indoor pool, hot tub, fitness room, grassy walking area,
1 mile to hillside walking area, www.bestwestern.com/ricehill

Richland, OR

Hitching Post Motel   541-893-6176
100 Main St   18 units, $67–$90
pet fee $5/day, rooms & cabins sleep up to 6, kitchenette or
coffeemaker & refrigerator, large yard, ¼ mile to park

Rockaway Beach, OR

Beachway Motel   503-355-2525
421 N Miller St   5 units, $79–$99
each pet $15/day, full kitchen or coffeemaker-microwave-
refrigerator, large open area for walking dogs, 1 block to beach,
4 blocks to public park, lots of walking trails

Covelle's Cove Beach House   503-556-5850
336 S Pacific   2 units, $75–$175
pet fee $27/stay, 2-bdrm duplex units, kitchens, can be rented
separately or together, ½ block to beach, www.pcez.com/~flyby

Getaway Oceanfront Lodging   503-355-2501, 800-756-5552
621 S Pacific Dr   13 units, $50–$125
1 to 2 dogs, $25 for 1st day, $5 each additional day, studios &
1-bdrm to 2-bdrm suites, kitchen, BBQ, picnic tables, crab
cookers, horseshoe pits, www.getawayoceanfront.com

Rockaway Beach, OR (continued)

Inn at Rockaway Beach   503-355-2400
104 S 4th Ave   10 units, $59–$69
each pet $5/stay, kitchenette, across street to beach

Northcoast Beach Rentals   503-368-4867, 866-355-0733
108 Hwy 101 S   11 units, $69–$359
1 to 3 dogs, pet fee varies, fully equipped vacation homes in
Manzanita & Rockaway Beach, most are a very short walk to
beach, www.northcoastbeachrentals.com

Sea Haven Motel   503-355-8101
520 Hwy 101 N   6 units, $53–$99
kitchen, BBQ, picnic area, lawn, 1 block to beach

Sea Treasures Inn   503-355-8220, 800-444–1864
301 N Miller St   14 units, $74–$90
each pet $10/stay, coffeemaker, microwave, refrigerator, gravel
walking area, ½ block to beach, another 4 units also available at
nearby Whale Watcher Inn, www.theseatreasuresinn.com

Silver Sands Resort Motel   503-355-2206, 800-457-8972
215 S Pacific Ave   39 units, $72–$146
each pet $10/day, kitchenette, indoor pool, sauna, hot tub,
short walk to beach, www.oregonsilversands.com

Surfside Oceanfront Resort Motel   503-355-2312, 800-243-7786
101 NW 11th Ave   56 units, $40–$169
1 to 2 dogs, $10/day each pet, kitchen, short walk to beach,
www.surfsideocean.com

Tradewinds Motel   503-355-2112, 800-824-0938
523 N Pacific St   19 units, $94–$149
1 to 2 dogs, $15/day each pet, kitchenette or coffeemaker &
refrigerator, short walk to beach, www.tradewinds-motel.com

Roseburg, OR

America's Best Value Inn   541-673-6000, 888-315-2378
760 NW Garden Valley Blvd Suite 125   55 units, $50–$95
each pet $10/day, coffeemaker, microwave, refrigerator,
continental breakfast, seasonal pool, picnic area, grassy walking
area, across street to public park, www.bestvalueinn.com

Best Western Garden Villa Inn   541-672-1601, 800-547-3446
760 NW Garden Valley Blvd   66 units, $80–$109
dogs under 30 lbs only, $25/day, coffeemaker, microwave,
refrigerator, full breakfast, freshly baked cookies, outdoor pool,
hot tub, across street to public park,
www.bestwestern.com/gardenvillainn

Budget 16 Motel   541-673-5556
1067 NE Stephens St   48 units, $45
kitchenette, pet walking area, 4 blocks to public park

C H Bailey House B & B   541-672-1500, 877-322-4539
121 Melton Rd   4 units, $125–$145
1 to 2 dogs, $20/stay each pet, guest rooms include private sitting
room, coffeemaker, full breakfast, hot tub, complimentary wine &
appetizers, on 50 acres for walking dogs, 1½ miles to park &
walking path, 8 miles to hiking trails, www.chbaileyhouse.com

Casa Loma Motel   541-673-5569
1107 NE Stephens St   18 units, $45
pet fee $5/day, coffeemaker, microwave, refrigerator, small pet
walking area

Comfort Inn   541-957-1100, 800-228-5150
1539 NW Mulholland Dr   50 units, $69–$99
each pet $15/day, coffeemaker, microwave, refrigerator,
continental breakfast, indoor pool, hot tub, fitness room, pet
walking area, ¼ mile to trail leading to public park,
www.comfortinn.com/hotel/or410

Douglas County Inn   541-673-6625
511 SE Stephens St   52 units, $60–$85
microwave, refrigerator, 2 public parks within ½ mile

Dunes Motel   541-672-6684, 800-260-9973
610 W Madrone St   43 units, $50–$70
microwave, refrigerator, continental breakfast, ½ block to public
park, www.dunesmotelroseburg.com

Hokanson's Guest House   541-672-2632
848 SE Jackson St   3 units, $85–$115
full breakfast, small pet walking area, short drive to public park,
www.hokansonsguesthouse.com

Roseburg, OR (continued)

Holiday Inn Express   541-673-7517, 800-898-7666
375 W Harvard Ave   100 units, $99–$139
pet fee $10/day, coffeemaker, microwave, refrigerator, full
breakfast, indoor pool, hot tub, fitness room, pet walking area,
close to walking & biking path, www.hiexpress.com/roseburgor-ex

Motel 6   541-464-8000, 800-466-8356
3100 NW Aviation Dr   82 units, $50–$70
microwave, refrigerator, coffee in lobby, grassy walking area,
1/2 mile to public park, www.motel6-roseburg.com

Quality Inn   541-673-5561, 800-626-1900
427 NW Garden Valley Blvd   70 units, $75–$120
pet fee $10/day, continental breakfast, outdoor pool, fitness room,
1 mile to waterfront park, www.qualityinn.com/hotel/OR125

Rose City Motel   541-673-8209
1142 NE Stephens St   12 units, $46–$56
pet fee $20/day, full kitchen or microwave & refrigerator, BBQ,
large open walking area, www.rosecitymotel.qwestdex.com

Shady Oaks Motel   541-672-2608
2954 Old Hwy 99 S   12 units, $45–$69
pet fee $8/day, coffeemaker, microwave, refrigerator, BBQ, picnic
tables, large yard for walking dogs, 1 mile to public park

Sleep Inn & Suites   541-464-8338
2855 Edenbower Blvd   108 units, $70–$125
pet fee $10/stay, coffeemaker, microwave, refrigerator, extended
continental breakfast, indoor pool, hot tub, fitness room, open field
for walking dogs, 1 mile to park, www.sleepinn.com/hotel/or091

Super 8 Motel   541-672-8880, 800-800-8000
3200 NW Aviation Dr   88 units, $65–$80
pet fee $10/stay, coffeemaker, microwave, refrigerator, continental
breakfast, indoor pool, hot tub, open field, www.super8.com

Travel Inn   541-672-3354
1627 SE Stephens St   12 units, $41–$44
small dogs only, $5/day, kitchen, next to walking trail

Travelodge   541-672-4836, 800-578-7878
315 W Harvard Ave   40 units, $55–$85
pet fee $10/day, continental breakfast, riverside picnic area,
outdoor pool, 1 block to park, www.travelodge.com/hotel/07076

Vista Motel   541-673-2736
1183 NE Stephens St   15 units, $38
each pet $5/day, microwave, refrigerator, small pet walking area,
1 mile to public park

Windmill Inn   541-673-0901, 800-547-4747
1450 NW Mulholland Dr   128 units, $63–$93
coffeemaker, microwave, refrigerator, continental breakfast & pet
treats delivered to your door, seasonal pool, sauna, hot tub, fitness
room, pet walking area, across street to walking trail, 2 blocks to
public park, www.windmillinns.com/ros.htm

Rufus, OR

Rufus Hillview Motel   541-739-8221
203 Wallace St   12 units, $86–$126
1 to 2 dogs under 50 lbs only, $15/day each pet, motel rooms &
cabins, full kitchen or microwave & refrigerator, grassy area for
walking dogs

Tyee Motel   541-739-2310
304 E 1st St   18 units, $45–$55
1 to 2 dogs, $10/stay, kitchenette, small grassy walking area,
1 mile to public park

Saint Helens, OR

Best Western Oak Meadows Inn   503-397-3000, 800-780-7234
585 S Columbia River Hwy   81 units, $68–$130
pet fee $10/stay, coffeemaker, microwave, refrigerator, continental
breakfast, indoor pool, large yard for walking dogs, 3 miles to
public park, www.bestwestern.com/oakmeadowsinn

Village Inn Motel   503-397-1490
535 S Hwy 30   50 units, $64–$72
1 to 2 dogs, $5/day each pet, microwave, refrigerator, restaurant,
lounge, RV sites, open field for walking dogs, 2 miles to park

Salem, OR

Best Western Black Bear Inn   503-581-1559, 877-594-1110
1600 Motor Ct NE   101 units, $69–$129
1 to 2 dogs, $10/day, coffeemaker, microwave, refrigerator, full
breakfast, indoor pool, steam room, sauna, hot tub, fitness room,
grassy area for walking dogs, www.bestwestern.com/blackbearinn

Salem, OR (continued)

Best Western Mill Creek Inn   503-585-3332, 800-346-9659
3125 Ryan Dr SE   109 units, $108–$120
1 to 2 dogs under 20 lbs only, $20/stay each pet, coffeemaker, microwave, refrigerator, full breakfast, indoor pool, steam room, hot tub, fitness room, deck, lawn for walking dogs, ¼ mile to walking trail, 2 miles to public park, www.bestwestern.com/millcreekinn

Best Western Pacific Highway Inn   503-390-3200, 800-832-8905
4646 Portland Rd NE   52 units, $67–$114
1 to 2 dogs, $20/day, coffeemaker, microwave, refrigerator, continental breakfast, indoor pool, hot tub, fitness room, across street to open field, www.bestwestern.com/pacifichighwayinn

Comfort Suites Airport   503-585-9705, 800-424-6423
630 Hawthorne Ave SE   85 units, $94–$170
1 to 2 dogs under 50 lbs only, $10/day each pet, coffeemaker, microwave, refrigerator, extended continental breakfast, indoor pool, sauna, hot tub, fitness room, grassy walking area, 2 miles to riverfront park, www.comfortsuites.com/hotel/or055

Crossland Economy Studios   503-363-7557
3535 Fisher Rd NE   129 units, $65–$99
1 to 2 dogs, $25/day ($75 maximum), kitchenette, lawn, ½ mile to public park, www.crosslandstudios.com/528

Howard Johnson Inn   503-375-7710, 877-375-7710
2250 Mission St SE   68 units, $55–$75
1 to 2 dogs under 30 lbs only, $15/day each pet, coffeemaker, refrigerator, extended continental breakfast, seasonal pool, fitness room, 10 blocks to public park, www.hojo.com/hotel/15400

Mar-Don Motel   503-585-2089
3355 Portland Rd NE   12 units, $44
1 to 2 dogs under 35 lbs only, $10/day each pet, kitchenette, small pet walking area, across street to open field for walking dogs

Motel 6   503-371-8026, 800-466-8356
1401 Hawthorne Ave NE   115 units, $48–$60
1 to 2 dogs, microwave, refrigerator, coffee in lobby, outdoor pool, grassy walking area, 8 blocks to park, www.motel6.com

Phoenix Inn Suites North Salem   503-581-7004, 888-239-9593
1590 Weston Ct NE   80 units, $99–$129
each pet $15/stay, coffeemaker, microwave, refrigerator,
extended continental breakfast, indoor pool, hot tub, fitness room,
small pet walking area, short drive to public park,
www.phoenixinn.com/north-salem

Phoenix Inn Suites South   503-588-9220, 800-445-4498
4370 Commercial St SE   89 units, $79–$109
each pet $15/day, coffeemaker, microwave, refrigerator,
extended continental breakfast, indoor pool, hot tub,
fitness room, small pet walking area, 2 blocks to public park,
www.phoenixinn.com/south-salem

Red Lion Hotel   503-370-7888, 800-248-6273
3301 Market St NE   150 units, $134–$154
1 to 2 dogs under 20 lbs only, $20/stay, coffeemaker, microwave,
refrigerator, restaurant, lounge, indoor pool, sauna, fitness room,
grassy walking area, 1 mile to public park, www.redlion.com/salem

Residence Inn   503-585-6500, 800-627-7648
640 Hawthorne Ave SE   99 units, $119–$179
pet fee $100/stay, kitchen, full breakfast, indoor pool, hot tub,
fitness room, Monday thru Thursday evenings complimentary
beverages & light dinner, lawn for walking dogs, short drive to
riverfront park, www.marriott.com/sleri

Rodeway Inn   503-393-6000, 877-424-6423
3340 Astoria Way NE   72 units, $50–$90
each pet $5/day, microwave, refrigerator, continental breakfast,
indoor pool, large open area for walking dogs, 2 miles to off-leash
dog park, www.rodewayinn.com/hotel/or057

Shilo Inn   503-581-4001
3304 Market St NE   90 units, $85–$120
pet fee $25/stay, coffeemaker, microwave, refrigerator, full
breakfast, indoor pool, sauna, hot tub, fitness room, paved area
for walking dogs, 3 miles to public park, www.shiloinns.com

Super 8 Motel   503-370-8888, 800-800-8000
1288 Hawthorne Ave NE   80 units, $60–$90
each pet $10/day, microwave & refrigerator available for additional
$5 fee, continental breakfast, indoor pool, hot tub, lawn for walking
dogs, www.super8.com

Salem, OR (continued)

Travelers Inn Motel   503-581-2444
3230 Portland Rd NE   29 units, $39–$69
pet fee $5/day, coffeemaker, microwave, refrigerator, 1 mile to
public park

Travelodge Salem Capitol   503-581-2466
1555 State St   42 units, $46–$80
each pet $10/day, continental breakfast, seasonal pool, short walk
to public park, www.travelodge.com/hotel/10917

Sandy, OR

Best Western Sandy Inn   503-668-7100, 888-882-1214
37465 Hwy 26   45 units, $101–$125
each pet $10/day, coffeemaker, microwave, refrigerator,
continental breakfast, indoor pool, hot tub, fitness room, grassy
walking area, close to open field, www.bestwestern.com/sandyinn

Brookside B & B   503-668-4766
45232 SE Paha Loop   5 units, $60–$75
dogs allowed with manager's approval only, full breakfast, on 7
acres with gardens & woods, large open area for walking dogs,
www.brooksidebandb.com

Scappoose, OR

Scappoose Creek Inn B & B   503-543-2740, 888-875-1670
53758 W Lane Rd   11 units, $69–$135
1 to 2 dogs, $15/day each pet, rooms in main house & separate
1-bdrm cottage, coffeemaker, microwave, refrigerator, full
breakfast, lawn for walking dogs, www.scappoosecreekinn.com

Seaside, OR

Beachhouse Vacation Rentals   503-738-9068, 800-995-2796
570 S Roosevelt Dr   20 units, $99–$500
pet fee $50/stay, fully equipped beach homes, short walk to beach,
www.beachhouse1.com

Best Western Ocean View Resort   503-738-3334, 800-234-8439
414 N Prom   107 units, $99–$499
each pet $20/day, kitchenette or coffeemaker-microwave-refrigerator,
restaurant, lounge, indoor pool, hot tub, pet treats-cleanup bags-local
pet activities guide, www.bestwestern.com/oceanviewresort

Budget Inn of Seaside   503-738-5221, 800-479-5191
521 Beach Dr   12 units, $50–$90
each pet $7-$10/day, kitchen or coffeemaker & microwave, ½ block
to beach, www.seasideteam.com/budgetinns/budgetinn.html

City Center Motel   503-738-6377
250 1st Ave   40 units, $49–$99
each pet $20/day, kitchen or coffeemaker-microwave-refrigerator,
indoor pool, 1½ blocks to beach, www.citycenterseaside.com

Comfort Inn   503-738-3011, 800-226-9518
545 Broadway Ave   65 units, $149–$189
dogs under 50 lbs only, $25/day each pet, continental breakfast,
freshly baked cookies, indoor pool, sauna, parking lot for walking
dogs, 2 blocks to beach, www.comfortinnseaside.com

Driftwood Motel   503-717-0331
825 N Holladay Dr   13 units, $45–$80
each pet $10/stay, kitchen, grassy walking area, 7 blocks to beach

Ebb Tide Motel   503-738-8371, 800-468-6232
300 N Prom   99 units, $120–$160
dogs under 25 lbs only, $20/day, coffeemaker, microwave,
refrigerator, indoor pool, sauna, hot tub, grassy walking area, next
to beach & beachside walkway, www.ebbtide.citysearch.com

Holiday Inn Express   503-717-8000, 800-465-4329
34 N Holladay Dr   79 units, $79–$399
dogs under 50 lbs only, $25/day, coffeemaker, microwave,
refrigerator, extended continental breakfast, indoor pool, sauna,
hot tub, fitness room, lawn for walking dogs, 3 blocks to beach,
www.hiexpress.com/seasideor

Inn at Seaside   503-738-9581, 800-699-5070
441 2nd Ave   47 units, $69–$199
each pet $10/day, kitchenette or coffeemaker & microwave,
continental breakfast, indoor pool, hot tub, 2 blocks to beach,
www.innatseaside.com

Inn at the Shore   503-738-3113, 800-713-9914
2275 S Prom   18 units, $69–$289
1 to 2 dogs, $20/stay each pet, rooms to 2-bdrm suites, kitchenette
or coffeemaker-microwave-refrigerator, terraces or balconies,
small grassy walking area, next to beach & beachside walkway,
www.innattheshore.com

Seaside, OR (continued)

Lanai at the Cove   503-738-6343, 800-738-2683
3140 Sunset Blvd   20 units, $100–$125
dogs under 25 lbs only, $10/day, kitchenette, outdoor pool, lawn
for walking dogs, next to beach, www.seasidelanai.com

Motel 6   503-738-6269, 866-738-6269
2369 S Roosevelt Dr   53 units, $58–$90
small dogs welcome, dogs over 50 lbs allowed with manager's
approval only, refrigerator, coffee in lobby, next to wetlands area
for walking dogs, 6 blocks to beach, www.motel6-seaside.com

Northwind Vacation Rentals   503-738-5532, 866-738-5532
948 N Roosevelt Dr   20+ units, $95–$325
fully equipped condos & vacation homes in Astoria-Gearhart-
Seaside, www.northwindrentals.com

Oceanside Vacation Rentals   503-738-7767, 800-840-7764
43 N Holladay Dr   32 units, $99–$550
pet fee $25/stay, kitchen, BBQ, fire pit, some with hot tub, small
pet walking areas, beachfront or less than 3 blocks to beach,
www.oceanside1.com

Rivertide Suites   503-717-1100, 877-871-8433
102 N Holladay Dr   70 units, $95–$350
1 to 2 dogs under 50 lbs only, $25/day each pet, studios to 2-bdrm
suites with kitchen, full breakfast, indoor pool, hot tub, fitness
room, lawn, 3 blocks to beach, www.rivertidesuites.com

Rogers Inn & Vacation Homes   503-738-7367, 888-717-7367
436 S Downing St   27 units, $95–$365
dogs allowed with advance approval only, $30/stay, fully equipped
cottages & vacation homes, some with hot tub, yard for walking
dogs, www.rogersinn.com

Royale Motel   503-738-9541
531 Avenue A   26 units, $89–$135
pet fee $10/stay, coffeemaker, microwave, refrigerator, 5 blocks to
beach

Sandy Cove Inn   503-738-7473
241 Avenue U   19 units, $44–$99
each pet $10/day, coffeemaker, microwave, refrigerator, pet treats
& cleanup bags available, gravel walking area, 2 blocks to beach,
www.sandycoveinn.biz

Seashore Inn on the Beach   503-738-6368, 888-738-6368
60 N Prom   54 units, $79–$189
dogs under 50 lbs only, $20/day each pet, kitchenette or
coffeemaker-microwave-refrigerator, continental breakfast, indoor
pool, sauna, hot tub, lawn, next to beach, www.seashoreinnor.com

Seaside International Hostel   503-738-7911, 888-994-0001
930 N Holladay Dr   12 units, $53–$59
each pet $10/stay, private rooms or dormitory-style shared rooms,
guest use of kitchen, backyard, 4 blocks to beach,
www.seasidehostel.net

Seaside Ocean Front Inn B & B   503-319-3300, 800-772-7766
581 S Promenade   14 units, $89–$109
1 to 2 dogs, $25/stay each pet, full breakfast, restaurant,
small pet walking area, next to paved beachside walkway

Seasider II Motel   503-717-1456, 866-917-8999
210 N Downing St   12 units, $69–$109
pets allowed with manager's approval only, $20/stay, coffeemaker,
microwave, refrigerator, grassy walking area, 1 block to beach

Shilo Inn Seaside East   503-738-0549, 800-222-2244
900 S Holladay Dr   59 units, $119–$169
1 to 2 dogs, $25/stay, coffeemaker, microwave, refrigerator,
continental breakfast, indoor pool, sauna, hot tub, 1 mile to beach,
www.shiloinns.com

Shilo Inn Seaside Oceanfront   503-738-9571, 800-222-2244
30 N Prom   143 units, $150–$500
1 to 2 dogs, $25/stay, coffeemaker, microwave, refrigerator,
restaurant, lounge, indoor pool, sauna, hot tub, fitness room, next
to beach, www.shiloinns.com

Tradewinds Motel & Condos   503-738-9468, 888-738-9468
1022 N Prom   15 units, $72–$115
each pet $10/day, kitchenette or coffeemaker-microwave-
refrigerator, grassy walking area, 50 feet to beach,
www.seaside-tradewinds.com

Windjammer Motel   503-738-3250, 800-479-5191
4253 Hwy 101 N   21 units, $45–$80
each pet $10/day, kitchen, grassy walking area, 1 mile to beach,
www.seasideteam.com/budgetinns/windjammer.html

Selma, OR

Illinois River Hideaway   541-592-9678
1 to 2 dogs allowed   1 unit, $125
400 sq ft cabin in the woods sleeps up to 6, kitchen with propane
powered appliances, solar- & hydro-generated electricity, hot tub,
friendly resident dogs, large riverfront walking area,
www.illinoisriverhideaway.com

Shady Cove, OR

Edgewater Inn   541-878-3171, 888-811-3171
7800 Rogue River Dr   54 units, $74–$199
each pet $7/day, coffeemaker, microwave, refrigerator, continental
breakfast, outdoor pool, sauna, hot tub, fitness room, deck
overlooking river, small pet walking area, next to riverfront park &
walkway, www.edgewater-inns.com

Royal Coachman Motel   541-878-2481
21906 Hwy 62   15 units, $54–$71
full kitchen or coffeemaker-microwave-refrigerator, lawn for
walking dogs, river access, great fishing spot, 2 blocks to public
park, www.royalcoachmanmotel.com

Silverton, OR

Oregon Garden Resort   503-874-2500, 800-966-6490
895 W Main St   103 units, $89–$199
1 to 2 dogs, $15/day each pet, coffeemaker, microwave, refrigerator,
restaurant, lounge, seasonal pool, hot tub, fitness room, private
patios or decks, full-service day spa, next to botanical gardens &
trails, www.moonstonehotels.com/Oregon-Garden-Resort.htm

Silverton Inn & Suites   503-873-5058
310 N Water St   16 units, $99–$199
1 to 2 dogs, $15/day, kitchen or kitchenette, ½ block to park

Sisters, OR

Best Western Ponderosa Lodge   541-549-0148, 888-549-4321
505 Hwy 20 W   75 units, $89–$134
each pet $15/day, coffeemaker, microwave, refrigerator,
continental breakfast, private patio or balcony, seasonal pool, hot
tub, pet treats-sheets-towel-cleanup bags, on 4 acres in the tall
pines for walking dogs, www.bestwestern.com/ponderosalodge

Black Butte Accommodations   541-549-3433, 866-617-0179
Black Butte Ranch   2 units, $190–$290
fully equipped 3-bdrm 2-bath houses on the golf course, restaurant,
lounge, outdoor pool, vacation homes also available in Bend & Inn
of the Seventh Mountain, www.rentalscentraloregon.com

Cascade Vacation Rentals   541-549-0792
581 N Larch St   1 unit, $150
pet fee $50/stay, fully equipped vacation home, 5-minute walk to
public park & national forest, www.cascadevacationrentals.net

FivePine Lodge & Conference Ctr   541-549-5900, 866-974-5900
1021 Desperado Trail   32 units, $149–$229
each pet $20/day, cabins with coffeemaker & refrigerator, full
breakfast, nightly wine reception, bicycles for guest use, pet
walking area, close to walking trail, www.fivepinelodge.com

Lodge at Suttle Lake   541-595-2628
13300 Hwy 20   13 units, $100–$130
1 to 2 dogs, $25/day each pet, dogs allowed in a few modern
cabins & in rustic cabins with electricity but no running water,
shared bathhouse, pet bowls-treats-toys-cleanup bags provided,
restaurant, www.thelodgeatsuttlelake.com

Sisters Vacation Rentals   541-977-9898
                                              23 units, $125–$225
dogs allowed with advance approval, $10/day, fully equipped
vacation homes, grassy walking areas, www.sistersvacation.com

Spray, OR

River Bend Motel & Retreat   541-468-2053
708 Willow St   5 units, $70–$180
each pet $5/day, motel rooms with microwave & refrigerator, large
open area for walking dogs, short walk to park; also off-site retreat
house with private hot tub sleeps 6, two 1-bdrm bungalows each
sleep 2, www.riverbendmotel.com and www.riverbendretreat.com

Springfield, OR

Best Western Grand Manor Inn   541-758-8571, 800-626-1900
971 Kruse Way   55 units, $92–$134
1 to 2 dogs, $10/day each pet, coffeemaker, microwave,
refrigerator, full breakfast, seasonal pool, sauna, fitness room,
1 mile to walking trail, www.bestwestern.com/prop_38119

Springfield, OR (continued)

Comfort Suites   541-746-5359, 877-746-5359
969 Kruse Way   77 units, $119–$159
1 to 2 dogs, $25/day each pet, coffeemaker, microwave,
refrigerator, continental breakfast, indoor pool, hot tub, fitness
room, lawn, 5 miles to park, www.comfortsuites.com/hotel/or095

Crossland Economy Studios   541-741-3908, 800-398-7829
520 Harlow Rd   127 units, $65–$75
1 to 2 dogs, $25/day, ($75 maximum), kitchenette or coffeemaker-
microwave-refrigerator, grassy walking area, next to open field,
www.crosslandstudios.com/529

Holiday Inn Express   541-746-8471, 800-465-4329
3480 Hutton St   85 units, $139–$169
each pet $10/day, coffeemaker, full breakfast, indoor pool, fitness
room, small lawn, 3/4 mile to park, www.hiexpress.com/eugeneor

Motel 6 Eugene/Springfield   541-741-1105, 800-466-8356
3752 International Ct   131 units, $45–$69
1 to 2 dogs, microwave, refrigerator, coffee in lobby, outdoor pool,
open field for walking dogs, 1 mile to park, www.motel6.com

Quality Inn & Suites   541-726-9266
3550 Gateway St   100 units, $90–$140
dogs under 40 lbs only, $5/day each pet, coffeemaker, microwave,
refrigerator, continental breakfast, seasonal pool, open field for
walking dogs, 2 miles to park, www.qualityinn.com/hotel/or164

Shilo Inn Eugene/Springfield   541-747-0332, 800-222-2244
3350 Gateway   141 units, $80–$180
pet fee $25/stay, full kitchen or coffeemaker, continental breakfast,
coffee-fruit-popcorn in lobby, restaurant, lounge, outdoor pool,
open field for walking dogs, www.shiloinns.com

Super 8 Motel Eugene/Springfield 541-746-1314, 800-800-8000
3315 Gateway St   71 units, $75–$88
pet fee $22/day, coffeemaker, microwave, refrigerator, continental
breakfast, hot tub, lawn, short drive to park, www.super8.com

Village Inn   541-747-4546, 800-327-6871
1875 Mohawk Blvd   67 units, $94
dogs under 20 lbs only, coffeemaker, microwave, refrigerator,
continental breakfast, restaurant, lounge, seasonal pool, hot tub,
lawn, 5 blocks to park & trail, www.springfieldvillageinn.com

Stayton, OR

Bird & Hat Inn B & B   503-769-7817
717 N 3rd Ave   3 units, $75
coffeemaker, microwave, refrigerator, full breakfast, large open
area for walking dogs, 1 block to public park

Gardner House B & B   503-769-5478
633 N 3rd Ave   1 unit, $95–$105
kitchenette, full breakfast, restaurant, lawn for walking dogs,
6 blocks to public park, www.gardnerhousebnb.com

Steamboat, OR

Steamboat Inn   541-498-2230, 800-840-8825
42705 N Umpqua Hwy   21 units, $170–$295
each pet $10/day, cottages & vacation homes, kitchen, restaurant,
www.thesteamboatinn.com

Sublimity, OR

Rodeway Inn & Suites   503-769-9579
300 SW Sublimity Blvd   50 units, $60–$65
dogs under 60 lbs only, $15/day each pet, coffeemaker,
microwave, refrigerator, continental breakfast, indoor pool, hot
tub, fitness room, across street to open field for walking dogs,
1 mile to public park, www.rodewayinn.com/hotel/or185

Summer Lake, OR

Lodge at Summer Lake   541-943-3993, 866-943-3993
53460 Hwy 31   12 units, $50–$100
pet fee $5/stay, lodge rooms & lakeside cabins, full kitchen or
coffeemaker-microwave-refrigerator, restaurant, pet beds available,
on 20 acres with 3-acre bass pond, designated pet walking area,
close to hiking trail, "horse hotel" & pasture also available,
www.thelodgeatsummerlake.com

Sumpter, OR

Depot Inn   541-894-2522, 800-390-2522
179 S Mill St   14 units, $75
dogs allowed with advance approval only, $5/stay, coffeemaker,
microwave, refrigerator, large open area for walking dogs, next to
park & walking path, www.thedepotinn-sumpter.com

Sunriver, OR

Bennington Properties   541-593-6300, 888-610-9700
56842 Venture Lane   150 units, $85–$495
1 to 2 dogs, $10/day each pet, fully equipped studios to 6-bdrm
vacation homes sleep up to 12, hot tub, walking & biking path,
10-minute drive to riverfront, www.benningtonproperties.com

Discover Sunriver Vacation Rentals 541-593-2482, 866-534-4668
Sunriver Village Mall #9   150 units, $81–$900
1 to 2 dogs, $35/stay each pet, fully equipped vacation homes,
kitchen or microwave & refrigerator, hot tub, community
swimming pool, www.discoversunriver.com

Mountain Resort Properties Inc.   541-593-8685, 800-346-6337
Sunriver Village Mall Bldg 11   12 units, $135–$395
pet fee $50/stay, cabins & vacation homes, natural area for walking
dogs, www.mtresort.com

REMAX Sunset Realty   541-593-5018, 800-541-1756
57100 Beaver Dr Bldg 2, Village Mall   250 units, $86–$800
each pet $10/day, condos & vacation homes, 35 miles of paved
walking trails, www.sunriverlodging.com

Sun Village Rentals   541-598-7898, 877-598-7898
56840 Venture Lane   30 units, $80–$320
each pet $10/day, condo units & vacation homes, full kitchen,
seasonal pool, walking trails, www.sunvillage.com sunvillage.com

Sunray Vacation Rentals Inc.   541-593-3225, 800-531-1130
56890 Venture Lane   170 units, $150–$800
pet fee $35/stay, fully equipped condos & vacation homes, close to
paved walking trails, www.sunrayinc.com

Sunriver Resort   541-593-1000, 800-801-8765
17600 Century Dr   600 units, $149–$589
pet fee $75/stay, lodge rooms with coffeemaker, vacation homes
with full kitchen, hot tub, 4 swimming pools, 4 restaurants,
35 miles of paved walking trails, www.sunriver-resort.com

Twin Lakes Resort   541-382-6432
11200 S Century Dr   14 units, $65–$160
pet fee $10/day, 1-room to 2-bdrm lakeside cabins, restaurant,
RV park, country store, surrounded by national forest & walking
trails, www.twinlakesresort.net

Village Properties   541-593-1653, 800-786-7483
Sunriver Village Mall Bldg 5   120 units, $95–$795
condos-townhouses-vacation homes, close to paved walking trails,
www.village-properties.com

Sutherlin, OR

Microtel Inn & Suites   541-459-6800, 800-635-5425
1400 Hospitality Way   80 units, $59–$69
microwave & refrigerator available upon request, continental
breakfast, large open area for walking dogs, short drive to
riverfront park, www.microtelinn.com

Relax Inn   541-459-9615
1386 W Central Ave   18 units, $45
pet fee $5-$10/day, full kitchen or coffeemaker-microwave-
refrigerator, small pet walking area, 1/2 mile to public park

Umpqua Regency Inn   541-459-1424
150 Myrtle St   62 units, $76–$97
each pet $10/day, coffeemaker, microwave, refrigerator,
continental breakfast, indoor pool, hot tub, fitness room, large
walking area, 1/4 mile to river, 6 blocks to new off-leash dog park

Sweet Home, OR

Sun Motel   541-367-2205
3026 Hwy 20   11 units, $53–$62
1 to 2 dogs, $10/day each pet, microwave, refrigerator, coffee in
lobby, lawn, 5-minute walk to park, www.sunmotelsweethomeor.com

Sweet Home Inn   541-367-5137
805 Long St   31 units, $69–$89
1 to 2 dogs, $15/day each pet, coffeemaker, microwave,
refrigerator, sauna, hot tub, lawn, 2 blocks to park,
www.sweethomeinn.com

Talent, OR

Good Night Inn   541-535-7234
210 N Pacific Hwy   20 units, $55–$72
dogs allowed with manager's approval only, fee varies depending
on size of dog & length of stay, kitchenette, small pet walking area,
next to greenway walking trail

Terrebonne, OR

Abaca Bed & Breakfast   541-504-1981
2121 NW Ice Ave   3 units, $95
pet-friendly room with private entrance, full breakfast, large yard
on 39 acres, 5 miles to state park

The Dalles, OR

American Hospitality Inn (Oregon Motor Motel) 541-296-9111
200 W 2nd St   54 units, $45–$55
each pet $10/day, microwave, refrigerator, coffee in lobby, grassy
walking area, 2 blocks to public park

Budget Inn   541-296-5464
118 W 4th St   24 units, $52–$55
each pet $10/day, microwave, refrigerator, small pet walking area,
short walk to public park

Cousins Country Inn   541-298-5161, 800-848-9378
2114 W 6th St   93 units, $65–$99
each pet $10/day, full kitchen or coffeemaker, restaurant, lounge,
seasonal pool, hot tub, lawn for walking dogs, short drive to public
park, www.cousinscountryinn.com

Hoffman Hills Guest Cottage & Lavender Farm   541-980-8222
6140 Mill Creek Rd   1 unit, $80–$95
dogs allowed with advance approval only, $25/day, cottage with
fully equipped kitchen sleeps 2, continental breakfast, on 40-acre
farm, 10-minute drive to park, www.hoffmanhillslavender.com

Motel 6   541-296-1191, 800-466-8356
2500 W 6th St   70 units, $39–$99
microwave, refrigerator, coffee in lobby, outdoor pool, grassy
walking area, short drive to public park, www.motel6.com

Shilo Inn   541-298-5502, 800-222-2244
3223 Bret Clodfelter Way   112 units, $79–$130
pet fee $25/stay, coffeemaker, microwave, refrigerator, coffee-fruit-
popcorn in lobby, seasonal pool, sauna, hot tub, fitness room, small
pet walking area, close to 2 public parks, www.shiloinns.com

Super 8 Motel   541-296-6888
609 Cherry Heights Rd   73 units, $65–$110
each pet $10/day, microwave, refrigerator, continental breakfast,
coffee in lobby, seasonal pool, lawn, 1 block to park, www.super8.com

The Dalles Inn 541-296-9107, 888-935-2378
112 W 2nd St 65 units, $59–$149
1 to 2 dogs, $10/day each pet, coffeemaker, microwave, refrigerator, continental breakfast, seasonal pool, pet bowls-sheets-treats-cleanup bags, small walking area, 4 blocks to park, www.thedallesinn.com

Tigard, OR

An Oregon Experience 503-620-0717, 866-445-4250
11330 SW Ambiance Place 24 units, $150–$500
fully equipped condos & vacation homes in Mount Hood area sleep 2 to 24, some with hot tub, www.anoregonexperience.com

Best Western Northwind Inn & Suites 503-431-2100
16105 SW Pacific Hwy 800-780-7234
pets up to 20 lbs $10/day, over 20 lbs $20/day 71 units, $92–$134
coffeemaker, microwave, refrigerator, continental breakfast, indoor pool, hot tub, fitness room, small pet walking area, 1 mile to public park, www.bestwestern.com/northwindinnandsuites

Embassy Suites Portland/Washington Square 503-644-4000
9000 SW Washington Sq Rd 800-586-5455
pet fee $49/day 356 units, $129–$209
coffeemaker, microwave, refrigerator, full breakfast, nightly reception with beverages & appetizers, restaurant, lounge, indoor pool, hot tub, fitness room, parking lot for walking dogs, 5-minute walk to public park, www.embassysuites.com

Homestead Studio Suites 503-670-0555, 800-398-7829
13009 SW 68th Parkway 137 units, $80–$115
1 to 2 dogs under 40 lbs only, $25/day ($150 maximum), full kitchen or kitchenette, lawn for walking dogs, short drive to public park, www.homesteadhotels.com/56

Motel 6 Portland/Tigard West 503-684-0760, 800-466-8356
17959 SW McEwan Ave 80 units, $55–$85
coffee in lobby, outdoor pool, grassy walking area, 1/2 mile to public park, www.motel6.com

Motel 6 Tigard East 503-620-2066
17950 SW McEwan Ave 117 units, $56–$62
1 to 2 dogs, 1st pet free, 2nd pet $10/day, microwave, refrigerator, coffee in lobby, outdoor pool, grassy walking area, 1/2 mile to public park, www.motel6.com

Tigard, OR (continued)

Phoenix Inn Suites   503-624-9000, 800-624-6884
9575 SW Locust St   101 units, $89–$200
dogs under 25 lbs only, $25/stay, coffeemaker, microwave,
refrigerator, extended continental breakfast, indoor pool, hot tub,
paved walking area, 1/4 mile to park, www.phoenixinn.com/tigard

Quality Inn   503-245-6421, 800-547-8828
11460 SW Pacific Hwy   115 units, $69–$94
1 to 2 dogs under 40 lbs only, $20/stay, coffeemaker, microwave,
refrigerator, continental breakfast, seasonal pool, fitness room,
short drive to off-leash dog park, www.qualityinn.com/hotel/or190

Shilo Inn Washington Square   503-620-4320, 800-222-2244
10830 SW Greenburg Rd   77 units, $70–$90
dogs under 20 lbs only, $15/day each pet, coffeemaker,
microwave, refrigerator, continental breakfast, restaurant, lounge,
sauna, hot tub, fitness room, paved walking area, short drive to
public park, www.shiloinns.com

Tigard Regency Inn   503-246-8451
11455 SW Pacific Hwy   50 units, $66–$77
1 to 2 dogs, $10/day each pet, microwave, refrigerator, continental
breakfast, small pet walking area, short drive to park

Tillamook, OR

Best Western Inn & Suites   503-842-7599, 800-299-4817
1722 Makinster Rd   51 units, $96–$270
1 to 2 dogs, $10/day each pet, coffeemaker, microwave,
refrigerator, continental breakfast, indoor pool, sauna, hot tub,
fitness room, sidewalks & open field for walking dogs, 10 miles to
beach, www.bestwestern.com/prop_38141

Happy Hollow House   503-842-3474
12140 Wilson River Hwy   5 units, $110–$250
fully equipped 3-bdrm riverfront vacation home, can also be rented
as 1-bdrm or 2-bdrm at reduced rate, open field for walking dogs,
next to river, www.guideshop.com/rental.html

Mar-Clair Inn   503-842-7571, 800-331-6857
11 Main Ave   47 units, $86–$135
1 to 2 small dogs only, $10/day each pet, kitchen, restaurant,
outdoor pool, sauna, hot tub, large open area, across street to park

Shilo Inn Suites 503-842-7971, 800-222-2244
2515 N Main St 101 units, $94–$179
1 to 3 dogs, $25/stay, coffeemaker, microwave, refrigerator, coffee
in lobby, restaurant, lounge, indoor pool, sauna, hot tub, fitness
room, fish cleaning station, small pet walking area, 10 miles to
beach, www.shiloinns.com

Western Royal Inn 503-842-8844, 800-624-2912
1125 N Main St (Hwy 101) 40 units, $76–$120
each pet $10/day, coffeemaker, microwave, refrigerator,
continental breakfast, grassy walking area, 10 miles to beach

Toledo, OR

Yaquina Bay Hotel 541-336-2830, 877-336-2830
160 N Main St 32 units, $55–$149
each pet $15/day, microwave, refrigerator, short walk to river, close
to off-leash dog park, 7 miles to beach, www.yaquinabayhotel.com

Troutdale, OR

Comfort Inn & Suites 503-669-6500, 800-824-6824
477 NW Phoenix Dr 73 units, $69–$159
1 to 2 dogs under 50 lbs only, $10/day each pet, coffeemaker,
microwave, refrigerator, continental breakfast, indoor pool, hot tub,
pet treats, field, 1 mile to park, www.comfortinn.com/hotel/or127

Holiday Inn Express Portland East 503-492-2900, 866-367-4667
1000 NW Graham Rd 77 units, $89–$109
dogs under 50 lbs only, $10 for 1st day, $5 each additional day,
coffeemaker, microwave, refrigerator, extended continental
breakfast, hot tub, fitness room, paved walking area, 1 mile to
public park, www.hiexpress.com/portlandeast

Motel 6 Portland East 503-665-2254, 800-466-8356
1610 NW Frontage Rd 123 units, $43–$66
coffee in lobby, outdoor pool, dog treats available, large open area
for walking dogs, 1 mile to public park, www.motel6.com

Tualatin, OR

Comfort Inn & Suites 503-612-9952, 866-394-8289
7640 SW Warm Springs St 59 units, $129–$150
1 to 2 dogs under 50 lbs only, $15/day, coffeemaker, refrigerator,
extended continental breakfast, freshly baked cookies, indoor pool,
hot tub, lawn, short drive to park, www.comfortinntualatin.com

Umatilla, OR

Desert River Inn   541-922-1000, 877-922-1500
705 Willamette St   67 units, $66–$85
pet fee $10/day, kitchenette or coffeemaker-microwave-
refrigerator, balcony or patio, restaurant, lounge, seasonal pool,
hot tub, fitness room, small pet walking area & nature trails,
½ mile to river, www.desertriverinn.com

Tillicum Motor Inn   541-922-3236, 800-806-1278
1481 6th St   79 units, $59–$70
pet fee $10/day, full kitchen or coffeemaker, seasonal pool, lawn
for walking dogs, 10-minute walk to waterfront walking area,
www.tillicuminn.com

Umatilla Inn & Suites   541-922-5396, 800-423-9913
1370 6th St   36 units, $65–$68
each pet $8/day, kitchenette or coffeemaker, grassy walking area,
3 blocks to public park, www.umatillainn.com

Union, OR

Historic Union Hotel   541-562-6135
326 N Main St   16 units, $39–$119
1 to 2 dogs under 125 lbs only, $15/stay, theme-decorated rooms,
restaurant, lounge, RV sites, on 5 acres with creek, next to public
park, www.theunionhotel.com

Vale, OR

Golden Wheel Motel   541-473-3947
350 A St E   14 units, $30–$40
microwave, refrigerator, grassy walking area, riverside walkway

Historic Goodrich Hotel   541-881-9636 or 541-212-4473,
229 A St   6 units, $59
suites with full kitchen, indoor kennel, outdoor dog runs, close to
walking trail, www.goodrichhotel.com

Vernonia, OR

Vernonia Inn B & B   503-429-4006, 800-354-9494
900 Madison Ave   13 units, $80–$115
rooms & suites with private entrance & deck, 3 with in-room spa
tub, refrigerator, continental breakfast, 2 public parks within 2
blocks, www.vernoniainn.com

Vida, OR

McKenzie River Inn B & B and Cabins   541-822-6260
49164 McKenzie Hwy   6 units, $95–$165
3 rooms in lodge, 3 cabins with fully equipped kitchen that sleep
up to 6, private deck, gourmet breakfast served in main lodge
(breakfast available at additional charge for guests in cabins),
trails & orchard for walking dogs, www.mckenzieriverinn.com

Wayfarer Resort   541-896-3613, 800-627-3613
46725 Goodpasture Rd   13 units, $105–$290
each pet $10/day, fully equipped studios to 2-bdrm cabins sleep
3 to 10, private hot tub in 1 unit, on 10 acres with creek & river for
swimming, short drive to hiking trail, www.wayfarerresort.com

Waldport, OR

America Inn & Suites   541-563-3249, 888-700-0503
190 SW Pacific Coast Hwy   20 units, $53–$143
pet fee $10/day, full kitchen or coffeemaker, grassy area, short
walk to bayfront, www.americainnandsuiteswaldport.com

Bayshore Rentals LLC   541-563-3162, 800-752-6321
2214 NW Bayshore Dr   75 units, $65–$550
fully equipped vacation homes in Seal Rock-South Beach-Waldport-
Yachats, close to beach, www.bayshore-rentals.com

Edgewater Cottages   541-563-2240
3978 SW Pacific Coast Hwy   9 units, $85–$200
dogs allowed with advance reservation only, $5-$15/day each pet,
kitchenette, private deck, beachfront lawn for walking dogs,
www.edgewatercottages.com

Soma on the Oregon Coast   541-547-3321
7365 SW Pacific Coast Hwy   12 units, $59–$75
1 to 2 dogs, kitchenette or coffeemaker & microwave, large open
area for walking dogs, 200 feet to beach, open Thursday thru
Sunday, www.markstewart.com/soma

Waldport Beach Resort   541-563-7700
902 NW Bayshore Dr   83 units, $79–$120
pet fee $12/stay, kitchenette, restaurant, lounge, seasonal pool,
fitness room, picnic area, private beach & bay access,
www.waldportbeachresort.com

Wallowa, OR

Minam Motel & Market 541-437-4475, 877-888-8130
72601 Hwy 82 8 units, $68–$78
kitchenette, BBQ, hammocks under the cottonwood trees,
fishing from the riverbank, grocery store, fishing supplies,
next to riverfront park, www.minammotel.com

Warm Springs, OR

Kah-Nee-Ta High Desert Resort & Casino 541-553-1112
100 Main St 800-554-4786
1 to 2 dogs, $15/day 171 units, $89–$249
kitchenette, restaurant, lounge, outdoor pool, fitness room, large
open area for walking dogs, www.kahneeta.com

Warrenton, OR

Shilo Inn Suites 503-861-2181, 800-222-2244
1609 E Harbor St 63 units, $119–$259
1 to 2 dogs, $25/stay, coffeemaker, microwave, refrigerator,
extended continental breakfast, restaurant, lounge, indoor pool,
sauna, hot tub, fitness room, next to beach, www.shiloinns.com

Welches, OR

All Seasons Property Management 503-622-1142, 800-622-1142
23804 E Greenwood Ave 39 units, $125–$800
each pet $30/stay, fully equipped cabins & vacation homes, some
with hot tub or sauna or outdoor pool, pet treats & cleanup bags
provided, close to off-leash hiking trail & public park,
www.mthoodrent.com

Beachcombers NW 503-622-1282, 888-333-4085
PO Box 686 200 units, $60–$575
fully equipped beach homes sleep up to 26, multiple locations
along the Oregon & Washington coast, www.beachcombersnw.com

Mount Hood Vacation Rentals 888-424-9168
24403 E Welches Rd, #104 26 units, $114–$339
pet fee $25/day, fully equipped cabins-condos-lodges located in
Brightwood-Government Camp-Rhododendron-Welches-Zigzag,
kitchen, BBQ, deck, yard, most have hot tub, pet towels & cleanup
bags provided, surrounded by national forest, close to hiking
trails, www.mthoodrentals.com

Mountain Air Motel 503-622-3169
65500 E Hwy 26 11 units, $60–$90
1 to 2 dogs, kitchen, small pet walking area, next to riverfront park
& walkway, www.mountainairmotel.com

Westlake, OR

Siltcoos Lake Resort & Motel 541-997-3741
82855 Fir St 8 units, $65–$85
dogs allowed with manager's approval only, rooms & riverfront
cabins, kitchen, RV & tent sites, fish cleaning station, canoe &
kayak rentals, riverside walking area, www.siltcooslakeresort.com

Westlake Resort 541-997-3722
4785 Laurel Ave 9 units, $50–$85
dogs allowed with advance approval only, cabins, full kitchen,
tackle shop, lakefront walking area, www.westlakeresort.com

Weston, OR

Tamarack Inn B & B 541-566-9348, 800-662-9348
62388 Hwy 204 4 units, $91–$127
dogs allowed with advance approval only, rustic A-frame lodge on
2 acres in mountain recreational area, full breakfast, hot tub, forest
roads & hiking trails for walking dogs, www.tamarackinnbb.com

Westport, OR

Westport Motel 503-455-2212
49238 Hwy 30 7 units, $54–$75
1 to 2 dogs, $10/day each pet, kitchen, close to playground

Wheeler, OR

Wheeler on the Bay Lodge 503-368-5858, 800-469-3204
580 Marine Dr 11 units, $80–$155
dogs under 20 lbs only, kitchenette, next to public park, 4 miles to
beach, www.wheeleronthebay.com

White City, OR

La Quinta Inn & Suites 541-826-0800, 866-928-2314
2020 Leigh Way 72 units, $95
1 to 3 dogs, coffeemaker, microwave, refrigerator, continental
breakfast, indoor pool, hot tub, fitness room, pet walking area,
1 mile to public park, www.lq.com

Willamina, OR

Wildwood Hotel   503-876-7100
150 NE Main St   6 units, $55–$65
1 to 2 small dogs only, $10/stay, turn-of-the-century hotel rooms,
kitchen available for guest use, restaurant, lounge, next to public
park, 30 miles to beach

Wilsonville, OR

Best Western Willamette Inn   503-682-2288, 888-682-0101
30800 SW Parkway Ave   63 units, $90–$105
1 to 2 dogs under 25 lbs only, coffeemaker, continental breakfast,
complimentary soup-freshly baked cookies-coffee-tea-cocoa in
lobby, seasonal pool, hot tub, fitness room, lawn, short walk to
park, www.bestwestern.com/willametteinn

Days Inn & Suites   503-682-9000, 800-228-5150
8855 SW Citizens Dr   64 units, $59/–$109
1 to 2 dogs, $15/day, microwave, refrigerator, continental
breakfast, indoor pool, hot tub, lawn, next to walking trail,
www.daysinn.com/hotel/31405

Holiday Inn Portland South   503-682-2211, 800-465-4329
25425 SW 95th Ave   170 units, $59–$125
1 to 3 dogs, $15/day, microwave, refrigerator, restaurant, lounge,
indoor pool, hot tub, fitness room, small pet walking area, close to
public park, www.hiportlandsouth.com

La Quinta Inn   503-682-3184, 800-213-8119
8815 SW Sun Place   76 units, $79–$109
1 to 4 dogs, $10/day, coffeemaker, microwave, refrigerator,
continental breakfast, outdoor pool, fitness room, lawn for walking
dogs, 1 mile to public park, www.wilsonvillelaquinta.com

SnoozInn   503-682-2333, 800-343-1553
30245 SW Parkway Ave   57 units, $53–$60
dogs up to 20 lbs $10/day, dogs over 20 lbs $20/day, continental
breakfast, seasonal pool, 1/2 mile to public park, www.snoozinn.com

Super 8 Motel   503-682-2088, 800-800-8000
25438 SW Parkway Ave   72 units, $60–$89
dogs under 30 lbs only, $10/stay, coffeemaker, microwave,
refrigerator, continental breakfast, small pet walking area,
1 1/2 miles to public park, www.super8.com

Wilsonville Inn & Suites   503-570-9700, 888-336-9700
29769 SW Boones Ferry Rd   56 units, $72–$99
pet fee $15/day ($45 maximum), coffeemaker, microwave,
refrigerator, extended continental breakfast, freshly baked
cookies, indoor pool, hot tub, fitness room, ¼ mile to public park,
www.wilsonvilleinn.com

Winchester Bay, OR

Bayside Vacation Rentals   541- 290-7317
115 8th St   6 units, $110–$125
pet fee $25/stay, fully furnished 1-bdrm beach apartments
overlooking bay, balcony, BBQ, 1 block to beach,
www.baysidevacationrentals.net

Discovery Point Resort   541-271-3443
242 Discovery Pt Lane   13 units, $98–$260
cabins & condos with full kitchen sleep up to 6, RV park, grassy
walking area, across street to bay, www.discoverypointresort.com

Harbor View Motel   541-271-3352
540 Beach Blvd   14 units, $40–$55
each pet $5/day, kitchen, alley for walking dogs, 1 block to park

Salmon Harbor Landing Motel   541-271-3742
265 8th St   7 units, $49–$140
theme-decorated rooms with coffeemaker-microwave-refrigerator,
3-bdrm 2-bath vacation home with full kitchen, lawn for walking
dogs, 2 blocks to harbor, www.salmonharborlanding.com

Winchester Bay Inn   541-271-4871, 800-246-1462
390 Broadway   50 units, $54–$115
1 to 2 dogs, $5/day each pet, kitchenette, continental breakfast,
BBQ, 1 block to harbor, 1 mile to beach, www.winbayinn.com

Winston, OR

Sweet Breeze Inn   541-679-2420, 888-672-2420
251 NE Main St   32 units, $54–$80
each pet $5/day, microwave, refrigerator, open field for walking
dogs, 7 blocks to public park

Woodburn, OR

Best Western Inn   503-982-6515, 800-766-6433
2887 Newberg Hwy   80 units, $100–$121
1 to 2 dogs, $10/day each pet, coffeemaker, microwave,
refrigerator, extended continental breakfast, outdoor pool, hot tub,
fitness room, lawn for walking dogs, 2 miles to public park,
www.bestwestern.com/woodburn

La Quinta Inn & Suites   503-982-1727, 800-531-5900
120 N Arney Rd   60 units, $89–$114
1 to 3 dogs, coffeemaker, microwave, refrigerator, continental
breakfast, seasonal pool, hot tub, fitness room, lawn for walking
dogs, 2 miles to public park, www.lq.com

Super 8 Motel   503-981-8881, 800-800-8000
821 Evergreen Rd   81 units, $55–$75
pet fee $10/day, coffeemaker, microwave, refrigerator, continental
breakfast, indoor pool, hot tub, www.super8.com

Woodburn Inn   503-982-9741
1025 N Pacific Hwy   20 units, $55–$61
1 to 2 dogs, coffeemaker, microwave, refrigerator, grassy walking
area, 2 blocks to public park

Yachats, OR

Adobe Resort   541-547-3141, 800-522-3623
1555 N Hwy 101   110 units, $107–$130
each pet $10/day, rooms-suites-condos, full kitchen or
coffeemaker-microwave-refrigerator, private porch, restaurant,
indoor pool, sauna, hot tub, fitness room, pet treats-towel–pooper
scooper-sheet to cover bed linens, rocky beach & walking trail,
www.adoberesort.com

Ambrosia Gardens B & B   541-547-3013
95435 Hwy 101 S   3 units, $110–$125
pets allowed in 1 suite only, kitchen, full breakfast, complimentary
beverages, hot tub, 1 block to beach, www.ambrosia-gardens.com

Beachcombers Cottages   541-547-3432
95500 Hwy 101 S   5 units, $60–$130
1 to 2 dogs, $10/day each pet, kitchen, picnic tables, fire pit, gift
shop, grassy walking area, private beach access

Dublin House Motel   541-547-3200, 866-922-4287
251 W 7th St   27 units, $49–$135
small adult dogs only, $10/day each pet, coffeemaker, microwave,
refrigerator, indoor pool, open field for walking dogs, 2 blocks to
beach, www.dublinhousemotel.com

Fireside Motel   541-547-3636, 800-336-3573
1881 N Hwy 101   43 units, $70–$140
1 to 2 dogs, $10/day each pet, coffeemaker, microwave,
refrigerator, hot tub, dog towels-scoopers-sheets to protect
furniture provided, small pet walking area beside rocky shore,
3/4-mile-long oceanfront walking trail, www.firesidemotel.com

Holiday Beachside Market & Motel   541-547-3120
5933 Hwy 101 N   7 units, $79–$89
1 to 2 dogs under 40 lbs only, $10/day, kitchen, lawn for walking
dogs, short walk to beach, www.holidayinyachats.com

Ocean Odyssey Vacation Rentals   541-547-3637
251 Pacific Coast Hwy   66 units, $100–$380
1 to 2 dogs, $30/stay each pet, 1-bdrm to 4-bdrm vacation homes,
some with hot tub or yard, close to beach, www.ocean-odyssey.com

Rock Park Cottages   541-547-3214
431 W 2nd St   5 units, $70–$130
pet fee $5/day, kitchen, next to beach & public park,
www.trillian.com/rockpark/rock.htm

Sea Nik Vacation Rentals   541-547-3036, 877-822-0436
3138 Hwy 101 N   8 units, $115–$200
pet fee $50/stay, fully equipped vacation homes sleep up to 10, some
with deck or yard, close to beach, www.seanikvacationrentals.com

See Vue Motel   541-547-3227, 866-547-3237
95590 Hwy 101 S   11 units, $95–$170
each pet $10/day, full kitchen or coffeemaker & refrigerator,
grassy walking area, 5-minute walk to beach, www.seevue.com

Silver Surf Motel   541-547-3175, 800-281-5723
3767 N Hwy 101   25 units, $79–$189
pet fee $10/day, rooms with coffeemaker-microwave-refrigerator
& private balcony, cabins with full kitchen sleep 6, indoor pool, hot
tub, on 3+ oceanfront acres with semi-secluded beach,
www.silversurf-motel.com

Yachats, OR (continued)

Sweet Homes Vacation Rentals   541-961-8835, 800-519-0437
6 units, $160–$495
1 to 3 dogs, $50/stay for 1st dog, $25/stay for each additional dog, fully equipped 2-bdrm to 3-bdrm vacation homes in Waldport & Yachats, one with hot tub, deck, BBQ, close to walking trails-public parks-sandy or rocky beaches, www.sweethomesrentals.com

Ya-Tel Motel   541-547-3225, 800-406-1338
640 Hwy 101   8 units, $50–$100
each pet $5/day, full kitchen or coffeemaker-microwave-refrigerator, grassy walking area, www.yatelmotel.com

Yachats Inn   541-547-3456, 888-270-3456
331 S Hwy 101   36 units, $85–$135
1 to 2 dogs, $10/day each pet, kitchen, indoor pool, hot tub, lawn for walking dogs, beachfront, www.yachatsinn.com

Yamhill, OR

Hideaway Hill B & B   503-662-4696, 866-662-4696
19355 NW Bear Lane   4 units, $125–$165
1 pet-friendly room with refrigerator, full breakfast, gardens & natural forest land for walking dogs, www.hideawayhill.biz

Zigzag, OR

River's Hideaway Cabin   503-939-9491, 800-524-9251
1 unit, $70–$220
pet fee $10/day, 1-bdrm riverside cabin sleeps 2, kitchen, hot tub, lawn for walking dogs, 3 miles to national forest, www.mt-hood-cabin.com/rivers-hideaway-cabin.html

Washington's Dog-Friendly Lodgings

Aberdeen, WA

America's Best Value Inn   360-532-5210, 888-315-2378
521 W Wishkah St   66 units, $53–$79
each pet $10/day, coffeemaker, microwave, refrigerator,
continental breakfast, grassy walking area, short drive to beach,
www.bestvalueinn.com

Central Park Motel   360-533-1210
6504 Olympic Hwy   9 units, $50–$60
small dogs allowed with manager's approval only, microwave,
refrigerator, large yard for walking dogs, 2 miles to riverfront park,
www.centralparkmotel.info

GuestHouse International Inn & Suites   360-537-7460
701 E Heron St   800-214-8378
each pet $10/day   60 units, $84–$109
kitchenette or coffeemaker-microwave-refrigerator, continental
breakfast, indoor pool, hot tub, fitness room, 1½-mile-long walking
trail, www.guesthouseintl.com/location-WA-Aberdeen.htm

Nordic Inn Motel   360-533-0100
1500 S Boone St   66 units, $65–$75
each pet $10/day, coffeemaker, microwave, refrigerator, wooded
area for walking dogs, www.nordicinnaberdeen.com

Olympic Inn   360-533-4200, 800-562-8618
616 W Heron St   55 units, $69–$89
each pet $10/day, kitchenette or microwave & refrigerator,
continental breakfast, small grassy walking area, 9 blocks to
public park, www.aberdeenolympicinn.com

Thunderbird Motel   360-532-3153
410 W Wishkah St   36 units, $59–$69
coffeemaker, microwave, refrigerator, close to open field, 1 mile to
riverfront park

Trave-Lure Motel   360-532-3280
623 W Wishkah St   24 units, $50–$55
pet fee $7/day, microwave, refrigerator

Airway Heights, WA

Days Inn & Suites Spokane Airport 509-244-0222, 800-329-7466
1215 S Garfield Rd   61 units, $69–$74
dogs under 25 lbs only, $10/stay, kitchenette or coffeemaker,
continental breakfast, fitness room, lawn & open field for walking
dogs, www.daysinn.com/hotel/22343

Lantern Park Motel   509-244-3653
13820 W Sunset Hwy   11 units, $49
pet fee $10/day, kitchenette or coffeemaker-microwave-
refrigerator, lawn for walking dogs, 1/2 mile to public park

Amanda Park, WA

Lake Quinault Inn   360-288-2714
8 N Shore Rd   8 units, $76–$87
pet fee $15/day, coffeemaker, microwave, refrigerator, grassy area
for walking dogs, 5-minute drive to lakefront

Quinalt River Inn   360-288-2237, 800-410-2237
8 River Dr   8 units, $69–$99
dogs allowed with manager's approval only, $15/day each pet,
coffeemaker, refrigerator, full breakfast, www.quinaultriverinn.com

Anacortes, WA

Anacortes Inn   360-293-3153, 800-327-7976
3006 Commercial Ave   44 units, $72–$128
1 to 2 dogs, $10/day each pet, full kitchen or coffeemaker-
microwave-refrigerator, outdoor pool, next to public park &
playground, www.anacortesinn.com

Bayside Inn   360-293-2655
2019 Commercial Ave   13 units, $50–$70
1 to 2 dogs allowed with manager's approval only, $10/day,
kitchenette, large courtyard, 2 blocks to beach & walking trail

Cap Sante Inn   360-293-0602, 800-852-0846
906 9th St   34 units, $70–$85
pet fee $10/day, microwave, refrigerator, continental breakfast, coffee
in lobby, dog treats, across street to marina, www.capsanteinn.com

Cottages by the Bay   360-588-1890
2802 Shannon Point   3 units, $150–$175
fully equipped 2-bdrm & 3-bdrm vacation homes, close to ocean,
www.vrbo.com/my/130571

Fidalgo Country Inn   360-293-3494, 800-244-4179
7645 State Route 20   50 units, $79–$300
dogs allowed with advance approval only, $20/day each pet,
kitchenette or coffeemaker-microwave-refrigerator, full breakfast,
outdoor pool, hot tub, large open area for walking dogs, 10-minute
drive to public park, www.fidalgocountryinn.com

Guemes Island Resort   360-293-6643, 800-965-6643
4268 Guemes Island Rd   13 units, $55–$400
each pet $10/day, well-mannered dogs only, fully furnished cabins-
yurts-vacation homes on 20 beachfront acres, kitchen, BBQ,
outdoor pool, sauna, hot tub, one of the longest walking beaches
in the San Juan islands, www.guemesislandresort.com

Holiday Motel   360-293-6511
2903 Commercial Ave   10 units, $50–$70
pet fee $10/day, microwave, refrigerator, across street to park

Islands Inn   360-293-4644, 866-331-3328
3401 Commercial Ave   36 units, $69–$130
coffeemaker, refrigerator, continental breakfast, restaurant,
seasonal pool, hot tub, 2 blocks to public park, www.islandsinn.com

Lake Campbell Lodging   360-293-5314, 888-399-1077
6676 State Route 20   10 units, $55–$105
each pet $10/day, full kitchen or coffeemaker-microwave-
refrigerator, large yard for walking dogs, 4 miles to state park,
www.lakecampbelllodging.com

Majestic Inn & Spa   360-299-1400, 877-370-0100
419 Commercial Ave   21 units, $114–$299
dogs under 25 lbs only, $50/stay, refrigerator, continental
breakfast, restaurant, lounge, guest pass to local fitness center,
2 blocks to off-leash dog park, www.majesticinnandspa.com

Ship Harbor Inn   360-293-5177, 800-852-8568
5316 Ferry Terminal Rd   28 units, $79–$189
each pet $10/day, full kitchen or coffeemaker-microwave-
refrigerator, extended continental breakfast, lawn for walking
dogs, 1 mile to public park, www.shipharborinn.com

Troll House Guest Cottage   360-293-5750
3895 Sea Breeze Lane   1 unit, $150
very private cabin, kitchen, BBQ, covered deck, hot tub, wooded
area for walking dogs, www.thetrollhouse.com

Anderson Island, WA

Anderson Island Inns   253-377-6467
10026 Selma Circle   20 units, $150–$195
dogs allowed with advance approval only, fully equipped 2-bdrm to
3-bdrm vacation homes, grassy area for walking dogs, close to
beachfront park, www.andersonislandinn.com

Arlington, WA

Arlington Motor Inn   360-652-9595
2214 State Route 530 NE   42 units, $65–$80
1 to 2 dogs, $15/stay, microwave, refrigerator, continental
breakfast, lawn for walking dogs, 2 miles to hiking trail

Crossroads Quality Inn   360-403-7222, 877-856-3751
5200 172nd St NE # E   52 units, $79–$89
pet fee $20/stay, coffeemaker, microwave, refrigerator, continental
breakfast, fitness room, lawn for walking dogs, 1/4 mile to park &
walking path, www.qualityinn.com/hotel/wa179

Smokey Point Motor Inn   360-659-8561
17329 Smokey Point Dr   54 units, $65–$70
pet fee $10-$15/day, kitchenette or coffeemaker-microwave-
refrigerator, hot tub, large open area for walking dogs, 1/2 mile to
lakefront park

Ashford, WA

Gateway Inn & Cabins   360-569-2506
38820 State Route 706 E   8 units, $109–$129
pet fee $15/day, dogs allowed in 1 log cabin that sleeps 4, BBQ,
bonfire pit, continental breakfast, RV & tent sites, restaurant,
general store, large yard for walking dogs, 2 miles to riverside
walkway, www.gatewayinnonline.com

Great Getaways   360-569-2799, 877-325-5881
35707 State Route 706 E   10+ units, $175
each pet $25/day, cabins & vacation homes, full kitchen, BBQ, hot
tub, www.greatgetaways.com

Mountain Meadows Inn B & B   360-569-2788
28912 State Route 706 E   6 units, $129–$165
pet fee $10/day, coffeemaker, microwave, refrigerator, full
breakfast, picnic lunches by request, hot tub, on 12 wooded acres
with pond-creek-trails, www.mountainmeadowsinn.com

Rainier Overland Lodge   360-569-0851, 800-582-8984
31811 State Route 706 E   12 units, $59–$89
dogs allowed by advance reservation only, $10/day, coffeemaker,
restaurant, open area for walking dogs, www.rainieroverland.net

Auburn, WA

Auburn Guesthouse Inn   253-735-9600, 800-443-7777
9 14th St NW   96 units, $59–$129
each pet $10/day, kitchenette or coffeemaker-microwave-
refrigerator, extended continental breakfast, hot tub, open field for
walking dogs, next to hiking trail, www.auburnguesthouseintl.com

Auburn Motel   253-833-7470
1202 Auburn Way S   28 units, $70–$80
1 to 2 dogs under 20 lbs only, $10/day each pet, microwave,
refrigerator, paved walking area, 2 blocks to public park

Best Western Peppertree Auburn Inn   253-887-7600
401 8th St SW   888-624-4854
dogs under 10 lbs only, $10/day each pet   124 units, $116–$199
coffeemaker, microwave, refrigerator, indoor pool, hot tub, fitness
room, lawn for walking dogs, 5-minute drive to public park,
www.bestwestern.com/peppertreeauburninn

Cedars Inn Auburn   253-833-8007, 866-833-8007
102 15th St NE   34 units, $59–$109
pet fee $10/day, microwave, refrigerator, continental breakfast,
large open area for walking dogs, www.cedarsinnauburn.com

Days Inn Auburn   253-939-5950
1521 D St NE   66 units, $65–$100
1 to 4 dogs, $15/day, coffeemaker, microwave, refrigerator,
continental breakfast, outdoor pool, sauna, hot tub, short drive to
public park, www.daysinn.com/hotel/10235

Travelodge Suites   253-833-7171, 866-871-2434
9 16th St NW   95 units, $55–$89
coffeemaker, microwave, refrigerator, coffee in lobby, extended
continental breakfast, fitness room, 1 mile to walking trail,
www.travelodge.com/hotel/14392

Bainbridge Island, WA

Arrow Point Guest House   206-842-0967
10159 Arrow Point Dr   1 unit, $150–$200
dogs allowed with advance approval, pet fee varies with length of
stay, private 2-bdrm guest house, full kitchen, covered deck,
bicycles for guest use, woods & meadow for walking dogs,
www.arrowpointguesthouse.com

Ashton Woods Retreat   206-780-0100
pet fee $40/stay   2 units, $175–$225
cottage sleeps 2, spa tub, mini-refrigerator & covered front porch;
loft sleeps 2, private entrance overlooking Zen garden & fountain;
fireplaces in both units, full breakfast basket delivered to your
door, pet beds-bowls-treats provided, on 10 wooded acres with
1-acre meadows & trails, ½ mile to several large public parks
connected by trails, www.ashtonwoodsretreat.com

Bainbridge Vacation Rentals   206-855-9763
pet fee $75-$95/stay   50 units, $125–$385
1-bdrm guesthouses to 3-bdrm vacation homes, hot tubs, near park
& swimming pool, www.bainbridgevacationrentals.com

Best Western Bainbridge Island Suites   206-855-9666
350 High School Rd NE   866-396-9666
1 to 2 dogs under 40 lbs only, $50/stay   51 units, $129
coffeemaker, microwave, refrigerator, continental breakfast, lawn,
short drive to ocean, www.bestwestern.com/bainbridgeislandsuites

Island Country Inn   206-842-6861, 800-842-8429
920 Hildebrand Lane NE   45 units, $89–$169
pet fee $15/day, full kitchen or microwave & refrigerator, extended
continental breakfast, seasonal pool, hot tub, open field for walking
dogs, 1 mile to public park, www.islandcountryinn.com

Kellerman Creek B & B   206-855-8081
10220 NE Roberts Rd   1 unit, $129–$149
dogs allowed by advance reservation only, $15/day, studio cottage
with kitchenette, full breakfast, on 1-acre English garden, short
walk to beach, 5-minute drive to park, www.kellermancreek.com

Saxon Cottage Guest House   206-842-0382
13671 Madison Ave NE   1 unit, $100–$125
1-bdrm private cottage with kitchen, full breakfast, on 10+ acres of
woodlands & fields, small fenced yard, www.saxoncottage.com

Waterfall Gardens Private Suites   206-842-1434
7269 NE Bergman Rd   4 units, $145–$230
1 to 2 dogs allowed with advance approval, $25/stay, coffeemaker,
microwave, refrigerator, on 5 landscaped acres, trails, "bobo golf,"
8-minute drive to public park, www.waterfall-gardens.com

Beaver, WA

Bear Creek Motel & RV Park   360-327-3225
Milepost 206   10 units, $55–$95
dogs allowed with advance approval only, $10/stay, kitchenette,
restaurant, lounge, RV sites, lawn for walking dogs, 1 block to
public park, www.hungrybearcafemotel.com

Belfair, WA

Belfair Motel   360-275-4485
23322 NE State Hwy 3   28 units, $71–$86
each pet $10/day, full kitchen or coffeemaker-microwave-
refrigerator, lawn, close to walking trail, www.belfairmotel.net

Hood Canal Vacation Rentals   360-277-9228, 877-275-7851
24070 NE State Route 3   12 units, $150–$350
dogs allowed with advance approval only, $25/day each pet,
waterfront vacation homes sleep up to 12, one with hot tub, beach
access, close to public parks, www.hoodcanalvacationrentals.com

Selah Inn & Cottages   360-275-0916, 877-232-7941
130 NE Dulalip Landing   2 units, $175
dog-friendly cottages, kitchen, breakfast & dinner available by
arrangement, lawn, close to state park, www.selahinn.com

Bellevue, WA

Bellevue Club Hotel   425-454-4424, 800-579-1110
11200 SE 6th St   67 units, call for current rates
dogs under 30 lbs only, $30/stay, restaurant, lounge, indoor &
outdoor pools, sauna, hot tub, athletic facility, day spa, lawn,
10 blocks to botanical gardens, www.bellevueclub.com

Days Inn   425-643-6644, 866-809-9800
3241 156th Ave SE   106 units, $89–$102
dogs under 50 lbs only, $25/stay, coffeemaker, refrigerator, coffee
in lobby, extended continental breakfast, hot tub, BBQ, picnic area,
parking lot for walking dogs, 5-minute walk to public park,
www.daysinn.com/hotel/06264

Bellevue, WA (continued)

Extended StayAmerica   425-453-8186, 800-326-5651
11400 Main St   148 units, $65–$115
pet fee $25/day ($150 maximum), kitchenette, parking lot for
walking dogs, 1 mile to park, www.extendedstayamerica.com/sbl

Homestead Studio Suites Seattle/Bellevue   425-865-8680
3700 132nd Ave SE   800-398-7829
pet fee $25/day ($75 maximum)   150 units, $89–$125
full kitchen, guest pass to local fitness center, grassy walking area,
www.homesteadhotels.com/blv extendedstayhotel.com

Homestead Studio Suites Seattle/Redmond   425-885-6675
15805 NE 28th St   800-804-3724
pet fee $25/stay ($75 maximum)   162 units, $70–$130
kitchenette, grassy walking area, www.homesteadhotels.com/rmd

La Residence Suite Hotel   425-455-1475
475 100th Ave NE   24 units, $95–$185
pet fee $10/day ($100 maximum), kitchen, continental breakfast,
fitness room, short walk to beach park, www.bellevuelodging.com

Larkspur Landing Bellevue Hotel   425-373-1212
15805 SE 37th St   132 units, $119–$139
pet fee $75/stay, kitchen, full breakfast, hot tub, fitness room,
freshly baked cookies & coffee in lobby, walking trails thru woods,
2 miles to off-leash dog park, www.larkspurlanding.com/bellevue

Red Lion Bellevue Hotel   425-455-5240, 800-733-5466
11211 Main St   181 units, $124–$235
pet fee $25/stay, restaurant, lounge, outdoor pool, fitness room,
grassy walking area, 1 mile to park, www.redlion.com/bellevue

Residence Inn Seattle/Bellevue Downtown   425-637-8500
605 114th Ave SE   231 units, $119–$239
1 to 2 dogs under 50 lbs only, $100/stay, kitchen, full breakfast,
complimentary evening beverages & appetizers twice weekly,
indoor pool, fitness room, dog treats & cleanup bags, lawn, 1 block
to walking trail, 4 block to public park, www.marriott.com/bvuri

Residence Inn Seattle/Bellevue East   425-882-1222
14455 NE 29th Place   800-331-3131
pet fee $75/stay   120 units, $119–$259
kitchen, full breakfast, seasonal pool, hot tub, pet walking area,
walking trail, www.marriott.com/bvuwa

Sheraton Bellevue 425-455-3330, 800-235-4458
100 112th Ave NE 178 units, $209–$299
dogs under 80 lbs only, coffeemaker, restaurant, fitness room,
1 mile to public park, www.sheratonbellevue.com

Westin Bellevue 425-638-1000
600 Bellevue Way NE 337 units, $159–$359
1 to 2 dogs under 40 lbs only, coffeemaker, restaurant, indoor pool,
hot tub, fitness room, walking trail, www.westin.com/bellevuewa

Bellingham, WA

Best Western Heritage Inn 360-647-1912, 888-333-2080
151 E Mcleod Rd 91 units, $99–$159
1 to 2 dogs, $20/day each pet, coffeemaker, microwave, refrigerator,
continental breakfast, seasonal pool, hot tub, small lawn, 15-minute
drive to off-leash dog park, www.bestwestern.com/prop_48090

Best Western Lakeway Inn 360-671-1011, 800-528-1238
714 Lakeway Dr 132 units, $129–$209
each pet $25/day, coffeemaker, microwave, refrigerator,
restaurant, lounge, indoor pool, sauna, hot tub, grassy walking
area, several parks within 6 blocks, www.bellingham-hotel.com

Cascade Inn 360-733-2520
208 N Samish Way 44 units, $45–$60
pet fee $15/day, full kitchen or coffeemaker-microwave-
refrigerator, hot tub, parking lot for walking dogs, 6 blocks to park

Coachman Inn 360-671-9000, 800-962-6641
120 N Samish Way 60 units, $55–$80
pet fee $10/day, refrigerator, continental breakfast, outdoor pool,
lawn, close to walking trail, www.coachmaninnmotel.com

Days Inn Bellingham 360-734-8830, 888-734-0888
215 N Samish Way 67 units, $84–$121
dogs under 25 lbs only, $20/day, coffeemaker, microwave,
refrigerator, extended continental breakfast, seasonal pool, guest
pass to local fitness center, lawn & parking lot for walking dogs,
www.daysinn.com/hotel/00996

Econo Lodge Inn & Suites 360-671-4600
3750 Meridian St 126 units, $62–$149
dogs under 10 lbs only, $10/day, microwave, refrigerator,
continental breakfast, seasonal pool, hot tub, 6 blocks to park &
walking path, www.econolodge.com/hotel/wa228

Bellingham, WA (continued)

Evergreen Motel   360-734-7671
1015 Samish Way   10 units, $50–$60
pet fee $5/day, kitchen, large yard for walking dogs

Fairhaven Village Inn   360-733-1311, 877-733-1100
1200 10th St   22 units, $159–$219
1 to 2 dogs under 30 lbs only, $20/day each pet, microwave,
refrigerator, coffee in lobby, extended continental breakfast,
walking trail to public park, 3 blocks to off-leash dog park,
www.fairhavenvillageinn.com

GuestHouse International Inn & Suites   360-671-9600
805 Lakeway Dr   800-443-7777
pet fee $10/day   82 units, $95–$140
coffeemaker, microwave, refrigerator, continental breakfast, hot
tub, lawn, 1 mile to park, www.bellinghamguesthouseintl.com

Holiday Inn Express   360-671-4800, 800-465-4329
4160 Meridian St   101 units, $110–$150
pet fee $15/stay, kitchenette or microwave & refrigerator, full
breakfast, indoor pool, hot tub, guest pass to local fitness center,
grassy walking area, www.hiexpress.com/bellinghamwa

Hotel Bellwether   360-392-3100, 877-411-1200
1 Bellwether Way   65 units, $136–$689
pet fee $20/day, coffeemaker, restaurant, lounge, fitness room, spa
tub in all guest rooms, private boat dock, lawn & waterfront
walking trails, ½ mile to public park, www.hotelbellwether.com

La Quinta Inn   360-671-6200, 800-531-5900
125 E Kellogg Rd   70 units, $89–$129
pet fee $7/day, kitchenette or coffeemaker, continental breakfast,
outdoor pool, hot tub, lawn, 1 mile to public park, www.lq.com

Mac's Motel   360-734-7570
1215 E Maple St   33 units, $40–$50
microwave, refrigerator, across street to grassy walking area

Motel 6   360-671-4494, 800-466-8356
3701 Byron St   60 units, $54–$80
coffee in lobby, seasonal pool, pet treats & cleanup bags provided,
small pet walking area, close to walking trail, 5 miles to state park
& waterfront, www.motel6.com

Quality Inn Baron Suites   360-647-8000, 800-900-4661
100 E Kellogg Rd   86 units, $90–$165
pet fee $25/stay, coffeemaker, microwave, refrigerator, continental
breakfast, outdoor pool, hot tub, fitness room, lawn for walking
dogs, 1 mile to public park, www.qualityinn.com/hotel/WA054

Rodeway Inn   360-738-6000, 800-476-5413
3710 Meridian St   74 units, $65–$109
pet fee $10/day, microwave, refrigerator, continental breakfast, hot
tub, 2 blocks to park & trail, www.rodewayinn.com/hotel/wa711

Shamrock Motel   360-676-1050
4133 W Maplewood Ave   38 units, $39–$65
each pet $5/day, full kitchen or microwave & refrigerator,
continental breakfast, www.shamrockmotels.com

The Guest House   360-671-0774
409 14th St   1 unit, $89
fully furnished apartment, large courtyard for walking dogs,
across street to public park, www.theguesthouse-bellingham.com

Birch Bay, WA

Driftwood Inn Resort Motel   360-371-2620, 800-833-2666
7394 Birch Bay Dr   13 units, $55–$190
each pet $15/day, studios-suites-cabins-condos, full kitchen or
coffeemaker-microwave-refrigerator, seasonal pool, bayfront lawn,
short walk to park & ocean, www.driftwoodinnmotel.com

Blaine, WA

Anchor Inn Motel   360-332-5539
250 Cedar St   13 units, $50–$75
dogs under 25 lbs only, $10/day, kitchenette or microwave &
refrigerator, lawn, ½ mile to marina, www.theanchorinnmotel.com

International Motel   360-332-8222
240 Martin St   23 units, $58–$82
dogs under 25 lbs only, $15/stay, coffeemaker, microwave,
refrigerator, 3 blocks to state park, 4 blocks to walking trail

Semiahmoo Resort   360-318-2000
9565 Semiahmoo Parkway   198 units, $189–$439
dogs allowed with manager's approval, $50/stay, rooms & suites,
coffeemaker, refrigerator, restaurant, lounge, outdoor pool, sauna,
steam room, hot tub, www.semiahmoo.com

Blaine, WA (continued)

Smugglers Inn Bed & Breakfast   360-332-1749
2480 Canada View Dr   8 units, $100–$350
kitchen, full breakfast, BBQ, hot tub, on 20 acres, 1 mile to beach
& off-leash dog park, www.smugglersinnblaine.com

Tide Catcher   360-223-2510
8076 Birch Bay Dr   7 units, $82–$96
dogs allowed with advance approval only, $75/stay, 2-bdrm to
3-bdrm beachfront cabins, private beach, www.tidecatcher.com

Bothell, WA

Extended Stay Deluxe Seattle/Bothell   425-482-2900
22122 17th Ave SE   123 units, $129
each pet $25/day, kitchenette, extended continental breakfast,
BBQ, seasonal pool, fitness room, small walking area, ½ mile to
park, 3 mile to riverfront park, www.extendedstaydeluxe.com/sbt

Extended StayAmerica Seattle/Bothell   425-402-4252
923 228th St SE   800-398-7829
pet fee $25/day ($150 maximum)   104 units, $104–$124
kitchenette, grassy area for walking dogs, 1 block to public park,
www.extendedstayamerica.com/scp

Residence Inn Seattle Northeast/Bothell   425-485-3030
11920 NE 195th St   800-331-3131
pet fee $75/stay   120 units, $89–$189
kitchen, full breakfast, Monday thru Wednesday complimentary
dinner, outdoor pool, hot tub, fitness room, 1½ miles to walking
trail around pond & business park, www.marriott.com/seabo

Bow, WA

Benson Farmstead B & B   360-757-0578, 800-441-9814
10113 Avon Allen Rd   6 units, $125–$200
each pet $25/stay, dog-friendly cottage sleeps 2 to 8, full breakfast,
BBQ, landscaped grounds, next to beach, also 3-bdrm beach
house sleeps 6, overlooking bay, www.bensonfarmstead.com

Bremerton, WA

Bird's Eye View B & B   360-698-2448
8226 Kaster Dr NE   3 units, $115–$150
pet fee $10/day, full breakfast, www.bremertonbb.com

Bremerton Inn & Suites   360-405-1111, 800-776-2291
4303 Kitsap Way   103 units, $90–$116
each pet $10/day, coffeemaker, microwave, refrigerator, continental
breakfast, seasonal pool, www.bremertoninnandsuites.com

Chieftain Motel   360-479-3111
600 National Ave N   45 units, $60
each pet $10/day, microwave, refrigerator, grassy walking area,
1 mile to public park, 6 blocks to state park

Comfort Inn & Suites   360-377-7666, 877-424-6423
5640 Kitsap Way   155 units, $120–$200
dogs under 30 lbs only, $50/stay, coffeemaker, microwave,
refrigerator, full breakfast, indoor pool, hot tub, fitness room,
1/4 mile to public park, www.comfortinn.com/hotel/wa218

Dunes Motel   360-377-0093
3400 11th St   64 units, $65–$70
pet fee $20/stay, kitchenette or microwave, continental breakfast,
small pet walking area, 3 blocks to public park

Flagship Inn   360-479-6566, 800-447-9396
4320 Kitsap Way   29 units, $75–$101
dogs under 20 lbs only, $6/day, coffeemaker, microwave,
refrigerator, continental breakfast, seasonal pool, small wooded
area for walking dogs, www.flagship-inn.com

Midway Inn   360-479-2909, 800-231-0575
2909 Wheaton Way   60 units, $84–$94
dogs under 20 lbs only, $25/stay, kitchenette or coffeemaker-
microwave-refrigerator, continental breakfast, lawn for walking
dogs, 1 mile to public park, www.midway-inn.com

Oyster Bay Inn   360-377-5510, 800-393-3862
4412 Kitsap Way   77 units, $77–$143
dogs allowed with advance approval only, $20 for 1st day, $10 each
additional day, kitchenette or microwave & refrigerator,
continental breakfast, restaurant, lounge, fitness room, enclosed
lawn for walking dogs, www.oysterbayinn.com

Super 8 Motel   360-377-8881, 800-800-8000
5068 Kitsap Way   75 units, $71–$96
pet fee $10/stay, coffeemaker, continental breakfast, open area for
walking dogs, 1 mile to public park, www.super8.com

Brewster, WA

Apple Avenue Motel   509-689-3000
16 Hwy 97 N   17 units, $65–$80
each pet $10/day, coffeemaker, microwave, refrigerator,
surrounded by orchards, walking trail, ¼ mile to riverfront
park & walkway

Brinnon, WA

Bayshore Motel   360-796-4220, 800-488-4230
306142 US Hwy 101   12 units, $55–$60
pet fee $10/stay, coffeemaker, microwave, refrigerator, open field
for walking dogs, across street to waterfront

Buckley, WA

Econo Lodge   360-829-1100, 800-582-4111
29405 Hwy 410 E   41 units, $70–$136
each pet $10/stay, microwave, refrigerator, continental breakfast,
outdoor pool, hot tub, lawn, across highway to walking trail that
leads to public park, www.econolodge.com/hotel/wa187

Mountain View Inn   360-829-1100, 800-582-4111
29405 Hwy 410 E   41 units, $70–$89
small dogs only, $20/stay, microwave, refrigerator, continental
breakfast, outdoor pool, hot tub, across highway to walking trail

West Main Motel   360-829-2400
466 W Main St   14 units, $65–$80
pet fee $25/stay, microwave, grassy walking area

Burlington, WA

Whispering Firs Motel   360-724-3477
1745 Old Hwy 99 N   13 units, $55–$65
pet fee $20/stay, coffeemaker, microwave, refrigerator, lawn &
gravel walking areas, 5 miles to lake

Carlton, WA

Country Town Motel & RV Park   509-997-3432, 800-658-5249
2266 Hwy 153   23 units, $69–$80
pet fee $5/day, full kitchen or coffeemaker-microwave-refrigerator,
restaurant, outdoor pool, hot tub, RV sites, convenience store,
miniature golf course, on 3 acres with lawn & trees, river access

Carson, WA

Sandhill Cottages   509-427-3464, 800 914-2178
932 Hot Springs Ave   6 units, $79–$99
each pet $15/stay, historic cottages, kitchenette, open field for
walking dogs, www.sandhillcottages.com

Cashmere, WA

Village Inn Motel   509-782-3522
229 Cottage Ave   21 units, $64–$79
1 small dog only, $10/day, coffeemaker, microwave, refrigerator,
2 blocks to riverfront park

Castle Rock, WA

7 West Motel   360-274-7526
864 Walsh Ave NE   24 units, $48–$58
each pet $5/day, 1/2-acre lawn for walking dogs, 4 blocks to
riverside walkway, www.sevenwest.8m.com

Timberland Inn & Suites   360-274-6002, 888-900-6335
1271 Mt St Helens Way NE   40 units, $70–$160
each pet $15/day, microwave, refrigerator, undeveloped area for
walking dogs, 5 miles to public park, www.timberland-inn.com

Centralia, WA

Econo Lodge   360-736-2875
702 W Harrison Ave   82 units, $50–$120
1 to 2 dogs under 50 lbs only, $10/day each pet, microwave,
refrigerator, continental breakfast, seasonal pool, next to public
park, 1 mile to state park with lake & trails,
www.econolodge.com/hotel/wa125

Ferryman's Inn & Suites   360-330-2094, 800-977-2094
1003 Eckerson Rd   82 units, $60–$70
each pet $10/day, full kitchen or coffeemaker-microwave-
refrigerator, continental breakfast, seasonal pool, hot tub, 2 public
parks within 2 blocks, www.ferrymaninnandsuites.com

Motel 6   360-330-2057, 800-466-8356
1310 Belmont Ave   122 units, $45–$60
microwave, refrigerator, coffee in lobby, seasonal pool, 6 blocks to
public park, www.motel6.com

Centralia, WA (continued)

Travel Inn Express   360-736-9344, 800-736-9344
1325 Lakeshore Dr   40 units, $55–$75
pet fee $5/day, coffeemaker, microwave, refrigerator, continental
breakfast, all rooms open onto grassy area & lake

Chehalis, WA

Best Western Park Place Inn & Suites   360-748-4040
201 Sw Interstate Ave   877-748-0008
dogs under 20 lbs only, $10/day   61 units, $95–$139
microwave, refrigerator, continental breakfast, indoor pool, hot
tub, fitness room, small pet walking area & walking trail, close to
playground, www.bestwestern.com/prop_48145

Chehalis Inn   360-740-5339, 877-740-5338
122 Interstate Ave   70 units, $50–$100
each pet $10/day, microwave, refrigerator, continental breakfast,
seasonal pool, lawn, 1 block to public park, www.chehalisinn.com

Relax Inn   360-748-8608, 800-843-6916
550 SW Parkland Dr   29 units, $65–$79
each pet $5-$10/day, coffeemaker, microwave, refrigerator,
continental breakfast, lawn, next to park, www.therelaxinn.com

Chelan, WA

Best Western Lakeside Lodge   509-682-4396, 800-468-2781
2312 W Woodin Ave   95 units, $89–$329
pets allowed with manager's approval only, $10/day, kitchenette or
coffeemaker-microwave-refrigerator, continental breakfast, indoor
& outdoor pools, hot tub, fitness room, private beach, next to
public park, www.bestwestern.com/prop_48136

Chelan Quality Vacation Properties 509-682-9782, 888-977-1748
123 E Johnson Ave   120 units, $250–$600
dogs allowed with advance approval only, $25/day, condos &
vacation homes, www.lakechelanvacationrentals.com

Kelly's Resort   509-687-3220, 800-561-8978
12800 S Lakeshore Rd   15 units, $130–$270
each pet $15/day, 20-acre resort on Lake Chelan, 1-bdrm to
2-bdrm cottages, full kitchen, BBQ, outdoor pool, walking trails,
sandy beach, convenience store, espresso bar, rowboats-canoes-
kayaks for guest use, www.kellysresort.com

Midtowner Motel   509-682-4051, 800-572-0943
721 E Woodin Ave   46 units, $40–$119
each pet $10/day, kitchenette or microwave & refrigerator, indoor
pool, hot tub, small pet walking area, 6 blocks to public park,
www.midtowner.com

Cheney, WA

AAA Inn   509-235-4058
12 Columbia St & 1st St   12 units, $45
pet fee $5/day, community kitchen for guest use, fitness room,
BBQ, picnic area, pet walking area, trail to lake & nature park

Bunker's Resort on Williams Lake   509-235-5212, 800-404-6674
36402 S Bunkers Landing Rd   4 units, $75–$90
rustic cabins with kitchen sleep 4 to 6, bring your own bedding &
cooking utensils, RV & tent sites, dock fishing, boat launch,
www.bunkersresort.com

Chewelah, WA

49er Motel & RV Park   509-935-8613, 888-412-1994
311 S Park St   13 units, $44–$68
pet fee $4/day, kitchenette or coffeemaker-microwave-refrigerator,
indoor pool, hot tub, RV sites, open field, www.49er-motel.com

Clarkston, WA

Best Western RiverTree Inn   509-758-9551, 800-597-3621
1257 Bridge St   62 units, $95–$119
pet fee $20/stay, coffeemaker, microwave, refrigerator, continental
breakfast, seasonal pool, sauna, steam room, hot tub, fitness room,
covered BBQ, picnic area, dog run available, 1 mile to public park,
www.bestwestern.com/rivertreeinn

Golden Key Motel   509-758-5566
1376 Bridge St   18 units, $40
dogs allowed with advance approval only, coffeemaker, microwave,
refrigerator, grassy walking area, 3 blocks to riverfront park,
www.thegoldenkeymotel.net

Motel 6   509-758-1631, 800-466-8356
222 Bridge St   86 units, $47–$55
refrigerator, coffee in lobby, indoor pool, next to riverside walkway,
www.motel6.com

Clarkston, WA (continued)

Quality Inn & Suites   509-758-9500, 800-424-6423
700 Port Dr   97 units, $99–$170
dogs allowed with advance approval only, $10/day each pet,
coffeemaker, microwave, refrigerator, full breakfast, restaurant,
lounge, espresso stand, outdoor pool, hot tub, fitness room, next to
riverfront park & walkway, www.qualityinnclarkston.com

Sunset Motel   509-758-2517
1200 Bridge St   10 units, $45–$65
microwave, refrigerator, courtyard with BBQ, lawn for walking
dogs, 1/4 mile to park & walking path

Cle Elum, WA

Aster Inn & Antiques   509-674-2551, 888-616-9722
521 E 1st St   10 units, $55–$125
1 to 2 dogs, $15/day each pet, full kitchen or coffeemaker-
microwave-refrigerator, grassy walking area, 8 blocks to walking
trail down to river, www.asterinn.com

Big Game Lodge at Elk Run Ranch   509-674-5969
4190 Teanaway Rd, Middle Fork   1 unit, call for current rates
pet fee $75/stay, 3-bdrm lodge sleeps 9, BBQ, picnic area, fire pit,
corrals (guests' horses welcome), riverfront walking areas, next to
forest service land, lots of hiking & riding trails

Cascade Mountain Inn   509-674-2380
906 E 1st St   43 units, $65–$105
each pet $20/day, kitchenette or coffeemaker-microwave-
refrigerator, continental breakfast, hot tub, open field for walking
dogs, 1 mile to public park, www.cascadeinncleelum.com

Cascade Mountain Rentals   509-852-0200, 800-324-8115
9614 Rainier Ave S, Seattle WA 98118   15 units, $250–$1400
each pet $25/day, fully equipped condos & vacation homes in
Cle Elum-Roslyn-San Juan Island-Suncadia Resort,
www.cascademtr.com

Stewart Lodge   509-674-4548, 877-233-5358
805 W 1st St   36 units, $86–$94
each pet $10/day, microwave, refrigerator, extended continental
breakfast, seasonal pool, hot tub, walking trail, 1 block to public
park, www.stewartlodge.com

Suncadia Resort   509-649-6400, 800-858-2400
3600 Suncadia Trl   14 units, $299–$399
dogs allowed by advance reservation only, pet fee $50/stay, lodge
rooms, 1-bdrm to 3-bdrm suites with kitchen, fully equipped
vacation homes on or near the golf course, restaurant, lounge,
indoor & outdoor pools, hot tub, fitness room,
www.suncadiaresort.com

Suncadia Resort Condominium #3047   360-701-4768
pet fee $50/stay   1 unit, call for current rates
privately owned studio suite with kitchenette sleeps 4, restaurant,
lounge, guest pass to athletic club-spa-swimming pool-water slides,
waterfront walking area, www.holidayescapes.net/suncadia.aspx

Timber Lodge Inn   509-674-5966
301 W 1st St   35 units, $70
pet fee $15/stay, microwave, refrigerator, continental breakfast,
hot tub, large open area for walking dogs, 2 blocks to a 2-mile-long
walking trail on an old railroad bed

Traveler's Inn   509-674-5535
1001 E 1st St   33 units, $52–$58
dogs under 20 lbs only, $5/day each pet, microwave, refrigerator,
coffeemaker available on request, small pet walking area

Clinton, WA

Heron Beach Cottage   360 319-5111
7495 Maxwelton Rd   1 unit, $150–$170
dogs allowed with advance approval, $20/day each pet, 2-bdrm
2-bath cottage sleeps 6, deck & BBQ, large yard, across street to
beach & boardwalk, short walk to park with softball field-picnic
tables-playground-boat launch, www.heronbeachcottage.com

Home by the Sea Cottages   360-321-2964
2388 E Sunlight Beach Rd   1 unit, $210
dogs under 30 lbs allowed by advance arrangement only, private
beachfront suite with separate entrance, kitchen, hot tub, gardens,
short walk to public park, www.homebytheseacottages.com

Lapis Lane Guest House   360-579-2009
3645 Lapis Lane   1 unit, $150–$170
dogs allowed by advance reservation only, $20/day, 2-bdrm house
sleeps 6, full kitchen, steam bath & hot tub, deck, on 6 acres with
organic garden, quiet yard, 1 mile to beach, www.lapislane.com

Clinton, WA (continued)

Sunlight SeaScape Retreat   206-525-1262 or 206-595-3498
6195 Barnacle Lane   3 units, $100–$165
dogs allowed with advance approval, $25-$50/stay, 2-story guest
house can be divided into 3 units with variable combinations of
rooms to accommodate up to 10 per unit; kitchenettes, private
entries & decks, BBQ, ½-acre landscaped yard & garden, 2 blocks
to beach, www.sunlightseascape.com

Sunset Cottages   360-579-4445
7359 Maxwelton Rd   2 units, $125–$275
dogs allowed by advance arrangement only, $20/day, 2-bdrm
cottage sleeps 6, 1-bdrm cottage sleeps 5, fenced backyard,
across street to beach, www.whidbeynet.net/beach

Sweetwater Cottage   360-341-1604
6111 S Cultus Bay Rd   1145 units, $150
pet fee $10/day, 2-bdrm cottage, kitchen, sauna, hot tub, on 22
acres with open areas & woods, www.whidbey.com/sweetwater

The Snug on Whidbey   206-612-3011
7905 Blakley   1 unit, $85
1 to 2 dogs allowed with advance approval only, 1-bdrm log cabin
with kitchen sleeps 3, deck, gardens & large yard for walking
dogs, 1 block to nature preserve, 10-minute drive to beach

Whidbey Getaways   206-550-3676
1 to 2 dogs, $50/stay   8 units, $100–$425
cabins & cottages sleep 8, kitchen, hot tub, access to community
swimming pool, short walk to beach, www.whidbeygetaways.com

Whidbey Island Beach Cottage   425-641-2765
7485 Humphrey Rd   1 unit, call for current rates
1 to 2 dogs under 20 lbs only, $10/day, rustic beachfront cabin
with kitchen & loft sleeps 4

Colfax, WA

Best Western Wheatland Inn   509-397-0397
701 N Main St   50 units, $89–$169
dogs under 35 lbs only, $10/stay, coffeemaker, microwave,
refrigerator, continental breakfast, indoor pool, hot tub, fitness
room, lawn, 1 mile to park, www.bestwestern.com/wheatlandinn

Colville, WA

Beaver Lodge Resort   509-684-5657
2430 Hwy 20 E   10 units, $55–$75
each pet $5/day, kitchenette, restaurant, RV & tent sites, lakeside
trails, fishing & swimming, canoes & rowboats available

Benny's Colville Inn   509-684-2517, 800-680-2517
915 S Main St   105 units, $57–$86
pet fee $6/stay, microwave, refrigerator, extended continental
breakfast, indoor pool, hot tub, guest pass to local fitness center,
gravel walking area, ½ block to public park, www.colvilleinn.com

Comfort Inn   509-684-2010, 800-228-5150
166 NE Canning Dr   53 units, $79–$200
pet fee $10/day, microwave, refrigerator, continental breakfast,
indoor pool, hot tub, grassy walking area, 2½ miles to public park,
www.comfortinn.com/hotel/wa717

Selkirk Motel   (509) 684-2565
369 S Main St   17 units, $46–$110
each pet $5/day, coffeemaker, microwave, refrigerator, grassy
walking area, 1½ blocks to public park

Whitetail Inn   509-684-8856
1140 Marble Valley Basin Rd   1 unit, $65–$75
dogs allowed with advance approval only, 2-room log cabin sleeps
2 to 4, kitchenette, hot tub, continental breakfast, on 40 acres for
walking dogs, www.inntravels.com/usa/wa/whitetail.html

Conconully, WA

Deer Haven Lodges   509-826-0108, 888-805-3337
117 N B Ave   3 units, $140–$190
1 to 2 dogs, $25/stay, 2-bdrm to 3-bdrm lodges, lawn for walking
dogs, state park & 2 lakes within 3 blocks, www.2deerhaven.com

Gibson's North Fork Lodge   509-826-1475, 800-555-1690
100 W Boone Ave   5 units, $80
1 to 2 dogs, fully equipped cabins, kitchen, linens provided, BBQ,
fire pit, creekside trails, www.gibsonsnorthforklodge.com

Kozy Kabins & RV Park   509-826-6780, 888-502-2246
111 E Broadway St   7 units, $40–$45
cabins, kitchen, tent sites, walking trails, across street to public
park, 2 lakes within 2 blocks

Conconully, WA (continued)

Liar's Cove Resort   509-826-1288, 800-830-1288
1835 Conconully Rd # A   28 units, $70–$90
lakefront cabins, kitchenette, BBQ, camping & RV sites, grassy
walking area, www.liarscr.com

Shady Pines Resort   509-826-2287, 800-552-2287
125 W Fork Salmon Creek Rd   10 units, $74–$84
1-room cabins, kitchenette, RV sites, large open area for walking
dogs, trail around lake, www.shadypinesresort.com

Concrete, WA

Cascade Mountain Lodge   360-853-8870, 800-251-3054
44618 State Route 20   14 units, $99–$125
pet fee $25/day, coffeemaker, microwave, refrigerator, restaurant,
lounge, large open area for walking dogs, across street to creek &
26-mile-long trail, www.cascademountainlodge.com

Eagles Nest Motel & RV Park   360-853-8662
46346 State Route 20   7 units, $50–$82
dogs allowed with manager's approval only, $10/stay, microwave,
refrigerator, grassy walking area, close to sandbar by river

Ovenell's Heritage Inn & Log Cabins   360-853-8494
46276 Concrete Sauk Valley Rd   866-464-3414
1 to 2 dogs, $10-$20/day   7 units, $135–$145
lodge rooms-cabins-guesthouse, full breakfast, on 580-acre cattle
ranch, 3/4 mile to river, www.ovenells-inn.com

Connell, WA

M & M Motel   509-234-8811, 800-353-9981
730 S Columbia Ave   43 units, $61–$74
each pet $5/day, microwave, refrigerator, continental breakfast,
large open walking area, 2 blocks to walking trail, 4 blocks to
public park

Tumbleweed Motel   509-234-2081
433 S Columbia Ave   20 units, $35–$60
coffeemaker, microwave, refrigerator, seasonal pool, grassy area
for walking dogs, trail, 2 blocks to public park,
www.cityofconnell.com/dt/profiles/info.php?id=39

Copalis Beach, WA

Beachwood Resort   360-289-2177
3009 State Route 109   18 units, $95–$155
pet fee $13/day, kitchen, outdoor pool, sauna, hot tub, small pet
walking area on 10 acres, short drive to walking trail

Iron Springs Resort   360-276-4230
3707 State Hwy 109   28 units, $60–$160
pet fee $20/day, rustic oceanview cottages, kitchen or kitchenette,
indoor & outdoor pools, http://ironspringsresort.tripod.com

Cougar, WA

Lone Fir Resort   360-238-5210
16806 Lewis River Rd   17 units, $55–$85
1 to 2 dogs, $10/day, kitchen or coffeemaker-microwave-
refrigerator, restaurant, seasonal pool, covered fire pit, children's
play area, RV sites, walking trail, www.lonefirresort.com

Coulee City, WA

Ala Cozy Motel   509-632-5703, 877-678-2918
9988 Hwy 2 E   11 units, $57–$77
each pet $10/day, coffeemaker, microwave, refrigerator, small pet
walking area, ½ mile to lakefront park, www.alacozymotel.com

Banks Lake Lodge   509-632-5596
109 N 6th St   13 units, $50–$75
pet fee $10/stay, kitchen or coffeemaker-microwave-refrigerator,
BBQ, fire pit, picnic tables, horseshoes, camping & RV sites, lawn,
walking trail, 3 blocks to lakeside park, www.bankslakelodge.com

Blue Lake Resort   509-632-5364, 877-287-7937
31199 Hwy 17 N   10 units, $50–$85
each pet $5/day, rustic cabins, full kitchen or refrigerator, RV &
tent sites, boat & pedal boat rentals, open field for walking dogs,
5 miles to public park, www.bluelakeresortwashington.com

Sun Lakes Park Resort   509-632-5291
34228 Park Lake Rd NE   169 units, $70–$169
each pet $10/day, cabins & mobile homes sleep up to 8, kitchenette,
outdoor pool, RV & tent sites, convenience store, gift shop, 9-hole
golf course & mini-golf, boat & pedal boat rental, waterfront
walking area, www.sunlakesparkresort.com

Coulee Dam, WA

Coulee House Inn & Suites   509-633-1101, 800-715-7767
110 Roosevelt Way   61 units, $54–$120
each pet $20/day, full kitchen or coffeemaker-microwave-
refrigerator, indoor pool, hot tub, fitness room, guest pass to local
fitness center, overlooking Grand Coulee Dam, near walking trails,
www.couleehouse.com

Coupeville, WA

Eagle's Aerie B & B   360-678-2217
dogs allowed with advance approval only   1 unit, $125
large studio with private entrance sleeps up to 4, coffeemaker,
refrigerator, continental breakfast, hot tub, on 14 acres inside
national historical reserve, trail to beach, www.eagleaerie.net

Jenne Farm Gathering House   360-678-4433
538 S Engle Rd   1 unit, $300–$500
well-behaved dogs allowed with advance approval, $50/stay,
4-bdrm 1908 farmhouse sleeps 10, on 146-acre working farm,
walking trails, close to beaches, www.jennefarm.homestead.com

Morris Farm House Bed & Breakfast   360-678-0939
105 W Morris Rd   866-440-1555
1 to 2 dogs, $7/day each pet   6 units, $85–$200
on 10 acres of landscaped gardens & walking paths in old growth
forest, www.morrisfarmhouse.com

Tyee Motel & Restaurant   360-678-6616
405 S Main St   9 units, $65–$80
pet fee $10/stay, restaurant, lounge, lawn for walking dogs,
2 blocks to walking trail, 1 mile to waterfront, www.tyeehotel.com

Willow Pond Lodge & Lake House   206-283-0746
dogs allowed with advance approval only   2 units, $500–$800
5-bdrm vacation homes sleep 15 to 20, on 60 acres with meadows-
ponds-hiking trails, www.willowpondlodge.com

Curlew, WA

Wolfgang's Riverview Inn   509-779-4252
2320 Hwy 21 N   4 units, $45–$60
full kitchen or coffeemaker-microwave-refrigerator, grocery store,
open field for walking dogs, trail to river, 2 miles to sandy beach on
river, www.wolfgangsriverviewinn.com

Cusick, WA

Blueslide Resort   509-445-1327
400041 State Route 20   9 units, $95–$115
pet fee $5/day, 1-bdrm to 2-bdrm cabins, kitchen, seasonal pool,
RV & tent sites, convenience store, on 8 riverside acres for walking
dogs, www.blueslideresort.com

Darrington, WA

Darrington Motor Inn   360-436-1776
1100 Seemann St   20 units, $49–$59
small dogs only, $10/day, kitchenette or microwave & refrigerator,
continental breakfast, pet walking area, across street to public park

Davenport, WA

Black Bear Motel   509-725-7700
30 Logan St   10 units, $50
dogs allowed with advance approval, $5/day, "Old West" theme-
decorated rooms, microwave, refrigerator, across street to park

Deer Meadows Motel   509-725-8425
41499 Gopher Lane N   16 units, $65–$75
pet fee $5/day, coffeemaker, restaurant, lounge, road around golf
course for walking dogs

Dayton, WA

Blue Mountain Motel   509-382-3040
414 W Main St   22 units, $44–$90
pet fee $10/stay, microwave, refrigerator, designated pet walking
area, 1 block to fairgrounds, 3 blocks to a 2-mile-long walking trail,
www.bluemountainmotel.net

Dayton Motel   509-382-4503
110 S Pine St   17 units, $40–$70
pet fee $8/day, kitchenette or coffeemaker, large open area for
walking dogs

Purple House B & B   509-382-3159, 800-486-2574
415 E Clay St   4 units, $95–$135
dogs under 15 lbs allowed by advance arrangement only, $15/day,
shared bath or private bath, kitchen & Japanese soaking tub in one
suite, full breakfast, picnic lunches & dinners also available,
outdoor pool, lawn, 4 blocks to park, www.purplehousebnb.com

Dayton, WA (continued)

Weinhard Hotel   509-382-4032
235 E Main St   15 units, $125–$180
each pet $20/stay, Victorian hotel, continental breakfast, walking trail, 5 blocks to park, 5 miles to state park, www.weinhard.com

Deer Harbor, WA

Deer Harbor Inn   360-376-4110, 877-377-4110
33 Inn Lane   13 units, $139–$385
each pet $15/day, 2-bdrm to 3-bdrm cottages & vacation homes, full kitchen, full breakfast, restaurant, hot tub, on 6 acres for walking dogs, ½ mile to beach & marina, www.deerharborinn.com

Maggie's Manor & Gnome House   360-376-2480
1 small dog allowed with advance reservation   3 units, $135–$375
4-bdrm 2-bath Manor House sleeps 8, alpine-chalet-style Gnome House sleeps 6, also 2-bdrm Seaside Cottage, kitchen, hot tub, on 140 acres with wildlife preserve, www.orcas-island-rentals.com

Place at Cayou Cove   360-376-3199, 888-596-7222
Olympic Lodge Lane   3 units, $195–$525
1 to 2 dogs, pet fee $25/day for 1st pet, $15/day for 2nd pet, secluded cottages, kitchen, private hot tub, full breakfast delivered to your door, on 5 waterfront acres, www.cayoucove.com

Deming, WA

Mount Baker Lodging & Properties   360-599-2453
7463 Mt Baker Hwy   800-709-7669
    18 units, $159–$289
rustic cabins to 4-bdrm executive vacation homes, private hot tubs, some have access to community swimming pools, close to national forest for walking dogs, www.mtbakerlodging.com

Dupont, WA

GuestHouse International Inn & Suites   253-912-8900
1609 McNeil St   800-214-8378
each pet $10/day   60 units, $135–$170
kitchenette or coffeemaker-microwave-refrigerator, extended continental breakfast, indoor pool, hot tub, fitness room, next to walking path, www.guesthouseintl.com/location-WA-DuPont.htm

East Wenatchee, WA

Cedars Inn	509-886-8000, 800-358-2074
80 9th St NE	94 units, $69–$150

pet fee $10/day, coffeemaker, microwave, refrigerator, full breakfast, indoor pool, hot tub, fitness room, across street to walking trail, www.eastwenatcheecedarsinn.com

Inn at the River	509-888-7378, 800-920-5406
580 Valley Mall Parkway	54 units, $45–$140

coffeemaker, microwave, refrigerator, continental breakfast, outdoor pool, hot tub, riverfront park & walkway, www.innattheriver.com

Easton, WA

CB's Motel & General Store	509-656-2248
1781 Railroad St	3 units, $70

1 to 2 dogs allowed with manager's approval, $5/day each pet, microwave, refrigerator, large walking area, 3/4 mile to public park

Silver Ridge Ranch	509-656-0275, 877-656-0275
182 Silver Ridge Ranch Rd	7 units, $80–$95

pet fee $10/day, dogs allowed in 1 lodge room only, full breakfast, kitchen for guest use, RV & tent sites, corrals for guests' horses, open field, hiking & riding trails, www.silverridgeranch.com

Eastsound, WA

Beach House at Massacre Bay	360-376-3733
2098 Deer Harbor Rd	2 units, $175–$215

each pet $10/day, full kitchen or coffeemaker-microwave-refrigerator, picnic table, hot tub, lawn, private beach, close to hiking trails, www.massacrebay.net

Blue Heron Bed & Breakfast	360-376-4198
982 Deer Harbor Rd	4 units, $95–$170

each pet $15/day, full breakfast, private deck, basket of pet supplies provided, 2 fenced yards, across street to beach access, public boat mooring, 15-minute drive to off-leash dog park, www.orcasblueheron.com

North Beach Inn	360-376-2660
650 Gibson Rd	13 units, $135–$210

1 to 2 dogs, $10/day each pet, fully equipped beachfront studios to 3-bdrm cottages, on 90 acres of woods & fields, 1/3-mile-long sand & pebble beach frontage, www.northbeachinn.com

Eastsound, WA (continued)

North Shore Cottages   360-376-5131, 866-743-3738
271 Sunset Ave   5 units, $220–$370
fully equipped waterfront cottages, full kitchen or coffeemaker-microwave-refrigerator, private hot tub, sauna, lawn & woods, ½ mile to off-leash dog park, www.northshore4kiss.com

Pebble Cove Farm   360-376-6161
3341 Deer Harbor Rd   2 units, $125–$225
dogs under 12 lbs only, $15/stay each pet, private waterfront suites, kitchenette, continental breakfast, resident farm animals, beachfront grassy walking area, www.pebblecovefarm.com

Sleeping Sea   360-376-7035
412 Eastman Rd   11 units, $125–$185
dogs allowed with advance approval, $35-$75/stay, suites & cottages with kitchen sleep up to 4, located on 35-acre organic farm emphasizing "eco-sustainable lifestyle"; 4-bdrm 3-bath Victorian beach home sleeps 12, on 1½ acres with boardwalk over wetlands to private beach; 1-bdrm cottage with full kitchen & deck plus separate 1-bdrm suite, located on hillside above Friday Harbor within walking distance of waterfront, www.sleepingsea.com

West Beach Resort   360-376-2240, 877-937-8224
190 Waterfront Way   18 units, $135–$245
dogs allowed by advance arrangement only, $18/day each pet, waterfront cabins, full kitchen or microwave & refrigerator, hot tub, RV & tent sites, list of island's dog-friendly activities available, 3 miles to off-leash dog park, www.westbeachresort.com

Windermere Real Estate Orcas Island   360-376-8000
18 Haven Rd   800-842-5770
1 to 2 dogs, $35/day   65+ units, $170–$843
fully equipped vacation homes on the waterfront or in the country, most with yard, close to walking trails, www.orcas-island.com

Eatonville, WA

Mill Village Motel   360-832-3200, 800-832-3248
210 Center St E   32 units, $80–$90
pet fee $10/stay, coffeemaker, microwave, refrigerator, continental breakfast, grassy walking area, across street to open field, www.whitepasstravel.com/millvillage.htm

Edmonds, WA

Best Western Edmonds Harbor Inn   425-771-5021
130 W Dayton St   800-441-8033
each pet $20/day   91 units, $120–$190
coffeemaker, microwave, refrigerator, continental breakfast,
seasonal pool, hot tub, fitness room, pet sitting service, walking
trail, near pet-friendly beach, www.bestwestern.com/prop_48168

Travelodge Seattle North/Edmonds   425-771-8008
23825 Hwy 99   800-771-8009
1 to 2 dogs under 60 lbs only, $25/stay   58 units, $64–$90
coffeemaker, microwave, refrigerator, continental breakfast, hot
tub, fitness room, lawn, 5-minute drive to waterfront,
www.travelodge.com/hotel/09538

Ellensburg, WA

4 W Ranch & Guest Cabins   509-933-2738, 888-497-2624
11670 Manastash Rd   2 units, $140–$150
each pet $10/day, cabins with kitchen, large open walking area,
horses welcome too, next to national forest, www.4wranch.net

Best Western Lincoln Inn & Suites   509-925-4244
211 W Umptanum Rd   866-925-4288
pets under 25 lbs only, $25/day each pet   55 units, $90–$150
coffeemaker, microwave, refrigerator, continental breakfast,
outdoor pool, hot tub, fitness room,
www.bestwestern.com/lincolninnandsuites

Comfort Inn   509-925-7037, 800-424-6423
1722 Canyon Rd   52 units, $69–$139
each pet $10/stay, microwave, refrigerator, continental breakfast,
indoor pool, hot tub, guest pass to local fitness center, lawn,
1/2 mile to lakeside park, www.comfortinn.com/hotel/wa069

Holiday Inn Express   509-962-9400, 800-664-9491
1620 Canyon Rd   66 units, $129–$145
pet fee $10/day, coffeemaker, extended continental breakfast, indoor
pool, hot tub, fitness center, www.hiexpress.com/ellensburgwa

I-90 Inn Motel   509-925-9844
1390 N Dolarway Rd   70 units, $62
pet fee $15/stay, coffeemaker, microwave, refrigerator, continental
breakfast, picnic tables, lakefront walking area, www.i-90inn.com

Ellensburg, WA

Nites Inn Motel   509-962-9600, 800-695-8284
1200 S Ruby St   32 units, $65–$72
pet fee $9/stay, coffeemaker, microwave, refrigerator, continental breakfast, riverfront trail, 1/2 mile to park, www.nitesinnmotel.com

Quality Inn & Conference Center   509-925-9800
1700 Canyon Rd   506 units, $78–$109
1 to 2 dogs, $10/stay, coffeemaker, microwave, refrigerator, restaurant, lounge, indoor pool, children's wading pool, fitness room, courtyard for walking dogs, 1/2 mile to public park, www.qualityinn.com/hotel/wa208

Super 8 Motel   509-962-6888
1500 Canyon Rd   102 units, $68–$99
pet fee $10/stay, coffeemaker, continental breakfast, indoor pool, hot tub, open field, 1 mile to public park, www.super8.com

Thunderbird Motel   509-962-5585
403 W University Way   72 units, $60–$100
each pet $10/day, microwave, refrigerator, seasonal pool, grassy walking area, 10-minute drive to waterfront walking area

Elma, WA

Parkhurst Motel   360-482-2541
208 E Main St   14 units, $70
full kitchen or coffeemaker-microwave-refrigerator, fenced yard, open grassy area for walking dogs, 1/4 mile to public park

Enumclaw, WA

King's Valu Inn   360-825-1626, 888-886-5118
1334 Roosevelt Ave E   44 units, $55–$85
dogs allowed with manager's approval only, $10/day each pet, kitchenette or coffeemaker, seasonal pool, www.kingsvaluinn.com

Ephrata, WA

Best Western Rama Inn   509-754-7111, 888-726-2466
1818 Basin St SW   46 units, $95–$170
pet fee $25/stay, coffeemaker, microwave, refrigerator, continental breakfast, indoor pool, sauna, steam room, hot tub, large walking area, 1/2 mile to public park, www.bestwestern.com/ramainn

Ephrata Inn   509-754-3575, 877-454-3575
848 Basin St SW   24 units, $35
dogs under 30 lbs only, $10/day, microwave, refrigerator, BBQ,
continental breakfast, 5-minute drive to park, www.ephratainn.com

Travelodge   509-754-4651, 800-578-7878
31 Basin St SW   28 units, $51–$60
each pet $10/day, coffeemaker, microwave, refrigerator,
continental breakfast, seasonal pool, grassy walking area,
www.travelodge.com/hotel/07055

Everett, WA

Days Inn Seattle/Everett   425-355-1570
1602 SE Everett Mall Way   76 units, $70–$120
pet fee $20/stay, coffeemaker, microwave, refrigerator, continental
breakfast, seasonal pool, 10-minute drive to off-leash dog park,
20-minute drive to beach park, www.daysinn.com/hotel/14457

Extended Stay Deluxe Everett/Silver Lake   425-337-1341
1431 112th St SE   800-398-7829
small dogs allowed with advance approval   88 units, $109–$114
$25/day ($150 maximum), kitchenette, extended continental
breakfast, BBQ, seasonal pool, grassy walking area, 3/4 mile to
lakefront walking trail, www.extendedstaydeluxe.com/esl

Extended StayAmerica   425-355-1923, 800-398-7829
8410 Broadway   109 units, $99–$110
pet fee $25/day ($150 maximum), kitchenette, extended
continental breakfast, 3/4 mile to waterfront park,
www.extendedstayamerica.com/evr

Holiday Inn Downtown   425-339-2000, 866-700-1188
3105 Pine St   250 units, $123–$159
pet fee $40/stay, extended continental breakfast, restaurant,
lounge, indoor pool, hot tub, fitness room, across street to grassy
area for walking dogs, 7-minute walk to park, www.hieverett.com

Inn at Port Gardner   425-252-6779, 888-252-6779
1700 W Marine View Dr   33 units, $90–$190
dogs under 50 lbs only, $25/day each pet, microwave, refrigerator,
continental breakfast delivered to your door, pet bedding-sheet-
treats provided, lawn for walking dogs, close to waterfront &
boardwalk, www.innatportgardner.com

Everett, WA (continued)

La Quinta Inn   425-347-9099, 800-434-9204
12619 4th Ave W   73 units, $84–$94
coffeemaker, continental breakfast, outdoor pool, hot tub,
walking trail, www.lq.com

Motel 6 North   425-347-2060
10006 Evergreen Way   118 units, $60–$75
microwave, refrigerator, coffee in lobby, outdoor pool, lawn,
10-minute walk to public park, www.motel6.com

Motel 6 South   425-353-8120
224 128th St SW   100 units, $60–$66
coffee in lobby, lawn for walking dogs, across highway to walking
trail, 4 blocks to public park, www.motel6.com

Travelodge   425-259-6141, 800-884-7083
3030 Broadway   29 units, $45–$75
each pet $5/day, coffeemaker, microwave, refrigerator, continental
breakfast, restaurant, lounge, outdoor pool, hot tub, fitness room,
1 block to park, www.travelodge.com/hotel/09451

Federal Way, WA

Clarion Hotel   253-941-6000, 877-315-1880
31611 20th Ave S   116 units, $99–$159
1 to 2 dogs under 25 lbs only, $25/stay, microwave, refrigerator,
full breakfast, lounge, seasonal pool, hot tub, guest pass to local
fitness center, grassy walking area, 3 blocks to public park,
www.clarionhotel.com/hotel/wa214

Comfort Inn   253-529-0101, 877-821-8618
31622 Pacific Hwy S   117 units, $69–$149
1 to 2 dogs under 80 lbs only, $10/day, coffeemaker, microwave,
refrigerator, extended continental breakfast, indoor pool, hot tub,
fitness room, pet walking area, close to park, 6 blocks to lake,
www.comfortinn.com/hotel/wa114

Days Inn   253-838-3164
34827 Pacific Hwy S   54 units, $60–$96
1 to 2 dogs under 30 lbs only, $20 for 1st day, $5 each additional
day, microwave, refrigerator, continental breakfast, guest pass to
local fitness center, parking lot for walking dogs, 5-minute drive to
public park, www.daysinn.com/hotel/17657

Econolodge   253-838-7700
1505 S 328th St   45 units, $60–$75
1 to 2 dogs, $10/day each pet, coffeemaker, microwave,
refrigerator, continental breakfast, paved walking area, short walk
to public park, www.econolodge.com/hotel/wa168

Extended StayAmerica   253-946-0553
1400 S 320th St   104 units, $70–$90
pet fee $25/day ($150 maximum), suites with kitchenette, paved
walking area, 1/2 mile to park, www.extendedstayamerica.com/862

New Horizon Motel   253-838-0762
33002 Pacific Hwy S   50 units, $50–$60
1 to 2 dogs, $25/stay, kitchenette, lawn for walking dogs,
3 blocks to public park

Quality Inn & Suites   253-835-4141
1400 S 348th St   65 units, $90–$135
1 to 2 dogs under 40 lbs only, $20/stay each pet, kitchenette,
continental breakfast, indoor pool, hot tub, fitness room, next to
vacant lot for walking dogs, 1½ miles to public park,
www.qualityinn.com/hotel/wa134

Super 8 Motel   253-838-8808, 800-800-8000
1688 S 348th St   90 units, $76
pet fee $20/stay, coffeemaker, refrigerator, continental breakfast,
small pet walking area, 1/2 mile to public park & aquatic center
with walking paths, www.super8.com

Ferndale, WA

Super 8 Motel   360-384-8881, 800-800-8000
5788 Barrett Rd   78 units, $77–$104
1 to 2 dogs, $15/stay, coffeemaker, microwave, refrigerator,
continental breakfast, indoor pool, hot tub, large yard for walking
dogs, 2 miles to public park, www.super8.com

Fife, WA

Baymont Inn & Suites   253-922-2500
5805 Pacific Hwy E   96 units, $65–$130
1 to 3 dogs, $10/day each pet, coffeemaker, microwave,
refrigerator, extended continental breakfast, hot tub, fitness room,
large open area for walking dogs, 1 mile to public park, 10-minute
drive to waterfront, www.guesthousefife.com

Fife, WA (continued)

Econo Lodge Inn & Suites   253-922-9520, 877-982-3781
3100 Pacific Hwy E   108 units, $60–$70
1 to 2 dogs under 50 lbs only, $10/day, coffeemaker, microwave,
refrigerator, continental breakfast, outdoor pool, small walking
area, 3 miles to park, www.econolodge.com/hotel/wa154

Emerald Queen Hotel & Casino   253-922-2000
5700 Pacific Hwy E   888-831-7655
pet fee $25/stay   139 units, $77–$109
coffeemaker, restaurant, lounge, small pet walking area,
3 miles to waterfront park, www.emeraldqueen.com

Extended StayAmerica   253-926-6316, 800-398-7829
2820 Pacific Hwy E   104 units, $70–$90
pet fee $25 ($150 maximum), kitchenette, small pet walking area,
5-minute drive to public park, www.extendedstayamerica.com/867

Howard Johnson Inn   253-926-1000
3501 Pacific Hwy E   96 units, $72–$171
pet fee $10/day, coffeemaker, microwave, refrigerator, continental
breakfast, fitness room, parking lot for walking dogs, 1/2 mile to
waterfront, 3 miles to public park, www.hojo.com/hotel/11154

Motel 6 Tacoma/Fife   253-922-1270, 800-466-8356
5201 20th St E   119 units, $40–$67
microwave, refrigerator, coffee in lobby, seasonal pool, lawn for
walking dogs, 5 miles to public park, www.motel6.com

Norman Bates Motel of Fife   253-922-5421
4221 Pacific Hwy E   26 units, $55–$65
1 to 2 dogs under 30 lbs only, $10/stay, microwave, refrigerator,
grassy walking area, 10-minute drive to public park

Quality Inn   253-926-2301, 800-424-6423
5601 Pacific Hwy E   68 units, $75–$135
1 to 2 dogs under 50 lbs only, $15 each pet for 1st day, $10 each pet
for each additional day, coffeemaker, microwave, refrigerator,
continental breakfast, parking lot for walking dogs, 5-minute drive
to open field, www.qualityinn.com/hotel/WA043

Sunshine Motel   253-926-0937
3801 Pacific Hwy E   40 units, $50–$80
small dogs only, $5/day, full kitchen or microwave & refrigerator,
lawn, 1 block to park, 3 blocks to river, www.sunshinemotel.us

Travelodge Port of Tacoma   253-922-0550
3518 Pacific Hwy E   79 units, $50–$60
pet fee $15/day, coffeemaker, microwave, refrigerator, continental
breakfast, small lawn for walking dogs, 2 miles to public park,
15-minute drive to state park, www.travelodge.com/hotel/14892

Forks, WA

A Cozy River House   360-374-4046, 866-543-4166
Steelhead Ave   2 units, $195–$235
3-bdrm vacation homes sleep up to 12, deck overlooking river,
BBQ, fire pit, fish cleaning station, www.acozyriverhouse.com

A Getaway Log Cabin   360-640-8902
dogs allowed with manager's approval only   1 unit, $230–$250
$20/day each pet, 3-bdrm 2-bath chalet sleeps 12, deck, fire pit,
RV sites, on 32 acres, trails & creek, www.agetawaylogcabin.com

Bagby's Town Motel   360-374-6231, 800-742-2429
1080 S Forks Ave   20 units, $45–$53
dogs allowed with advance approval only, $6/day each pet, coffee
in lobby, BBQ, picnic tables, large yard, landscaped gardens,
close to beaches-trails-state parks, www.bagbystownmotel.com

Brightwater House B & B   360-374-5453
440 Brightwater Dr   4 units, $115–$125
each pet $10/day, kitchenette, continental breakfast, courtyard &
large yard, on 60 secluded acres with 3/4-mile river frontage,
www.brightwaterhouse.com

Dew Drop Inn   360-374-4055, 888-433-9376
100 Fernhill Rd   24 units, $64–$81
pet fee $11/stay, coffeemaker, microwave, refrigerator, continental
breakfast, private balconies or patios, large open area for walking
dogs, 1/4 mile to public park, www.dewdropinnmotel.com

Forks Motel   360-374-6243, 800-544-3416
351 S Forks Ave   73 units, $52–$150
each pet $15/day, kitchenette, outdoor pool, grassy walking area,
1/2 mile to park, 20-minute drive to beaches, www.forksmotel.com

Hoh Humm Ranch   360-374-5337
171763 Hwy 101   3 units, $40–$70
each pet $5/day, full breakfast, guest use of kitchen, riverside
walking area, on 200-acre ranch, www.olypen.com/hohhumm

Forks, WA (continued)

Kalaloch Lodge   360-962-2271, 866-525-2562
157151 Hwy 101   64 units, $181–$299
pet fee $15/day, rustic cabins with kitchenette sleep 2 to 7, RV &
tent sites, restaurant, short walk to beach, www.visitkalaloch.com

Manitou Lodge B & B   360-374-6295
813 Kilmer Rd   7 units, $99–$159
pet fee $10/day, full breakfast, on 10 wooded acres for walking
dogs, 4 miles to pet-friendly beach, www.manitoulodge.com

Miller Tree Inn   360-374-6806, 800-943-6563
654 E Division St   8 units, $90–$195
pet fee $10/day, kitchenette, full breakfast, hot tub, large yard for
walking dogs, 20-minute drive to beach, www.millertreeinn.com

Olson's Vacation Cabin   360-374-3142
2423 Mora Rd   1 unit, $80
pet fee $10/day, fully equipped 1-bdrm cabin with kitchen, BBQ,
landscaped & fenced yard, secluded 4-acre meadow for walking
dogs, 2 miles to beach & park, www.olsonscabin.com

Olympic Suites   360-374-5400, 800-262-3433
800 Olympic Dr   33 units, $54–$119
1 to 2 dogs allowed with advance approval only, $10/day, 1-bdrm to
2-bdrm suites, full kitchen, gravel walking area, 1 mile to public
park & trails, 14 miles to ocean, www.olympicsuitesinn.com

Sol Duc Cabin Fever   360-374-6481
198 Shuwah Rd   1 unit, $89–$109
1 to 2 dogs allowed with advance approval, $25/stay, 1-room cabin
sleeps 4, covered porch, BBQ, doggie day care available, large
yard, 2-minute walk to river, www.solduccabinfever.com

Three Rivers Resort   360-374-5300
7764 LaPush Rd   6 units, $59–$99
each pet $10/day, 1-bdrm to 2-bdrm cabins, kitchenette, RV & tent
sites, restaurant, groceries & gasoline, large open area for walking
dogs, 1 block to river, 4 miles to ocean beaches,
www.forks-web.com/threerivers/lodging.htm

Twilight Eclipse Cabin 360-374-6781
each pet $10/day 1 unit, $120–$150
creekside cabin with kitchen, BBQ, doggie day care available,
gravel & grassy walking areas, close to hiking trail,
www.searchforks.com/haags-cabin.html

Freeland, WA

A Tuscan Lady Vacation Rental 360-331-5057
619 Dolphin Dr 2 units, $120–$179
1 dog under 20 lbs allowed by advance arrangement only, $30/day
($100 maximum), 2-bdrm-plus-loft cottage, 3-bdrm cottage, self-
serve breakfast, gardens, 1 block to beach, www.atuscanlady.com

Harbour Inn Motel 360-331-6900
1606 E Main St 20 units, $87–$115
1 to 2 dogs, $15/day, kitchenette, continental breakfast, picnic
tables, on 2 acres of lawn & trees, 5 blocks to waterfront park,
2 miles to off-leash beach, www.harbourinnmotel.com

Island Getaways 360-331-7707
397 Cardinal Way 3 units, $150–$250
1 to 2 pets allowed with advance approval, $30/stay, cottages,
kitchen, private hot tub, BBQ, lawn for walking dogs, 1 block to
beach, www.whidbeynet.net/getaways

Tara Vacation Rentals 360-331-7100, 800-260-4158
18205 State Route 525 Suite 5 30 units, $150–$600
dogs under 20 lbs only, $25/day each pet, fully equipped cabins-
cottages-vacation homes, beach access, www.whidbeyvacation.com

Friday Harbor, WA

Argyle House B & B 360-378-4084, 800-624-3459
685 Argyle Ave 5 units, $100–$250
dogs allowed in cottage with advance approval only, full breakfast,
hot tub, lawn for walking dogs, 1/4 mile to off-leash dog park,
www.argylehouse.net

Elements San Juan Islands Hotel & Spa 360-378-4000
410 Spring St 800-793-4756
each pet $15/day 72 units, $137–$314
coffeemaker, microwave, refrigerator, indoor pool, sauna, hot tub,
fitness room, day spa, grassy walking area, 3 blocks to off-leash
dog park, 4 blocks to harbor, www.hotelelements.com

Friday Harbor, WA (continued)

Harrison House Suites   360-378-3587, 800-407-7933
235 C St   5 units, $115–$375
1 to 2 dogs, $25/day, suites with private outdoor jacuzzi tubs, also
communal hot tub, full kitchen or coffeemaker & microwave, full
breakfast, grassy walking area, ½ block to public park, 1 block to
ferry, www.harrisonhousesuites.com

Lakedale Resort & Campground   360-378-2350, 800-617-2267
4313 Roche Harbor Rd   9 units, $189–$339
1 to 4 dogs, $25/stay each pet, 2-bdrm cabins, kitchen, large deck,
BBQ, picnic tables, hot tub, on 82 acres for walking dogs, ½ mile
to public park, www.lakedale.com

San Juan Escapes Vacation Homes 509-852-0200, 800-324-8115
9614 Rainier Ave S, Seattle WA 98118   3 units, $300–$800
fully equipped vacation homes located on San Juan Island
www.sanjuanescapes.com

Sandpiper Condominiums   360-378-5610
250 Tucker Ave   10 units, $69–$119
1 to 2 dogs, $10/stay each pet, studios & 1-bdrm condos, kitchen,
seasonal pool, hot tub, grassy & gravel walking areas, 3 miles to
off-leash dog park, www.sandpiper-condos.com

Snug Harbor Marina Resort   360-378-4762
1997 Mitchell Bay Rd   10 units, $129–$239
1 to 2 dogs, $20/day each pet, waterfront cabins, full kitchen or
coffeemaker-microwave-refrigerator, BBQ, beach access, grassy
walking area, 5-minute drive to beach, www.snugresort.com

Trumpeter Inn B & B   360-378-3884, 800-826-7926
318 Trumpeter Way   7 units, $110–$175
small dogs preferred but dogs over 50 lbs may be allowed with
advance approval, $25/stay, full breakfast, private patio, guest use
of kitchen, hot tub, on 5 acres with pond & meadows for walking
dogs, 4 miles to off-leash dog park, www.trumpeterinn.com

Tucker House B & B   360-378-2783
260 B St   5 units, $99–$350
1 to 2 dogs, $25/stay, dogs allowed in 3 cottages, kitchenette or
microwave & refrigerator, full breakfast, hot tub, grassy walking
area, ½ mile to public park, www.tuckerhouse.com

Wayfarer's Rest   360-378-6428
35 Malcolm St   5 units, $70–$80
pet fee $10/stay, private rooms or shared dormitory rooms, shared
bath, linens provided, common room with fully equipped kitchen
for guest use, gardens, short walk to open field, ½ mile to
off-leash dog park, www.rockisland.com/~wayfarersrest

Windermere Vacation Rentals   360-378-3601, 800-391-8190
100 1st St   80 units, $230–$840
pet fee $35/day, condos & vacation homes located on Orcas Island-
San Juan Island-Lopez Island-Friday Harbor, BBQ, hot tub, deck,
close to waterfront & trails, www.windermeresji.com

Fruitland, WA

White Willow Motel & Camp   509-722-3640
6161 Hwy 25 S   15 units, $55–$85
1 to 2 dogs, $8/day, coffeemaker, microwave, refrigerator, on 60
wooded acres with walking trails, 5 miles to Fort Spokane &
Lake Roosevelt, www.whitewillowmotel.com

Gig Harbor, WA

Best Western Wesley Inn   253-858-9690, 888-462-0002
6575 Kimball Dr   81 units, $139–$280
1 to 2 dogs, $10/day each pet, coffeemaker, microwave,
refrigerator, continental breakfast, seasonal pool, hot tub, guest
pass to local fitness center, dog treats, small pet walking area,
1 block to trail, ½ mile to park, www.wesleyinn.com

Cottage at Gig Harbor   253-509-0064
7614 Pioneer Way   1 unit, $125–$195
pet fee $10/day, 2-bdrm cottage sleeps 4, full kitchen, patio,
2 blocks to harbor, www.gigharborcottage.com

Harborside B & B   253-851-1795
8708 Goodman Dr NW   1 unit, $100–$125
dogs under 20 lbs only, waterfront suite sleeps 3, kitchen, large
yard, ½ mile to off-leash dog park, 1 mile to harbor

Inn at Gig Harbor   253-858-1111, 800-795-9980
3211 56th St NW   64 units, $154
pet fee $5/stay, coffeemaker, microwave, refrigerator, continental
breakfast, restaurant, lounge, hot tub, fitness room, grassy walking
area, 2 miles to harbor & park, www.innatgigharbor.com

Gig Harbor, WA (continued)

No Cabbages B & B   253-858-7797
10319 Sunrise Beach Dr NW   3 units, $80–$135
full breakfast, on 1,000 acres for off-leash walking, "prayer
labyrinth" meditation path thru the woods, short walk to beach
park, www.nocabbages.com

Old Glencove Hotel B & B   253-884-2835
9418 Glencove Road Kp N   4 units, $75–$95
coffeemaker, microwave, refrigerator, full breakfast, waterfront
walking area, 7 miles to public parks, www.glencovehotel.com

Westwynd Motel   253-857-4047, 800-468-9963
6703 144th St NW   24 units, $44–$72
kitchen, children's play area, lawn for walking dogs, 1 block to
bayfront, ¼ mile to public beach, www.westwyndmotel.com

Glacier, WA

The Logs at Canyon Creek   360-599-2711
7577 Canyon View Dr   7 units, $125–$300
each pet $5/day, 2-bdrm log cabins, 2-bdrm to 3-bdrm vacation
homes sleep up to 10, full kitchen or coffeemaker & refrigerator,
grassy walking area, 5-minute walk to creek & trails,
www.thelogs.com

Glenwood, WA

Flying L Ranch Country Inn   509-364-3488
25 Flying L Lane   16 units, $165–$190
1 to 2 dogs allowed with advance approval only, $15/stay, cabins
sleep 4 to 6, kitchen, continental breakfast, hot tub, picnic area,
off-leash dog walking area, on 80 acres with pond, several miles of
marked trails, www.mt-adams.com

Gold Bar, WA

Steven's Pass Motel   360-793-6633
809 Croft Ave   18 units, $44–$88
dogs allowed with manager's approval only, $10/day each pet,
BBQ, small pet walking area, short drive to hiking trail,
www.stevenspassmotel.com

Goldendale, WA

Ponderosa Motel   509-773-5842
775 E Broadway St   38 units, $60–$90
pet fee $10-$15/day, kitchenette or coffeemaker-microwave-
refrigerator, continental breakfast, small pet walking area,
3 blocks to public park

Quality Inn & Suites   509-773-5881
808 E Simcoe Dr   48 units, $85–$120
1 to 2 dogs, $10/day each pet, coffeemaker, microwave,
refrigerator, restaurant, seasonal pool, picnic area, open field,
3/4 mile to park, www.qualityinn.com/hotel/wa178

Graham, WA

Sky Song B & B Retreat   253-875-7775
10006 255th St Ct E   3 units, $75
1 to 2 dogs, coffeemaker, microwave, refrigerator, full breakfast,
private entrance to living room, den, deck, on 6 acres with 1-acre
garden area, 2 miles to public park, www.skysongbandb.com

Grand Coulee, WA

Grand Coulee Center Lodge   509-633-2860, 866-633-2860
404 Spokane Way   32 units, $49–$145
dogs allowed with advance approval only, $10/day, full kitchen or
coffeemaker-microwave-refrigerator, continental breakfast, BBQ,
gift shop, grassy walking area, 1 mile to public park, 2 state parks
within 5 miles, www.grandcouleemotel.com

Trail West Motel   509-633-3155, 866-633-8157
108 Spokane Way   26 units, $55–$120
1 to 2 dogs, $10/day each pet, kitchenette, seasonal pool,
open field for walking dogs, 1 1/2-mile-long walking trail to
Grand Coulee Dam, www.trailwestmotel.com

Grandview, WA

Apple Valley Motel   509-882-3003
903 W Wine Country Rd   16 units, $49–$65
each pet $10/stay, microwave, refrigerator, seasonal pool,
grassy walking area, 1/4 mile to public park

Grandview, WA (continued)

Grandview Motel   509-882-1323
522 E Wine Country Rd   20 units, $48–$68
small dogs only, $20/day each pet, microwave, refrigerator, grassy
walking area, close to walking trails

Grayland, WA

Beachy Day Vacation Rentals   360-267-3234, 866-654-4666
1624 State Route 105   45 units, $99–$290
each pet $10/day, cabins, kitchen, hot tub, close to beach,
www.beachyday.com

Ocean Acres B & B Horse Hotel   360-267-5521, 877-869-4728
3079 State Route 105   7 units, $135
pet fee $15/day, microwave, refrigerator, full breakfast, grassy
walking area, short walk to miles of open beach, stables for guests'
horses, www.horsebeachcamp.com

Ocean Spray Motel   360-267-2205
1757 State Route 105   10 units, $65–$95
1 to 2 dogs, $10/day each pet, 1-bdrm to 2-bdrm cottages sleep up
to 8, full kitchen or coffeemaker-microwave-refrigerator, beach
access road for walking dogs, www.oceanspraymotel.com

Walsh Motel   360-267-2191
1593 State Route 105   24 units, $50–$105
each pet $10/stay, dogs allowed in cottages but not motel rooms,
full kitchen or coffeemaker & refrigerator, large area for walking
dogs, short walk to beach, www.westport-walshmotel.com

Greenbank, WA

Lagoon Point Log Home   360-632-4853, 800-929-7464
3617 Marine View Dr   1 unit, $95
1 to 2 dogs, 3-bdrm log home sleeps 6, available as B & B style
2-bdrm suite with continental breakfast or as complete vacation
home rental, kitchen, BBQ, wraparound deck, large yard,
5-minute walk to beach, www.lagoonpoint-bandb.com

Spring Hill Inn   360-678-5210, 800-475-0192
24811 State Route 525   2 units, $115–$175
dogs allowed with advance approval only, $10/day, full breakfast,
on 5 landscaped acres, lawn furniture, badminton, horseshoes,
croquet, 3-minute drive to public park, www.springhillinn.com

Greenwater, WA

Alta Crystal Resort at Mt Rainier   360-663-2500, 800-277-6475
68317 State Route 410 E   23 units, $143–$270
dogs allowed in spring & fall only, pet fee $25-$40/day, kitchen,
outdoor pool, hot tub, on 22 acres surrounded by national forest,
creek & miles of walking trails, www.altacrystalresort.com

Hoodsport, WA

Creekside Inn   360-877-9686
27131 Hwy 101 N   4 units, $75–$95
small to medium dogs only, $10/day each pet, full kitchen or
coffeemaker-microwave-refrigerator, wooded area for walking
dogs, 1 mile to hiking trail, www.hoodsportwa.com/Creekside/

Sunrise Motel & Dive Resort   360-877-5301
24520 N Hwy 101   15 units, $60–$90
each pet $10/stay, waterfront location, kitchenette, RV sites,
espresso bar, water sports, lawn & beach for walking dogs, 1 mile
to public park, www.hctc.com/~sunrise/

Hoquiam, WA

Econo Lodge Inn & Suites   360-532-8161, 866-532-8161
910 Simpson Ave   65 units, $50–$100
pet fee $5-10/day, kitchenette, continental breakfast, grassy
walking area, riverfront park, www.econolodge.com/hotel/wa213

Sandstone Motel   360-533-6383
2424 Aberdeen Ave   24 units, $50–$60
small dogs only, $7/day each pet, small grassy pet walking area,
3/4 mile to public park

Tops Motel   360-532-7373
2403 Simpson Ave   11 units, $48–$68
dogs under 20 lbs only, $10/day, coffeemaker, microwave,
refrigerator, parking lot for walking dogs, 3-minute drive to park

Husum, WA

Husum Riverside B & B and European Cafe   509-493-8900
866 State Hwy 141   5 units, $129–$149
pet fee $20/stay, full breakfast, restaurant, hot tub, large yard for
walking dogs, next to walking trails, www.gorge-rooms.com

Ilwaco, WA

101 Haciendas   360-642-8459
US Hwy 101 & Brumbach Ave   8 units, $50–$185
full kitchen or coffeemaker-microwave-refrigerator, continental
breakfast, BBQ, picnic area, crab cooker, fish freezer, pet walking
area, 4 blocks to public park, www.101haciendas.com

Col-Pacific Motel   360-642-3177
214 S 1st St   16 units, $55–$180
dogs allowed by advance arrangement only, $15 for 1st day,
$10 each additional day, coffeemaker, microwave, refrigerator,
open area for walking dogs, 2 blocks to port, 1½ miles to ocean,
www.colpacificmotel.com

Harbor Lights Motel   360-642-3196
147 SE Howerton Way   20 units, $50–$98
each pet $5/day, microwave, refrigerator, restaurant, lounge, close
to beach & parks, ½ mile to harbor, www.harbor-lights-ilwaco.com

Heidi's Inn   360-642-2387, 800-576-1032
126 E Spruce St   25 units, $55–$150
small pets only, $6/day each pet, coffeemaker, microwave,
refrigerator, small wooded area for walking dogs, 3 blocks to
harbor, www.heidisinnmotel.com

Inchelium, WA

Hartman's Log Cabin Resort   509-722-3543
178 Twin Lakes Rd   59 units, $45–$70
each pet $6/day, motel rooms & log cabins, kitchenette or
coffeemaker & refrigerator, restaurant, RV & tent sites, lakefront
wooded area for walking dogs, www.hartmanslogcabin.com

Rainbow Beach Resort   509-722-5901, 888-862-0978
18 N Twin Lakes Rd   26 units, $48–$162
each pet $20/stay, lakefront cabins, kitchen, large open area &
walking trails, swimming in lake, www.rainbowbeachresort.net

Index, WA

Wild Lily Ranch   360-793-2103
pet fee $15/day   3 units, $105–$175
main house with kitchen sleeps 6, riverside cedar log cabins sleep
2 to 4, breakfast included, separate bathhouse, sauna & hot tub, in
national wilderness area, www.wildlilyranch.com

Ione, WA

Box Canyon Motel   509-442-3728
8612 State Route 31   9 units, $55–$72
1 to 2 dogs, $10/day each pet, kitchenette or coffeemaker &
microwave, riverfront walking area, 1 mile to trail around lake

Ione Motel & Trailer Park   509-442-3213
301 S 2nd St   11 units, $40–$85
1 to 2 dogs allowed by advance reservations only, motel rooms to
2-bdrm suite, kitchenette or coffeemaker-microwave-refrigerator,
500 ft river frontage, short walk to public park

Porter's Plaza Motel   509-442-3534
103 S 2nd Ave   7 units, $50–$60
coffeemaker, microwave, refrigerator, fitness room, 2 blocks to
riverfront park, http://users.potc.net/portersplaza/

Issaquah, WA

Motel 6 Seattle East/Issaquah   425-392-8405
1885 15th Place NW   103 units, $99
coffee in lobby, seasonal pool, grassy walking area, across street to
state park, www.motel6.com

Kalama, WA

Kalama River Inn   360-673-2855, 888-412-2855
602 NE Frontage Rd   44 units, $49–$65
1 to 2 small dogs only, $5/day each pet, microwave, refrigerator,
2 blocks to river

Kelso, WA

Best Western Aladdin Motor Inn   360-425-9660, 800-764-7378
310 Long Ave   78 units, $90–$140
dogs under 10 lbs only, $15/day each pet, full kitchen or
coffeemaker-microwave-refrigerator, continental breakfast,
restaurant, lounge, indoor pool, hot tub, pet walking area, 2 blocks
to riverfront park, www.bestwestern.com/prop_48070

Econo Lodge   360-636-4610
505 N Pacific Ave   49 units, $45–$65
1 to 2 dogs, $20/day each pet, microwave, refrigerator, continental
breakfast, grassy walking area, trail to river,
www.econolodge.com/hotel/wa197

Kelso, WA

GuestHouse International Inn & Suites   360-414-5953
501 Three Rivers Dr   800-214-8378
each pet $15/day   60 units, $90–$96
rooms & 1-bdrm to 2-bdrm suites, kitchenette or coffeemaker-
microwave-refrigerator, continental breakfast, indoor pool, hot tub,
fitness room, grassy walking area, 1/4 mile to waterfront trail,
1/2 mile to park, www.guesthouseintl.com/location-WA-Kelso.htm

Motel 6   360-425-3229, 800-466-8356
106 N Minor Rd   63 units, $53–$65
coffee in lobby, seasonal pool, grassy walking area, 2 blocks to
public park, www.motel6.com

Red Lion Hotel   360-636-4400, 800-733-5466
510 Kelso Dr   161 units, $119–$146
each pet $20/day, coffeemaker, microwave, refrigerator,
restaurant, lounge, seasonal pool, children's pool, hot tub, fitness
room, grass & gravel walking areas, 1/2 block to public park,
www.redlion.com/kelsolongview

Super 8 Motel   360-423-8880, 800-800-8000
250 Kelso Dr   84 units, $66–$102
1 to 2 dogs, $10/day each pet, coffeemaker, microwave,
refrigerator, continental breakfast, indoor pool, hot tub, next to
public park, short walk to riverside walkway, www.super8.com

Kennewick, WA

Best Western Kennewick Inn   509-586-1332, 800-780-7234
4001 W 27th Ave   87 units, $99–$166
pet fee $10/stay, all pet rooms are on ground floor with outside
entrances, coffeemaker, microwave, refrigerator, full breakfast,
freshly baked cookies, indoor pool, sauna, hot tub, fitness room,
lawn for walking dogs, 5-minute drive to riverfront park &
walkway, www.bestwestern.com/kennewick

Cabin Suites B & B   509-374-3966, 866-374-3966
115 N Yelm St   3 units, $85–$95
pet fee $10/day ($30 maximum), 3-bdrm home sleeps up to 12, full
breakfast, dog run available, grassy walking area, across street to
public park, www.cabinsuites.com

Clover Island Inn   509-586-0541, 800-586-0542
435 Clover Island   151 units, $89–$129
pet fee $25/stay, coffeemaker, microwave, refrigerator, extended
continental breakfast, restaurant, lounge, outdoor pool, hot tub,
riverfront walking area, next to 24-mile bike trail, short drive to
public park, www.cloverislandinn.com

Comfort Inn   509-783-8396, 800-424-6423
7801 W Quinault Ave   56 units, $85–$130
1 to 2 dogs, $10/day, coffeemaker, microwave, refrigerator,
continental breakfast, indoor pool, hot tub, grassy walking area,
½ mile to public park, www.comfortinn.com/hotel/wa701

Days Inn   509-735-9511, 888-783-5733
2811 W 2nd Ave   103 units, $69–$95
1 to 2 dogs under 25 lbs only, $10/day each pet, kitchenette or
coffeemaker-microwave-refrigerator, continental breakfast,
seasonal pool, fitness room, lawn for walking dogs, 1 mile to public
park, www.daysinn.com/hotel/14603

Fairfield Inn   509-783-2164, 800-228-2800
7809 W Quinault Ave   63 units, $95–$135
each pet $15/day ($75 maximum), coffeemaker, microwave,
refrigerator, continental breakfast, indoor pool, hot tub, fitness
room, grassy walking area, 1 mile to walking & biking path,
www.marriott.com/kwcfi

Guesthouse International Inn & Suites   509-735-2242
5616 W Clearwater Ave   800-214-8378
each pet $10/stay   56 units, $62–$79
coffeemaker, microwave, refrigerator, extended continental
breakfast, fitness room, gravel walking area, 5-minute drive to
park, www.guesthouseintl.com/location-WA-Kennewick.htm

La Quinta Inn & Suites   509-736-3326
4220 W 27th Ave   53 units, $89–$109
1 to 2 dogs, full kitchen or coffeemaker-microwave-refrigerator,
extended continental breakfast, indoor pool, sauna, hot tub, grassy
walking area, 3 blocks to public park, www.lq.com

Quality Inn   509-735-6100, 800-205-6938
7901 W Quinault Ave   124 units, $89–$140
1 to 2 dogs under 25 lbs only, $15/day, coffeemaker, microwave,
refrigerator, full breakfast, indoor pool, hot tub, large yard,
1½ miles to waterfront park, www.qualityinn.com/hotel/wa190

Kennewick, WA (continued)

Red Lion Hotel Columbia Center 509-783-0611, 800-733-5466
1101 N Columbia Center Blvd 162 units, $120–$130
coffeemaker, microwave, refrigerator, restaurant, lounge, seasonal
pool, fitness room, grassy area for walking dogs, ½ mile to
waterfront park & walking trail, www.redlion.com/columbiacenter

Super 8 Motel 509-736-6888
626 N Columbia Center Blvd 95 units, $64–$85
1 to 2 dogs, $10/day, coffeemaker, microwave, refrigerator,
continental breakfast, indoor pool, hot tub, grassy walking area,
7 blocks to waterfront park, www.super8.com

Kent, WA

Comfort Inn 253-872-2211, 877-424-6423
22311 84th Ave S 102 units, $90–$130
each pet $25/day, coffeemaker, microwave, refrigerator,
continental breakfast, indoor pool, hot tub, fitness room, small
lawn, 3 miles to park, www.comfortinn.com/hotel/wa020

Crossland Economy Studios Seattle/Kent 253-946-1744
25104 Pacific Hwy S 135 units, $65–$75
pet fee $25/day ($75 maximum), coffeemaker, microwave,
refrigerator, 3 miles to public park, www.crosslandstudios.com/540

Days Inn South Seattle 253-854-1950, 800-329-7466
1711 W Meeker St 80 units, $58–$68
pet fee $15/day, coffeemaker, microwave, refrigerator, continental
breakfast, restaurant, fitness room, open field, 1 block to riverside
park & walking trail, www.daysinn.com/hotel/05570

Extended StayAmerica 253-872-6514, 800-398-7829
22520 83rd Ave S 120 units, $75–$89
pet fee $25/day ($150 maximum), suites with kitchenette, lawn,
1 mile to walking trail, www.extendedstayamerica.com/866

Golden Kent Motel 253-872-8372
22203 84th Ave S 22 units, $75–$105
small dogs only, $10/day, kitchenette, lawn & open field for
walking dogs, ½ mile to walking trail, www.goldenkentmotel.com

Hawthorn Suites Seattle South   253-395-3800, 800-527-1133
6329 S 212th St   152 units, $99–$169
dogs under 25 lbs only, $250/stay, kitchenette or coffeemaker &
microwave, extended continental breakfast, seasonal pool, hot tub,
fitness room, 3-acre nature preserve, www.hawthorn.com

Howard Johnson Inn   253-852-7224, 800-446-4656
1233 Central Ave N   85 units, $80–$102
1 to 2 small dogs only, $10/day each pet, coffeemaker, microwave,
refrigerator, continental breakfast, seasonal pool, sauna, hot tub,
lawn, 2 blocks to public park, www.hojo.com/hotel/10234

Quality Inn & Suites   253-520-6670, 877-424-6423800-470-8081
25100 74th Ave S   60 units, $90–$100
dogs under 15 lbs, $10/day, coffeemaker, extended continental
breakfast, indoor pool, sauna, hot tub, small pet walking area, bike
trail, close to public park, www.qualityinn.com/hotel/wa136

TownePlace Suites Seattle Southcenter   253-796-6000
18123 72nd Ave S   152 units, $99–$159
1 to 2 dogs, $10/day each pet, full kitchen or coffeemaker &
microwave, continental breakfast, beverages & appetizers on
Tuesday & Wednesday evenings, seasonal pool, hot tub, fitness
room, paved walking trail, close to park, www.marriott.com/seakt

Kettle Falls, WA

America's Best Value Inn   509-738-6514
205 E 3rd Ave (Hwy 395)   24 units, $47–$60
1 to 2 dogs, $10/day, full kitchen or coffeemaker-microwave-
refrigerator, sauna, hot tub, grassy walking area, 2 blocks to
lakefront park, www.bestvalueinn.com

Blue Moose Cabins   509-738-6950
24387 Hwy 395 N   3 units, $65
pets allowed with manager's approval, $10/stay, modern cabins
sleep up to 4, kitchenette, BBQ, fire pit, covered decks, on 10
wooded acres, 4-minute walk to lake, www.bluemoosecabins.com

Bull Hill Guest Ranch   509-732-1171, 877-285-5445
3738 Bull Hill Rd   8 units, $190
2-story cabins, rate shown is per person & includes 3 meals per
day, coffeemaker, restaurant, lounge, hot tub, on 50,000 acres with
private lake, boating, horseback riding, www.bullhill.com

Kettle Falls, WA

Grandview Inn Motel & RV Park   509-738-6733, 888-488-6733
978 Hwy 395 N   13 units, $52–$67
1 to 2 dogs, $3/day each pet, kitchenette or coffeemaker-
microwave-refrigerator, grassy walking area, 1/2 mile to public
park, www.grandviewinnandrv.com

Kingston, WA

Blue Water Inn   360-297-3622, 866-895-7645
11045 NE State Hwy 104   21 units, $62
microwave, refrigerator, grassy walking area, 1/2 block to baseball
field for walking dogs, 1/2 mile to public park,
www.bluewaterinn.net

Kirkland, WA

Baymont Inn   425-822-2300, 800-332-4800
12223 NE 116th St   105 units, $94
1 to 2 dogs under 40 lbs only, $15/stay, coffeemaker, microwave,
refrigerator, continental breakfast, seasonal pool, hot tub, small pet
walking area, 1 mile to lakefront, 10-minute drive to public park,
www.baymontinns.com/hotel/wa17835

La Quinta Inn   425-828-6585, 800-531-5900
10530 Northup Way   121 units, $115–$155
coffeemaker, microwave, refrigerator, continental breakfast,
seasonal pool, fitness room, grassy walking area, 2 blocks to
walking trail, 3 miles to off-leash park, www.lq.com

Motel 6 Seattle North/Kirkland   425-821-5618
12010 120th Place NE   123 units, $65–$80
small dogs only, coffee in lobby, seasonal pool, 2 blocks to
lakefront park, several public parks within 1 mile, www.motel6.com

Woodmark Hotel, Yacht Club & Spa   425-822-3700
1200 Carillon Point   800-822-3700
pet fee $100/stay   100 units, $265–$2000
coffeemaker, microwave, refrigerator, restaurant, lounge, fitness
room, day spa, private pier, pet room service menu & grooming
available, lakefront lawn for walking dogs, www.thewoodmark.com

La Conner, WA

Estep's Residences   360-466-2116
610 S 1st St   4 units, $150–$175
pet fee $50/stay, 1-bdrm condos, full kitchen, private deck or
garden, hot tub, large yard, www.estep-properties.com

Heron Inn & Watergrass Day Spa   360-466-4626, 877-883-8899
117 Maple Ave   11 units, $99–$199
1 to 2 dogs under 50 lbs only, $25/day each pet, gourmet breakfast
buffet, BBQ, private deck, hot tub, landscaped garden, lawn for
walking dogs, 1 mile to public park, www.theheron.com

Katy's Inn   360-466-9909, 866-528-9746
503 Third St   4 units, $79–$159
small dogs only, $25/day, full breakfast, hot tub, deck, landscaped
yard for walking dogs, www.katysinn.com

La Conner Country Inn   360-466-3101, 888-466-4113
107 S 2nd St   28 units, $119–$209
pet fee $50/stay, coffeemaker, refrigerator, extended continental
breakfast, restaurant, lounge, pet bed-treats-bowls, lawn for
walking dogs, 8 blocks to public park, www.laconnerlodging.com

La Conner on the Water Guest House   360-466-7494
17022 Island View Lane   360-770-0903
                                              1 unit, $175–$285
dogs under 15 lbs allowed with advance approval only, $20/day,
available as either 1-bdrm or 2-bdrm cottage with full kitchen, pet
walking area, 1 block to beach, www.laconneronthewater.com

La Push, WA

Quileute Oceanside Resort   360-374-5267, 800-487-1267
320 Ocean Dr   70 units, $45–$175
pet fee $10/stay, motel rooms (Thunderbird Motel), 1-room rustic
camper cabins, 2-bdrm townhouses, kitchen, convenience store,
grassy area for walking dogs, beach, www.quileuteoceanside.com

Lacey, WA

Candlewood Suites   360-491-1698, 888-226-3539
4440 3rd Ave SE   62 units, $140–$150
dogs under 80 lbs only, pet fee $75/stay up to 6 days, $150/stay for
7 or more days, kitchenette, BBQ, fitness room, convenience
store, small pet walking area, 1 mile to park, www.cwlacey.com

Lacey, WA

La Quinta Inn　　　　　　　　　360-412-1200, 800-957-9163
4704 Park Center Ave NE　　　　　　　　63 units, $99–$120
1 to 2 dogs, coffeemaker, microwave, refrigerator, continental breakfast, indoor pool, fitness room, walking area, www.lq.com

Lodge at Long Lake　　　　　　　　　　　　360-701-4768
pet fee $50/stay　　　　　　　　　　1 unit, $200–$300
fully equipped 4-bdrm 4-bath lakeside vacation home, huge deck, BBQ, canoes, lawn, www.holidayescapes.net/lakehouse.aspx

Quality Inn & Suites　　　　　　360-493-1991, 800-282-7028
120 College St SE　　　　　　　　　　77 units, $69–$110
1 to 2 dogs under 25 lbs only, $15/day each pet, coffeemaker, microwave, refrigerator, continental breakfast, sauna, fitness room, trails thru the woods for walking dogs, next to public park, www.qualityinn.com/hotel/wa161

Super 8 Motel　　　　　　　　　360-459-8888, 800-800-8000
112 College St SE　　　　　　　　　100 units, $66–$102
1 to 3 dogs, $10/day each pet, coffeemaker, microwave, refrigerator, continental breakfast, indoor pool, hot tub, 1 block to public park, www.super8.com

Lakewood, WA

La Quinta Inn　　　　　　　　　　　　　　253-582-7000
11751 Pacific Hwy SW　　　　　　　　120 units, $139–$219
dogs under 50 lbs only, coffeemaker, microwave, refrigerator, extended continental breakfast, indoor pool, hot tub, fitness room, small pet walking area, 4 miles to off-leash dog park, www.lq.com

Langley, WA

Angels Guest Suite　　　　　　　360-730-1138, 800-319-2181
3789 Morning Glory Lane　　　　　　　　1 unit, $100–$125
1 to 2 dogs, $25/day each pet, secluded garden suite with full kitchen, continental breakfast provided for first 2 days of stay, close to beach access, www.angelsguestsuite.com

Carol Lee's Attic　　　　　　　　　　　　360-730-1955
3704 S Saratoga Rd　　　　　　　　　　1 unit, $95–$120
1 to 2 dogs, 1-room suite sleeps 4, kitchen stocked with breakfast supplies, large yard for walking dogs, www.carolleesattic.com

Country Cottage of Langley   360-221-8709, 800-713-3860
215 6th St   6 units, $139–$189
pet fee $25/day, cottages, coffeemaker, microwave, refrigerator,
private deck, full breakfast, 1½-acre lawn & garden, 6 blocks to
beach, www.acountrycottage.com

Crabtrapper Beach House   360-321-4353
5941 Norton Lane   1 unit, $120–$150
pet fee $25/stay, 2-bdrm beach house sleeps 6, full kitchen, BBQ,
next to beach & boardwalk, www.vacationhomes.com/22681

Drake's Landing   360-221-3999
203 Wharf St   4 units, $90–$110
pet fee $25/stay, coffeemaker, microwave, refrigerator, beach
access for walking dogs, across street to park, 20-minute drive to
off-leash dog park, www.langleydrakeslanding.hotels.officelive.com

Inn at Langley   360-221-3033
400 1st St   28 units, $275–$595
1 to 2 dogs, $50/stay each pet, beachfront guest rooms & cottages,
coffeemaker, refrigerator, continental breakfast, restaurant, private
deck or balcony overlooking water, walking trails, beachfront,
www.innatlangley.com

Langley Motel   360-221-6070, 866.276.8292
526 Camano Ave # B   4 units, $95–$125
pet fee $10/day, dogs allowed in 1 suite only, kitchen, garden
terrace with outdoor table, open area for walking dogs, 4 blocks to
marina, www.langleymotel.com

Morning Glory Cottage B & B   206-601-8244 or 360-341-2867
3795 Morning Glory Lane   1 unit, $150–$175
dogs allowed with advance approval only, 1-bdrm cottage sleeps 4,
bottle of wine & breakfast fixings provided for 1st day of stay,
deck, BBQ, lawn, short walk to beach, www.cottageonwhidbey.com

Rabbit On The Green   360-321-7254
3018 Quigley Rd   1 unit, $125–$175
cottage with kitchen, continental breakfast, very large lawn, on 10
acres with pond, ¼ mile to lake, 2 miles to park

Langley, WA (continued)

Sunlight Seascape Retreat   206-525-1262 or 206-595-3498
dogs allowed with advance approval only   3 units, $100–$165
$25-$50/stay, 3 units (guesthouse-library-annex-children's play
space) sleep a combined total of 10, kitchenette, continental
breakfast, BBQ, private deck, on ½-acre garden overlooking bay,
2 blocks to beach access, www.sunlightseascape.com

Leavenworth, WA

59er Diner & Cabins   509-763-2267
15361 US Hwy 2   3 units, $180
dogs under 30 lbs only, $10/day each pet, themed cabins sleep up
to 4, kitchenette, hot tub, RV sites, restaurant, grassy & wooded
walking areas, 5-minute drive to river, www.59erdiner.com

Alpine River Hideaway   425-985-6455
pet fee $50/stay   1 unit, $180
2-bdrm 2-bath riverview cabin sleeps 8, kitchen, BBQ, covered
deck, hot tub, on 4 acres, www.alpineriverhideaway.com

Aspen Suites Condominiums at Icicle Village Resort
525 Junction Lane   509-888-2776, 800-961-0162
1 to 2 dogs under 35 lbs only   92 units, $129–$179
each pet $25/stay, 1-bdrm to 3-bdrm condos, coffeemaker,
microwave, refrigerator, extended continental breakfast, seasonal
pool, hot tub, 5 blocks to beach, ½ mile to park, www.aspensuites.us

Bavarian Orchard House B & B   509-293-6693
11001 US Hwy 2   3 units, $159–$199
dogs under 35 lbs only, full breakfast, coffeehouse on premises,
wine tasting, pool table, www.bavarianorchardhouse.com

Bavarian Ritz Hotel   509-548-5455, 800-854-6365
633 Front St   16 units, $89–$299
pet fee $10/day, kitchenette or coffeemaker-microwave-
refrigerator, restaurant, sun deck overlooking river & mountains,
across street to riverside walkway, www.bavarianritz.com

Beaver Valley Lodging   509-763-9012, 800-763-5215
18623 Beaver Valley Rd   7 units, $82–$130
small to medium dogs only, $32/stay, full kitchen or coffeemaker-
microwave-refrigerator, on 50 acres for walking dogs, 20-minute
walk to river, 5 miles to lakefront, www.beavervalleylodge.com

Best Western Icicle Inn   509-548-7000, 800-558-2438
505 W Hwy 2   92 units, $108–$170
dogs under 35 lbs only, $25/stay, coffeemaker, microwave,
refrigerator, extended continental breakfast, restaurant, outdoor
pool with seasonal domed cover, hot tub, fitness room, next to
mini-golf & movie theater, grassy area for walking dogs, 2 blocks
to waterfront park, www.icicleinn.com

Bindlestiffs Riverside Cabins   509-548-1685
1600 US Hwy 2   8 units, $89–$99
pet fee $10/day, 1-room cabins, coffeemaker, microwave,
refrigerator, private riverside deck, small pet walking area,
8 blocks to island for walking dogs, www.bindlestiffcabins.com

Chiwawa River Lodging   509-763-3767, 877-700-3767
Lake Wenatchee area   2 units, $135–$650
pet fee $25/stay, lodges sleep 6 to 14, full kitchen, BBQ, covered
porch, lawn for walking dogs, close to river & walking trails,
www.chiwawalodging.com

Comfy Cabins   206-612-5761 or 425-218-8592
1 to 2 dogs, $10/day each pet   27 units, $99–$375
fully equipped cabins to 5-bdrm 3-bath lodge sleep up to 16,
kitchen, linens provided, most have hot tub, close to walking trails
& river, www.comfycabins.com

Der Ritterhof Motor Inn   509-548-5845, 800-255-5845
190 US Hwy 2   51 units, $75–$107
1 to 2 dogs, $10/day each pet, kitchenette, continental breakfast,
seasonal pool, hot tub, BBQ, picnic area, large yard for walking
dogs, 3 blocks to waterfront park, www.derritterhof.com

Destination Leavenworth   509-548-4230, 866-904-7368
940 US Hwy 2 # A1   40+ units, $175–$375
1 to 2 dogs, $20/day, cabins-condos-vacation homes, kitchen, hot
tub, some units located on acreage, close to walking areas & public
parks, www.destinationleavenworth.com

Dirty Face Lodge   253-722-2409
16705 Brown Rd   1 unit, $549
each pet $35/day, 10-bdrm lodge sleeps up to 30, full kitchen, hot
tub, seasonal pool, on 3 wooded acres with open field for walking
dogs, 1 mile to lakefront, www.dirtyfacelodge.com

Leavenworth, WA (continued)

Evergreen Inn   509-548-5515, 800-327-7212
1117 Front St   40 units, $79–$139
1 to 3 dogs, $10/stay each pet, kitchenette or coffeemaker-
microwave-refrigerator, continental breakfast, hot tub, on private
park, 3 blocks to riverfront trails, www.evergreeninn.com

Howard Johnson Express Inn   509-548-4326, 800-423-9380
405 W US Hwy 2   41 units, $76–$94
each pet $12/day, coffeemaker, microwave, refrigerator,
continental breakfast, seasonal pool, hot tub, guest pass to indoor
pool at nearby Quality Inn, grassy walking area, across street to
public park & walking trails, www.hojo.com/hotel/14251

Natapoc Lodging   509-763-3313, 888-628-2762
12348 Bretz Rd   5 units, $225
dogs allowed with advance approval only, $25/day, fully furnished
lodges sleep 2 to 22, kitchen, hot tub, lawn & wooded riverfront
walking area, close to public park & walkway, www.natapoc.com

Obertal Inn   509-548-5204, 800-537-9382
922 Commercial St   27 units, $89–$179
each pet $15/day, coffeemaker, microwave, refrigerator,
continental breakfast, hot tub, across street to open field, 2 blocks
to riverfront park, www.obertal.com

Osprey Nest Cabin   425-881-6814
pet fee $50/stay   1 unit, $180
riverview cabin with 2 open loft bedrooms & full kitchen sleeps 8,
BBQ, covered deck, hot tub, on 12 wooded acres for walking dogs,
www.hcwlodge.com

Quality Inn & Suites   509-548-7992, 800-693-1225
185 W Hwy 2   78 units, $69–$150
1 to 2 dogs under 100 lbs only, $15/day each pet, coffeemaker,
microwave, refrigerator, continental breakfast, indoor pool, hot
tub, fitness room, grassy walking area, close to riverfront park &
1½-mile-long trail thru town, www.leavenworthqualityinn.com

River's Edge Lodge   509-548-7612, 800-451-5285
8401 Hwy 2   23 units, $69–$195
1 to 2 dogs, $15/day each pet, coffeemaker, microwave,
refrigerator, continental breakfast, seasonal pool, hot tub, large
lawn & riverside walkway, www.riversedgelodge.net

Sleeping Lady Mountain Resort   509-548-6344, 800-574-2123
7375 Icicle Rd   58 units, $200–$300
coffeemaker, restaurant, lounge, seasonal pool, hot tub, nightly
rate includes breakfast & dinner in restaurant (summer rate also
includes lunch), dog bed & bowls provided, on 67 wooded acres,
large open area & trails for walking dogs, www.sleepinglady.com

Liberty Lake, WA

Best Western Peppertree Liberty Lake Inn   509-755-1111,
1816 Pepper Lane   800-274-7750
1 to 2 dogs under 10 lbs, $10/day each pet   76 units, $79–$129
coffeemaker, microwave, refrigerator, extended continental
breakfast, indoor pool, hot tub, fitness room, lawn, 1-minute walk
to open field for exercising dogs, www.peppertreelibertylake.com

Cedars Inn   509-340-3333, 866-609-2148
2327 N Madison Rd   69 units, $59–$139
each pet $15/stay, coffeemaker, microwave, refrigerator,
continental breakfast, indoor pool, hot tub, small walking area,
short walk to park, short drive to trail, www.cedarsinnspokane.com

Long Beach, WA

Accommodation Long Beach   360-642-7829, 877-642-7829
405 Ocean Beach Blvd N   6 units, $99–$199
1 to 3 dogs under 100 lbs only, $25/stay, 1-bdrm to 5-bdrm fully
equipped condos & vacation homes, continental breakfast, deck,
BBQ, fire pit, yard for walking dogs, short walk to beach,
www.accommodationlongbeach.com

Akari Bungalows   360-642-5267
203 W Bolstad Ave   8 units, $85–$175
pet fee $15/stay, 1930s studios with kitchenette to 2-bdrm cottages
with full kitchen, restaurant, grassy walking area, short walk to
beach, www.akaribungalows.com

Anchorage Cottages   360-642-2351, 800-646-2351
2209 Ocean Beach Blvd N   10 units, $70–$128
1 to 2 dogs, $10/day each pet, 1-bdrm to 2-bdrm cottages sleep up
to 9, kitchen, BBQ, sport courts, playground, small grassy walking
area, private trail to beach, www.theanchoragecottages.com

Long Beach, WA (continued)

Anthony's Home Court   360-642-2802, 888-787-2754
1310 N Pacific Hwy   8 units, $80–$125
1 to 2 dogs, $10/day each pet, studios to 2-bdrm bungalows,
full kitchen or coffeemaker & microwave, picnic tables, RV sites,
grassy walking area, 2 blocks to beach,
www.anthonyshomecourt.com

Breakers Hotel   360-642-4414, 800-219-9833
210 26th St NE   116 units, $88–$139
1 to 2 dogs, $10/day, hotel rooms with coffeemaker-refrigerator-
microwave or oceanview suites with full kitchen, patio or balcony,
indoor pool, hot tub, on 24 beachfront acres, trails thru the dunes,
www.breakerslongbeach.com

Cedars Ocean View Inn   360-642-5400, 888-886-9111
208 Bolstad Ave W   42 units, $80–$115
each pet $10/stay, full kitchen or coffeemaker-microwave-
refrigerator, continental breakfast, ocean view, large yard for
walking dogs, easy beach access, www.cedarsoceanviewinn.com

Chautauqua Lodge   360-642-4401, 800-869-8401
304 NW 14th St   120 units, $69–$249
each pet $10/day, rooms & suites, full kitchen or coffeemaker-
microwave-refrigerator, restaurant, lounge, indoor pool, sauna, hot
tub, recreation room, BBQ, picnic tables, horseshoe pits,
basketball & volleyball courts, large open area for walking dogs,
100 feet to beach, www.chautauqualodge.com

Discovery Coast Cottage Inn   360-642-2613, 877-642-2613
405 Ocean Beach Blvd N   8 units, $49–$219
each pet $10/day, rooms, studios, 1-bdrm to 2-bdrm suites,
vacation homes, porch, private hot tub, full kitchen or
coffeemaker-microwave-refrigerator, continental breakfast, BBQ,
picnic tables, children's play area, greenbelt area for walking dogs,
short walk to beach, www.discoverycoastonline.com

Edgewater Inn   360-642-2311, 800-561-2456
409 Sid Snyder Dr SW   84 units, $64–$99
1 to 2 dogs, $10/day each pet, coffeemaker, restaurant, sand &
grassy walking area, across street to boardwalk & trails to beach,
www.edgewaterinnlongbeachwa.com

Inn at Discovery Coast   360-642-5265, 866-843-5782
421 11th St SW   12 units, $85–$199
1 to 3 dogs allowed with advance approval only, $15/stay each pet,
coffeemaker, microwave, refrigerator, private deck & ocean view,
breakfast basket delivered to your door, beach cruiser bikes for
guest use, 2-minute walk to beach, www.innatdiscoverycoast.com

Lighthouse Oceanfront Resort   360-642-3622, 877-220-7555
12417 Pacific Way   36 units, $55–$155
1 to 2 dogs allowed with advance approval only, $15/day each pet,
1-bdrm to 3-bdrm rustic cottages & modern townhouses, full
kitchen or coffeemaker & microwave, BBQ, picnic area, indoor
pool with retractable roof in summer, hot tub, fitness room, grassy
walking area, trail to beach, www.lighthouseresort.net

Our Place at the Beach   360-642-3793, 800-538-5107
1309 S Ocean Beach Blvd   26 units, $59–$140
each pet $5/day, oceanview rooms & apartments, full kitchen or
coffeemaker-microwave-refrigerator, continental breakfast, sauna,
hot tub, fitness room, open field, www.ourplacelongbeach.com

Riptide Motel   360-642-3455, 800-214-1379
620 S Pacific   10 units, $60–$180
1 to 2 dogs, $7/day each pet, full kitchen or coffeemaker-
microwave-refrigerator, recreation room with ping pong table &
pool table, grassy walking area, close to dunes, 2 blocks to beach

Rodeway Inn   360-642-3714, 800-753-3750
115 3rd St SW   42 units, $62–$115
1 to 2 dogs under 30 lbs only, $7/day each pet, coffeemaker,
microwave, refrigerator, continental breakfast, seasonal pool, lawn,
3 blocks to beach & boardwalk, www.rodewayinn.com/hotel/wa192

Super 8 Motel   360-642-8988, 888-478-3297
500 Ocean Beach Blvd N 5th St   50 units, $69–$119
1 to 2 dogs, $10/day, coffeemaker, microwave, refrigerator,
continental breakfast, freshly baked cookies, pet treats & toys
available, grassy walking area, across street to dunes, 5-minute
walk to beach, www.longbeachsuper8.com

Thunderbird Motel   360-642-5700
201 N Ocean Beach Blvd N   15 units, $45–$138
1 to 2 dogs, $8/day each pet, 1-bdrm to 2-bdrm suites sleep up to 6,
kitchenette, continental breakfast, open area for walking dogs,
2 blocks to beach & boardwalk

Long Beach, WA (continued)

Yett Beach House   360-642-8069, 888-642-8069
601 N Ocean Beach Blvd   1 unit, $150
1 to 2 dogs allowed with advance approval, $25/stay, 125-year-old
3-bdrm beachfront cottage sleeps 6, covered porch, large fenced
yard, trail thru dunes to beach, www.boreasinn.com/pu-yett.html

Longview, WA

Hudson Manor Inn & Suites   360-425-1100
1616 Hudson St   25 units, $60–$80
pet fee $15/stay, coffeemaker, microwave, refrigerator, continental
breakfast, BBQ, grassy walking area, 1 block to park, 4 blocks to
lake, 2 miles to off-leash dog park, www.hudsonmanorinn.com

Quality Inn & Suites   360-414-1000, 800-424-6423
723 7th Ave   50 units, $70–$189
1 to 2 dogs, $25 for 1st day, $15 each additional day, coffeemaker,
microwave, refrigerator, continental breakfast, indoor pool, hot
tub, grassy walking area, 2 blocks to open field, 1 mile to lake &
walking trail, www.qualityinn.com/hotel/WA183

Rodeway Inn   360-423-6980
1808 Hemlock St   34 units, $70–$75
1 to 3 dogs under 30 lbs only, $7/day each pet, coffeemaker,
microwave, refrigerator, continental breakfast, lawn for walking
dogs, 6 blocks to lake, 3 miles to off-leash dog park,
www.rodewayinn.com/hotel/WA200

Town Chalet Motor Hotel   360-423-2020
1822 Washington Way   24 units, $40–$60
pet fee $3/day, kitchenette, lawn for walking dogs, 2 blocks to
public park, 6 blocks to lake, 6 miles to off-leash dog park

Town House Motel   360-423-7200
744 Washington Way   28 units, $50–$60
pet fee $5/day, coffeemaker, microwave, refrigerator, outdoor pool,
lawn, 1 block to fairgrounds, www.townhousemo.com

Travelodge   360-423-6460, 800-578-7878
838 15th Ave   32 units, $55–$80
1 to 2 dogs, $15/day each pet, coffeemaker, microwave,
refrigerator, continental breakfast, ½ block to public park,
www.travelodge.com/hotel/08802

Loon Lake, WA

Loon Lake Motel   509-233-2916
3945 Hwy 292   8 units, $48–$56
1 to 2 dogs, $5/day each pet, coffeemaker, microwave, refrigerator,
grassy walking area, 5 miles to lake

Robbins Cottages   509-276-2839
40750 Robbins Rd   2 units, $72
small dogs only, 2-bdrm lakefront cottages sleep 6, full kitchen,
quiet country road & trail around lake for walking dogs

Lopez Island, WA

Bay House & Garden Cottages   360-468-4889
                                                    3 units, $150–$200
1-bdrm to 2-bdrm cottages, full kitchen, bay view, landscaped yard,
½ block to off-leash beach, www.interisland.net/cc

Blue Fjord Cabins   360-468-2749, 888-633-0401
862 Elliott Rd   2 units, $130–$150
1 to 2 dogs, $25/day each pet, secluded waterfront cabins sleep 2,
kitchenette, deck, on 6 wooded acres, short trail to private beach,
open April thru October, www.bluefjord.com/

Lopez Islander Resort & Marina   360-468-2233, 800-736-3434
2864 Fisherman Bay Rd   30 units, $99–$135
pet fee $20 for 1st day, $5 each additional day, rooms to 3-bdrm
suites, full kitchen or coffeemaker, restaurant, lounge, seasonal
pool, hot tub, RV & tent sites, grassy walking area, access to good
clamming beach, www.lopezislander.com

Lopez Village Properties   360-468-5055, 888-772-9735
122 Lopez Rd #A   42 units, $93–$370
pet fee $50/stay, rustic cabins with kitchenette to 5-bdrm vacation
homes with full kitchen, some with yard or on the waterfront for
walking dogs, close to parks & trails, www.lopezisproperties.com

Lummi Island, WA

Seaside Lodging Northwest   360-758-7064, 888-758-7064
1695 Seacrest Dr   10 units, $150–$1500
fully equipped vacation homes sleep 4 to 20, BBQ, hot tub, on the
waterfront or with water view, www.seasidelodgingnw.com

Lummi Island, WA (continued)

Willows Inn B & B   360-758-2620, 888-294-2620
2579 W Shore Dr   5 units, $135–$190
1 to 2 dogs under 50 lbs only, $30/day, 2-bdrm cottage with full
kitchen sleeps 2, fully equipped guest house sleeps 6, full breakfast
provided, massage therapy available, hot tub, waterfront deck,
across street to beach, www.willows-inn.com

Lyle, WA

Lyle Hotel   509-365-5953, 800.447.6310
100 7th St   10 units, $85–$105
1 to 2 dogs, $10/day each pet, 100-year-old hotel, private rooms
with shared baths, continental breakfast, restaurant, lounge, on 28
open acres for walking dogs, www.lylehotel.com

Morning Song Acres B & B   509-365-3600
6 Oda Knight Rd   6 units, $40–$85
full breakfast, on 45 acres for walking dogs, close to hiking trails,
www.morningsongacres.com

Lynden, WA

Windmill Inn   360-354-3424
8022 Guide Meridian Rd   15 units, $49–$129
dogs under 10 lbs only, $5/day, rooms to 2-bdrm suites, full
kitchen or coffeemaker-microwave-refrigerator, lawn, 8-minute
drive to off-leash dog park, www.windmillinnlynden.com

Lynnwood, WA

Best Western Alderwood   425-775-7600, 800-205-6935
19332 36th Ave W   141 units, $89–$135
dogs under 20 lbs only, $25/stay, coffeemaker, microwave,
refrigerator, extended continental breakfast, seasonal pool, hot
tub, fitness room, grassy walking area, 4 blocks to high school
field for walking dogs, www.bestwestern.com/alderwood

Extended StayAmerica   425-670-2520, 800-398-7829
3021 196th St SW   104 units, $70–$90
pet fee $25/day ($150 maximum), studios with kitchenette,
5 blocks to public park, www.extendedstayamerica.com/869

La Quinta Inn   425-775-7447
4300 Alderwood Mall Blvd   101 units, $89–$139
1 to 2 dogs, coffeemaker, refrigerator, extended continental
breakfast, indoor pool, hot tub, fitness room, grassy walking area,
1/3 mile to public park, 5 miles to beach, www.lq.com

Residence Inn Seattle North/Lynnwood/Everett 425-771-1100
18200 Alderwood Mall Parkway   120 units, $149–$199
1 to 2 dogs, $75/stay, kitchen, full breakfast, Monday thru
Thursday complimentary evening reception, seasonal pool, hot
tub, list of local off-leash dog parks provided, grassy walking area,
close to school field for walking dogs, www.marriott.com/sealw

Mansfield, WA

Jameson Lake Resort   509-683-1929
580 N Jameson Lake Rd   6 units, $30–$100
mobile homes & travel trailers sleep 2 to 6, kitchenette, bring your
own linens & cooking utensils, RV sites, restaurant, paddle boat
rentals, open desert area for walking dogs,
www.jamesonlakeresort.com

Manson, WA

Mountain View Lodge   509-687-9505, 800-967-8105
25 Wapato Point Parkway   31 units, $65–$155
each pet $15/day, microwave, refrigerator, continental breakfast,
seasonal pool, hot tub, BBQ, fire pit, volleyball, pet walking area,
5 blocks to waterfront, www.mountainviewlakechelan.com

Marysville, WA

Village Inn & Suites   360-659-0005, 877-659-0005
235 Beach Ave   47 units, $69–$159
dogs under 15 lbs only, $15/day each pet, coffeemaker,
microwave, refrigerator, continental breakfast, lawn, 1 block to
open field for walking dogs, www.villageinnsuite.com

Mazama, WA

Freestone Inn & Cabins at Wilson Ranch   509-996-3906
31 Early Winters Dr   800-639-3809
1 to 2 dogs, $30/stay   12 units, $175–$365
kitchenette or coffeemaker & refrigerator, private deck or veranda
with soaking tub, miles of trails, www.freestoneinn.com

Mazama, WA (continued)

Lost River Resort　　　　　　　　　　509-996-2537
681 Lost River Rd　　　　　　　　　　6 units, $85–$160
rustic log cabins with fully equipped kitchen sleep up to 8, RV
sites, wooded off-leash walking areas next to national forest,
2-minute walk to riverfront, www.lostriverresort.com

Mazama Country Inn　　　509-996-2681, 800-843-7951
15 Country Rd　　　　　　　　　　22 units, $140–$300
each pet $25/stay, cabins & vacation homes with full kitchen sleep
6 to 8, wooded walking areas, www.mazamacountryinn.com

Rock 'n' River Guest House　　　　　509-996-8144
Lost River Rd　　　　　　　　　　1 unit, $150–$250
1 to 2 dogs, $25/day, fully equipped log vacation home sleeps 8,
kitchen, BBQ, patio, fitness room, riverside walking area,
surrounded by national forest, www.rocknriverhouse.com

Metaline Falls, WA

Circle Motel　　　　　　509-446-4343, 877-206-6835
15802 Hwy 31　　　　　　　　　　10 units, $53–$83
each pet $10/day, rooms & mobile homes, full kitchen or
coffeemaker-microwave-refrigerator, hot tub, BBQ, picnic tables,
fire pit, on 20 country acres with trails for walking dogs,
www.circlemotel.com

Washington Hotel　　　　　　　　　509-446-4415
225 E 5th Ave　　　　　　　　　　18 units, $40–$60
historic building, microwave, across street to public park

Moclips, WA

Gull Wing Inn　　　　　　　　　　360-276-0014
4852 Pacific Ave　　　　　　　　　　3 units, $60–$85
pet fee $3-6/day, available as 3 separate suites or as a 4-bdrm inn,
full kitchen, sleeps 14, 100 feet to beach, www.gullwinginn.com

Hi-Tide Ocean Beach Resort　　360-276-4142, 800-662-5477
4890 Railroad Ave　　　　　　　　　25 units, $75–$230
1 to 2 dogs, $12-$15/day each pet, full kitchen or coffeemaker-
microwave-refrigerator, grassy walking area, 100 yards to beach,
www.hi-tide-resort.com

Moonstone Beach Motel   360-276-4346 or 360-276-4228
4849 Pacific Ave   888-888-9063
each pet $10/day   8 units, $75–$125
beachfront studios with kitchenette to 2-bdrm suites with full
kitchen, yard for walking dogs, www.moonstonemoclips.com

Ocean Crest Resort   360-276-4465, 800-684-8439
4651 State Route 109   45 units, $69–$209
1 to 2 dogs, $18/day each pet, full kitchen or coffeemaker-
microwave-refrigerator, restaurant, lounge, indoor pool, sauna, hot
tub, fitness room, stairway to beach, www.oceancrestresort.com

Monroe, WA

Best Western Sky Valley Inn   360-794-3111, 877-794-3111
19233 Hwy 2   58 units, $90–$120
each pet $20/day, full kitchen or microwave & refrigerator,
continental breakfast, seasonal pool, hot tub, fitness room, grassy
walking area, www.bestwestern.com/skyvalleyinn

Fairgrounds Inn   360-794-5401
18950 State Route 2   60 units, $45–$65
dogs under 30 lbs only, $9/day each pet, microwave, refrigerator,
continental breakfast, lawn, 10-minute walk to park, www.zzzinn.com

GuestHouse International Inn & Suites   360-863-1900
19103 State Route 2   800 214-8378
pet fee $20/day   66 units, $114–$134
coffeemaker, microwave, refrigerator, indoor pool, hot tub, fitness
room, small grassy walking area, 2 miles to public park,
www.guesthouseintl.com/location-WA-Monroe.htm

Monroe Motel   360-794-6751
20310 Old Owen Rd   15 units, $50–$70
dogs allowed with manager's approval only, $5-$10/day,
kitchenette, on 3 acres for walking dogs, 1 mile to fairgrounds,
www.betterlodging.com/Monroe-Washington-Hotels.htm

Montesano, WA

Monte Square Motel   360-249-4424
100 Brumfield Ave W   37 units, $59–$90
pet fee $10/stay, coffeemaker, microwave, refrigerator, pet walking
area, 2 miles to state park,
www.nwwebessentials.com/monte_square_motel

Morton, WA

Seasons Motel   360-496-6835, 877-496-6835
200 Westlake Ave   49 units, $70–$100
pet fee $10/stay, coffeemaker, microwave, refrigerator, continental breakfast, grassy walking area, 2½ blocks to public park, ½ mile to riverfront park, www.whitepasstravel.com/seasons.htm

Stiltner Motel   360-496-5103
250 State Route 7   7 units, $60
1 to 2 dogs under 30 lbs only, cabins, full kitchen, lawn & field for walking dogs, www.stiltnermotel.com

Moses Lake, WA

Ameristay Inn & Suites   509-764-7500
1157 N Stratford Rd   60 units, $81–$89
pet fee $25/stay, coffeemaker, microwave, refrigerator, continental breakfast, indoor pool, hot tub, fitness room, gravel walking area, 1 mile to public park, www.ameristayinn.com

Best Western Lake Front Hotel   509-765-9211, 800-235-4255
3000 W Marina Dr   157 units, $64–$140
pet fee $20/stay, coffeemaker, refrigerator, restaurant, lounge, outdoor pool, sauna, steam room, hot tub, fitness room, pet walking area, trail around lake to state park, www.bestwestern.com/prop_48045

Moses Lake, WA

Comfort Suites   509-765-3731, 866-765-8090
1700 E Kittleson Rd   60 units, $120–$150
1 to 2 dogs under 25 lbs only, $25/day each pet, coffeemaker, microwave, refrigerator, full breakfast, indoor pool, hot tub, fitness room, gravel & paved walking areas, 5-minute drive to public park, www.comfortsuites.com/hotel/wa189

El Rancho Hotel   509-765-9173
1214 S Pioneer Way   20 units, $50–$80
pet fee $5/day, coffeemaker, microwave, refrigerator, BBQ, picnic area, lawn for walking dogs

Heritage Suites   509-765-7707
511 S Division St   24 units, $99–$139
pet fee $50/stay, kitchen, grassy area for walking dogs, 5 blocks to public park, www.heritagesuites.com

Inn at Moses Lake   509-766-7000
1741 Kittleson Rd   44 units, $79–$89
pet fee $10/stay, microwave, refrigerator, continental breakfast,
small pet walking area, 5 miles to public park

Lakeshore Resort Motel   509-765-9201
3206 W Lakeshore Ct   35 units, $25–$70
pet fee $7/day, lakefront bungalows, full kitchen, BBQ, picnic area,
outdoor pool, boat launch, large yard for walking dogs, short drive
to public park, www.lakeshoreresortmotel.com

Motel 6   509-766-0250
2822 W Driggs Dr   89 units, $40–$57
pet fee $10/stay, microwave, refrigerator, coffee in lobby, seasonal
pool, open field, 2 blocks to public park, www.motel6.com

Motel Oasis   509-765-8636
466 Melva Lane   36 units, $47–$75
pet fee $10/day, kitchenette or coffeemaker-microwave-
refrigerator, continental breakfast, outdoor pool, hot tub, BBQ,
picnic area, large lawn, 2 blocks to lake, www.moteloasisinn.com

Ramada Inn   509-766-1000
1745 E Kittleson Rd   155 units, $90–$110
pet fee $10/day, microwave, refrigerator, extended continental
breakfast, indoor pool, lawn for walking dogs, 2 miles to public
park, www.ramada.com/hotel/23268

Sage 'n' Sand Motel   509-765-1755, 800-336-0454
1011 S Pioneer Way   37 units, $32–$65
kitchenette or coffeemaker-microwave-refrigerator, outdoor pool,
vacant lot for walking dogs, ½ mile to lakeside walking trails

Shilo Inn   509-765-9317, 800-222-2244
1819 E Kittleson Rd   100 units, $73–$124
coffeemaker, microwave, refrigerator, continental breakfast, indoor
pool, sauna, hot tub, fitness room, dog treats available at front
desk, grassy walking area, 1 mile to park, www.shiloinns.com

Sunland Motor Inn   509-765-1170
309 E 3rd Ave   22 units, $34–$52
pet fee $25/stay, kitchenette or microwave & refrigerator, 1 block
to public park, www.sunlandinn.com

Moses Lake, WA (continued)

Super 8 Motel   509-765-8886, 800-800-8000
449 Melva Lane   63 units, $59–$85
1 to 2 dogs, $10/day each pet, coffeemaker, microwave,
refrigerator, continental breakfast, indoor pool, open walking area,
across street from walking trail to lake, www.super8.com

Travel Inn Moses Lake   509-765-8631
316 S Pioneer Way   40 units, $50–$80
pet fee $10/day, coffeemaker, microwave, refrigerator, continental
breakfast, outdoor pool, hot tub, fitness room, next to city park

Mount Vernon, WA

Best Western College Way Inn   360-424-4287, 800-793-4024
300 W College Way   66 units, $67–$79
each pet $20/day, full kitchen or coffeemaker-microwave-
refrigerator, continental breakfast, seasonal pool, hot tub, grassy
walking area, 1/4 mile to riverfront park & walkway,
www.bestwestern.com/collegewayinn

Best Western Cottontree Inn   360-428-5678, 800-662-6886
2300 Market St   120 units, $99–$159
1 to 3 dogs, $25/stay, coffeemaker, microwave, refrigerator, full
breakfast, freshly baked cookies, restaurant, lounge, seasonal pool,
hot tub, fitness room, lawn, 1 block to riverfront park & trails,
www.bestwestern.com/cottontreeinnmtvernon

Days Inn   360-424-4141, 800-882-4141
2009 Riverside Dr   67 units, $93–$100
each pet $10/day, coffeemaker, microwave, refrigerator, continental
breakfast, restaurant, lounge, outdoor pool, fitness room, open lot
for walking dogs, 4 miles to park, www.daysinn.com/hotel/04735

Quality Inn   360-428-7020, 800-228-5150
1910 Freeway Dr   68 units, $80–$160
each pet $10/day, full kitchen or coffeemaker, extended
continental breakfast, indoor pool, hot tub, small pet walking area,
1/2 mile to public park, www.mvqi.com

Tulip Inn   360-428-5969, 800-599-5969
2200 Freeway Dr   40 units, $60–$89
pet fee $10/day, coffeemaker, continental breakfast, barkdust
walking area, 2-minute drive to public park, www.tulipinn.net

West Wind Motel 360-424-4224, 800-695-8284
2020 Riverside Dr 40 units, $55–$60
pet fee $10 for 1st day, $5 each additional day, microwave,
refrigerator, coffee in lobby, grassy walking area, ½ mile to park

Mountlake Terrace, WA

Studio 6 425-771-3139, 888-897-0202
6017 244th St SW 119 units, $68–$76
pet fee $10/day, kitchenette, grassy walking area, short walking
trail, 10-minute drive to beach, www.staystudio6.com

Mukilteo, WA

Extended StayAmerica 425-493-1561
3917 Harbour Pointe Blvd SW 94 units, $70–$90
pet fee $25/stay ($150 maximum), kitchenette, parking lot for
walking dogs, www.extendedstayamerica.com/870

Hogland House 425-742-7639, 888-681-5101
917 Webster St 3 units, $85–$125
kitchen, full country breakfast, hot tub, on 5 acres for walking
dogs, trail to beach, www.hoglandhouse.com

Towneplace Suites Seattle North 425-551-5900, 800-257-3000
8521 Mukilteo Speedway 128 units, $79–$159
1 to 2 dogs, $10/day, kitchen, continental breakfast, outdoor pool,
hot tub, BBQ, picnic area, wooded area for walking dogs, close to
state park, www.marriott.com/seats

Naches, WA

Agape Mountain Sunshine B & B 509-658-1500, 877-958-1500
10121 State Route 410 3 units, $125–$199
full breakfast provided, kitchen for guest use, fitness room, deck
overlooking river & waterfall, close to walking trail, 2 miles to
river, www.agapemtsunshine.com

Natchez Hotel 509-653-1317, 888-282-1317
213 Naches Ave 6 units, $69–$139
1 to 2 dogs allowed with manager's approval only, $10/day,
coffeemaker, microwave, refrigerator, restaurant, hot tub,
1½ blocks to public park

Naches, WA (continued)

Silver Beach Resort   509-672-2500
40350 US Hwy 12   17 units, $49–$80
pet fee $5/day, motel rooms & cabins sleep up to 6, RV & tent
sites, restaurant, store, boat rentals, lakefront walking trail, open
mid-April thru mid-September, www.silverbeach.biz

Snug Harbor at Rimrock Lake   509-672-2460
37590 US Hwy 12   6 units, $125–$300
cabins with kitchenette sleep up to 8, RV & tent sites, restaurant,
on 5 acres for walking dogs

Squaw Rock Resort   509-658-2926, 866-415-5817
15070 State Route 410   10 units, $85–$140
small dogs only, $10/day, motel rooms, riverside cabins,
kitchenette or coffeemaker-microwave-refrigerator, restaurant, RV
sites, store, gas station, walking trails, www.squawrockresort.net

Nahcotta, WA

Moby Dick Hotel   360-665-4543, 800-673-6145
25814 Sandridge Rd   10 units, $90–$150
each pet $10/day, full breakfast, restaurant, sauna, on 7-acre oyster
farm with woods & trails for off-leash walking, ½ mile to beach &
parks, www.mobydickhotel.com

Naselle, WA

Sleepy Hollow Motel   360-484-3232
1032 State Route 4   7 units, $40–$50
coffeemaker, microwave, refrigerator, close to river & small park

Neah Bay, WA

Cape Motel & RV Park   360-645-2250, 866-744-9944
1510 Bay View Ave   10 units, $50–$85
pet fee $10/day, motel rooms, full kitchen or coffeemaker,
RV & tent sites, across street to beach

Nespelem, WA

Reynold's Resort   509-633-1092
Buffalo Lake Access Rd   4 units, $20–$25
rustic fishing cabins with refrigerator but no running water,
tent sites, large area for walking dogs

Newman Lake, WA

Sutton Bay Resort   509-226-3660
12016 N Sutton Bay Rd   10 units, $10
dogs allowed with advance reservation only, $5/day, rustic cabins
with kitchenette sleep 6, trails for walking dogs, open mid-April
thru mid-October, www.suttonbayresort.net

Newport, WA

Golden Spur Motel   509-447-3823, 800-913-7787
924 W Hwy 2   24 units, $50–$73
pet fee $10/day, full kitchen or coffeemaker, restaurant, across
street to walking trail, 1/4 mile to public park,
www.goldenspurmotorinn.com

Newport City Inn   509-447-3463
220 N Washington Ave   13 units, $50–$56
pet fee $10/stay, coffeemaker, microwave, refrigerator, picnic area,
lawn behind motel for walking dogs, 6 blocks to park & riverfront

North Bend, WA

Mount Si Motel   425-888-1621
43200 SE North Bend Way   4 units, $45
each pet $5/day, coffeemaker, refrigerator, grassy walking areas,
1/3 mile to walking trail on old railroad bed

North Salt Lake, WA

Healing Water Inn   509-246-0292
21058 Hwy 17   24 units, $95–$135
small to medium dogs only, $10/day, guest use of kitchen,
gravel pet walking area, close to beach, 3 miles to public park,
www.thesundownermotelwa.com/healingwater.nxg

Oak Harbor, WA

Candlewood Suites   360-279-2222, 877-226-3539
33221 State Route 20   80 units, $99–$139
dogs under 80 lbs only, $75/stay, kitchenette, gazebo with BBQ,
fitness room, convenience store, small pet walking area, close to
beach & public park, www.candlewoodsuites.com

Oak Harbor, WA (continued)

Coachman Inn   360-675-0727, 800-635-0043
32959 State Route 20   100 units, $89–$105
each pet $8/day, coffeemaker, microwave, refrigerator, continental breakfast, seasonal pool, hot tub, fitness room, lawn, 1½ miles to beach & off-leash dog park, www.thecoachmaninn.com

Oaktown Cottages   360-279-8013
475 SE Barrington Dr   5 units, $80–$108
each pet $50/stay, 2-bdrm cottages, kitchen, lawn for walking dogs, 5-minute walk to public park, www.oaktowncottages.com

Queen Ann Motel   360-675-2209
450 SE Pioneer Way   20 units, $49–$75
pet fee $20/stay, coffeemaker, microwave, refrigerator, restaurant, lounge, indoor pool, grassy walking area, 1 block to beach & public park

Ocean City, WA

North Beach Motel   360-289-4116
2601 State Route 109   12 units, $45–$100
1 to 2 dogs, $10/stay each pet, microwave, refrigerator, grassy walking area, 5-minute walk to beach, 2-minute drive to public park, www.northbeachmotel.com

Pacific Sands Resort Motel   360-289-3588
2687 State Route 109   9 units, $61–$87
each pet $10/day, condos-cabins-vacation homes, full kitchen or coffeemaker-microwave-refrigerator, seasonal pool, grassy walking area, ¼ mile trail to beach, www.pacific-sands.net

Summerhome   206-697-2587
2 2nd Ave   1 unit, $165–$195
historic 6-bdrm home sleeps 12, small pet walking area, 3 blocks to beach, www.thesummerhomellc.com

West Winds Resort Motel   360-289-3448, 800-867-3448
2537 State Route 109   10 units, $60–$120
1 to 2 dogs, $10/day, 1-bdrm to 2-bdrm cabins-condos-vacation homes, kitchen, fish cleaning station, on 3 acres with creek & grassy walking area, ½ mile to beach, www.wa-accommodations.com/nw/westwinds.htm

Ocean Park, WA

Charles Nelson Guest House 360-665-3016, 888-862-9756
26205 Sandridge Rd 3 units, $80–$180
1 to 2 dogs allowed by advance reservation only, $25/stay, full
breakfast, across street to open field for walking dogs, 1 mile to
beach, www.charlesnelsonbandb.com

Coastal Cottages of Ocean Park 360-665-4658
1511 264th Place 4 units, $65–$150
1 to 3 dogs, $5/stay, 1930s cottages, fully-stocked kitchen, BBQ,
picnic area, fire pit, fish cleaning station, large yard, 5-minute walk
to beach, www.coastalcottagesofoceanpark.com

Harbor View Motel 360-665-4959
3204 281st St 8 units, $80–$130
each pet $5/day, rooms & 1-bdrm cottage with kitchen, courtyard
picnic area with BBQ, fire pit, grassy walking area, 1 block to bay,
www.harborviewmotel.net

Ocean Park Resort 360-665-4585, 800-835-4634
25904 R St 14 units, $65–$120
1 to 2 dogs, $7/day, motel rooms & mobile homes, full kitchen or
coffeemaker-microwave-refrigerator, seasonal pool, hot tub, RV &
tent spaces, fish cleaning station, basketball & volleyball courts,
on 9 acres for walking dogs, 4 blocks to ocean, www.opresort.com

Oceanfront Getaways 360-665-3633
1 to 2 dogs, $20/stay 11 units, $165–$315
2-bdrm to 5-bdrm vacation homes in Long Beach area sleep up to
10, most are oceanfront, some with hot tub, easy beach access,
www.oceanfrontgetaways.us

Shakti Cove Cottages 360-665-4000
25301 Park Ave 10 units, $80–$130
each pet $5/day, cottages, kitchen, on 3 acres for walking dogs,
5-minute walk thru dunes to beach, 8 miles to state park,
www.shakticove.com

Sunset View Resort 360-665-4494, 800-272-9199
25517 Park Ave 52 units, $60–$115
1 to 3 dogs, $15/stay each pet, rooms-studios-2-bdrm suites, full
kitchen or coffeemaker & microwave, sauna, hot tub, most have
ocean view, on 6½ landscaped acres, 400 feet to beach for walking
dogs, www.sunsetviewresort.com

Ocean Shores, WA

At the Beach Family Vacation Rentals   360-289-4297
659 Ocean Shores Blvd NW   800-303-4297
each pet $10/day   70 units, $75–$495
beachfront cabins-condos-vacation homes sleep 2 to 16, hot tub,
beach access for walking dogs, www.oceanshoreswashington.com

Canterbury Inn Luxury Beach   360-289-3317, 800-562-6678
643 Ocean Shores Blvd NW   46 units, $82–$278
1 to 2 dogs under 75 lbs only, $15/day each pet, kitchen, BBQ,
indoor pool, hot tub, fitness room, lawn, www.canterburyinn.com

Echoes of the Sea   360-289-3358, 866-999-3246
3208 State Route 109   8 units, $47–$105
each pet $15/day, 1-bdrm to 2-bdrm suites sleep up to 6, full kitchen
or coffeemaker, picnic tables, fire rings, RV & tent sites, on 3½
wooded acres, www.wa-accommodations.com/nw/echoes.htm

Grey Gull Resort   360-289-3381, 800-562-9712
651 Ocean Shores Blvd NW   37 units, $130–$350
pet fee $15/stay, beachfront condos with full kitchen sleep up to
10, outdoor pool, sauna, hot tub, www.thegreygull.com

Huckleberry Inn   360-289-3169
839 Ocean Shores Blvd NW   7 units, $68–$148
1 to 2 dogs, $20/day each pet, kitchen, picnic area, fire pit,
horseshoes, tetherball, next to beach, www.oceanbch.com

Nautilus Condos   360-289-2722
835 Ocean Shores Blvd NW   24 units, $80–$160
1 to 2 dogs, $20/stay, fully equipped 1-bdrm condos, kitchen, hot
tub, pet towels provided, designated pet walking area, trail to
beach, www.nautiluscondos.com www.nautiluscondos.com

Oasis Motel   360-289-2350, 800-290-2899
686 Ocean Shores Blvd NW   17 units, $49–$199
1 to 2 dogs, $10/day, microwave, refrigerator, kitchen, grassy
walking area, next to golf course, across street to beach

Ocean Shores Ocean View Resort Homes   360-289-4416
123 Taurus Blvd SW   800-927-6394
pet fee varies depending on particular unit   15 units, $120–$350
rustic cabins-condos-contemporary homes, kitchen, hot tub,
easy beach access, www.oceanbeachfronthomes.com

Ocean Shores Reservations   360-289-2430, 800-562-8612
899 Point Brown Ave NW   60 units, $119–$250
pet fee $10-20/day, condos & vacation homes sleep 2 to 16, full
kitchen or coffeemaker, indoor pool, hot tub, easy beach access for
walking dogs, www.oceanshoresreservation.com

Polynesian Resort   360-289-3361, 800-562-4836
615 Ocean Shores Blvd NW   69 units, $59–$119
each pet $15/day, studios to 2-bdrm units, kitchen, continental
breakfast, restaurant, lounge, indoor pool, sauna, hot tub, game
room, sports courts, oceanfront park area & trails to the beach for
walking dogs, www.thepolynesian.com

Sands Resort   360-289-2444, 800-841-4001
801 Ocean Shores Blvd NW   196 units, $49–$269
pet fee $10/day, beachfront motel rooms & condos, full kitchen or
coffeemaker, continental breakfast, BBQ, picnic tables, sundeck,
game room, indoor & outdoor pools, sauna, hot tub, beach &
dunes for walking dogs, www.thesandsonline.com

Shilo Beachfront Resort   360-289-4600, 800-222-2244
707 Ocean Shores Blvd NW   113 units, $94–$240
1 to 2 dogs, $25/stay, kitchenette, indoor pool, sauna, hot tub,
www.shiloinns.com

Silver King Motel   360-289-3386
1070 Discovery Ave SE   25 units, $50–$90
dogs allowed with advance approval, $10/day, kitchen, BBQ,
picnic area & outdoor fireplace, children's play area, walking trail
to bird sanctuary, close to bayfront, www.silverkingmotel.com

Westerly Motel   360-289-3711
870 Ocean Shores Blvd NW   8 units, $40–$89
pet fee $10/stay, full kitchen or microwave & refrigerator, pet
walking area, 2 blocks to beach

Odessa, WA

La Collage Inn   509-982-2412
609 E 1st Ave   12 units, $44–$63
each pet $11/day, rooms to 2-bdrm suites, kitchenette or
coffeemaker-microwave-refrigerator, creekside walking trail, close
to public swimming pool & spa, 6 blocks to public park,
www.lacollageinn.com

Okanogan, WA

Okanogan Inn   509-422-6431, 877-422-7070
1 Appleway   77 units, $50–$65
1 to 3 dogs, $5/day, full kitchen or microwave & refrigerator,
continental breakfast, restaurant, lounge, outdoor pool, fitness
room, large walking area, 1/4 mile to park, www.okanoganinn.com

Olga, WA

Doe Bay Resort & Retreat   360-376-2291
107 Doe Bay Rd   39 units, $35–$650
each pet $20/day, studios to 1-bdrm cabins, kitchen, restaurant,
sauna, hot tub, yurts & tent sites, massage & yoga studio, on 33
waterfront acres, lawn & gravel areas for walking dogs, close to
state park, 8 miles to off-leash dog park, www.doebay.com

Olympia, WA

Clarion Hotel   360-352-7200, 800-528-1234
900 Capitol Way S   99 units, $75–$115
1 to 2 dogs under 25 lbs only, $25/day each pet, coffeemaker,
microwave, refrigerator, extended continental breakfast, restaurant,
seasonal pool, hot tub, fitness room, barkdust walking area,
4 blocks to off-leash dog park, www.clarionhotel.com/hotel/wa186

Governor Hotel   360-352-7700, 877-352-7701
621 S Capitol Way   119 units, $99–$140
1 to 2 dogs, $50/stay, coffeemaker, microwave, refrigerator,
restaurant, lounge, seasonal pool, sauna, hot tub, fitness room,
across street to park, 1 block to lakefront trail, www.olywagov.com

La Quinta Inn Olympia/Lacey   360-412-1200, 800-957-9163
4704 Park Center Ave NE   63 units, $86–$159
coffeemaker, microwave, refrigerator, continental breakfast, indoor
pool, hot tub, fitness room, lawn for walking dogs, www.lq.com

Olympia Inn   360-352-8533
909 Capitol Way S   27 units, $50–$55
pet fee $10/day, microwave, refrigerator, 2 blocks to park & lake

Quality Inn   360-943-4710
1211 Quince St SE   62 units, $75–$95
each pet $15/day, coffeemaker, microwave, refrigerator, extended
continental breakfast, outdoor pool, fitness room, 3 blocks to
lakefront trail, www.qualityinn.com/hotel/wa130

Red Lion Hotel   360-943-4000, 866-896-4000
2300 Evergreen Park Dr SW   192 units, $69–$169
pet fee $20/day, coffeemaker, restaurant, lounge, seasonal pool,
hot tub, fitness room, lawn for walking dogs, ½ mile to public park
with trail around lake, www.redlion.com/olympia

Omak, WA

Best Western Pepper Tree Inn   509-422-2088, 888-280-2088
820 Koala Ave   77 units, $81–$160
dogs under 10 lbs only, $10/day each pet, coffeemaker,
microwave, refrigerator, extended continental breakfast, indoor
pool, hot tub, fitness room, small pet walking area, open field
across street, 1 mile to public park, www.peppertreeomak.com

Motel Nicholas   509-826-4611
527 E Grape St   21 units, $47
1 to 2 dogs, $10/day, coffeemaker, microwave, refrigerator,
grassy walking area, 2 miles to public park

Omak Inn   509-826-3822, 800-204-4800
912 Koala Ave   66 units, $65–$125
pet fee $25/stay, coffeemaker, microwave, refrigerator, continental
breakfast, indoor pool, hot tub, open field & country road for
walking dogs, www.omakinnwa.com

Rodeway Inn   509-826-0400, 888-700-6625
122 N Main St   61 units, $40–$75
1 to 2 dogs, $10/day each pet, coffeemaker, microwave,
refrigerator, extended continental breakfast, seasonal pool, freshly
baked cookies, lawn for walking dogs, several public parks within
3 blocks, www.rodeway.com/hotel/wa115

Royal Motel   509-826-5715
514 Riverside Dr   11 units, $40–$60
each pet $5/day, kitchenette or coffeemaker-microwave-
refrigerator, picnic area, grassy walking area, 2 blocks to riverside
walking trail, ¼ mile to public park

Stampede Motel   509-826-1161
215 W 4th St   14 units, $35–$45
1 to 2 dogs, coffeemaker, microwave, refrigerator, grassy walking
area, across street to park & walking path

Orcas, WA

All Dream Cottages   360-376-2500
5 units, $187–$297
dogs allowed October thru April only (not in summer), $10/day,
1-bdrm to 2-bdrm cottages, kitchen, deck, hot tub, BBQ, on 3 acres
overlooking East Sound, short walk to private beach,
www.alldreamcottages.com

Oroville, WA

Camaray Motel   509-476-3684
1320 Main St   38 units, $41–$61
pet fee $10/day, coffeemaker, microwave, refrigerator, seasonal
pool, grassy walking area, ½ block to public park

Eden Valley Guest Ranch   509-485-4002
31 Eden Valley Lane   10 units, $95–$110
pet fee $5/day, 1-bdrm cabins sleep 2 to 4, full kitchen, 10 corrals
for guests' horses, guided trail riding available, open field & miles
of walking trails, ½ mile to swimming pond, 5 miles to old ghost
town of Molson, www.edenvalleyranch.net

Veranda Beach Cottages   509.476.4000, 888-476-4001
1 to 2 dogs, $5/day   110 units, $200–$800
2-bdrm to 4-bdrm lakeside cottages, kitchen, restaurant, seasonal
pool, hot tub, fitness room, both adult & children's swimming
pools, open fields for walking dogs on 280-acre resort,
www.verandabeach.com

Othello, WA

Best Western Othello Inn   509-488-5671, 800-240-7865
1020 E Cedar St   50 units, $81–$100
1 to 2 dogs, $15/stay, full kitchen or coffeemaker, continental
breakfast, seasonal pool, steam room, fitness room, freshly baked
cookies, bird cleaning station for hunters, ½ block to public park,
www.bestwestern.com/othelloinn

Cabana Motel   509-488-2605, 800-442-4581
665 E Windsor St   50 units, $50–$75
dogs allowed with manager's approval only, $10/stay, kitchenette
or coffeemaker-microwave-refrigerator, seasonal pool, field for
walking dogs, across street from public park

Cimarron Motel 5   509-488-9619
1490 E Main St   69 units, $50–$75
microwave, refrigerator, ¼ mile to public park

Mardon Resort   509-346-2651, 800-416-2736
8198 Hwy 262 SE # 1   300 units, $40–$200
pet fee $5/day, lakefront motel rooms & cottages, restaurant,
lounge, RV & tent sites, tackle & gift shop,
www.mardonresort.com

Otis Orchards, WA

Oxford Suites   509-847-1000, 866-668-7848
22624 E Heroy Ave   127 units, $119–$195
pet fee $25/stay, coffeemaker, microwave, refrigerator, full
breakfast, evening reception with beverages & appetizers, outdoor
pool, sauna, steam room, hot tub, fitness room, pet walking area,
next to walking trail, www.oxfordsuitesspokanevalley.com

Pacific Beach, WA

Pacific Beach & Beyond   360-276-0215
1st St at Central Ave   12 units, $110–$295
1 to 2 dogs, $10/day each pet, 1-bdrm cottages to 3-bdrm vacation
homes with full kitchen sleep up to 12, located in Pacific Beach-
Moclips-Taholah, most are only a short walk from the beach, also
1-bdrm units with kitchenette at the Sweet Alice Inn in
Pacific Beach, www.pacificbeachandbeyond.com

Pacific Beach Inn   360-276-4433
12 1st St S   10 units, $49–$119
1 to 2 dogs allowed with manager's approval only, $10/day each
pet, full kitchen or coffeemaker-microwave-refrigerator, BBQ,
1 block to beach, www.pbinn.com

Sand Dollar Inn & Cottages   360-276-4525
56 Central Ave   11 units, $55–$195
each pet $10/day, 1-bdrm to 3-bdrm suites & cottages with full
kitchen sleep 2 to 6, across road to beach, www.sanddollarinn.net

Sandpiper Beach Resort   360-276-4580, 800-567-4737
4159 State Route 109   31 units, $75–$250
pet fee $13/day, oceanfront studios with kitchenette to 3-bdrm
suites & cottages with full kitchen that sleep up to 12, beachfront
for walking dogs

Packwood, WA

Cowlitz River Lodge   360-494-4444, 888-305-2185
13069 US Hwy 12   31 units, $60–$90
each pet $10-$20/day, continental breakfast, hot tub, open field for
walking dogs, 3 blocks to public park, close to hiking trails,
www.escapetothemountains.com

Crest Trail Lodge   360-494-4944, 800-477-5339
12729 US Hwy 12   27 units, $70–$90
dogs under 25 lbs only, $10/stay, coffeemaker, microwave,
refrigerator, continental breakfast, lawn for walking dogs, next to
walking trail, www.cresttraillodge.com

Elk Trail Lodge   360-273-8710
530 Rochester 98579   2 units, $295–$350
3-bdrm fully equipped vacation homes sleep up to 8, kitchen, hot
tub, BBQ, fire pit, on 2½ creekside acres for walking dogs &
watching elk, www.lawrencevacationrentals.com

Great Northwest Cabins   503-492-8783 or 503-888-6173
dogs allowed with advance approval, $25/stay   4 units, $99–$225
3-bdrm 1-bath modern cabins, kitchen, hot tub, on 1 acre with
large yard for walking dogs, www.greatnorthwestcabins.com

Mountain View Lodge   360-494-5555, 877-277-7192
13163 US Hwy 12   23 units, $45–$150
each pet $5/day, rustic lodge rooms sleep up to 6, full kitchen or
coffeemaker, seasonal pool, hot tub, picnic tables, lawn & wooded
area for walking dogs, close to hiking trails, www.mtvlodge.com

Packwood Inn   360-494-5500, 877-496-9666
13032 US Hwy 12   34 units, $50–$145
pet fee $15/day, full kitchen or coffeemaker-microwave-
refrigerator, continental breakfast, indoor pool, hot tub, picnic
area, large yard for walking dogs, 2 blocks to riverside walkway,
close to national park, www.innofpackwood.com

Tall Pines Vacation Cabins   360-623-0457
dogs allowed with advance approval only   1 unit, $130–$200
fully equipped 3-bdrm 2-bath vacation cabin on wooded lot,
kitchen, BBQ, fire pit, hot tub, www.tallpinescabins.com

Tatoosh Motel   360-494-7379
12880 Hwy 12   12 units, $35–$75
1 to 2 dogs under 100 lbs only, $5/stay, coffeemaker, microwave,
continental breakfast, on 1 acre for walking dogs

TMC Properties   360-494-2311, 800-294-2311
each pet $25/stay   25 units, $125–$550
fully equipped cabins & vacation homes, www.tmcproperties.com

Pasco, WA

Best Western Pasco Inn & Suites   509-543-7722, 866-313-7599
2811 N 20th Ave   110 units, $109–$162
dogs under 10 lbs only, $10/stay, coffeemaker, microwave,
refrigerator, extended continental breakfast, sauna, hot tub, fitness
room, www.bestwestern.com/pascoinnandsuites

Holiday Inn Express   509-543-7000, 888-465-4329
4525 Convention Place   85 units, $129–$169
dogs under 30 lbs only, $20/day each pet, kitchenette or
coffeemaker, extended continental breakfast, indoor pool, hot tub,
fitness room, grassy walking area, 5-minute drive to public park,
www.hiexpress.com/pascowa

King City Knights Inn   509-547-3475
2100 E Hillsboro St   36 units, $39–$64
pet fee $10/day, coffeemaker, restaurant, lounge, picnic area,
grassy walking area, 10 miles to public park, www.knightsinn.com

Motel 6   509-546-2010
1520 N Oregon Ave   106 units, $39–$69
outdoor pool, open walking area, 1 mile to park, www.motel6.com

Red Lion Hotel   509-547-0701, 800-733-5466
2525 N 20th Ave   279 units, $109–$140
pet fee $25/stay, coffeemaker, microwave, refrigerator, restaurant,
lounge, outdoor pool, hot tub, fitness room, grassy walking area,
www.redlion.com/pasco

Sleep Inn   509-545-9554, 866-892-0202
9930 Bedford St   62 units, $65–$110
pet fee $10/stay, coffeemaker, microwave, refrigerator, extended
continental breakfast, indoor pool, hot tub, freshly baked cookies,
open area for walking dogs, 5-minute walk to riverfront park,
www.gorgehotels.com/pasco

Pasco, WA (continued)

Starlite Motel　　　　　　　　　　　　　509-547-7531
2634 N 4th Ave　　　　　　　　　　　　18 units, $40–$60
pet fee $10/day, microwave, refrigerator, open area for walking dogs

Pateros, WA

Lake Pateros Motor Inn　　　509-923-2203, 866-444-1985
115 S Lake Shore Dr　　　　　　　　　30 units, $55–$102
pet fee $10/day, rooms overlooking waterfront, coffeemaker, microwave, refrigerator, outdoor pool, BBQ, picnic tables, boat rentals, large yard, 1 block to park, www.lakepaterosmotorinn.com

Peshastin, WA

Alpine Chalets　　　　　　　　　　　　509-548-5674
3601 Allen Lane　　　　　　　　　　2 units, $125–$150
fully equipped A-frame cabins with kitchen sleep 6, walking path to river, close to riverfront park, 1 mile to dog-friendly hiking trail, www.alpineleavenworth.com

Pomeroy, WA

Pioneer Motel　　　　　　　　　　　　509-843-1559
1201 Main St　　　　　　　　　　　13 units, $45–$70
microwave, refrigerator, open field for walking dogs, close to trails & public park with swimming pool, www.pomeroymotel.com

Port Angeles, WA

Days Inn　　　　　　　　　360-452-4015, 877-438-8588
1510 E Front St　　　　　　　　　109 units, $49–$129
1 to 2 small to medium dogs only, $10/stay, coffeemaker, microwave, refrigerator, continental breakfast, seasonal pool, hot tub, small grassy walking area, across street to waterfront trail, www.daysinn.com/hotel/32328

Eagle's Flight Bed, Breakfast Inn & Barn　　　360-417-6797
1053 S Bagley Creek Rd　　　　　　　　866-692-9159
　　　　　　　　　　　　　　　　　　2 units, $85–$145
1 to 2 dogs allowed, studio & 2-bdrm suite with kitchenette, full breakfast, hot tub, on 5 acres for walking dogs, guests' horses also welcome, 5 miles to waterfront walking area, www.efbbb.com

Flagstone Motel   360-457-9494, 888-304-3465
415 E 1st St   45 units, $63–$84
small dogs only, $10/day each pet, microwave, refrigerator,
continental breakfast, small grassy area for walking dogs,
2½ blocks to public park, www.flagstonemotel.com

Indian Valley Motel   360-928-3266
235471 Hwy 101   8 units, $65–$110
1 dog under 20 lbs only, $15/day, microwave, refrigerator,
restaurant, grassy walking area, 5-minute drive to national park,
www.grannyscafeandmotel.com/motel.htm

Inn at Rooster Hill   360-452-4933, 877-221-0837
112 Reservoir Rd   6 units, $119–$189
dogs allowed with advance approval, $15-$25/stay, coffeemaker,
microwave, refrigerator, full breakfast, on 2½ acres with flower
gardens & walking paths, short drive to public park,
www.innatroosterhill.com

La Place Sur La Mer   360-565-8029, 888-248-1277
2026 Place Rd   4 units, $129–$250
dogs allowed with advance approval only, 1 pet-friendly suite with
full kitchen, hot tub, on 1¾ acres with walking paths & fenced
area for off-leash play, ocean views, short walk to beach,
www.magicalbeach.com

Lake Crescent Lodge   360-928-3211
416 Lake Crescent Rd   52 units, $132–$231
1 to 3 dogs allowed in 1-room to 2-bdrm cottages only, $15/day
each pet, coffeemaker, microwave, refrigerator, restaurant, lounge,
open meadow for walking dogs, next to national park,
www.lakecrescentlodge.com

Michael's Inn   360-461-5197
604 W 8th St   8 units, $75–$175
1 to 2 dogs under 15 lbs only, $20/day each pet, full kitchen or
coffeemaker-microwave-refrigerator, fenced yard, 3 blocks to
public park, 1 mile to beach, www.ptangeles.com/michaelsinn

Northwest Manor B & B   360-452-5839, 888-229-7052
1320 Marie View Dr   2 units, $115–$130
1 to 2 small dogs only, $15/day each pet, resident dog, full
breakfast, private deck, field for walking dogs, 6 blocks to
waterfront walking area, www.northwestmanor.com

Port Angeles, WA (continued)

Quality Inn Uptown   360-457-9434, 800-858-3812
101 E 2nd St   35 units, $70–$189
1 to 2 dogs under 20 lbs only, $10/day each pet, coffeemaker,
microwave, refrigerator, continental breakfast, hot tub, freshly
baked cookies, grassy walking area, 3 blocks to public pool &
waterfront park, www.qualityinn.com/hotel/wa099

Riviera Inn   360-417-3955
535 E Front St   38 units, $59–$149
1 to 2 small dogs allowed with advance approval only, $15/day
each pet, microwave, refrigerator, continental breakfast, lawn,
2 blocks to waterfront walking area, www.rivierainn.net

Sol Duc Hot Springs Resort   360-327-3583, 866-476-5382
Sol Duc Rd & Highway 101   32 units, $147–$179
pet fee $15/day, cabins sleep up to 5, full kitchen, RV & tent sites,
restaurant, outdoor swimming pool, 4 mineral water soaking pools,
woods & riverfront walking areas, www.visitsolduc.com

Super 8 Motel   360-452-8401, 800-800-8000
2104 E 1st St   63 units, $66–$96
1 to 2 dogs, $15/day each pet, coffeemaker, microwave,
refrigerator, continental breakfast, lawn, short drive to
several parks, www.super8.com

Port Hadlock, WA

Hadlock Motel   360-385-3111, 888-360-3111
175 Chimacum Rd   18 units, $80–$90
pet fee $10/day, coffeemaker, grassy walking area, short drive to
beach, www.hadlockmotel.com

Inn at Port Hadlock   360-385-7030, 800.785.7030
310 Hadlock Bay Rd   47 units, $99–$349
each pet $25/day, full kitchen or coffeemaker & microwave,
restaurant, lounge, close to park, www.innatporthadlock.com

Port Ludlow, WA

Resort at Port Ludlow   360-437-7000, 800-732-1239
1 Heron Rd   2 units, $109–$229
pet fee $35-$50/stay, coffeemaker, refrigerator, restaurant, hot tub,
1/2 block to beach, www.portludlowresort.com

Pullman, WA (continued)

Country B & B   509-334-4453
2701 Staley Rd   2 units, $100
1 to 2 dogs, continental breakfast, hot tub, lawn, fields & country roads for walking dogs

Hilltop Inn   509-332-0928, 866-333-8400
928 NW Olsen St   59 units, $79–$169
1 to 2 dogs, $15/day each pet, kitchenette, full breakfast, freshly baked cookies, complimentary soup & soda on Wednesday evenings, restaurant, lounge, indoor pool, sauna, hot tub, fitness room, lawn & open field for walking dogs, 2 blocks to public park, www.hotelonthehill.com

Holiday Inn Express   509-334-4437, 800-465-4329
1190 SE Bishop Blvd   130 units, $99–$139
dogs allowed by advance arrangement only, $10-$20/day, microwave, refrigerator, full breakfast, indoor pool, hot tub, fitness room, pet walking area, ¼ mile to trail, ½ mile to park, www.hiexpress.com/pullmanwa

Mendels Inn   509-332-2646
15 E Main St   59 units, $45–$89
1 to 2 small dogs only, $20/day, kitchenette, continental breakfast, across street from college campus, 1 block to public park

Quality Inn Paradise Creek   (509) 332-0500, 800-669-3212
1000 SE Bishop Blvd   66 units, $70–$105
coffeemaker, microwave, refrigerator, continental breakfast, seasonal pool, sauna, hot tub, grassy walking area, close to paved walking trail, www.qualityinn.com/hotel/WA015

Town Centre Inn   509-334-2511
SE Paradise St   31 units, $46–$68
pet fee $10/day, coffeemaker, microwave, refrigerator, grassy walking area, 2 blocks to public park, www.thetowncentreinn.com

Puyallup, WA

Best Western Park Plaza   253-848-1500, 888-204-5804
S Hill Park Dr   100 units, $109–$154
pet fee $25/stay, coffeemaker, microwave, refrigerator, continental breakfast, seasonal pool, hot tub, small pet walking area, ¼ mile to waterfront trail, 2 miles to parks, www.bestwesternparkplaza.com

Port Orchard, WA

Comfort Inn   360-895-2666, 800-424-6423
1121 Bay St   63 units, $85–$120
1 to 2 dogs under 25 lbs only, $25/stay, coffeemaker, microwave, refrigerator, continental breakfast, hot tub, BBQ, picnic tables, www.comfortinn.com/hotel/wa167

Days Inn   360-895-7818, 800-329-7466
220 Bravo Terrace   55 units, $89–$129
1 to 2 dogs under 25 lbs only, $20/day each pet, coffeemaker, microwave, refrigerator, continental breakfast, indoor pool, hot tub, 5 miles to public park, www.daysinn.com/hotel/14080

Port Townsend, WA

Aladdin Motor Inn   360-385-3747, 800-281-3747
2333 Washington St   30 units, $70–$140
1 to 2 dogs, $10/day each pet, coffeemaker, microwave, refrigerator, extended continental breakfast, beachfront for walking dogs, www.aladdinmotorinnpt.com

Ann Starrett Mansion Victorian   360-385-3205, 800-321-0644
744 Clay St   9 units, $115–$175
pet fee $25/day, dogs allowed in separate 2-bdrm cottage, coffeemaker, lawn, 2 blocks to park, www.starrettmansion.com

Big Red Barn   360-301-1271
40 Vancouver Dr   1 unit, $160–$185
pet fee $35/stay, 2-room romantic getaway sleeps 2, kitchenette & jacuzzi tub, breakfast basket provided, dog treats, fenced yard, 1 block to public park, www.bigredbarngetaway.com

Bishop Victorian Hotel   360-385-6122, 800-824-4738
714 Washington St   16 units, $109–$199
1 to 3 dogs, $20/day each pet, coffeemaker, microwave, refrigerator, continental breakfast, breakfast basket delivered to your door each morning, lawn & gardens, 1 block to waterfront & walking paths, www.rainshadowproperties.com/bishop

Chevy Chase Inn & Beach Cabins   360-385-1270
3710 S Discovery Rd   7 units, $100–$300
1 to 2 dogs, $20/day each pet, studios with coffeemaker-microwave-refrigerator to 3-bdrm cabins with kitchen, lawn, trail to beach, www.chevychasebeachcabins.com

Port Townsend, WA (continued)

Harborside Inn   360-385-7909, 800-942-5960
330 Benedict St   63 units, $80–$160
each pet $15/day, kitchenette or microwave & refrigerator,
continental breakfast, outdoor pool, hot tub, grassy walking area,
2 blocks to beach, www.harborside-inn.com

Morgan Hill Getaways   360-385-2536, 800-490-9070
606 Roosevelt St   5 units, $100–$175
each pet $20/day, suites with microwave & refrigerator to 4-bdrm
2-bath vacation home with full kitchen, close to beach for walking
dogs, www.morganhillgetaways.com

Palace Hotel   360-385-0773, 800-962-0741
1004 Water St   19 units, $59–$159
pet fee $10/stay, kitchen, continental breakfast, ½ block to beach,
www.palacehotelpt.com

Port Townsend Inn   360-385-2211, 800-216-4985
2020 Washington St   36 units, $69–$168
1 dog under 25 lbs allowed in smoking rooms only, $10/stay,
kitchenette, continental breakfast, indoor pool, hot tub, lawn,
1 block to public park, 7 blocks to small lake & walking trail,
www.porttownsendinn.com

Swan Hotel   360-385-1718, 800-824-4738
216 Monroe St   9 units, $99–$175
1 to 3 dogs, $20/day each pet, first floor rooms & studio cottages,
coffeemaker, microwave, refrigerator, guest pass to local fitness
center, lawn, across street from beach, www.theswanhotel.com/

Valley View Motel   360-385-1666
162 State Route 20   5 units, $50–$75
1 to 2 dogs, $10/stay, full kitchen or coffeemaker, on 40 acres for
walking dogs, 1 mile to lakefront trails

Poulsbo, WA

Brauer Cove Guest House   360-779-4153
16709 Brauer Rd NE   1 unit, $125
2-bdrm waterfront apartment, kitchen stocked with breakfast
supplies, lawn & quiet neighborhood for walking dogs, 1-mile
bayside walk to town, www.brauercove.com

Foxbridge Bed & Breakfast   360-598-5599, 866-2
30680 State Hwy 3 NE   3 un
full breakfast, pedal bike available for guest use, on 5 coun
acres, close to beach & walking trail, www.foxbridge.com

Holiday Inn Express   360-697-4400, 800
19801 7th Ave NE   63 units, $
1 to 2 dogs, $10-$30/day each pet, coffeemaker, microwa
refrigerator, full breakfast, hot tub, picnic tables, grassy
area, short drive to public park, www.hiexpress.com/po

Poulsbo Inn   360-779-3921, 8
18680 State Hwy 305 NE   83 unit
each pet $15/day, coffeemaker, microwave, refrigerato
continental breakfast, complimentary soup bar Tuesda
Thursday evenings in winter, seasonal pool, hot tub, fi
lawn, 6 blocks to waterfront park, www.poulsboinn.co

Prosser, WA

Barn Motor Inn
490 Wine Country Rd   30 u
1 to 2 small dogs only, $15/stay each pet, microwave
coffee in lobby, restaurant, lounge, seasonal pool, R
area for walking dogs, 2 blocks to trail, ½ mile to ri
www.barnmotorinn.com

Best Western Inn at Horse Heaven 509-786-79
259 Merlot Dr   8
dogs under 50 lbs only, $10/day, coffeemaker, mi
refrigerator, continental breakfast, indoor pool, h
½ block to trail, www.bestwestern.com/theinnat

Prosser Motel
1206 Wine Country Rd
each pet $3/day, coffeemaker, refrigerator, gras

Pullman, WA

Cougar Land Motel
150 W Main St
1 to 2 dogs, microwave, refrigerator, continen
walking area, 1 block to walking trail

Crossland Economy Studios Tacoma/Puyallup
2101 N Meridian   253-445-5945, 800-326-5651
1 to 2 dogs under 20 lbs only   133 units, $60–$75
$25/day ($150 maximum), suites, kitchenette, grassy walking
area, 5-minute walk to public park, www.crosslandstudios.com/539

Holiday Inn Express   253-848-4900, 888-465-4329
812 S Hill Park Dr   96 units, $159–$199
pet fee $25/stay, coffeemaker, microwave, refrigerator, continental
breakfast, indoor pool, hot tub, small grassy area for walking dogs,
5-minute drive to lakefront trail, www.hiexpress.com/puyallup

Motel Puyallup   253-845-8825, 800-921-2700
1412 Meridian St S   64 units, $59–$70
pet fee $15/day for 1st pet, $5/day each additional pet, full kitchen
or coffeemaker-microwave-refrigerator, continental breakfast,
gravel area & field for walking dogs, 2 blocks to fairgrounds,
3 blocks to public park, www.motelpuyallup.com

Northwest Motor Inn   253-841-2600, 800-845-9490
1409 Meridian St S   52 units, $49–$80
each pet $10/day, kitchen or microwave & refrigerator, continental
breakfast, gravel area & vacant lot for walking dogs, 3 blocks to
public park, www.nwmotorinn.com

Quilcene, WA

Maple Grove Motel   360-765-3410
61 Maple Grove Rd   12 units, $55–$65
pet fee $10/day, kitchen or coffeemaker, grassy walking area, next
to national forest & hiking trails, guests' horses can also be
accommodated

Quinault, WA

Lake Quinault Lodge   360-288-2900, 800-562-6672
345 S Shore Rd   92 units, $70–$183
lodge rooms & boathouses, pet fee varies up to $25/day depending
on particular unit, restaurant, indoor pool, sauna, ping pong table,
boat/canoe/kayak rentals, wooded walking area & trails, daily
lake tours (dogs welcome too), www.visitlakequinault.com

Quincy, WA

Cave B Inn at Sagecliffe   509-785-2283, 888-785-2283
344 Silica Rd NW   30 units, $135–$235
pet fee $30/stay, full breakfast, kitchenette, seasonal pool,
dramatic inn overlooking river, open walking areas,
www.cavebinn.com

Country Cabin Motel & RV Park   509-787-3515
711 2nd Ave SW   21 units, $60
each pet $10/day, coffeemaker, microwave, refrigerator,
grassy walking area

Sundowner Motel   509-787-3587
414 F St SE   24 units, $39–$83
each pet $5/day, full kitchen or coffeemaker-microwave-
refrigerator, seasonal pool, gravel area for walking dogs, 2 blocks
to public park, www.thesundownermotelwa.com

Villager Inn Motel   509-787-3515
711 2nd Ave SW   21 units, $50–$60
1 to 2 dogs, $5/stay each pet, coffeemaker, microwave,
refrigerator, seasonal pool, small pet walking area next door in RV
park, 7 blocks to public park

Randle, WA

Tall Timber Motel   360-497-2991
10023 Hwy 12   8 units, $48–$75
1 to 2 dogs, $10/day, refrigerator, restaurant, lounge, lawn for
walking dogs, 5-minute drive to lakes & walking trails,
www.talltimberrestaurantloungemotel.com

Woodland Motel   360-494-6766
11890 US Hwy 12   6 units, $45–$60
full kitchen or microwave & refrigerator, lawn & wooded area for
walking dogs, close to national forest & walking trails

Raymond, WA

Golden Lion Inn   360-942-5571
24 3rd St   26 units, $55–$60
1 to 2 dogs, $5-$10/day, full kitchen or coffeemaker-microwave-
refrigerator, large yard, 2 blocks to walking trail

Holiday Inn Express   509-737-8000, 888-890-0245
1970 Center Parkway   82 units, $109–$139
each pet $10/day, kitchenette, extended continental breakfast,
indoor pool, outdoor pool, hot tub, across street to 10-acre open
walking area, short walk to park, www.hiexpress.com/richlandwa

Motel 6   509-783-1250, 800-466-8356
1751 Fowler St   93 units, $46–$55
seasonal pool, pet walking area, 1 block to riverside public park,
www.motel6.com

Red Lion Hotel   509-946-7611
802 George Washington Way   149 units, $139–$159
1 to 2 dogs, $35/stay each pet, coffeemaker, microwave,
refrigerator, restaurant, lounge, seasonal pool, hot tub, fitness
room, grassy walking area, close to riverside park & trails,
www.redlion.com/richland

Shilo Inn   509-946-4661, 800-222-2244
50 Comstock St   151 units, $68–$115
1 to 2 dogs, $25/stay, coffeemaker, microwave, refrigerator, full
breakfast, restaurant, lounge, seasonal pool, sauna, hot tub, fitness
room, pet beds & treats, next to riverside park, www.shiloinns.com

Ritzville, WA

America's Best Value Inn Colwell   509-659-1620
501 W 1st Ave   25 units, $45–$85
1 to 2 dogs, $10/day each pet, coffeemaker, microwave,
refrigerator, continental breakfast, seasonal pool, sauna, small pet
walking area, 1 mile to public park, www.bestvalueinn.com

Best Western Bronco Inn   509-659-5000
105 W Galbreath Way   63 units, $84–$99
pet fee $10/stay, coffeemaker, microwave, refrigerator, extended
continental breakfast, indoor pool, hot tub, fitness room, grassy
walking area, ¼ mile to park, www.bestwestern.com/broncoinn

Empire Motel   509-659-1030
101 W 1st Ave   19 units, $30–$52
each pet $5-$10/day, coffeemaker, microwave, refrigerator, next to
vacant lot for walking dogs, 10 blocks to trail

Ritzville, WA (continued)

La Quinta Inn   509-659-1007
1513 S Smittys Blvd   54 units, $59–$129
coffeemaker, microwave, refrigerator, continental breakfast,
seasonal pool, hot tub, lawn for walking dogs, across street to
public park, www.lq.com

Top Hat Motel   509-659-1100
210 E 1st Ave   11 units, $42–$64
1 to 2 small to medium dogs allowed with manager's approval only,
$5/day, microwave, refrigerator, continental breakfast, small pet
walking area, 1 mile to fairgrounds

Rockport, WA

Clark's Skagit River Resort   360-873-2250, 800-273-2606
58468 Clark Cabin Rd   40 units, $79–$169
1 to 2 dogs, $10/day each pet, 1-bdrm to 3-bdrm cabins & travel
trailers with kitchen sleep up to 7, also B & B lodge, restaurant,
"bunny-hole" golf, lawn for walking dogs, riverside walking trails,
www.northcascades.com

Grace Haven   360-873-4106
9303 Dandy Place   5 units, $85–$105
each pet $10/day, 1-bdrm cabins sleep up to 8, fully equipped
kitchen, picnic area, fire pit, horseshoes, badminton, croquet,
ping pong, riverside trails, www.gracehavenretreat.com

Totem Trail Motel   360-873-4535
57627 State Route 20   8 units, $55–$65
1 to 2 dogs allowed with manager's approval only, $5-$20/stay each
pet, coffeemaker, refrigerator, BBQ, picnic tables, basketball court,
walking trails on 7½ acres, 10-minute walk to riverfront park,
www.totemtrail.com

Ronald, WA

Starlite Resort   509-649-2222
14254 Salmon la Sac Rd   12 units, $63–$75
motel rooms & cabins, RV sites, restaurant, lounge, general store,
grassy walking area, ¼ mile to lake, www.starliteresort.com

Roslyn, WA

All Seasons Vacation Rentals   509-649-3099
80 Coralbell Lane   22 units, $190–$500
each pet $25/day, fully equipped cabins & vacation homes in
Cle Elum & Roslyn, www.allseasonsvacationrents.com

Roslyn Rooms   509-649-2551, 866-476-7596
105½ Pennsylvania Ave   8 units, $70–$200
pet fee $15 for 1st day, $10 each additional day, rooms-condos-
vacation homes sleep up to 8, fully equipped kitchen, some have
BBQ-deck-yard, www.roslynrooms.com

Saint John, WA

Creekside Farm B & B   509-648-4042
15742 State Route 23   3 units, $80–$150
dogs allowed in suite with sleeping loft that sleeps 6, coffeemaker,
microwave, refrigerator, full breakfast, on 20 acres for walking
dogs, 1 mile to public park

Margarita's Villa   509-648-3676
501 W Fairway Lane   2 units, $50
1 to 2 dogs, rooms with private entrances, full breakfast, grassy
walking area, across street to golf course, 2 blocks to public park

SeaTac, WA

Clarion Hotel SeaTac Airport   206-242-0200, 800-252-7466
3000 S 176th St   214 units, $75–$115
dogs under 20 lbs only, $20/day each pet, coffeemaker,
microwave, refrigerator, restaurant, lounge, indoor pool, hot tub,
fitness room, lawn, 5-minute drive to park, www.clarionseattle.com

Doubletree Hotel Airport   206-246-8600
18740 International Blvd   850 units, $129–$159
dogs under 100 lbs only, coffeemaker, refrigerator, restaurant,
lounge, outdoor pool, hot tub, fitness room, lawn, 1 block to
lakeside park, www.seattleairport.doubletree.com

Econo Lodge SeaTac Airport S   206-824-1350, 888-326-6644
19225 International Blvd   94 units, $64–$129
1 to 2 dogs under 20 lbs only, $10/day, coffeemaker, microwave,
refrigerator, continental breakfast, restaurant, across street from
lakeside park, www.econolodge.com/hotel/wa716

SeaTac, WA (continued)

Hilton Seattle Airport   206-244-4800
17620 International Blvd   396 units, $219–$269
1 to 2 dogs under 25 lbs only, $50/stay, coffeemaker, restaurant,
lounge, outdoor pool, hot tub, fitness room, lawn for walking dogs,
www.seattleairport.hilton.com/

Holiday Inn Airport   206-248-1000, 800-465-4329
17338 International Blvd   259 units, $99–$179
dogs under 20 lbs only, $20/day, coffeemaker, restaurant, lounge,
indoor pool, hot tub, fitness room, residential streets for walking
dogs, 1 mile to public park, www.holidayinn.com

Holiday Inn Express Airport   206-824-3200, 888-890-0245
19621 International Blvd   171 units, $89–$139
pet fee $50/stay, full kitchen or coffeemaker-microwave-
refrigerator, continental breakfast, fitness room, across street to
lakeside walking area, www.hiexpress.com/seattleairport

La Quinta Inn & Suites   206-241-5211, 800-531-5900
2824 S 188th St   143 units, $89–$124
coffeemaker, continental breakfast, outdoor pool, hot tub, fitness
room, pet walking area, ¼ mile to public park, www.lq.com

Motel 6 Airport   206-246-4101
16500 Pacific Hwy S   109 units, $40–$65
dogs under 50 lbs only, coffee in lobby, lawn, across street to
walking trails, www.motel6.com

Motel 6 Airport South   206-241-1648, 800-466-8356
18900 47th Ave S   145 units, $40–$57
microwave, refrigerator, coffee in lobby, outdoor pool, 2 blocks to
public park, www.motel6.com

Motel 6 Seattle South   206-824-9902, 800-466-8356
20651 Military Rd S   124 units, $50–$70
microwave, refrigerator, coffee in lobby, outdoor pool, hot tub,
lawn for walking dogs, www.motel6.com

Red Lion Hotel Airport   206-246-5535, 800-733-5466
18220 International Blvd   144 units, $99–$219
pet fee $25/day, restaurant, lounge, seasonal pool, hot tub, fitness
room, small grassy areas for walking dogs, 3 blocks to public park,
www.redlion.com/seattleairport

Red Roof Inn Airport   206-248-0901, 800-733-7663
16838 International Blvd   152 units, $50–$90
microwave, refrigerator, coffee in lobby, fitness room, lawn, across
street to walking trails, www.redroof.com

Rodeway Inn   206-246-9300, 877-424-6423
2930 S 176th St   59 units, $40–$70
1 to 2 dogs, $10/day each pet, continental breakfast, lawn, 5 blocks
to lakeside park, www.rodewayinn.com/hotel/wa075

Super 8 Motel Airport   206-433-8188, 800-800-8000
3100 S 192nd St   119 units, $72–$92
pet fee $25/day, coffeemaker, continental breakfast, lawn for
walking dogs, 3 blocks to lakeside park, www.super8.com

Sutton Suites Hotel   206-431-6884, 877-900-6884
3423 S 160th St   70 units, $69–$90
pet fee $25/day, kitchen, continental breakfast, parking lot for
walking dogs, www.suttonsuites.com

Seattle, WA

Ace Hotel   206-448-4721
2423 1st Ave   28 units, $85–$225
coffeemaker, refrigerator, extended continental breakfast, guest
pass to local fitness center, parking lot for walking dogs, 2 blocks
to off-leash dog park, www.acehotel.com/seattle

Alexis Hotel   206-624-4844, 800-426-7033
1007 1st Ave   121 units, $195–$395
coffeemaker, complimentary wine hour, restaurant, lounge, steam
room, hot tub, pet bowls & treats, dog walking & dog sitting
services available, 2 blocks to waterfront, 7 blocks to public park,
www.alexishotel.com

Andra Hotel   206-448-8600, 877-448-8600
2000 4th Ave   119 units, $186–$309
dogs under 30 lbs only, coffeemaker, restaurant, fitness room,
sidewalks for walking dogs, 4 blocks to off-leash dog park,
www.hotelandra.com

Arctic Club Hotel   206-340-0340
700 3rd Ave   120 units, $179–$500
dogs under 40 lbs only, coffeemaker, restaurant, lounge, hot tub,
fitness room, paved pet walking area, 5-minute walk to waterfront,
25-minute walk to public park, www.arcticclubhotel.com

Seattle, WA (continued)

Bacon Mansion   206-329-1864, 800-240-1864
959 Broadway E   11 units, $99–$234
1 to 2 well-behaved dogs allowed in separate carriage house only,
microwave, refrigerator, extended continental breakfast, sidewalks
for walking dogs, 2 blocks to public park, www.baconmansion.com

Boulevard Motel   206-241-0066
14440 Pacific Hwy S   30 units, $55–$65
1 to 2 small dogs only, $15/day each pet, coffeemaker, microwave,
refrigerator, small grassy walking area

Capitol Hill Guest House   206-412-7378
1808 E Denny Way   14 units, $85–$165
dogs under 25 lbs allowed with advance approval only, $10/day,
guest use of gourmet kitchen, continental breakfast, bicycle
rentals available, guest pass to local fitness center, pet beds
provided, grassy walking area, www.capitolhillguesthouse.com

Chambered Nautilus B & B   206-522-2536, 800-545-8459
5005 22nd Ave NE   4 units, $134–$204
1 to 2 dogs, $15/day, pet-friendly suites, kitchenette, private
entrance across garden from main house, basket of pet supplies
provided, www.chamberednautilus.com

Comfort Inn   206-361-3700, 800-213-6308
13700 Aurora Ave N   72 units, $86–$160
1 to 2 dogs under 35 lbs allowed with manager's approval only,
$15/day, full kitchen or refrigerator, continental breakfast, sauna,
hot tub, fitness room, residential streets for walking dogs,
1½ miles to off-leash dog park, www.comfortinn.com/hotel/wa217

Crowne Plaza Downtown   206-464-1980, 800-521-2762
1113 6th Ave   415 units, $109–$280
pet fee $50/stay, coffeemaker, refrigerator, continental breakfast,
restaurant, lounge, fitness room, across street from public park,
www.crowneplazaseattle.com

Dibble House B & B   206-783-0320
7301 Dibble Ave NW   2 units, $55–$65
coffeemaker, refrigerator, continental breakfast, fenced backyard,
1 mile to zoo & off-leash dog park

Doubletree Guest Suites Airport Southcenter   206-575-8220
16500 Southcenter Parkway   218 units, $109–$249
1 to 2 dogs under 15 lbs only, $35/stay, coffeemaker, microwave,
refrigerator, restaurant, lounge, indoor pool, sauna, hot tub, fitness
room, www.seattle.doubletree.com

Edgewater Hotel   206-728-7000, 800-624-0670
2411 Alaskan Way # 67   236 units, $149–$2500
rooms-suites-penthouse overlooking bay, coffeemaker,
refrigerator, restaurant, lounge, fitness room, 50 yards to public
park, www.edgewaterhotel.com

Executive Hotel Pacific   206-623-3900, 888-388-3932
400 Spring St   153 units, $104–$160
coffeemaker, restaurant, fitness room, paved walking area,
www.executivehotelpacific.com

Extended StayAmerica   206-365-8100, 800-398-7829
13300 Stone Ave N   130 units, $70–$90
pet fee $25/day ($150 maximum), suites, kitchenette, 2 blocks to
public park, www.extendedstayamerica.com/861

Fairmont Olympic Hotel   206-621-1700, 800-332-3442
411 University St   450 units, $299–$845
dogs under 15 lbs only, continental breakfast, restaurant, lounge,
indoor pool, sauna, hot tub, fitness room, sidewalks for walking
dogs, 2 blocks to public park, www.fairmont.com/seattle

Homewood Suites Downtown   206-281-9393, 800-225-5466
206 Western Ave W   161 units, $119–$279
dogs under 70 lbs only, $20/day, kitchen, full breakfast, fitness
room, small grassy areas for walking dogs, 5 blocks to waterfront
park, www.homewoodsuites.com

Hotel 1000   206-957-1000, 877-315-1088
1000 1st Ave   120 units, $199–$309
1 to 2 dogs under 40 lbs only, $40/stay, coffeemaker, refrigerator,
restaurant, lounge, hot tub, fitness room, parking lot for walking
dogs, 1 block to waterfront, www.hotel1000seattle.com

Hotel Max   206-728-6299, 866-986-8087
620 Stewart St   163 units, $129–$349
pet fee $40/stay, coffeemaker, refrigerator, restaurant, fitness
room, 6 blocks to waterfront park, www.hotelmaxseattle.com

Seattle, WA (continued)

Hotel Monaco   206-621-1770, 800-546-7866
1101 4th Ave   189 units, $195–$725
coffeemaker, hosted evening reception, restaurant, lounge, fitness
room, pet room service menu, dog walking service available,
3 blocks to park, 6 blocks to waterfront, www.monaco-seattle.com

Hotel Nexus   206-365-0700, 800-435-0754
2140 N Northgate Way   169 units, $99–$159
pet fee $50/stay, kitchen, extended continental breakfast,
restaurant, lounge, seasonal pool, hot tub, fitness room, small pet
walking area, 2 blocks to park, www.hotelnexusseattle.com

Hotel Vintage Park   206-624-8000, 800-624-4434
1100 5th Ave   126 units, $175–$285
coffeemaker, wine reception each evening, restaurant, lounge,
"pet survival kit" provided, dog walking & dog sitting services
available, short drive to off-leash dog park,
www.hotelvintagepark.com

Howard Johnson SeaTac Airport   206-244-6464
14110 Pacific Hwy S   68 units, $65–$85
1 to 2 dogs, $10/day each pet, coffeemaker, microwave,
refrigerator, continental breakfast, outdoor pool, parking lot for
walking dogs, 10-minute drive to public park,
www.hojo.com/hotel/18447

La Quinta Inn & Suites Downtown   206-624-6820, 800-437-4867
2224 8th Ave   72 units, $89–$199
1 to 2 dogs, kitchenette or coffeemaker-microwave-refrigerator,
continental breakfast, sauna, hot tub, fitness room, parking lot for
walking dogs, 1 block to public park, www.lq.com

Pan Pacific Hotel   206-264-8111
2125 Terry Ave   160 units, $200–$300
1 to 2 dogs, $50/stay, coffeemaker, refrigerator, restaurant, lounge,
hot tub, fitness room, parking lot for walking dogs, 2 blocks to
public park, www.panpacific.com/Seattle

Pensione Nichols B & B   206-441-7125
1923 1st Ave # 300   12 units, $130–$230
1 to 2 dogs, $15/stay, rooms, suites with full kitchen & sitting
room, continental breakfast, 1 block to public park, 2 blocks to
off-leash dog park, www.pensionenichols.com

Quality Inn & Suites   206-728-7666, 800-255-7932
618 John St   159 units, $79–$129
1 to 2 dogs under 20 lbs only, pet fee $25 1st day, $10 each
additional day, coffeemaker, microwave, refrigerator, continental
breakfast, indoor & outdoor pools, hot tub, fitness room, sidewalks
for walking dogs, 4 blocks to public park,
www.qualityinn.com/hotel/WA155

Quality Inn SeaTac Airport   206-241-9292, 800-393-1856
2900 S 192nd St   105 units, $69–$120
1 to 2 dogs under 40 lbs only, $10/day each pet, coffeemaker,
microwave, refrigerator, continental breakfast, 1 block to lakeside
park, www.qualityinn.com/hotel/wa153

Red Lion Hotel on Fifth Ave   206-971-8000
1415 5th Ave   297 units, $155–$290
1 to 2 dogs under 35 lbs only, $50/stay, coffeemaker, refrigerator,
restaurant, lounge, fitness room, parking lot for walking dogs,
4 blocks to off-leash dog park, www.redlion.com/5thavenue

Renaissance Seattle Hotel   206-583-0300, 800-546-9184
515 Madison St   553 units, $149–$259
1 to 2 dogs, $100/stay, coffeemaker, refrigerator, restaurant,
lounge, indoor pool, hot tub, parking lot for walking dogs,
6 blocks to trail, www.marriott.com/seasm

Residence Inn Downtown/Lake Union   206-624-6000
800 Fairview Ave N   234 units, $120–$350
each pet $10/day, full kitchen or coffeemaker, full breakfast,
indoor pool, hot tub, fitness room, BBQ, picnic area, lawn,
lakefront walking trail, www.marriott.com/sealu

Roosevelt Hotel   206-621-1200
1531 7th Ave   151 units, $149–$269
1 to 2 dogs under 50 lbs only, $50/stay, coffeemaker, refrigerator,
restaurant, parking lot for walking dogs, 4 miles to public park,
www.roosevelthotel.com

Seattle Pacific Hotel   206-441-0400, 888-451-0400
325 Aurora Ave N   59 units, $80–$179
1 to 2 dogs, $10/day each pet, coffeemaker, microwave,
refrigerator, continental breakfast, seasonal pool, hot tub, grassy
walking area, 4 blocks to public park, www.seattlepacifichotel.com

Seattle, WA (continued)

Sheraton Seattle Hotel   206-621-9000, 800-325-3535
1400 6th Ave   1,258 units, $199–$299
dogs under 80 lbs only, coffeemaker, microwave, refrigerator,
restaurant, lounge, indoor pool, hot tub, fitness room, pet welcome
kit provided, barkdust area, next to park, www.sheratonseattle.com

Sorrento Hotel   206-622-6400, 800-426-1265
900 Madison St   76 units, $299–$550
dogs under 100 lbs only, $60/stay, dog must be kept in travel crate
when in room, coffeemaker, refrigerator, restaurant, lounge,
fitness room, small petwalking area, 10 blocks to public park,
www.hotelsorrento.com

Three Tree Point B & B   206-669-7646
17026 33rd Ave SW   2 units, $150–$250
pet fee $25/day, kitchen, breakfast supplies provided, lawn for
walking dogs, 1 block to beach, www.3treepointbnb.com

University Inn   206-632-5055, 800-733-3855
4140 Roosevelt Way NE   102 units, $125–$160
1 to 2 dogs under 75 lbs only, $20/stay, coffeemaker, microwave,
refrigerator, extended continental breakfast, restaurant, seasonal
pool, hot tub, parking lot for walking dogs, 4 blocks to walking
trail, close to public parks, www.universityinnseattle.com

W Hotel Seattle   206-264-6000
1112 4th Ave   424 units, $229–$349
refrigerator, coffee in lobby, restaurant, lounge, fitness room, pet
treats & featherbeds, dog walking service available, next to grassy
walking area, 2 blocks to public park, www.whotelsseattle.com

Westin Seattle   206-728-1000
1900 5th Ave   891 units, $165–$310
1 to 2 dogs under 40 lbs only, coffeemaker, microwave,
refrigerator, restaurant, lounge, indoor pool, hot tub, fitness room,
dog beds, lawn, 8 blocks to waterfront, 1 mile to park,
www.westin.com/seattle

Seaview, WA

Bloomer Estates Vacation Rentals   360-642-8598, 800-747-2096
1004 41st Place   6 units, $195–$575
1 to 2 dogs, $20/day each pet, beachfront studios to 6-bdrm mansion, full kitchen, BBQ, deck, hot tub, lawn for walking dogs, close to ocean, www.bloomerestates.com

Historic Sou'wester Lodge & Cabins   360-642-2542
3728 J Place   28 units, $79–$199
dogs allowed with advance approval, lodge rooms, cabins, spartan trailers, kitchens, tent sites, musical & theatrical events, fireside discussions, close to dunes & beach, www.souwesterlodge.com

Seaview Motel & Cottages   360-642-2450, 866-288-2849
3728 Pacific Way   14 units, $39–$99
no fee for 1st pet, each additional pet $5/day, full kitchen or coffeemaker-microwave-refrigerator, grassy walking area, close to park & trails, 3 blocks to ocean, www.seaviewmotelandcottages.com

Sedro Woolley, WA

South Bay B & B   360-595-2086, 877-595-2086
4095 S Bay Dr   6 units, $139–$175
1 to 2 dogs, $20/stay each pet, full breakfast, common area with kitchen for guest use, jetted tub in each room, across street to beach & public park, 5 miles to off-leash dog park, www.southbaybb.com

Three Rivers Inn   360-855-2626, 800-221-5122
210 Ball St   40 units, $79–$89
1 to 2 dogs, $10/stay, coffeemaker, microwave, refrigerator, some rooms have private patio, full breakfast, restaurant, seasonal pool, hot tub, lawn & courtyard for walking dogs, 1 block to trail

Sekiu, WA

Bay Motel   360-963-2444
15562 Hwy 112   16 units, $62–$92
each pet $6/day, coffeemaker, microwave, refrigerator, full kitchen or kitchenette, grass & gravel walking areas, across street to beach, ½ mile to county park

Sequim, WA

Brigadoon Vacation Rentals   360-683-2255
62 Balmoral Ct   30 units, $95–$300
dogs allowed with advance approval only, fully equipped 1-bdrm to
3-bdrm vacation homes sleep 2 to 6, full kitchen or coffeemaker &
microwave, hot tub, most with yard for walking dogs, short drive
to river & beach, www.sequimrentals.com

Econo Lodge   360-683-7113, 800-488-7113
801 E Washington St   43 units, $55–$129
1 to 2 dogs under 20 lbs only, $10/day each pet, coffeemaker,
microwave, refrigerator, continental breakfast, free miniature golf,
very small grassy pet walking area, 5-minute walk to public park,
www.sequimeconolodge.com

Greywolf Inn   360-683-5889, 800-914-9653
395 Keeler Rd   1 unit, $550
1 to 2 dogs, $50/stay each pet, 5-bdrm 5-bath vacation home on 5
acres, hot tub, close to bay, www.greywolfinn.com

Groveland Cottage & Sequim Vacation Rentals   360-683-3565
4861 Sequim Dungeness Way   800-879-8859
1 to 2 dogs, $25-$45/stay each pet   48 units, $100–$250
rooms in B & B include full breakfast, also fully equipped vacation
homes, ¼ mile to riverside trail, ½ mile to beach,
www.sequimvalley.com

Juan De Fuca Cottages   360-683-4433, 866-683-4433
182 Marine Dr   9 units, $109–$405
1 to 2 dogs under 90 lbs allowed with advance approval only,
$20/day each pet, rooms-cottages-fully equipped vacation homes,
kayak rentals, lawns, 1-minute walk to beach, www.juandefuca.com

Quality Inn & Suites   360-683-2800, 800-424-6423
134 River Rd   60 units, $89–$125
1 to 2 dogs, $10/day each pet, coffeemaker, microwave,
refrigerator, continental breakfast, indoor pool, hot tub, fitness
room, small walking area & trail, www.qualityinn.com/hotel/wa151

Rancho Llamro B & B   360-683-8133
1734 Woodcock Rd   2 units, $75–$85
dogs under 25 lbs only, kitchenette, coffee in lobby, on 2¼ acres
with fenced yard, 5-minute drive to beaches & walking trails

Red Ranch Inn   360-683-4195
830 W Washington St   55 units, $54–$100
1 to 2 dogs, $10/day each pet, coffeemaker, microwave,
refrigerator, continental breakfast, open field for walking dogs,
1 mile to off-leash dog park, www.redranchinn.com

Sequim Bay Lodge   360-683-0691, 800-622-0691
268522 Hwy 101   54 units, $63–$149
1 to 2 dogs, $10/day each pet, coffeemaker, microwave,
refrigerator, restaurant, lounge, seasonal pool, on 17 wooded acres
for walking dogs, ½ mile to state park, www.sequimbaylodge.com

Sequim Inn & Suites   360-683-1775, 800-683-1775
1095 E Washington St   60 units, $89–$140
1 to 2 dogs, $10/day each pet, coffeemaker, microwave,
refrigerator, continental breakfast, indoor pool, hot tub, open field
for walking dogs, www.sequiminn.com

Sequim West Inn & RV Park   360-683-4144
740 W Washington St   36 units, $54–$160
1 to 2 dogs, $10/day each pet, rooms with coffeemaker-microwave-
refrigerator, 2-bdrm to 3-bdrm cottages with full kitchen, lawn,
4 blocks to park, 10-minute drive to beach, www.sequimwestinn.com

Sundowner Motel   360-683-5532, 800-325-6966
364 W Washington St   33 units, $35–$99
small dogs only, $10/day each pet, microwave, refrigerator, coffee
in lobby, grassy walking area, 5-minute drive to public park &
swim center, www.sequimsundowner.com

Sunset Marine Resort   360-681-4166
40 Buzzard Ridge Rd   7 units, $110–$250
1 to 2 dogs, $20/day each pet, fully equipped beachfront cabins
with kitchen sleep up to 6, canoe & kayak rentals, beach access,
9 miles to off-leash dog park, www.sunsetmarineresort.com

Shelton, WA

City Center Best Rates Motel   360-426-3397, 866-574-8715
128 E Alder St   13 units, $39–$64
each pet $6/day, coffeemaker, microwave, refrigerator, continental
breakfast, designated pet walking area, 5-minute walk to public
park, www.citycenterbestratesmotel.net

Shelton, WA (continued)

Little Creek Casino Resort   360-427-4579, 800-667-7711
91 W State Route 108   190 units, $95–$145
pet fee $30/day, rooms & suites, coffeemaker, microwave,
refrigerator, restaurant, lounge, indoor pool, hot tub,
close to golf course & hiking trails, www.little-creek.com

Shelton Inn   360-426-4468, 800-451-4560
628 W Railroad Ave   30 units, $58–$73
1 to 2 dogs, $10/day each pet, coffeemaker, microwave,
refrigerator, open field for walking dogs, 5-minute walk to park

Super 8 Motel   360-426-1654, 800-800-8000
2943 Northview Circle   39 units, $55–$80
1 to 2 dogs, $10/stay, coffeemaker, microwave, refrigerator,
continental breakfast, fenced yard, 5-minute drive to public park,
1 mile to walking trail, www.super8.com

Silverdale, WA

Forest Enchantment Cottage   360-692-5148
7448 NW Ioka Dr   2 units, $100–$120
each pet $10/stay, 1-bdrm & 2-bdrm suites sleep up to 9, full
kitchen or kitchenette, stocked with breakfast supplies, wooded
setting, steep trail to beach, www.forestenchantmentcottage.com

Oxford Inn   360-692-7777, 800-273-5076
9734 Silverdale Way NW   63 units, $79–$99
1 to 2 small dogs only, $20/stay, coffeemaker, microwave,
refrigerator, kitchenette, continental breakfast, barkdust walking
area, 2 blocks to waterfront trail, www.oxfordinnsilverdale.com

Oxford Suites   360-698-9550, 888-698-7848
9550 Silverdale Way NW   104 units, $129–$159
1 to 2 dogs under 20 lbs only, $20/stay each pet, coffeemaker,
microwave, refrigerator, full breakfast, complimentary evening
appetizers & beverages, restaurant, lawn, 2 blocks to waterfront
park & trail, www.oxfordsuitessilverdale.com

Silverdale Beach Hotel   360-698-1000, 800-544-9799
3073 NW Bucklin Hill Rd   151 units, $79–$99
pet fee $20/day, microwave, refrigerator, restaurant, lounge,
indoor pool, sauna, hot tub, fitness room, short walk to waterfront
park & trail, www.silverdalebeachhotel.com

Silverlake, WA

Silver Lake Motel & Resort   360-274-6141
3201 Spirit Lake Hwy   13 units, $80–$175
each pet $5/day, lakefront cabins sleep 2 to 6, kitchen, go fishing
right off your private balcony or deck, fire pit, RV & tent sites, boat
rentals, tackle shop, lakeside walking area, 6 miles to riverfront
park, www.silverlake-resort.com

Skykomish, WA

Cascadia Inn   360-677-2030, 866-677-2030
210 Railroad Ave E   14 units, $60–$85
pet fee $20/day, rooms in historic inn with private or shared bath,
coffeemaker-microwave-refrigerator available in guest lounge,
restaurant, lounge, surrounded by national forest, 1/4 mile to public
park, 4 miles to hiking trails, www.historiccascadia.com

Snohomish, WA

Country Man Bed & Breakfast   360-568-9622, 800-700-9622
119 Cedar Ave   4 units, $105–$135
Victorian home, coffeemaker, refrigerator, full breakfast, next to
public park, 3 blocks to riverfront trails,
www.countrymanbandb.com

Snohomish Inn   360-568-2208
323 2nd St   22 units, $80–$120
1 to 2 small dogs allowed with advance approval only, dogs must
stay in travel crate while in room, coffeemaker, microwave,
refrigerator, across street to grassy walking area,
www.snohomishinn.com

Snoqualmie Pass, WA

Summit Lodge at Snoqualmie Pass   425-434-6300
603 State Route 906   800-557-7829
1 to 2 dogs only, $25/stay each pet   81 units, $135–$229
coffeemaker, microwave, refrigerator, restaurant, lounge, outdoor
pool, sauna, hot tub, open field for walking dogs, 1/4 mile to
walking trail, www.snoqualmiesummitlodge.com

Soap Lake, WA

Inn at Soap Lake   509-246-1132, 800-557-8514
226 Main Ave E   29 units, $59–$130
1 to 3 dogs, $5/day each pet, lodge rooms & cottages sleep 2 to 6,
coffeemaker, microwave, refrigerator, most rooms have private
mineral water soaking tubs, lawn & trails, www.innsoaplake.com

Masters Inn & Retreat   509-246-1831, 888-412-8515
404 4th Ave NE   17 units, $42–$75
dogs allowed with advance approval only, $7-$10/day each pet, full
kitchen or coffeemaker-microwave-refrigerator, open field, across
street to lakefront, www.mastersinn-retreat.com

Notaras Lodge   509-246-0462
236 E Main   15 units, $51–$125
1 to 2 dogs, $10/stay, full kitchen or coffeemaker-microwave-
refrigerator, restaurant, lounge, all rooms have mineral baths, next
to lakefront trail, 1 block to park, www.notaraslodge.com

Tumwata Lodge   509-246-1416
340 Main Ave W   6 units, $45
studios & 1-bdrm apartments, kitchen, outdoor pool, RV sites,
grassy area & lakeside trail for walking dogs

South Bend, WA

Chen's Motel & Restaurant   360-875-5548
206 E Robert Bush Dr   16 units, $63–$87
1 to 2 dogs, $10/stay, full kitchen or microwave & refrigerator,
restaurant, lounge, RV sites, parking lot for walking dogs, close to
"Rails to Trails" walking trail, www.nopwa.com/chensmotel.htm

Seaquest Motel   360-875-5349
801 W 1st St   16 units, $35–$65
pet fee $10/day, full kitchen, across street to grassy walking area,
trail thru historic neighborhood, ½ mile to riverfront park,
20-minute drive to ocean beaches, www.seaquestmotel.com

Spokane, WA

Apple Tree Inn Motel   509-466-3020, 800-323-5796
9508 N Division St   71 units, $50–$80
small dogs allowed with advance approval only, $10/day each pet,
kitchen or microwave & refrigerator, continental breakfast, BBQ,
seasonal pool, 2 blocks to park, www.appletreeinnmotel.com

Bel Air 7 Motel   509-535-1677
1303 E Sprague Ave   17 units, $45–$55
each pet $8/day, microwave, refrigerator, espresso stand, open
field for walking dogs, www.belairsevenmotel.com

Best Western Peppertree Airport Inn   509-624-4655
3711 S Geiger Blvd   866-627-7191
small dogs only, $10/day each pet   100 units, $89–$199
coffeemaker, microwave, refrigerator, extended continental
breakfast, indoor pool, hot tub, fitness room, lawn for walking
dogs, www.peppertreespokane.com

Cedar Village Motel & RV Park   509-838-8558, 800-700-8558
5415 W Sunset Hwy   30 units, $49–$55
each pet $3/day, full kitchen or coffeemaker-microwave-
refrigerator, BBQ, picnic tables, gazebo, large lawn

Comfort Inn   509-535-9000
923 E 3rd Ave   105 units, $82–$105
1 to 2 dogs under 100 lbs only, $10/stay, coffeemaker, microwave,
refrigerator, full breakfast, indoor pool, hot tub, pet beds & treats,
small pet walking area, www.comfortinn.com/hotel/wa215

Comfort Inn North   509-467-7111, 800-424-6423
7111 N Division St   96 units, $53–$150
each pet $10/day, extended continental breakfast, outdoor pool,
sauna, hot tub, fitness room, small pet walking area, quiet streets
for longer walks, www.comfortinn.com/hotel/wa016

Davenport Hotel & Tower   509-455-8888, 800-899-1482
10 S Post St   611 units, $169–$2500
restaurant, lounge, indoor pool, hot tub, fitness room, pet bowls
provided, complimentary pet walking service available, 2 blocks to
public park, www.thedavenporthotel.com

Days Inn   509-747-2011, 800-329-7466
120 W 3rd Ave   89 units, $60–$112
1 to 2 dogs, $10/day each pet, coffeemaker, microwave,
refrigerator, continental breakfast, outdoor pool, open area across
street for walking dogs, 7 blocks to riverside park & Centennial
Trail, www.daysinn.com/hotel/18280

Spokane, WA (continued)

Doubletree Hotel   509-455-9600, 888-222-8733
322 N Spokane Falls Ct   375 units, $89–$500
dogs under 80 lbs only, $25/stay, coffeemaker, restaurant, lounge,
seasonal pool, sauna, hot tub, fitness room, small pet walking area
behind motel, close to riverfront park,
www.spokane.doubletree.com

Econo Lodge & Suites   509-747-2021, 888-318-2611
4212 W Sunset Blvd (1503 Russell St)   132 units, $52–$80
1 to 2 dogs under 30 lbs only, $10/day each pet, coffeemaker,
microwave, refrigerator, continental breakfast, seasonal pool,
courtyard & open area for walking dogs, 4 miles to riverfront park,
www.econolodge.com/hotel/wa002

Holiday Inn   509-838-1170, 877-816-1699
1616 S Windsor Rd   200 units, $129–$139
dogs under 70 lbs only, restaurant, lounge, indoor pool, hot tub,
fitness room, parking lot for walking dogs, 10 miles to public park,
www.holidayinn.com

Holiday Inn Express Downtown   509-328-8505, 877-816-1699
801 N Division St   120 units, $79–$140
small dogs only, pet-friendly rooms have outside entrances,
coffeemaker, microwave, refrigerator, full breakfast,
complimentary beverages & light dinner served 4 evenings/week,
fitness room, close to public park, www.hiexpress.com

Howard Johnson Airport/Downtown   509-838-6630
211 S Division St   888-271-4190
dogs under 40 lbs only, $25/day each pet   79 units, $79–$109
coffeemaker, microwave, refrigerator, extended continental
breakfast, fitness room, grassy area for walking dogs, 6 blocks to
riverfront park, www.hojo.com/hotel/06661

Howard Johnson Spokane North   509-326-5500, 800-621-8593
3033 N Division St   63 units, $61–$100
coffeemaker, microwave, refrigerator, continental breakfast, indoor
pool, hot tub, 2 blocks to public park, www.hojo.com/hotel/17764

Liberty Motel   509-467-6000, 800-705-4755
6801 N Division St   17 units, $49–$65
pet fee $10/day, kitchenette, seasonal pool, lawn for walking dogs,
www.libertymotel.com

Madison Inn   509-474-4200, 800-538-0375
15 W Rockwood Blvd   80 units, $80–$90
1 to 2 dogs, $10/day for 1st pet, $15/day for 2nd pet, coffeemaker,
microwave, refrigerator, continental breakfast, fitness room, lawn,
8 blocks to park, www.the-madison-inn.com

Motel 6 Spokane West/Airport   509-459-6122, 800-466-8356
1508 S Rustle Rd   120 units, $43–$53
microwave, refrigerator, coffee in lobby, outdoor pool, lawn for
walking dogs, 3 miles to riverfront park, www.motel6.com

Odell House   509-838-9140
2325 W 1st Ave   6 units, $85–$155
apartments, 1-bdrm bungalow, 4-bdrm mansion, full kitchen,
grassy pet walking area, close to several public parks,
www.odellhouse.com

Oxford Suites   509-353-9000, 800-774-1877
115 W North River Dr   125 units, $149–$159
pet fee $25/stay, coffeemaker, microwave, refrigerator, full
breakfast, evening reception with beverages & appetizers, indoor
pool, sauna, hot tub, fitness room, grassy walking area, close to
public park, www.oxfordsuitesspokane.com

Pheasant Hill Inn & Suites   509-926-7432, 800-269-0061
12415 E Mission Ave   104 units, $69–$189
pet fee $15/day, coffeemaker, microwave, refrigerator, continental
breakfast, indoor pool, hot tub, fitness room, lawn for walking
dogs, 5-minute drive to public park, 3 miles to riverside walking
trail, www.pheasanthillgrand.com

Ramada Limited Downtown   509-838-8504, 800-210-8456
123 S Post St   46 units, $50–$75
pet fee $25/day, coffeemaker, microwave, refrigerator, extended
continental breakfast, fitness room, 5 blocks to riverfront park,
6 blocks to Centennial Trail, www.ramada.com/hotel/10046

Ramada Limited Suites   509-468-4201, 800-210-8975
9601 N Newport Hwy   76 units, $59–$129
pet fee $25/stay, coffeemaker, microwave, refrigerator, extended
continental breakfast, indoor pool, sauna, hot tub, fitness room,
BBQ, pet walking area, 5-minute drive to public park, 15-minute
drive to Mount Spokane hiking trails,
www.ramada.com/hotel/10087

Spokane, WA (continued)

Ramada Spokane Airport & Indoor Waterpark   509-838-5211
8909 Airport Dr   161 units, $117–$130
1 to 2 dogs under 50 lbs only, $10/day each pet, coffeemaker,
microwave, refrigerator, restaurant, lounge, indoor& outdoor
pools, indoor water slide, hot tub, lawn for walking dogs,
www.ramada.com/hotel/00207

Ranch Motel   509-456-8919
1609 S Lewis St   10 units, $29–$40
kitchen, lawn & wooded area for walking dogs, ½ mile to
arboretum & walking trails

Red Lion Hotel at the Park   509-326-8000, 800-733-5466
303 W North River Dr   400 units, $104–$199
each pet $20/day, coffeemaker, refrigerator, restaurant, lounge,
indoor pool, outdoor swimming lagoon & water slide, sauna, hot
tub, across street to riverfront park, www.redlion.com/park

Red Lion River Inn   509-326-5577, 800-733-5466
700 N Division St   245 units, $107–$150
pet fee $20/stay, pet-friendly room with outside entrance,
coffeemaker, microwave, refrigerator, restaurant, lounge,
seasonal pool, hot tub, fitness room, grassy walking area,
next to riverside Centennial Trail, www.redlion.com/riverinn

Shangri-La Motel   509-747-2066, 800-234-4941
2922 W Hartson Ave   20 units, $35–$85
pet fee $30/stay, microwave, refrigerator, kitchen, outdoor pool,
1-acre lawn & children's play area, greenbelt walking trail to river,
www.shangrilamotel.us

Spokane House Hotel   509-838-1471
4301 W Sunset Blvd   86 units, $46–$100
pet fee $10/day, coffeemaker, microwave, refrigerator, restaurant,
lounge, seasonal pool, sauna, hot tub, fitness room, grassy walking
area, next to public arboretum & trails

Super 8 Spokane West/Airport   509-838-8800, 888-288-1878
11102 W Westbow Blvd   80 units, $60–$84
pet fee $15/stay, microwave, refrigerator, continental breakfast,
indoor pool, hot tub, fitness room, open field for walking dogs,
www.super8.com

Travelodge at the Convention Center   509-623-9727
33 W Spokane Falls Blvd   888-824-0292
pet fee $12/day   80 units, $80–$119
coffeemaker, microwave, refrigerator, full breakfast, fitness room,
lawn, 4 blocks to public park, www.travelodge.com/hotel/08872

Spokane Valley, WA

Crossland Economy Studios   509-928-5948
12803 E Sprague Ave   800-326-5651
                                         115 units, $55–$90
pet fee $25/day, kitchenette, designated pet walking area, 4-minute
drive to walking trail, www.crosslandstudios.com/538

Holiday Inn Express   509-927-7100, 800-465-4329
9220 E Mission Ave   103 units, $69–$149
coffeemaker, microwave, refrigerator, continental breakfast, indoor
pool, hot tub, lawn & field for walking dogs, short drive to public
park, www.hiexpress.com

La Quinta Inn & Suites   509-893-0955, 800-531-5900
3808 N Sullivan Rd   59 units, $89–$129
coffeemaker, microwave, continental breakfast, indoor pool,
hot tub, fitness room, grassy pet walking area, 2 blocks to riverside
Centennial Trail, www.lq.com

Mirabeau Park Hotel   509-924-9000, 866-584-4674
1100 N Sullivan Rd   236 units, $99–$129
pet fee $25/stay, coffeemaker, restaurant, lounge, outdoor pool,
hot tub, fitness room, 1½ blocks to riverside Centennial Trail,
www.mirabeauparkhotel.com

Motel 6 Spokane East   509-926-5399, 800-466-8356
1919 N Hutchinson Rd   92 units, $56–$69
microwave, refrigerator, coffee in lobby, grassy area for walking
dogs, 1 mile to public park, www.motel6.com

Oxford Suites   509-847-1000, 866-668-7848
15015 E Indiana Ave   127 units, $119–$165
dogs under 20 lbs only, $25/stay, coffeemaker, microwave,
refrigerator, full breakfast, evening reception with appetizers &
beverages, indoor pool, sauna, hot tub, fitness room, close to
public park, www.oxfordsuitesspokanevalley.com

Spokane Valley, WA (continued)

Park Lane Motel Suites & RV Park   509-535-1626
4412 E Sprague Ave   27 units, $65–$80
rooms & suites with kitchen, 1 suite has 2-person Cal Spa sauna,
continental breakfast, RV sites, fenced grassy play area, 3/4 mile to
fairgrounds, www.parklanemotel.com

Quality Inn Valley Suites   509-928-5218, 800-777-7355
8923 E Mission Ave   128 units, $78–$250
coffeemaker, microwave, refrigerator, full breakfast,
complimentary evening beverages & snacks, indoor pool, sauna,
hot tub, fitness room, courtyard for walking dogs, close to
riverside Centennial Trail, www.spokanequalityinn.com

Ramada Inn   509-924-3838, 800-228-5150
905 N Sullivan Rd   45 units, $65–$100
pet fee $10/day, continental breakfast, seasonal pool, sauna,
hot tub, www.ramada.com/hotel/25893

Red Top Motel   509-926-5728
7217 E Trent Ave   35 units, $40–$125
pet fee $5/day, kitchen, outdoor pool, small pet walking area,
close to school field for walking dogs

Residence Inn East Valley   509-892-9300
15915 E Indiana Ave   84 units, $139–$189
dogs under 30 lbs only, $75/stay, full breakfast, Monday thru
Thursday complimentary beverages & appetizers, kitchenette,
BBQ, picnic area, www.marriott.com/gegri

Rodeway Inn   509-535-7185, 800-237-8466
6309 E Broadway Ave   70 units, $49–$150
1 to 2 dogs, $10/day, full kitchen or coffeemaker-microwave-
refrigerator, continental breakfast, outdoor pool, hot tub, fitness
room, large pet walking area, close to fairgrounds,
www.rodewayinn.com/hotel/wa139

Super 8 Motel   509-928-4888, 800-800-8000
2020 N Argonne Rd   181 units, $56–$76
pet fee $15/stay, coffeemaker, microwave, refrigerator, extended
continental breakfast, indoor pool, hot tub, fitness room, open field
for walking dogs, 1/2 mile to public park, www.super8.com

Sprague, WA

Purple Sage Motel   509-257-2507
405 W 1st St   7 units, $50–$120
coffeemaker, microwave, refrigerator, small lawn & open fields for
walking dogs, 2 miles to lake, www.purplesagemotel.com

Sprague Motel & RV Park   509-257-2615
312 E 1st St   9 units, $58–$75
pet fee $8/stay, full kitchen or coffeemaker-microwave-refrigerator,
RV sites, lawn, next to walking trail, 2 blocks to public park,
www.spraguemotel.com

Stanwood, WA

Camano Cliff Cabins   360-387-4050
                                                  3 units, $135–$195
secluded cottages sleep 2 to 4, full kitchen, breakfast basket
provided, decks, hot tub, on 3 waterfront acres, day & overnight
pet boarding available (dogs sleep right in the house), short drive
to beach & waterfront park, www.camanocliffcabins.com

Stehekin, WA

Rainbow Falls Lodge   206-219-7512
66 Rainbow Lane   2 units, $155–$195
pet fee $20/day, 1-room cabin with kitchen & screened deck for
pets, studio apartment & 3-bdrm main lodge, large open area for
walking dogs overlooking river & waterfall, access is by boat or
seaplane (no roads), www.rainbowfallslodge.com

Stevenson, WA

Columbia Gorge Riverside Lodge   509-427-5650
200 Sw Cascade Ave   12 units, $79–$199
1 to 2 dogs, $10/day each pet, kitchenette or coffeemaker-
microwave-refrigerator, hot tub, lawn for walking dogs, next to
riverfront park, www.cgriversidelodge.com

Skamania Lodge   509-427-7700, 800-221-7117
1131 Skamania Lodge Dr   254 units, $99–$250
pet fee $50/stay, coffeemaker, restaurant, lounge, indoor pool, hot
tub, tennis-volleyball-basketball courts, on 175 wooded acres,
1/2 mile to public park, www.skamania.com

Stevenson, WA (continued)

Wind Mountain Resort   509-427-5152
50561 State Road 14   3 units, $79–$99
pet fee $10/day, motel rooms, kitchenette, RV sites, restaurant,
convenience store, 1/2 mile to beach, grassy walking area, across
road to riverfront park, www.windmountainresort.com

Sultan, WA

Dutch Cup Motel   360-793-2215
819 Main St   20 units, $64–$88
1 to 2 small to medium dogs only, $8-$10/day, coffeemaker,
microwave, refrigerator, large lawn, 1 mile to riverfront park,
www.dutchcup.com

Sumas, WA

B & B Border Inn   360-988-5800
121 Cleveland Ave   21 units, $59–$69
each pet $5/day, microwave, refrigerator, continental breakfast,
next to grassy lot for walking dogs, 2½ blocks to public park,
www.sumasborderinn.com

Sumner, WA

Sumner Motor Inn   253-863-3250
15506 Main St E   39 units, $60–$75
each pet $10/day, microwave, refrigerator, coffee in lobby, grassy
walking area, 4 miles to walking trail, short drive to fairgrounds-
parks-lakes, www.sumnermotorinn.com

Sunnyside, WA

Best Western Grapevine Inn   509-839-6070, 800-915-6070
1849 Quail Lane   54 units, $90–$110
dogs under 20 lbs only, $20/stay, coffeemaker, microwave,
refrigerator, full breakfast, indoor pool, hot tub, fitness room,
grassy walking area, 3 miles to off-leash dog park,
www.bestwestern.com/grapevineinn

Country Inn & Suites   509-837-7878, 877-896-7878
408 Yakima Valley Hwy   73 units, $55–$65
pet fee $10/day for 1st dog, $5/day for each additional dog,
kitchenette or coffeemaker-microwave-refrigerator, continental
breakfast, restaurant, outdoor pool, next to public park, 1 mile to
paved walking trail, www.sunnysidecountryinn.com

Rodeway Inn   509-837-5781
3209 Picard Place   46 units, $79–$89
each pet $11/stay, coffeemaker, microwave, refrigerator,
continental breakfast, indoor pool, hot tub, fitness room, lawn for
walking dogs, 1 block to trail, www.rodewayinn.com/hotel/WA004

Sunnyside Inn B & B   509-839-5557, 800-221-4195
804 E Edison Ave   12 units, $89–$109
dogs allowed with advance approval only, $10/day, coffeemaker,
microwave, refrigerator, full breakfast, lawn for walking dogs,
close to park & walking path, www.sunnysideinn.com

Travel Inn   509-837-4721
724 Yakima Valley Hwy   40 units, $49–$60
well-behaved dogs only, microwave, full kitchen or refrigerator,
continental breakfast, seasonal pool, gravel pet walking area,
1 mile to public park, www.travelinnsunnyside.com

Suquamish, WA

Suquamish Clearwater Casino Resort   360-598-8700
15347 Suquamish Way NE   866-609-8700
pet fee $20/day   85 units, $129–$199
coffeemaker, microwave, refrigerator, continental or full breakfast,
outdoor pool, hot tub, fitness room, lawn for walking dogs, beach
access, www.clearwatercasino.com

Tacoma, WA

Blue Spruce Motel   253-531-6111
12715 Pacific Ave S   27 units, $45–$60
1 to 2 dogs under 30 lbs only, $5/day, full kitchen or microwave,
grassy walking area, 3 blocks to public park

Budget Inn South Tacoma   253-588-6615
9915 S Tacoma Way   50 units, $40–$85
1 to 2 dogs under 25 lbs only, $20/day each pet, kitchen, grassy
walking area, 1 mile to public park

Tacoma, WA (continued)

Crossland Economy Studios Tacoma/Hosmer   253-538-9448
8801 S Hosmer St   90 units, $69–$80
pet fee $25/day, kitchenette, grassy walking area, 1 mile to public
park, www.crosslandstudios.com/541

Days Inn Tacoma Mall   253-475-5900, 800-329-7466
6802 Tacoma Mall Blvd   123 units, $62–$80
pet fee $20/day, coffeemaker, microwave, refrigerator, continental
breakfast, outdoor pool, fitness room, grassy walking area,
10-minute drive to public park, www.daysinn.com/hotel/06315

Days Inn Tacoma/North Fife   253-922-3500, 866-922-3500
3021 Pacific Hwy E   190 units, $77–$87
dogs under 25 lbs only, $5/day, kitchenette, continental breakfast,
outdoor pool, open area for walking dogs, 5-minute drive to public
park, www.daysinn.com/hotel/04876

Extended StayAmerica   253-475-6565
2120 S 48th St   94 units, $80–$99
pet fee $25/day ($150 maximum), kitchenette, 8-minute walk to
public park, www.extendedstayamerica.com/865

Hotel Murano   253-238-8000, 888-862-3255
1320 Broadway   319 units, $139–$469
1 to 2 dogs under 35 lbs only, $35/stay each pet, coffeemaker,
refrigerator, restaurant, lounge, hot tub, fitness room, pet bed-
bowls-toy-treats provided, lawn, 7 blocks to public park,
www.hotelmuranotacoma.com

La Quinta Inn & Suites   253-383-0146, 800-531-5900
1425 E 27th St   155 units, $99–$149
1 to 3 dogs, coffeemaker, continental breakfast, restaurant, lounge,
outdoor pool, hot tub, fitness room, grassy walking area, 10-minute
drive to public park, www.lq.com

Motel 6 Tacoma South   253-473-7100, 800-466-8356
1811 S 76th St   119 units, $50–$80
outdoor pool, hot tub, lawn, 1 mile to public park, www.motel6.com

Red Lion Hotel   253-548-1212, 866-548-3434
8402 S Hosmer St   119 units, $69–$249
dogs under 30 lbs only, $20/day each pet, coffeemaker, microwave,
refrigerator, extended continental breakfast, indoor pool, hot tub,
fitness room, 1 mile to public park, www.redlion.com/tacoma

Shilo Inn   253-475-4020, 800-222-2244
7414 S Hosmer St   132 units, $100–$170
each pet $25/stay, full kitchen or coffeemaker-microwave-
refrigerator, continental breakfast, indoor pool, sauna, hot tub,
fitness room, grassy walking area, 1 block to public park,
www.shiloinns.com

Tacoma Center Motel   253-272-7720
1220 Puyallup Ave   22 units, $46–$65
dogs under 20 lbs only, $30/stay, grassy walking area, 10-minute
drive to public park

Western Inn Lakewood/Tacoma   253-588-5241, 800-600-9751
9920 S Tacoma Way   103 units, $58–$64
each pet $25/stay, full kitchen or coffeemaker-microwave-
refrigerator, continental breakfast, restaurant, lounge, lawn,
1½ miles to public park, www.westerninntacoma.com

Tahuya, WA

Summertide Resort & RV Park   360-275-9313
15781 NE North Shore Rd   7 units, $65–$150
1 to 2 dogs, $5/day each pet, rustic cabins, RV sites, on 14 wooded
acres with walking trails, boat launch & fishing dock

Tenino, WA

Bear Creek Lodge   360-754-3843
3211 143rd Ave SW   3 units, $125
1 to 2 dogs, coffeemaker, microwave, refrigerator, continental or
full breakfast, hot tub, on 120 acres with woods & open fields for
walking dogs, 10 miles to beach

Tokeland, WA

Tokeland Hotel & Restaurant   360-267-7006
100 Hotel Rd   18 units, $44–$95
1 to 2 small dogs only, historic 120-year-old hotel, shared baths,
restaurant, lawn, across street to beach, www.tokelandhotel.com

Tradewinds on the Bay   360-267-7500
4305 Pomeroy Lane   18 units, $99–$199
1 to 2 dogs under 30 lbs only, $50/stay, fully equipped 1-bdrm
condos, party room with kitchen & fireplace, BBQ, seasonal pool,
large yard, 300 feet to beach & trail, www.tradewindsonthebay.com

Tonasket, WA

Bonaparte Lake Resort & Restaurant   509-486-2828
615 Bonaparte Lake Rd   10 units, $45–$65
1 to 2 dogs, $3/day each pet, rustic lakeside log cabins, kitchen, BBQ, RV & tent sites, restaurant, store & gas station, grassy walking area, woods & trail, www.bonapartelakeresort.com

Junction Motel   509-486-4500
23 W 6th St   8 units, $60–$77
1 to 2 dogs, $10-$20/day each pet, coffeemaker, microwave, 4 blocks to riverside walkway

Red Apple Inn   509-486-2119
20 S Whitcomb Ave   21 units, $56–$76
1 to 2 well-behaved adult dogs only, $5/day, full kitchen or microwave & refrigerator, grassy walking area, 3 blocks to public park, www.redappleinnmotel.com

Spectacle Lake Resort   509-223-3433
10 McCammon Rd   16 units, $62–$170
1 to 2 dogs allowed with advance approval only, waterfront motel rooms & suites, kitchen, RV & tent sites, horsehoe pits, volleyball, fitness room, seasonal pool, children's play area, boat launch & rentals, large open area for walking dogs, 3 miles to national forest, www.spectaclelakeresort.com

Toppenish, WA

Best Western Toppenish Inn   509-865-7444, 877-509-7444
515 S Elm St   40 units, $80–$130
1 to 2 dogs, $10/day each pet, coffeemaker, microwave, refrigerator, continental breakfast, freshly baked cookies, indoor pool, hot tub, fitness room, lawn, across street to public park, www.bestwestern.com/toppenishinn

El Corral Motel   509-865-1874
61731 US Hwy 97   17 units, $40–$50
pet fee $10/stay, microwave, refrigerator, lawn, 3 blocks to park

Quality Inn & Suites   509-865-5800
511 S Elm St   44 units, $79–$159
each pet $10/stay, coffeemaker, microwave, refrigerator, continental breakfast, fitness room, grassy walking area, across street to public park, www.qualityinn.com/hotel/wa227

Trout Lake, WA

Kelly's Trout Creek Inn B & B   509-395-2769
25 Mount Adams Rd   3 units, $75–$100
full breakfast, guest use of kitchen, hot tub, on 1 acre with creek &
waterfalls, open field for walking dogs, 3 miles to national forest,
www.kellysbnb.com

Trout Lake Motel   509-395-2300
2300 Hwy 141   13 units, $80–$89
1 to 2 dogs, $10/stay for 1 dog, $15/stay for 2 dogs, microwave,
refrigerator, continental breakfast, close to walking trail, bicycle &
snowshoe rentals, www.troutlakemotel.com

Tukwila, WA

Econo Lodge SeaTac Airport   206-244-0810, 800-446-6661
13910 Tukla Intl Blvd   47 units, $65–$121
1 to 2 dogs under 40 lbs only, $20/day each pet, coffeemaker,
microwave, refrigerator, continental breakfast, hot tub, fitness
room, sidewalks for walking dogs, 1/4 mile to public park,
www.econolodge.com/hotel/wa703

Extended StayAmerica   206-244-2537, 800-326-5651
15451 53rd Ave S   94 units, $70–$90
pet fee $25/day, ($150 maximum), kitchenette, grassy walking
area, www.extendedstayamerica.com/863

Homestead Studio Suites Seattle/Southcenter   425-235-7160
15635 W Valley Hwy   94 units, $85–$99
dogs under 45 lbs only, $25/day ($150 maximum), kitchenette,
grassy walking area, across street from 2-block-long trail that leads
to public park, www.homesteadhotels.com/125

Homewood Suites   206-433-8000, 800-225-5466
6955 Fort Dent Way   106 units, $129–$269
dogs under 30 lbs only, $20/day each pet, kitchenette, continental
breakfast, seasonal pool, hot tub, fitness room, pet walking area,
walking trail, across street to park, www.homewoodsuites.com

Ramada Limited Tukwila/SeaTac   206-244-8800, 877-972-6232
13900 International Blvd   38 units, $80–$95
each pet $20-$40/day, coffeemaker, microwave, refrigerator,
continental breakfast, fitness room, sidewalks for walking dogs,
3 miles to public park, www.ramada.com/hotel/08911

Tukwila, WA (continued)

Residence Inn Seattle South/Tukwila   425-226-5500
16201 W Valley Hwy   800-331-3131
1 to 2 dogs, $75/stay   144 units, $109–$199
suites, full kitchen, extended continental breakfast, complimentary
evening reception, seasonal pool, hot tub, BBQ, picnic area, small
pet walking area, next to 27-mile-long walking trail,
www.marriott.com/seaso

Riverside Residences   206-762-0300, 866-762-0300
11244 Tukwila International Blvd   118 units, $59–$99
1 to 2 dogs, $20/stay, coffeemaker, microwave, refrigerator,
restaurant, seasonal pool, fitness room, grassy area for walking
dogs, next to walking trail, www.riversideresidences.com

Tumwater, WA

Best Western Tumwater Inn   360-956-1235
5188 Capitol Blvd SE   90 units, $58–$96
1 to 2 dogs, $15/day each pet, coffeemaker, microwave,
refrigerator, continental breakfast, sauna, hot tub, fitness room,
small grassy walking area, 1/2 mile to public park & trail,
www.bestwestern.com/tumwaterinn

Comfort Inn   360-352-0691
1620 74th Ave SW   58 units, $90–$119
1 to 2 dogs under 25 lbs only, $10/day each pet, coffeemaker,
microwave, refrigerator, continental breakfast, indoor pool, hot
tub, fitness room, lawn, www.comfortinn.com/hotel/wa126

Extended StayAmerica   360-754-6063, 800-398-7829
1675 Mottman Rd SW   104 units, $70–$90
pet fee $25/day ($150 maximum), kitchenette, lawn, 6-minute
drive to 3-mile-long trail, www.extendedstayamerica.com/864

GuestHouse International Inn & Suites   360-943-5040
1600 74th Ave SW   877-847-7152
1 to 2 dogs under 25 lbs, $10/day each pet   59 units, $90–$135
rooms & 1-bdrm suites, coffeemaker, microwave, refrigerator,
extended continental breakfast, indoor pool, hot tub, fitness room,
quiet street for walking dogs, 5-minute drive to public park,
www.guesthouseintl.com/location-WA-Tumwater.htm

Motel 6 Tumwater/Olympia   360-754-7320, 800-466-8356
400 Lee St SW   119 units, $46–$51
1 to 2 dogs, microwave, refrigerator, coffee in lobby, seasonal pool,
picnic tables, lawn for walking dogs, 5-minute drive to riverside
park & walking trails, www.motel6.com

Twisp, WA

Blue Spruce Motel   509-997-5000
1321 N Methow Valley Hwy   16 units, $50–$54
pet fee varies depending on size of dog, kitchenette, large open
area for walking dogs, 1/4 mile to riverfront park & walkway

Idle-a-While Motel   509-997-3222
505 N Hwy 20   25 units, $68
each pet $6/day, motel rooms & cottages sleep up to 6, full kitchen
or coffeemaker-microwave-refrigerator, sauna, hot tub, BBQ,
picnic area, tennis court, on 41/2 acres for walking dogs, 1/2 mile to
public park, www.idle-a-while-motel.com

Twisp River Inn B & B   509-997-4011
894 Twisp River Rd   3 units, $85–$105
1 to 2 dogs, $10/stay each pet, full breakfast, riverside walking
area, 1 mile to hiking trail, horses boarded for $10/day,
www.twispriverinn.com

Union, WA

Alderbrook Resort & Spa   360-898-2200, 800-622-9370
10 E Alderbrook Dr   93 units, $130–$500
each pet $25/day, guest rooms & cottages, coffeemaker,
refrigerator, restaurant, lounge, indoor pool, outdoor pool, sauna,
hot tub, fitness room, BBQ, picnic area, paved pet walking area,
5 miles to public park, www.alderbrookresort.com

Hood Canal Cottages at Robin Hood Village   360-898-2163
6780 E State Route 106   8 units, $135–$195
1 to 2 dogs under 100 lbs only, $20/stay each pet, cottages with full
kitchen or kitchenette, most with private hot tub, picnic area, RV
sites, restaurant, lounge, on 15 secluded acres with walking trails,
www.robinhoodvillage.com

Union, WA (continued)

Hood Canal Hideaway	360-701-4768
3815 Walthew Dr SE	1 unit, $250–$400

pet fee $50/stay, fully equipped 4-bdrm waterfront vacation home & separate guest house sleep up to 15, covered deck & BBQ, lawn for walking dogs, www.holidayescapes.net/hc_beachhouse.aspx

Union Gap, WA

Super 8 Motel	509-248-8880, 800-800-8000
2605 Rudkin Rd	95 units, $78–$114

pet fee $15/stay, coffeemaker, continental breakfast, indoor pool, lawn, 2 blocks to greenway riverside trail, www.super8.com

Uniontown, WA

Churchyard Inn B & B	509-229-3200, 800-227-2804
206 Saint Boniface St	7 units, $75–$180

dogs allowed with advance approval only, $25/stay, full breakfast, landscaped lawn & gardens, park nearby, www.churchyardinn.com

Valley, WA

Jump Off Joe Resort & RV Park	509-937-2133
3290 E Jump Off Joe Rd	4 units, $45–$75

each pet $5/day, lakefront cabins, kitchen, RV & tent sites, woods & trails for walking dogs, www.ewra.org/jumpoff.html

Silver Beach Resort	509-937-2811
3323 Waitts Lake Rd	7 units, $90–$105

dogs allowed with advance approval only, $5/day each pet, fully equipped lakeside cabins sleep 6, RV sites, restaurant, on 4 acres, open mid-April thru September, www.silverbeachresort.net

Winona Beach Resort	509-937-2231
33022 Winona Beach Rd	8 units, $50–$65

1 to 2 dogs under 100 lbs only, $5/day each pet, cabins, kitchen, RV & tent sites, fishing dock, general store, on 450 wooded acres

Vancouver, WA

Briar Rose Inn	360-694-5710
314 W 11th St	4 units, $85

dogs under 20 lbs only, full breakfast, lawn for walking dogs, 3 blocks to public park, www.briarroseinn.com

Comfort Inn & Suites 360-696-0411, 800-222-2244
401 E 13th St 114 units, $90–$100
1 to 2 dogs under 25 lbs only, $25/day each pet, coffeemaker,
microwave, refrigerator, continental breakfast, seasonal pool,
sauna, hot tub, dog beds & treats available at front desk, grassy
walking area, 4 blocks to park, www.comfortinn.com/hotel/wa198

Days Inn 360-253-5000, 800-272-6232
9107 NE Vancouver Mall Dr 55 units, $54–$76
1 to 3 dogs, $15/day, coffeemaker, microwave, refrigerator,
continental breakfast, indoor pool, hot tub, grassy walking area,
short drive to public park, www.daysinn.com/hotel/15134

Days Inn & Suites Salmon Creek/Vancouver 360-574-6000
13207 NE 20th Ave 866-647-6886
1 to 2 dogs, $15/day 58 units, $59–$99
coffeemaker, microwave, refrigerator, continental breakfast, indoor
pool, hot tub, fitness room, lawn for walking dogs, 1 mile to public
park, www.daysinn.com/hotel/31406

Econo Lodge 360-693-3668
601 Broadway St 40 units, $50–$81
1 to 2 dogs, $10/day each pet, coffeemaker, microwave,
refrigerator, continental breakfast, small walking area, 1 block to
public park, www.econolodge.com/hotel/wa164

Extended StayAmerica 360-604-8530, 800-398-7829
300 NE 115th Ave 116 units, $75–$100
pet fee $25/day ($150 maximum), kitchenette, parking lot for
walking dogs, short drive to riverfront park,
www.extendedstayamerica.com/van

Hilton Hotel 360-993-4500, 800-445-8667
301 W 6th St 226 units, $99–$219
dogs under 50 lbs only, $35/stay, coffeemaker, restaurant, indoor
pool, hot tub, fitness room, across street to public park,
www.vancouverwashington.hilton.com

Homewood Suites 360-750-1100, 800-225-5466
701 SE Columbia Shores Blvd 104 units, $99–$179
1 to 2 dogs, $25 for 1st day, $10 each additional day, suites sleep 4,
kitchen, full breakfast, Monday thru Thursday evenings
complimentary beverages & appetizers, seasonal pool, hot tub,
lawn, close to riverside walking trail, www.homewoodsuites.com

Vancouver, WA (continued)

La Quinta Inn & Suites   360-566-1100, 877-566-1101
1500 NE 134th St   89 units, $69–$169
1 to 2 dogs under 45 lbs only, coffeemaker, microwave,
refrigerator, extended continental breakfast, indoor pool,
fitness room, grassy walking area, 5-minute drive to walking trail,
www.lq.com

Motel 6   360-253-8900, 800-426-5110
221 NE Chkalov Dr   116 units, $56–$62
1 to 2 dogs allowed, 1st dog free, 2nd dog $10/day, microwave,
refrigerator, coffee in lobby, indoor pool, hot tub, grassy area for
walking dogs, ½ mile to public park, www.motel6.com

Phoenix Inn Suites   360-891-9777, 888-988-8100
12712 SE 2nd Circle   98 units, $119–$154
1 to 2 dogs, $15/day each pet, coffeemaker, microwave,
refrigerator, extended continental breakfast, freshly baked
cookies, indoor pool, hot tub, fitness room, 1½ miles to public
park, www.phoenixinn.com/vancouver

Quality Inn & Suites   360-696-0516, 800-424-6423
7001 NE Hwy 99   72 units, $70–$90
pet fee $10/day, full kitchen or coffeemaker-microwave-
refrigerator, continental breakfast, seasonal pool, hot tub, fitness
room, large grasssy area for walking dogs, 4 blocks to public park,
www.qualityinn.com/hotel/WA708

Red Lion Hotel at the Quay   360-694-8341, 800-733-5466
100 Columbia St   160 units, $79–$130
1 to 2 dogs under 30 lbs only, $20/day each pet, coffeemaker,
microwave, refrigerator, restaurant, lounge, seasonal pool, fitness
room, grassy walking area, riverside trail, 5 blocks to public park,
www.redlion.com/vancouver

Residence Inn Portland North/Vancouver   360-253-4800
8005 NE Parkway Dr   800-331-3131
pet fee $75/stay   120 units, $79–$139
kitchen, extended continental breakfast, BBQ, picnic area,
seasonal pool, hot tub, fitness room, grassy walking area, close to
walking paths thru business park, www.marriott.com/vanwa

Riverside Motel 360-693-3677
4400 Columbia House Blvd 18 units, $38–$48
1 to 2 dogs, $10/day, kitchenette, lawn for walking dogs, ½ mile to public park & riverside boardwalk

Rodeway Inn 360-254-0900, 866-680-3045
9201 NE Vancouver Mall Dr 63 units, $65–$85
1 to 2 dogs, $25/stay each pet, coffeemaker, microwave, refrigerator, continental breakfast, indoor pool, hot tub, grassy walking area, close to park, www.rodewayinn.com/hotel/WA018

Shilo Inn & Suites Salmon Creek 360-573-0511, 800-222-2244
13206 NE Hwy 99 66 units, $92–$131
pet fee $25/stay, full kitchen or coffeemaker-microwave-refrigerator, extended continental breakfast, indoor pool, sauna, hot tub, ½ mile to public park, pet beds & dog treats available, small grassy pet walking area, www.shiloinns.com

Staybridge Suites 360-891-8282, 877 238 8889
7301 NE 41st St 117 units, $69–$150
pet fee $75/stay, studios, 1-bdrm to 2-bdrm suites, kitchenette, full breakfast, Tuesday thru Thursday evenings complimentary light dinner, BBQ, seasonal pool, hot tub, fitness room, pet walking area, next to public park, www.staybridge.com

Vantage, WA

Vantage Riverstone Resort 509-856-2800
551 Main St 18 units, $65–$99
1 to 3 dogs, $10/day, motel rooms with kitchenette, 3-bdrm vacation homes with full kitchen, RV & tent sites, seasonal outdoor pool, convenience store, boat launch, open field & riverside area for walking dogs, open Memorial Day thru Labor Day, www.vantagewa.com

Vashon, WA

Castle Hill Lodging & Reservation Service 206-463-3556
26734 94th Ave SW 1 unit, $85
dogs allowed by advance arrangement only, carriage house with full kitchen, 5 acres of open field surrounded by woods for walking dogs, reservation service provided for other local lodgings

Vashon, WA (continued)

Maury Cottage   206-463-4558
5313 SW Point Robinson Rd   1 unit, $100
1 to 2 pets allowed (combined weight not over 70 lbs), $20 for 1st
day, $5 each additional day, cottage with full kitchen sleeps 2,
private setting on 1 acre, 1 mile to beach, www.maurycottage.com

Swallow's Nest Guest Cottages   206-463-2646, 800-269-6378
6030 SW 248th St   7 units, $105–$290
dogs allowed with advance approval only, $15/day each pet,
cottages in various locations on the island, full kitchen or
kitchenette, one with private hot tub, close to public parks &
beaches, www.vashonislandcottages.com

Waitsburg, WA

Waitsburg Inn   509-337-8455, 800-718-9025
731 Preston Ave   6 units, $50
1 to 2 dogs under 50 lbs only, coffeemaker, microwave,
refrigerator, large lawn for walking dogs, ½ mile to public park

Walla Walla, WA

Best Western Walla Walla Suites Inn   509-525-4700
7 E Oak St   78 units, $89–$149
1 to 3 dogs, $10/day each pet, coffeemaker, microwave, refrigerator,
continental breakfast, restaurant, indoor pool, hot tub, fitness room,
lawn, walking trail, www.bestwestern.com/wallawallasuitesinn

Budget Inn   509-529-4410, 888-529-4161
305 N 2nd Ave   58 units, $30–$75
1 to 2 dogs, $5/day each pet, microwave, refrigerator, continental
breakfast, seasonal pool, pet walking area, 10-minute drive to
public park, www.wallawallabudgetinn.com

Capri Motel   509-525-1130, 800-451-1139
2003 Melrose St   35 units, $48
each pet $8/stay, coffeemaker, microwave, refrigerator, seasonal
pool, pet walking area, ½ mile to park, www.wallawallamotel.com

City Center Motel   509-529-2660, 800-453-3160
627 W Main St   20 units, $49–$59
pet fee $5/day, coffeemaker, microwave, refrigerator, seasonal
pool, lawn, 2 blocks to park, www.citycentermotel.net

Colonial Motel   509-529-1220
2279 E Isaacs Ave   17 units, $59–$80
dogs under 25 lbs only, coffeemaker, microwave, refrigerator, large
landscaped yard, 1 block to park & trail, www.colonial-motel.com

Fat Duck Inn & Guest Rooms   509-526-3825, 888-526-8718
527 Catherine St   6 units, $145–$185
1 to 2 dogs, $25/day each pet, 1 pet-friendly suite with full kitchen
sleeps 6, continental breakfast, complimentary wine hour, lawn,
2 blocks to park, ½ mile to off-leash dog park, www.fatduckinn.com

Holiday Inn Express   509-525-6200, 877-816-1699
1433 W Pine St   81 units, $119–$129
1 to 2 dogs, $20/day each pet, coffeemaker, microwave,
refrigerator, continental breakfast, indoor pool, hot tub, fitness
room, lawn, walking trail, www.wwhie.com

Inn at Abeja   509-522-1234
2014 Mill Creek Rd   4 units, $245–$265
dogs allowed in 1 cottage by advance arrangement only, $15/stay,
kitchen, full breakfast, creekside walking area on 35-acre vineyard
& winery, www.abeja.net

La Quinta Inn   509-525-2522, 800-531-5900
520 N 2nd Ave   61 units, $79–$159
coffeemaker, microwave, refrigerator, continental breakfast, indoor
pool, hot tub, fitness room, lawn, 1 mile to public park, www.lq.com

Marcus Whitman Hotel   509-525-2200, 866-826-9422
6 W Rose St   127 units, $119–$169
pet fee $20/stay, coffeemaker, refrigerator, full breakfast,
restaurant, lounge, fitness room, parking lot for walking dogs,
4 blocks to public park, www.marcuswhitmanhotel.com

Super 8 Motel   509-525-8800, 800-800-8000
2315 Eastgate St   101 units, $77–$103
1 to 2 dogs, $10/day, coffeemaker, microwave, refrigerator,
continental breakfast, indoor pool, hot tub, open field for walking
dogs, ¼ mile to park, 1 mile to trail & creek, www.super8.com

Travelodge   509-529-4940
421 E Main St   39 units, $65–$99
1 to 2 dogs, $7/day, coffeemaker, microwave, refrigerator,
continental breakfast, seasonal pool, grassy walking area, 1 block
to public park, www.travelodge.com/hotel/07059

Walla Walla, WA (continued)

Walla Walla Grape Havens 509-540-9513
335 S 3rd Ave 4 units, $140–$425
pet fee $20/stay, fully equipped 2-bdrm to 3-bdrm vacation homes,
hot tub, air-conditioned dog house, lawns, 5-minute drive to
lakefront trail, www.wallawallagrapehavens.com

Walla Walla Vineyard Inn 509-529-4360, 877-747-8713
325 E Main St 85 units, $78–$159
1 to 2 dogs, $25/stay each pet, full kitchen or coffeemaker-
microwave-refrigerator, continental breakfast, seasonal pool,
sauna, fitness room, lawn for walking dogs, 1 mile to public park,
www.thewallawallavineyardinn.com

Waterville, WA

Waterville Historic Hotel 509-745-8695, 888-509-8180
102 E Park St 10 units, $59–$125
dogs allowed with advance approval, $10/day each pet, hotel
rooms with private bath or shared bath, kitchenette, continental
breakfast, across street to public park, 8 miles to riverfront,
open April thru October, www.watervillehotel.com

Wenatchee, WA

Apple Country Bed & Breakfast 509-664-0400
524 Okanogan Ave 6 units, $85–$120
1 to 2 dogs under 25 lbs only, $15/day each pet, full breakfast, hot
tub, lawn for walking dogs, 1 mile to riverfront park & walkway,
www.applecountryinn.com

Avenue Motel 509-663-7161, 800-733-8981
720 N Wenatchee Ave 38 units, $50–$80
pet fee $5/day, full kitchen or coffeemaker-microwave-refrigerator,
continental breakfast, seasonal pool, hot tub, picnic area in park-
like setting, 4 blocks to public park, www.avenuemotel.com

Coast Wenatchee Center Hotel 509-662-1234, 800-663-1144
201 N Wenatchee Ave 147 units, $71–$155
1 to 2 dogs, $10/stay, coffeemaker, restaurant, lounge, indoor &
outdoor pools, hot tub, fitness room, grassy walking area, 2 blocks
to riverfront park, www.wenatcheecenter.com

Comfort Inn   509-662-1700, 866-973-7839
815 N Wenatchee Ave   81 units, $62–$78
1 to 2 dogs under 25 lbs only, $20/day each pet, coffeemaker,
microwave, refrigerator, full breakfast, indoor pool, hot tub, fitness
room, grassy walking area, ½ mile to public park & trail,
www.comfortinn.com/hotel/wa082

Econo Lodge   509-663-7121
232 N Wenatchee Ave   37 units, $40–$80
1 to 2 dogs under 25 lbs only, $10/day each pet, coffeemaker,
microwave, refrigerator, continental breakfast, seasonal pool, small
grassy pet walking area, 3 blocks to riverfront park,
www.econolodge.com/hotel/wa185

Holiday Inn Express   509-663-6355, 800-465-4329
1921 N Wenatchee Ave   90 units, $117–$159
small dogs only, coffeemaker, microwave, refrigerator, continental
breakfast, indoor pool, hot tub, fitness room, small pet walking
area, paved walking trail, www.wenatcheeexpress.com

Holiday Lodge   509-663-8167, 800-722-0852
610 N Wenatchee Ave   59 units, $55–$65
1 to 2 dogs under 15 lbs only, $10/day each pet, microwave,
refrigerator, continental breakfast, seasonal pool, hot tub, lawn,
2 blocks to public park, www.wenatcheeholidaylodge.com

IvyWild Inn   509-293-5517, 866-608-8808
410 N Miller St   4 units, $115–$135
dogs under 25 lbs only, full breakfast, complimentary wine tasting,
outdoor pool, hot tub, on landscaped half-acre for walking dogs,
⅓ mile to riverfront park, www.theivywildinn.com

La Quinta Inn & Suites   509-664-6565, 800-531-5900
1905 N Wenatchee Ave   65 units, $64–$124
coffeemaker, microwave, refrigerator, continental breakfast,
indoor pool, sauna, hot tub, fitness room, small pet walking area,
walking trail, www.lq.com

Lyles Motel   509-663-5155, 800-582-3788
924 N Wenatchee Ave   24 units, $35–$45
coffeemaker, microwave, refrigerator, outdoor pool, hot tub,
fitness room, grassy walking area, across street to public park

Wenatchee, WA (continued)

Red Lion Hotel   509-663-0711, 800-733-5466
1225 N Wenatchee Ave   149 units, $100–$170
1 to 2 dogs, $20/day each pet, coffeemaker, microwave,
refrigerator, full breakfast, restaurant, lounge, seasonal pool, hot
tub, fitness room, grassy area for walking dogs, 1 mile to public
park, www.redlion.com/wenatchee

Value Inn   509-663-8115, 800-668-1862
1640 N Wenatchee Ave   34 units, $40–$79
1 to 4 dogs, $15/stay, coffeemaker, microwave, refrigerator,
extended continental breakfast, outdoor pool, sauna, small pet
walking areas, 2 blocks to park, www.wenatcheevalueinn.com

Wenatchee Travelodge   509-662-8165, 800-578-7878
1004 N Wenatchee Ave   48 units, $70–$129
1 to 3 dogs, $10/day each pet, coffeemaker, microwave,
refrigerator, extended continental breakfast, seasonal pool, sauna,
hot tub, close to walking trail, www.wenatcheetravelodge.com

Westport, WA

Alaskan Motel & Apartments   360-268-9133, 866-591-4154
708 N 1st St   12 units, $50–$160
pet fee $10/stay, rooms-suites-houses sleep 6 to 13, full kitchen or
coffeemaker-microwave-refrigerator, BBQ, picnic area, fish
cleaning station, on 1 acre, www.westportwa.com/alaskan

Albatross Motel   360-268-9233
200 E Dock St   13 units, $49–$64
dogs under 25 lbs only, $15/day, kitchenette or coffeemaker &
refrigerator, fish cleaning station, grassy area for walking dogs,
close to public park, http://users.techline.com/lbatross/

All Seasons Beach Cabin   800-932-3472
585 Winston OR 97496   1 unit, $250–$300
pet fee $30/day, 2-bdrm plus loft vacation cabin sleeps 10, fully
equipped kitchen, wraparound deck, 300-ft private dune trail to
beach, www.allseasonsbeachcabin.com

Breakers Boutique Inn   360-268-0848, 800-898-4889
971 N Montesano St   4 units, $74–$210
1 to 2 small dogs preferred, $10/day each pet, rooms & suites
sleep up to 17, full kitchen or kitchenette, next to city park,
www.breakersmotel.com

Chateau Westport   360-268-9101, 800-255-9101
710 W Hancock St   104 units, $89–$130
1 to 2 dogs, pet fee $25 for 1st day, $10 each additional day,
microwave, continental breakfast, indoor pool, hot tub, large yard,
short walk to beach, www.chateauwestport.com

Glenacres Historic Inn   360-268-0958, 800-996-3048
222 N Montesano St   8 units, $50–$140
pet fee $10/day, 3 pet-friendly rooms & 1 studio cottage with full
kitchen sleep up to 4, coffee in lobby, outdoor pool, on 2½ acres
for walking dogs, ½ mile to ocean & 3-mile-long beach trail,
www.glenacresinn.com

Harbor Resort   360-268-0169
871 E Neddie Rose Dr   14 units, $59–$170
dogs allowed with advance approval only, $10/day each pet, motel
rooms, cottages sleep up to 4, full kitchen or coffeemaker-
microwave-refrigerator, close to waterfront area with paved beach
trail for walking dogs, www.harborresort.com

Islander Resort   360-268-9166, 800-322-1740
421 E Neddie Rose Dr   32 units, $79–$159
pet fee $40/stay, coffeemaker, restaurant, lounge, large yard, close
to waterfront walking area, www.westport-islander.com

Mariners Cove Inn   360-268-6000 or 360-268-0631, 877-929-9096
303 W Ocean Ave   9 units, $49–$74
pet fee $20/stay, kitchenette or coffeemaker-microwave-
refrigerator, BBQ, large open walking area, 6 blocks to beach,
close to 2 state parks & nature trail, www.marinerscoveinn.com

Ocean Avenue Inn   360-268-9400, 888-692-5262
275 W Ocean Ave   12 units, $49–$135
each pet $10/day, rooms, 1-bdrm to 3-bdrm suites & cottage sleep
up to 9, full kitchen or kitchenette, lawn for walking dogs, ½ mile
to ocean, www.westportwa.com/oceaninn

Westport, WA (continued)

Pacific Bay Motel & RV Park   360-268-2675
1500 S Montesano St   10 units, $55–$75
1 to 3 dogs, $10-$12/day, 3-room cabins, full kitchen or
coffeemaker-microwave-refrigerator, sauna, hot tub, crab cooker &
fish cleaning station, walking trails thru nature area,
www.pacificbaymotel.com

Pacific Motel & RV Park   360-268-9325
330 S Forrest St   12 units, $49–$64
pet fee $10/day, kitchen, recreation room with kitchen, seasonal
pool, RV sites, fire pit, fish cleaning station, close to walking trails,
www.pacificmotelandrv.com

Vacations by the Sea   360-268-1119, 877-332-0090
1600 W Ocean Ave   58 units, $139–$279
1 to 2 dogs, $30/stay, kitchen, seasonal pool, hot tub, recreation
center & sport court, beachfront, www.vacationbythesea.com

Windjammer Motel   360-268-9351, 866-208-7371
461 E Pacific Ave   12 units, $55–$60
pet fee $10/day, coffeemaker, microwave, refrigerator, on 1 acre
for walking dogs, 1 mile to ocean, www.windjammermotel.net

White Salmon, WA

Lothlorien Woods Hide-a-Way   509-493-8733
222 Staats Rd   1 unit, $135–$149
dogs allowed with advance approval only, secluded 1-bdrm
"treehouse" with full kitchen sleeps 4, hot tub, open field
surrounded by woods, walking trails, www.lothlorienwoods.com

Wilbur, WA

Eight Bar B Motel   509-647-2400
718 SE Main St   154285 units, $30–$75
each pet $10/stay, full kitchen or coffeemaker-microwave-
refrigerator, seasonal pool, barkdust walking area, 3/4 mile to
public park, www.wa-accommodations.com/ne/8barb/

Willows Motel   509-647-2100
303 NE Main St   11 units, $45–$65
kitchenette or coffeemaker-microwave-refrigerator, picnic area,
landscaped grounds & creek, www.wilburwillowsmotel.com

Winthrop, WA

A Bend in the River Lodge	509-996-2797, 800-854-2834
386 W Chewuch Rd	2 units, $189–$869

pet fee $65/stay, lodge with full kitchen sleeps 30, screened porch, adjacent cabin sleeps 5, river access, close to hiking trails

America's Best Value Cascade Inn	509-996-3100, 800-468-6754
1006 Hwy 20	63 units, $68–$142

1 to 2 dogs, $10/day each pet, coffeemaker, microwave, refrigerator, continental breakfast, BBQ, picnic area, outdoor pool, hot tub, open field for walking dogs, 10-minute drive to park, www.winthropwa.com

Central Reservations	509-996-2148, 800-422-3048
pet fee varies depending on particular unit	50 units, $65–$869

hotels-motels-vacation homes in Greenbank-Leavenworth-Mazama-Winthrop, some with pool or hot tub or yard, close to trails for walking dogs, www.centralreservations.net

Eagle Pine Chalets	509-996-2109, 800-422-3048
345 Twin Lakes Rd	2 units, $95–$115

small to medium dogs allowed in summer only, $10/day, studio chalets sleep 2, kitchenette, fields & hiking trails, 5-minute drive to lake, www.methownet.com/eaglepinechalets

KOA Winthrop/North Cascades National Park	
1114 Hwy 20	509-996-2258
1 to 2 dogs allowed	17 units, $40–$62

1-room to 2-room kamping kabins, coffee in lobby, seasonal pool, RV & tent sites, western-style playground, riverfront walking area, www.koa.com/where/wa/47145/

Mount Gardner Inn	509-996-2000
611 State Hwy 20	9 units, $59–$89

1 to 2 dogs, $10/day each pet, coffeemaker, microwave, refrigerator, open field for walking dogs, www.mtgardnerinn.com

River Run Inn	509-996-2173, 800-757-2709
27 Rader Rd	15 units, $105–$180

dogs allowed with advance approval only, $15/day, rooms-cabins-houses, full kitchen or coffeemaker-microwave-refrigerator, BBQ, patio or private deck, indoor pool, hot tub, on 11 riverfront acres, close to dog-friendly cross-country ski trail, www.riverrun-inn.com

Winthrop, WA (continued)

Spring Creek Ranch   509-996-2495
22 Belsby Rd   3 units, $75–$320
pet fee $20/day, studios to 2-bdrm cabins sleep up to 4, full kitchen, riverfront acreage with large open area for walking dogs, www.springcreekwinthrop.com

Winthrop Inn   509-996-2217, 800-444-1972
960 Hwy 20   30 units, $70–$90
each pet $10/day, microwave, refrigerator, continental breakfast, BBQ, picnic area, outdoor pool, hot tub, volleyball & basketball courts, on 4½ acres for walking dogs, close to hiking trails, www.winthropinn.com

Winthrop Mountain View Chalets   509-996-3113, 800-527-3113
1120 Hwy 20   6 units, $75–$110
1 to 2 dogs allowed in summer only, $15–$30/stay each pet, cabins with private decks, coffeemaker, microwave, refrigerator, next to national forest for walking dogs, www.winthropchalets.com

Wolfridge Resort   509-996-2828, 800-237-2388
412 Wolf Creek Rd # B   17 units, $89–$245
dogs allowed with advance approval only, $10/day each pet plus $25 cleaning fee, rooms to 2-bdrm townhouses, full kitchen or coffeemaker-microwave-refrigerator, outdoor pool, hot tub, on 40 riverside acres, walking trails, www.wolfridgeresort.com

Woodinville, WA

Willows Lodge   425-424-3900, 877-424-3930
14580 NE 145th St   84 units, $169–$369
pet fee $25/stay, coffeemaker, continental breakfast, restaurant, lounge, sauna, hot tub, fitness room, pet treats & toys, courtyard & natural riverside area for walking dogs, close to 30-mile-long walking trail, 15-minute drive to park, www.willowslodge.com

Woodland, WA

Cedars Inn   360-225-6548, 800-444-9667
1500 Atlantic Ave   60 units, $60–$67
each pet $10/day, microwave, refrigerator, continental breakfast, indoor pool, hot tub, fitness room, lawn, 5-minute drive to riverfront park & walkway, www.woodland-cedarinnexpress.com

Lakeside Motel 360-225-8240
785 Lakeshore Dr 13 units, $55–$65
1 to 2 dogs, $5/day each pet, microwave, refrigerator, public park

Lewis River Inn 360-225-6257, 800-543-4344
1100 Lewis River Rd 49 units, $67–$77
each pet $10/day, microwave, refrigerator, continental breakfast, grassy walking area, 6 blocks to park, www.lewisriverinn.com

Scandia Motel 360-225-8006
1123 Hoffman St 13 units, $40–$44
1 to 2 dogs, $6/day, kitchenette, grassy walking area, 10-minute walk to public park

Yakima, WA

All Star Motel 509-452-7111
1900 N 1st St 50 units, $35–$70
1 to 2 dogs, $10-$50/stay, microwave, refrigerator, open field for walking dogs, 1/4 mile to public park

Apple Country Bed & Breakfast 509-972-3409, 877-788-9963
4561 Old Naches Hwy 5 units, $79–$95
small dogs allowed with advance approval only, $15/day, coffeemaker, microwave, refrigerator, full breakfast, gazebo & picnic tables, on 40-acre fruit orchard for walking dogs, www.applecountryinnbb.com

Best Western Lincoln Inn 509-453-8898, 800-834-1649
1614 N 1st St 75 units, $109–$119
1 to 2 dogs under 10 lbs only, $25/day, coffeemaker, microwave, refrigerator, continental breakfast, indoor pool, hot tub, fitness room, paved walking area, 5-minute drive to public park, www.bestwestern.com/prop_48140

Birchfield Manor Country Inn 509-452-1960, 800-375-3420
2018 Birchfield Rd 11 units, $119–$219
dogs allowed in 2 rooms with private fenced patios, full breakfast, dinner served Thursday thru Saturday evenings, picnic area, outdoor pool, lawn for walking dogs, next to game reserve, short drive to public park, www.birchfieldmanor.com

Yakima, WA (continued)

Cedars Suites at Yakima Convention Center   509-452-8101
1010 East A St   866-952-8100
pet fee $10/day   47 units, $73–$109
microwave, refrigerator, continental breakfast, freshly baked
cookies, spa & swimming pool across street, guest pass to local
fitness center, quiet neighborhood for walking dogs, 3-minute
drive to public park, www.cedarssuites.com

Clarion Hotel   509-248-7850, 800-896-7966
1507 N 1st St   208 units, $37–$120
1 to 2 dogs under 25 lbs only, $10/day each pet, coffeemaker,
microwave, refrigerator, BBQ, picnic tables, restaurant, lounge,
outdoor pool, hot tub, fitness room, lawn for walking dogs,
10-minute drive to public park, www.yakimaclarion.com

Comfort Suites   509-249-1900, 866-423-8960
3702 Fruitvale Blvd   59 units, $89–$229
dogs under 15 lbs only, $15–$25/day each pet, coffeemaker,
microwave, refrigerator, full breakfast, freshly baked cookies,
indoor pool, hot tub, fitness room, gravel walking area, 1 block to
open field for walking dogs, 2 blocks to riverside greenway trail,
www.comfortsuites.com/hotel/wa104

Days Inn   509-248-3393, 800-248-3360
1504 N 1st St   61 units, $75–$95
pet fee $15/day, coffeemaker, continental breakfast, outdoor pool,
parking lot for walking dogs, 2-minute drive to public park,
www.daysinn.com/hotel/10258

Econo Lodge   509-453-8981
1405 N 1st St   53 units, $45–$52
1 to 2 dogs, $10/day each pet, microwave, refrigerator, continental
breakfast, indoor pool, hot tub, lawn for walking dogs, 1 mile to
riverside greenway trail, www.econolodge.com/hotel/wa188

Economy Inn   509-457-6155, 888-925-6633
510 N 1st St   36 units, $45–$55
1 to 2 dogs, $10/day, microwave, refrigerator, continental
breakfast, outdoor pool, 3 blocks to park, www.economyinn.info

Fairfield Inn & Suites   509-452-3100, 800-228-2800
137 N Fair Ave   81 units, $84–$124
pet fee $25/day ($75 maximum), coffeemaker, microwave,
refrigerator, continental breakfast, dog treats, indoor pool, hot tub,
lawn, 3-minute drive to public park, www.marriott.com/ykmfi

Holiday Inn Express   509-249-1000, 800-465-4329
1001 East A St   87 units, $99–$149
1 to 2 dogs under 30 lbs only, $20/day, coffeemaker, microwave,
refrigerator, extended continental breakfast, indoor pool, hot tub,
fitness room, paved walking area, 1 mile to greenway walking trail,
www.hiexpress.com/yakimawa

Howard Johnson Plaza   509-452-6511, 800-733-5466
9 N 9th St   171 units, $79–$99
each pet $15/day, coffeemaker, microwave, refrigerator,
restaurant, lounge, outdoor pool, hot tub, fitness room, grassy
walking area, 2 blocks to riverside greenway trail,
www.hojo.com/hotel/17592

Knights Inn   509-453-0391
818 N 1st St   58 units, $59–$99
each pet $15/day, coffeemaker, microwave, refrigerator,
continental breakfast, freshly baked cookies, seasonal outdoor
pool, hot tub, lawn, 1 mile to public park, 3 miles to greenway trail,
www.knightsinn.com/hotel/14602

Motel 6   509-454-0080, 800-446-8356
1104 N 1st St   95 units, $44–$52
dogs under 20 lbs only, coffee in lobby, outdoor pool, lawn, 2 miles
to riverside greenway trail, www.motel6.com

Orchard Inn B & B   509-966-1283, 866-966-1283
1207 Pecks Canyon Rd   4 units, $119–$139
pet fee $15/day, coffeemaker, microwave, refrigerator, full
breakfast, outdoor dining area, dog house available, 1-minute walk
to open field for walking dogs, www.orchardinnbb.com

Oxford Inn   509-457-4444, 800-521-3050
1603 E Yakima Ave   95 units, $70–$109
pet fee $20/stay, full kitchen or coffeemaker-microwave-
refrigerator, extended continental breakfast, outdoor pool, hot tub,
fitness room, lawn for walking dogs, next to riverfront park &
10-mile-long paved greenway trail, www.oxfordinnyakima.com

Yakima, WA (continued)

Oxford Suites   509-457-9000, 800-404-7848
1701 E Yakima Ave   107 units, $105–$115
pet fee $20/stay, coffeemaker, microwave, refrigerator, full
breakfast, Monday thru Saturday evenings complimentary light
appetizers, indoor pool, hot tub, fitness room, grassy walking area,
next to 10-mile-long riverside trail, www.oxfordsuitesyakima.com

Quality Inn   509-248-6924, 800-510-5670
12 E Valley Mall Blvd   85 units, $60–$90
dogs under 15 lbs only, $10/day each pet, coffeemaker,
microwave, refrigerator, continental breakfast, freshly baked
cookies, seasonal pool, gravel walking area, 2 miles to riverside
greenway trail, 10-minute drive to several parks,
www.qualityinnyakima.com

Red Apple Motel   509-248-7150
416 N 1st St   59 units, $40–$50
1 to 2 dogs under 20 lbs only, $10/day each pet, microwave,
refrigerator, continental breakfast, seasonal pool, lawn for walking
dogs, 5-minute walk to public park, www.redapplmotel.com

Red Carpet Inn   509-457-1131
1608 Fruitvale Blvd   29 units, $45–$65
coffee in lobby, outdoor pool, sauna, small open area for walking
dogs, 2 blocks to riverside trail & public park

Red Lion Hotel   509-248-5900
607 E Yakima Ave   156 units, $96–$219
each pet $15/day, coffeemaker, restaurant, lounge, outdoor pool,
fitness room, lawn for walking dogs, 1/4 mile to public park &
riverside greenway trail, www.redlion.com/yakimacenter

Sun Country Inn   509-248-5650, 800-559-3675
1700 N 1st St   71 units, $52–$64
pet fee $8/day, microwave, refrigerator, continental breakfast,
Sunday thru Thursday evenings complimentary appetizers,
seasonal pool, fitness room, lawn for walking dogs, 1/2 mile to
off-leash dog park, http://suncountryinn.tripod.com

Yelm, WA

Blueberry Hill Farm Guest House — 360-458-4726
12125 Blueberry Hill Lane SE — 1 unit, $115
private suites, kitchen, continental breakfast, on 8-acre working
berry farm, creek & waterfall,
www.blueberryhillfarmguesthouse.com

Prairie Motel — 360-458-8300
700 Prairie Park Lane — 23 units, $60–$125
1 to 2 dogs, $5/day each pet, coffeemaker, hot tub, private decks,
7-acre natural area for walking dogs, 3 blocks to walking trail,
www.prairiehotel.com

Zillah, WA

Comfort Inn — 509-829-3399, 800-501-5433
911 Vintage Valley Parkway — 40 units, $105–$159
1 to 2 dogs, $10/day each pet, next to 3-mile scenic walking trail
thru town, coffeemaker, microwave, refrigerator, extended
continental breakfast, complimentary crockpot chili & freshly
baked cookies, picnic area, sun deck, indoor pool, hot tub, fitness
room, open field for walking dogs, 1/2 mile to public park,
www.comfortinnzillah.com

A: Business Name Index

Morris Farm House B & B,
  Coupeville WA, 230
Motel 6 Airport South,
  SeaTac WA, 302
Motel 6 Airport, SeaTac WA, 302
Motel 6 Eugene South,
  Eugene OR, 109
Motel 6 Eugene/Springfield,
  Springfield OR, 190
Motel 6 Mall 205/Airport,
  Portland OR, 168
Motel 6 North, Everett WA, 238
Motel 6 North,
  Medford OR, 146
Motel 6 Portland Central,
  Portland OR, 168
Motel 6 Portland Downtown,
  Portland OR, 168
Motel 6 Portland East,
  Troutdale OR, 197
Motel 6 Portland North,
  Portland OR, 169
Motel 6 Portland/Tigard West,
  Tigard OR, 195
Motel 6 Seattle East/Issaquah,
  Issaquah WA, 251
Motel 6 Seattle North,
  Kirkland WA, 256
Motel 6 Seattle South,
  SeaTac WA, 302
Motel 6 South, Everett WA, 238
Motel 6 South, Medford OR, 146
Motel 6 Spokane East,
  Spokane Valley WA, 319
Motel 6 Spokane West/Airport,
  Spokane WA, 317
Motel 6 Tacoma South,
  Tacoma WA, 324
Motel 6 Tacoma/Fife,
  Fife WA, 240

Motel 6 Tigard East,
  Tigard OR, 195
Motel 6 Tumwater/Olympia,
  Tumwater WA, 329
Motel 6, Albany OR, 73
Motel 6, Bellingham WA, 216
Motel 6, Bend OR, 87
Motel 6, Centralia WA, 221
Motel 6, Clarkston WA, 223
Motel 6, Coos Bay OR, 100
Motel 6, Corvallis OR, 102
Motel 6, Gold Beach OR, 117
Motel 6, Grants Pass OR, 119
Motel 6, Hermiston OR, 123
Motel 6, Kelso WA, 252
Motel 6, Klamath Falls OR, 132
Motel 6, Lincoln City OR, 139
Motel 6, Moses Lake WA, 273
Motel 6, Ontario OR, 159
Motel 6, Pasco WA, 287
Motel 6, Pendleton OR, 162
Motel 6, Portland OR, 168
Motel 6, Redmond OR, 175
Motel 6, Richland WA, 299
Motel 6, Roseburg OR, 180
Motel 6, Salem OR, 182
Motel 6, Seaside OR, 186
Motel 6, The Dalles OR, 194
Motel 6, Vancouver WA, 332
Motel 6, Yakima WA, 345
Motel Del Rogue,
  Grants Pass OR, 120
Motel Nicholas, Omak WA, 283
Motel Oasis,
  Moses Lake WA, 273
Motel Puyallup,
  Puyallup WA, 295
Motel West, Bend OR, 87
Mount Bachelor Motel,
  Bend OR, 87

B: Topics Index